THE CENTER OF THE WORLD

THE CENTER

COMMUNIS

Robert S. Elegant

OF THE WORLD
AND THE MIND OF CHINA

Revised Edition

Funk & Wagnalls
New York

THE CENTER OF THE WORLD

Published by Funk & Wagnalls,
A Division of Reader's Digest Books, Inc.

Printed in the United States of America

FOR MY PARENTS

PREFACE TO THE REVISED EDITION

If each nation possessed a single, conscious will, outsiders could hardly doubt that for the past two years China had been deliberately demonstrating her utter distinctness from all other nations.

The phenomenon called the Great Proletarian Cultural Revolution is unique in the annals of mankind. Never before 1966 had the respected leaders of a major nation deliberately destroyed the machinery through which authority was exercised. Never before the proclamation of the Cultural Revolution had such leaders directed their idealistic fervor to the creation of perfect mass democracy that would make their own functions superfluous. Although commitment to absolute political goals has been characteristic of the Chinese for at least two millennia, China's previous rulers had tempered their purposes with realism. Moving against the current of an age that historians may later judge to have been as troubled as it feels itself to be, the youth and the intelligentsia of China have demanded an ordered hierarchy of authority, principles, and standards.

The youthful intelligentsia of most of the world has been in revolt against authority in the 1960s. The group of nations under the aegis of the Soviet Union has been impelled by such protest toward progressive relaxation of economic and political repression. A generation in the West, which experienced neither personal peril nor personal deprivation, has protested vehemently against the comfortably cushioned futility affluence inflicts upon the majority while inflicting inequities upon some minorities. Both groups seek comprehensive change, and both question established standards of morality and behavior.

In China authority itself commanded the destruction of "every aspect of the old civilization." More than 700 million Chinese were to be transformed into "perfect" Communist men and women by inner self-cultivation—and the mechanisms of control that men call government were to become superfluous. But the tormented youth of China, supported by the intelligentsia, has rejected the official nihilism, which sought the dissolution of all formal political, economic, and social institutions. With the Chinese, as usual carrying all matters to hyperlogical extremes, the contrast between developments in that country and developments elsewhere could not have been more marked.

As I have indicated, the behavior of that influential portion of the Chinese leadership that adhered to the transcendental doctrines of Mao Tse-tung was consistent with the psychological and historical compulsions that had shaped Chinese Communism. The response of the majority of the Chinese people, led by the youthful intelligentsia, was a renewed manifestation of the protestant tradition that, since 220 B.C., has checked the extremist compulsions of the orthodox tradition. In the first edition of this book, published in 1964, I described the primary influences, which, it appeared to me, had determined the character of Maoism. I also noted that China was at that time in a state of suspended political development. Since their doctrines and their purposes demanded constant movement, the Maoists discerned in that suspension a profound threat to their total authority and to the attainment of their ultimate goals. They proclaimed the Cultural Revolution in order to restore their spiritual authority by destroying both their enemies and the institutions that sustained their enemies.

Those phenomena are described in the material added to this revised edition. A great volume of information on both the Great Proletarian Cultural Revolution and earlier events has become available in the polemics accompanying that upheaval. Historians will mine that material for decades to come. My own purpose has been not to write a history, but to illuminate the sources of Chinese political behavior. Although no one could have foreseen its exact character, the Cultural Revolution has been consistent with the past. The chief obstacle to comprehension has been neither a paucity of information nor the difficulty of analysis, but the inherent skepticism of Western minds. Westerners have been reluctant to credit developments that appeared irrational in terms of our own logic.

The reader will himself assess my successes and failures in describing phenomena that are all but incredible to the West. I must, however, apologize for the tentative character of some judgments, while pleading in mitigation that I am writing about the incomplete present, rather than events that may, however arbitrarily, be judged complete because they took place in the past.

American intervention in South Vietnam—however mismanaged and however reviled—has, I believe, had a significant effect on China. The Maoists preached "liberation of all mankind through people's war and designated South Vietnam the "focus of the worldwide liberation struggle." Their opponents argued against total Chinese sponsorship of North Vietnam's ambitions. They contended that South Vietnam was not a vital Chinese interest, but was a drain on Chinese resources and a dangerous flashpan of direct and disastrous conflict with the United States. American intervention not only prevented Hanoi's conquest of the south; it also refuted the Maoist thesis of the "inevitable victory of people's war." The costs and hazards loomed larger in the consciousness of many influential Chinese than the "sacred mission of liberation." The Chinese view of the outside world began to change, and the danger of nuclear confrontation between Peking and Washington receded. A China that recognized the limits of her own power and her own interests was less inclined to use her burgeoning nuclear arsenal for ideological or territorial expansion, while, of course, determined to use those weapons to defend China herself.

As I write these prefatory words the outcome of the negotiations just begun between Washington and Hanoi is quite unclear. If those negotiations should end in a substantial success for Hanoi and its sponsor, Peking, they could set in motion events even more portentous than the fate of the suffering people of South Vietnam or the future of American influence in Southeast Asia.

Maoist doctrines—so perfectly idealistic as to be perfectly

inhuman—have by and large been discredited in China. But a substantial success in South Vietnam could impel the successor Communist regime to rededicate itself to the Maoist ideal of "world liberation." While rejecting Mao Tse-tung's domestic policies, the anti-Maoists might yield to the temptation to remake the outside world. Rekindled by a victory in South Vietnam, Messianic Maoism and the instinctive Chinese movement outward could together seek a violent consummation. The danger of nuclear confrontation between the United States and China could once again become acute.

Most men hope that the contending powers will reach a settlement that neither commits the South Vietnamese people to totalitarian rule nor renews the danger of nuclear war. China, however, remains central to the problem of Asia and the problem of world peace. No nation so large and so potentially powerful can be ignored.

China has begun to change, though no external force can direct the process. But the United States can influence the process by resolutely refuting the Chinese conviction of Messianic invincibility that threatens the world with a nuclear conflict. The United States can further influence the process by offering friendship to an embittered and isolated nation. Although they are long overdue, diplomatic recognition and American sponsorship of Peking's entry into the United Nations—sustained by normal commercial and cultural relations between the two countries—can still assist China's transformation. China can become a force that makes for stability and progress in the tumultuous years of technological, social, and psychological change that lie ahead of us all.

Although repetition has robbed them of much of their meaning, I must employ the usual formulae of thanks and self-abnegation. Sincerity may restore some of the original meaning when I acknowledge with gratitude the assistance of friends and colleagues and confess that blame for the errors and caprices in which I have persisted lies on my own head. I should also like to express my appreciation to the respective editors for their permission to use again material that originally appeared in journals like *Foreign Affairs, The Reporter, The Nation, The New Leader,* and

L'Espresso of Rome. My employers, *The Los Angeles Times,* have given me both time and freedom to devote myself to the sometimes esoteric study of China with understanding and generosity that are, in my experience, unique among the editors of daily newspapers. I must, finally, express my gratitude to my wife and apologize to her for breaking my solemn promise not to become involved with another book on China until the situation was clarified. She will, I trust, forgive me, since she knows that strict observance of that promise might have meant never.

Hong Kong
June, 1968

CONTENTS

PREFACE TO THE REVISED EDITION vii

Part One

ALL UNDER HEAVEN 1
China Encompasses the World

 1 Paradise Gained 3
   Daily Life in People's China

 2 The Road to Damascus 18
   The Communists' Revelation of the
   Purposes and Compulsions that Move Them

Part Two

THE OUTER DARKNESS (1600–1900) 27
Western Aggressiveness Penetrates the Glorious
Isolation of Imperial China

 3 China or Cathay? 29
   The West's First Contact with an
   Affluent Chinese Empire

 4 The Rich Impoverished, the Poor Starving 52
   A New Dynasty's Magnanimity Produces
   Overpopulation, Hardship, and Revolt

xiii

5 Salesmen with Muskets   67

   *The West's Militant Approach to China
   in the Nineteenth Century*

6 Cannon, Science, and Democracy   81

   *China Adopts Various Means from the West to Meet
   the Challenge of Western Material Supremacy*

Part Three

SHAPING THE WEAPON (1900–1963)   103

*Twentieth-century China Experiments with Sweeping
Internal Changes, Determined to Confront the West
on Terms of Equality—or Supremacy*

7 The Blade Shatters   105

   *A Republican Revolution Destroys the Empire, but
   Parliamentary Democracy Fails*

8 The Sword of Wrath   133

   *The Communist Party: Its Birth, Struggles,
   Victory, and a Brief Account of Its Conduct in Power*

Part Four

THE MYSTIQUE   175

*The Sinocentricity, Authoritarianism, and
Utopianism Evident in Traditional and
Communist Patterns of Thought*

9 What Is a Man?   177

   *The Confucian State-Ideology that
   Shaped the Chinese Mind*

10 The Vision of Mao Tse-tung   199

   *The Communist Chieftain's Thought,
   Shaped by Traditional Chinese as Well
   as Marxist Influences*

Part Five

PRESSURE, PURGE, AND MENTAL PARALYSIS   223

*The Communist Pattern of Government
Before the Cultural Revolution*

11   Guerrillas with Epaulettes   225

*The Structure and Functioning of the
Communist Party of China Before
Its Destruction in 1966*

12   Government with Mirrors   255

*The Organization and Working of the
People's Government Before It Was Shattered by
the Great Proletarian Cultural Revolution*

13   Government by Upheaval   270

*The Periodic Campaigns Which
Convulsed China Before the Catharsis of
the Cultural Revolution*

14   The Paper Heart   293

*The Attempt to Make All Men Think
as the Communists Wish*

Part Six

THE SHAPE OF PARADISE   315

What the Communists Wrought

15   Ladder to Heaven   317

*The First Climacteric: the Great Leap Forward and
the Great People's Communes*

16   The Kaleidoscope Stops   344

*The Shape of China (After the First Climacteric):
Economy, Education, Art, and Religion*

17 The World Beyond   383

China's Foreign Relations: the Sino-Soviet Quarrel, the United States, and Asia

EPILOGUE   415

18 The Grand Climacteric   417

The Great Proletarian Cultural Revolution, Beginning in 1966, Overturns All Structures of Power and Almost All Institutions

19 The Center of the World?   443

Can China Become a Normal Member of the Comity of Nations?

Bibliography   460

Index   465

Part One

ALL UNDER HEAVEN

China Encompasses the World

In the narrow harbor, enclosed on one side by Portuguese Macao and on the other by the shores of Communist China, the angular little tugboat darted, busy as a dolphin, among the fishing junks rolling like surfaced whales on the swell. From its stovepipe funnel hung a vertical banner reading: "The People's Communes Are the Ladder to Heaven! The Chinese People's Republic Is Paradise!"

1

Paradise Gained

Daily Life in People's China

Mrs. Lee woke reluctantly in the big chamber that had once been the formal parlor, sacred to eminent guests and family rituals. Still half-asleep, she felt a sudden pang, as for something vital lost. The mood, which began her every day, was dismissed in the same instant it was evoked and by the same agency—her first glimpse of the pale panels on the walls where her father-in-law's precious scrolls had once hung.

She glanced into the big courtyard, preferring to guess the hour rather than thread her way across the room to the watch under her husband's pillow. Besides, he could never remember that the new Peace brand stopped unless it was wound twice a day. The black rim of the ornamental fishpond loomed in the darkness, reassuringly familiar but breathing the benign enchantment that had for years made this courtyard in Peking in the hours before dawn the most beautiful place in the world for her. A pearl-gray shadow was just twining itself around the bare boughs of the willow tree. Since all the rest was blackness, it could not be later than four-thirty.

Mrs. Lee wondered what had awakened her. The two boys slept, and Little Woo's cough sounded no worse than it had all winter. Her mother-in-law snored quietly in the inner corner of the parlor, while her husband, as usual, lay with his face to the wall. Her feeling of uneasiness persisted, though she normally en-

3

joyed the sense of stolen leisure an early awakening gave her. The elder boy should have left for the market a half-hour earlier, but she did not bother to shake him awake. For six days he had invariably found, when he came to the head of the queue, that he could not buy the half-ounce of green tea his grandmother coveted. Mrs. Lee's stomach rumbled angrily, but hunger alone could not have awakened her. It was too old and too familiar an acquaintance.

Glancing around again, she saw that the Wong family who lived in the inner room had left the courtyard door ajar. During the two years that had passed since their arrival the Wongs had failed to close the door at least once a week. She was, once more, dismayed at how important that open door had become to her. She recalled with shame that she had pleaded, wept, and screamed at the Wongs before giving up hope of ever compelling them to remember to close the door. She slid out of bed, her body shaking with the cold, while her mind dreamed of a world without Wongs. After easing the door to, she slipped back under the thin quilt. But the light was creeping through the uncurtained windows, and she could neither sleep nor abandon herself wholly to pleasant reveries.

For more than an hour Mrs. Lee lay shivering between sleep and full wakefulness. It was that bleakest hour, when fears besiege the half-slumbering mind like beasts with leering devil-faces. Mrs. Lee had learned years earlier that she could turn her mind from the unsatisfactory present by remembering the past or by recasting the future after her own desire.

Although she knew that it was dangerous to the family's security—and to her own equilibrium—to dwell upon her greater fears and thwarted hopes, she could at least permit herself to dream that she might this morning find a sliver of pork in her millet gruel. She emphatically rejected her favorite fantasy in which the entire family sat down together to a full meal—not a holiday feast such as even rickshaw coolies had formerly enjoyed at Lunar New Year, but merely a simple dinner. Wai-ding, her husband, had explained why it was impossible that they should, even once, satisfy their constant hunger.

"China has discovered statistics," he had said. "If every family in the nation should just once eat to repletion, they would consume untold tons of the grain, the pork, the eggs, and the vegetables which must purchase the sinews of industrialization. Before 'liberation,' before we discovered statistics, we did not know —and almost everyone could eat his fill at least once a year."

She never reminded Wai-ding of the impassioned lectures he had delivered before the arrival of the Communists' People's Liberation Army. Recalling the thousands he had seen starving by the roadsides on his trips, he would then speak of "the crying need for fair distribution of food and goods—in a new atmosphere of freedom from the corruption of the bankrupt Nationalist regime." There seemed little point in asking why the new regime, so gladly welcomed, had produced equality of deprivation. Besides, Wai-ding and she did not talk as freely as they had in the old days, though even then he would lock the servants out before speaking his mind.

She must not think about food beyond the not impossible shred of pork that might appear in her gruel. Besides, if some miracle should produce the ingredients of a proper meal, she had neither pots, a stove, nor even a charcoal brazier. Even the thermos bottle of hot water—the family's only refreshment before leaving their room each morning—came from the public mess hall.

The blue suits hanging on the wall stirred in a draught, their limp, headless forms like the embodied fears of her reverie. All five were identical in pattern, though they were graduated in size from Wai-ding's through her own and her mother-in-law's to the boys' miniatures. All were so patched and darned that her servants would have disdained them for rough work in the old days. She could not help thinking about daring to wear the one silk-brocade dress she had carefully hidden, for the temptation was too sweet. Just once, she mused, to dress like a lady, instead of a dedicated worker; to see a motion picture that was all moonlight and music; to hear a Peking opera in its original form, unmarred by "social comments" from the painted players; or to dawdle away an afternoon over a light novel. She clung to the dream, for once warmed by the glow of memory.

Someday they might travel again. All they had known in the

past five years was a Sunday at the Imperial City, spoiled by Little Woo's parroting of diatribes. "The Empress Dowager," he had said, "sinned against the people by using naval funds to build the vast stone ship before us." She remembered her honeymoon in the glowing city of Hangchow, its inhabitants so different it was hard to believe that they, too, were Chinese. Wai-ding and she had stayed at an inn overlooking the West Lake and had strolled along the wisteria-decked causeway built by a great poet-official eight hundred years earlier. It had been a good life before "liberation," though they had welcomed the Communists ardently. No decent person could, after all, justify the privileges they had known under Chiang Kai-shek's Nationalist regime at the price of widespread deprivation and insecurity for the masses.

She wondered if her future daughters-in-law would know the tremulous joy of weddings amid clouds of incense and all the clans gathered for the feast. But the boys would probably marry shapeless creatures in blue "liberation suits," bowing before a portrait of Chairman Mao Tse-tung of the Communist Party beside a hundred other couples in the new mass marriage ceremony.

The boys . . . she usually did not dare wonder what might become of them. As Wai-ding had said, "It is quite enough to keep alive and out of trouble today, and perhaps next week, without thinking of six months, a year, or—let us not be ridiculous—five years from now." He had added a bitter aside, his sarcasm, as always, cast in language so formal it sounded stilted: "The shape of the anticipated future has changed so often in the last decade that we can only wait breathless for the next revelation. To plan ahead is feckless."

Mrs. Lee wondered, as she had so often in the past, why it was the little, almost intangible things that she most resented about the new order. The glorious goals toward which her generation had always yearned were now the goals of the government: a reborn, respected China, where all men and women could live amid plenty. But her own daily concerns were petty in the extreme: avoiding a slip of the tongue that might reveal ideological error; scheming for a half-ounce of tea; memorizing new slogans; or concealing a hoarded lipstick. Worst of all, she mused, was the way politics and their consequences now dominated her every waking thought—and even her half-waking dreams. But what else, after all, remained to think about?

She truly regretted that she could not rejoice in sacrificing every lighthearted moment for future steel mills; she tried hard to believe that a glorious future would unfold for her sons. Meanwhile, they seemed to walk with assurance through the mazes of a world wholly changed since her own school days. Little Woo, class monitor at nine, flaunted the red bandanna of the Young Pioneers. He saw his personal idol each day when the monitors reported to the school's Party Secretary. She had not been able to tell whether Wai-ding was hurt when Little Woo asserted with characteristic pomposity, "I want to be a leader in educational circles! Not principal like Daddy used to be, but Party Secretary like Comrade Lin."

Was she pleased, she wondered, that her elder son, inevitably nicknamed Big Woo, felt no real enthusiasm for the new ways? A year ago Big Woo, consulting neither Wai-ding nor herself, had informed his class monitor that he could no longer "offer voluntary labor" to repair streets or dig ditches. "It simply does not leave me time to study," he had said. "And I must work hard if I am to become a good scientist." The turmoil that followed shook them all, and Wai-ding's colleagues reproached him "in a comradely manner" for his son's attitude. The worst moment was Big Woo's coming home, sobbing, "The Comrade Party Secretary says . . . if I do not reform my thoughts, I must go to the students' reform camp—or a work group in Tibet, maybe for years. He says the state cannot nourish vipers in its breast."

He gulped and asked, "Mama, am I a viper?"

Wai-ding and she had never discussed their distress in prevailing upon the boy to reject the conclusions of his own logic, for there would have been no comfort in mutually confessing their own intellectual surrender.

The storm had finally passed. Big Woo had won the formal accolade of Model Student. He was assiduous in patching culverts, attending political lectures, and cleaning latrines, but his mathematics were weak, and he no longer bothered to study at home.

It was, curiously, her mother-in-law who encouraged Big

Woo in his self-reformation. "Don't be ashamed, Son, of the smell of honest labor," she said consolingly when he came home stinking like a latrine coolie.

Yet Wai-ding's mother had once been the embodiment of reaction, despising change and manual labor equally. "Respect, girl, respect!" the old lady would snap when Mrs. Lee was a new bride. "I remember how my mother-in-law treated me . . . and how hard I worked. . . . If I were you, I would thank heaven for such a considerate mother-in-law." But the older Mrs. Lee, widow of "an enemy of the people, a bureaucratic capitalist," had become an impassioned "progressive" and a champion of women's rights. She often spoke at mass rallies, where she was invariably hailed by the cadres as a model for all women.

The metamorphosis had begun when a delegation implored old Mrs. Lee to "draw on your vast knowledge of household administration and advise us on the nurseries we are establishing to serve the people." Appointed Deputy Director of Child Welfare for the urban Commune, the old lady was so busy that she showed hardly any concern when Wai-ding's younger brother, a graduate civil engineer, was sent to Manchuria to improve *his* ideological consciousness by laboring among the farming masses.

"Mama," Wai-ding had said in another aside, "is so intoxicated by her victory over herself that she acts as if this overcrowded room were an ideological battlefield—and devotes her every waking hour to mutual criticism."

It was, Mrs. Lee reflected with amusement, a new kind of mother-in-law trouble, and she felt herself given a touch of true distinction. The tales her mother and grandmother had told her—and their grandmothers had told them—had always centered upon the exacting mother-in-law. Throughout history it had always been that imperious figure, asserting the force of tradition and her own authority, which had enslaved Chinese women, not masculine domination. Her own mother-in-law now displayed progressive enthusiasm and unconcern for the household in equal measure.

There, at least, Mrs. Lee mused, she had it over her sister May-ying in Hong Kong. Married to the son of a wealthy Shanghai textile family, which had left in time to salvage most of its possessions, May-ying led a life of consummate idleness. Even in the old days, she and Wai-ding, the earnest intellectuals, had been disgusted with the self-indulgent silliness of the scented hedonists they called the Shanghai crowd. But May-ying had a mother-in-law straight out of the Chinese wife's immemorial tale of woe—grasping, petty, and domineering. She had consented to have May-ying's ailing father live with them only after her own son had shamed her for trying to prevent proper filial behavior—that foremost virtue of traditional morality. There was no question that the women of the new China had been relieved of one heavy burden, the old-fashioned mother-in-law.

But, Mrs. Lee thought, the Communists would be horrified if they knew how superficial was the transformation of her own mother-in-law, the woman they proudly characterized as "this aged representative of the exploiting classes who has penetratingly acquired proletarian consciousness." The old lady's enthusiasm did not extend to that hard-working cadre Comrade Wong, manager of the District Store of the Red Star People's Commune, nor to Mrs. Wong, whom she called "common as rice-gleanings," nor to the Wongs' boisterous brood.

Her mother-in-law's resentment of the Wongs had the same roots as Mrs. Lee's own. Though other families lived in the forty rooms and five courtyards which had once belonged to Wai-ding's father, the Lees saw them only as vague figures at a distance. When the government began billeting other families in their house, the Lees had managed to retain the bridal apartments, to which both women had come as brides of eldest sons. Although Mrs. Lee had resented paying seven People's Dollars a month for rent and electricity in order to live in a small corner of her own house, she had not felt the full indignity until the newly established Urban Great People's Commune pre-empted her own bedroom for the Wongs. The Wongs' advent—and their infuriating carelessness with the outside door—had become the focus for her resentment of the new order.

"Since families no longer need cook separately in a semifeudal manner," the Housing Assignment Officer had said, "two families can easily live in this space. Besides, Comrade Wong will welcome the opportunity to give ideological guidance to a bourgeois family. I know you will welcome the opportunity to learn."

Actually, Comrade Wong behaved better than they had expected. He tried to avoid invading their privacy and delivered few ideological homilies. The poor man was much too busy with the District Store, the nerve center of the Urban Commune. They were all ceaselessly busy. All the Wongs, and all the Lees as well, habitually left the house at six in the morning, rarely returning before eleven at night. Her own boys would, like the Wongs' children, have been sleeping at school rather than at home had their dormitory not been undermined by rainstorms.

"Our new lives are a welcome relief from domestic monotony," Wai-ding had remarked after drinking too much *bygar*, the fiery, white liquor sometimes distributed during the Spring Festival, which had been the Lunar New Year.

Reluctant to rise, Mrs. Lee stirred unhappily. She took little joy in her recent promotion to Section Leader at the Street Workshop, where women and old men made ball bearings. Although she was a trained schoolteacher, she preferred the workshop, which required little concentration and no parroting of slogans. The authorities, apparently doubting her reliability, had not asked her to teach.

When the boys awoke and began scuffling as they dressed, she gave up the attempt to pull the few remaining shreds of sleep around her. Washing rapidly, she went over the coming day in her mind. Her shift, starting at six in the morning, would be over at eight that evening. Wai-ding, who was scheduled to attend the faculty's weekly Mutual and Self-criticism Meeting, would not be home until midnight. As she left, she realized that she should have awakened him. But he did not have to be at school until seven, and they really had little to say to each other nowadays.

Mrs. Lee suffered her fit of wakefulness on a winter morning early in the second decade of the People's Republic of China. She told her story after fleeing to Hong Kong on the pretext that her father's acute illness required her to care for him there.

"I don't know why they let me out and kept so many others back," she later explained. "But, you know, there are no fixed rules

. . . different offices in different places behave in quite different ways. Maybe they thought I was no use to them."

Little Woo, who was permitted to visit her during school vacation, happily returned to Peking, as he phrased it, "to resume my place in the front ranks of reconstruction." But she still hopes that Wai-ding and Big Woo will join her some day. She does not think they would wish to return.

While the hardships Mrs. Lee endured were not remarkable by Chinese standards of the time, many circumstances changed for the better after 1960. There was more food, for one thing, and the Urban Communes were suspended in practice, though not always in name.

Nonetheless, tens of millions of women continued to live Mrs. Lee's life across the broad expanses of China until 1966, when the convulsions of the Great Proletarian Cultural Revolution began to change the essential character of the country. Their circumstances varied superficially from Mrs. Lee's. Most homes were in the countryside, rather than the city; only an infinitesimal portion of the Chinese people belonged to the educated classes; and fewer had known wealth before the Communist "liberation" of 1949. But regardless of where they lived, what they knew, or the conditions under which they had previously lived, more than 700 million Chinese men and women passed their days in remarkably similar circumstances until 1966. A surreptitious "liberalization" —economic, political, and ideological—had relieved many of the tensions between 1960 and 1966. That "liberalization" was tacitly permitted by a group of senior officials who had become disillusioned with the constant excesses and constant pressures of Maoism. They had, in effect, taken much of the power of decision out of the hands of the fanatical Maoists, and in 1966 the Maoists stimulated the great—and, probably, final—climacteric called the Cultural Revolution in order to restore their power and to reinforce their visions.

If the Maoists had been as efficient in execution as they were daring in conception, no distinctions whatsoever would exist in China. Every individual would be both a manual and an intellectual worker; the countryside would be indistinguishable from the city, every civilian would be a soldier; and no child would say to another "my family," but only "our family—the Chinese people." The Maoist regime sought the perfect harmony which, the Chinese tradition holds, springs from ordered uniformity. In pursuit of this goal—and its other grand objective, a China once more predominant in the world—the regime subjected the country to a series of political and economic convulsions—beginning with land reform in 1951 and reaching one climax in the People's Communes of 1958. After 1958, a completely altered Chinese society displayed striking uniformity, but the Communists had not succeeded in creating perfect uniformity. Thwarted by its own inefficiency, by popular resistance, and by the laws of nature, the Maoists continually tested new devices. Behind these experiments lay mankind's most sweeping attempt to remake society by fiat. In 1966 the Maoists recognized that their fiat was ineffective. Stubbornly determined, they ordered the Chinese people to remake themselves through the Cultural Revolution. The Maoists abandoned the normal organs of power and went directly to the masses. All that had been was to be destroyed—even the Communist Party itself—to make way for a new and perfect order of mankind.

Almost all the Chinese people had been organized into People's Communes, "autonomous, wholly new social, economic, cultural and military organisms," which were to combine the benevolent regimentation of the *allyu* of the Incas with the compulsive industriousness of the beehive. A society that had endured for two millennia because its broad workings were in practice remarkably flexible, though authoritarian in theory, became the most rigid and oppressive in history. All conscious activities—and man's most private thoughts as well—were "guided" for the benefit of the state, at whose apex sat the Chairman of the Communist Party, surrounded by his "cadres," [1] like the Great Inca among his attendant Incas. Most Chinese ate in communal mess halls, which doled out to a nation of gourmets unappetizing fare so meager that it barely sustained their frenzied activity. Almost all Chinese

[1] In Chinese: *kan-pu*, literally "the doers." The term "cadre" or "cadres" is applied to all servants of the state.

were driven to heroic tasks whose every fulfillment merely laid the basis for an endless proliferation of new tasks.

When he realized in 1965 that the communal experiment had failed "because of the corruption of the cadres," Mao determined to create a wholly new administrative structure. Modeled on the Paris Commune of 1871, it was to be a perfect instrument through which the people ruled themselves directly. It was his greatest failure.

The model for the traditional Chinese state had been the family—hallowed as the basis of society by the dominant Confucian ideology. Although the individual's standing within the clan was rigorously defined according to his place on the ladder of the generations—and horizontally to the twentieth degree of consanguinity—the theoretical rigidity of relationships within the formal structure was suffused by affection and tolerance. So complete was the acceptance of the family's paramount interest that direct compulsion was normally employed within the family to a much lesser extent than it is in the individualistic West. The clan as a bulwark of the old order was naturally one of the first institutions the Communists sought to destroy. Their war cry was: "Destroy the feudal family—the basis of inequality and subjection!" The regime sought to purge from men's breasts all those emotions which the West considers natural affection, but which the Chinese leaders describe as "the slave and master psychology deliberately inculcated by bourgeois society." Their practical purpose was to disperse the "small family" composed of parents and children around the common hearth. Brought up in nurseries and boarding schools, children were taught to despise filial love, and parents were told: "All children belong to the state!"

China's civilization had survived for two thousand years, while her hegemony—political, economic, and cultural—had extended over the entire Orient. The Chinese had been predominant because they were compulsively industrious and astonishingly ingenious—when they were working for themselves or for the family-clan. But the Communist regime deliberately destroyed traditional incentives for the exercise of talent. Buoyed by the tremendous enthusiasm that greeted their expulsion of the corrupt and inefficient Nationalist regime, the Communists apparently felt that the masses had been completly imbued with their own messianic idealism. For the clan they substituted the abstraction of the state; for tangible rewards they substituted promises to posterity. The people were denied all but the barest of material satisfactions so that the food and goods thus saved might be applied to capital construction. To millions of women in medieval street workshops, to laborers in modern plants, and to farmers working the communal land fourteen hours a day, the knowledge that they produced more but consumed much less was the most galling aspect of the new regime.

A nation that had shown all religions tolerance verging on indifference was taught that there was but one truth—the Marxist canons as interpreted by the Communist Party of China. Even the elaborate Chinese ideographs were transformed. The regime quite sincerely sought to make them easier to learn, as had the Japanese earlier. Some of the new characters were actually more difficult than the old because the nationalistic Communists, rejecting the simplified forms already worked out by the Japanese, were forced to oversimplify to the point where characters were sometimes almost indistinguishable from one another.[2] The chief damage was cultural. Becoming mere shapes—instead of abstract pictures—the new characters lost the integral grace which had invested the old with so much reverence and had made them the chief unifying force of the world's oldest living culture.

The principal expression of Chinese spirituality had been reverence for the land as the source of life. Every small farm had been enshrined in men's hearts as the cradle of the generations of

[2] Take, for example, the name of the Communist leader, Mao Tse-tung, conventionally written 毛澤東. The Japanese short form is 毛沢東, the new Chinese form 毛澤东. The last character, which means East, is remarkably similar to 本 and 车, which have quite different sounds and meanings. The original forms of the three characters are quite distinct. The result is that the new forms are quite simple for scholars, who know the old forms and the historical principles upon which the new are based. But they are exceedingly difficult for the neophyte, for whose benefit they are designed.

mankind, whose eternal flow through the world was that single manifestation of supernatural power to which the normal Chinese paid devotion. Today, in Hong Kong—that curious combination of treaty port, refugee camp, and free marketplace run wild— natty young businessmen respond alike when asked where their homes are. They will name remote farming villages in Kiangsi, Chekiang, or Anhwei provinces, though their families may have lived in Shanghai for generations before fleeing to Hong Kong to escape the Communists.

Reverence for the ancestral acres is universal, embracing all classes. On a snowy night in 1952 South Korean litter-bearers trudged into a dugout on the west-central front, carrying a Chinese private who had just been wounded in a clash between patrols. The prisoner displayed neither fear of his captors nor concern for the immediate future. Relieved to find someone with whom he could communicate in his own language, he asked only: "Can the doctors fix my leg? Will I be able to follow the plow again?"

During their protracted assault on the seats of power the Communists exploited this mystical devotion to the land with their slogans: "Land to the landless! The tiller shall own his fields!" They promised the farmer not merely a plot of land, but those fields where lay the sacred graves of his ancestors. Once secure in power, the Communists deprived the farmer of his land because the tiny individual plots were undeniably inefficient. Shortly thereafter the Party deliberately desecrated the graves, in part because the considerable areas they occupied were required for cultivation, but in greater part because it wished to destroy the old loyalties whose visible symbol the grave mounds were.

All that had been was to perish. Beauty, frivolity, piety, affection, individuality—all were systematically expunged by a regime dedicated to power and conformity. Determined to create a nation of producers rather than consumers, the Communist Party sought to shape the individual into a "producing unit" with as much wayward emotion as a fine lathe.

But the Chinese people did not become automata responsive only to the Communist Party's will. The masses' genuine enthusiasm, freely given, sustained the Communists until the excesses of 1958–59. Before that time of overwhelming troubles, almost all the Chinese people were committed to the regime's purposes, and the great majority believed in the Communist Party's leadership. Thereafter, most Chinese still approved of the Party's ultimate goals, but they had lost faith in its wisdom.

The Communists were shocked to discover that they had not created a wholly compliant nation. Mrs. Lee had not become an automaton, nor had her husband, Wai-ding, nor their hundred million cousins. If they had truly been transformed, there would have been no need for the unceasing campaigns against "rightists, counter-revolutionaries, bourgeois elements, and anti-Party groups within the Party." The intensity of the repressive effort remained the surest evidence that the Communists were still far from transforming human beings into "producing units." They believed until 1964 that they had destroyed the old society, but the Maoists could not pretend even to themselves that they had created a new society that functioned effectively. Nor had they discovered how to transform a medieval farming nation into a modern industrial power. The task might have been barely possible of fulfillment if they had been receiving enormous quantities of aid from outside; the niggardly assistance they actually got from the Soviet Union on stringent terms raised vain hopes, rather than satisfying real needs.

In 1960 the realists within the Chinese hierarchy began to retreat from the excesses of 1958, the climactic year of the Communes. Though they clung to the slogans and their ambitions never abated, the administrators were forced to reverse many of the most extreme measures. The People's Communes deteriorated into agricultural cooperatives. Peasants, no longer susceptible to complete regimentation through coercion, were once more given title to small garden plots and allowed to sell their produce in free markets. The Urban Communes, never more than an inspired blueprint outside a few major cities, simply disappeared as functioning economic units, though the administrative fiction was retained and many city dwellers still ate in communal mess halls because their cooking utensils had been melted down for the metal. Tens of millions were transferred from cities and factories to the countryside in obedience to the new policy of concentrating upon agriculture. Industrial production dropped radically as men and material were diverted to agriculture. New construction virtually ceased. Uniformity and crash industrialization were still the regime's goals, but pressure was relaxed, since the realists saw that they had pushed the people as far as they could—for the moment. By 1965 the combination of relaxation and more rational policies had produced a remarkable improvement in the standard of living. Besides, slow but marked progress was discernible in industrial construction, and the people were relatively content. Those accomplishments were the work of the pragmatists within the hierarchy.

But in 1966 the Maoists, still consecrated to their obsessive and unattainable goals, realized that they were losing almost all power. Mao Tse-tung therefore unleashed the adolescent fanatics of the hastily organized Red Guard against the structure of the government and the Party he had created. He was determined to prevent the *embourgeoisement* of China as the Soviet Union had by his analysis become bourgeois. He was, at the age of seventy-three, determined to insure the continuity of his hand-wrought policies—whatever the cost to existing Chinese society. The bright spirit of Communist man was to be preserved untarnished—although men's minds, men's bodies, and men's works were destroyed.

2

*The Communists' Revelation of the Purposes
and Compulsions that Move Them*

Western writers on the People's Republic of China fall into three broad groups. Fellow travelers and avowed Communists exalt the benevolent wisdom and the vast achievements of the Peking regime. Men who understand political necessity, but do not really care for people, report with appreciative cynicism. Others, whose emotions are intimately engaged with the old China, tend to see nothing but horror.

Since suffering, death, and degradation are but by-products of the regime, considering them alone can hardly lead to understanding. The Chinese Communists have never been infatuated with terror for terror's sake. The man who made the People's Republic, Chairman Mao Tse-tung, in particular, has always avoided *unnecessary* bloodshed, although he has not hesitated when he thought violence advantageous. Mao and his intimates are impelled by transcendent idealism, not by blood lust. They are not indifferent to the people's welfare, but the fate of the transcendent entity called China has always been their overriding concern. Determination to restore China to her ancient glory is the source of their beliefs and their behavior; their excesses stem from that purpose, which they seek through methods determined by the most rigid dogmas.

The task is monumental. When an emperor died, Imperial scribes would broadcast the classical euphemism to the far corners of the realm: "The Son of Heaven has mounted the dragon!" When the Chinese People's Republic was proclaimed on October 1, 1949, Communist publicists might well have proclaimed that Chairman Mao Tse-tung had challenged the hydra. As soon as he lops off the head of one difficulty, ten problems ten times more vicious spring from the same neck.

Like every other major Asian leader, Mao is convinced that he must modernize his country by building a heavy industrial force and powerful armed forces. In order to attain those goals, he must institute an effective public health service, universal education, and mechanized agriculture. Mao must also unravel two of his country's basic problems, each embodying a paradox: the rate of the population's increase and the persistence of traditional Chinese civilization.

China's population, somewhere between 600 and 650 million in 1957, was increasing by 15 to 20 million a year until 1958. Public health measures had accelerated the rate of increase, but near famine and natural disasters checked it sharply from 1958 to 1962. Although the appearance of new consumers in ever increasing numbers threatened to devour all his economic gains, Mao knew that his chief strength—both economic and military—was human labor. He therefore rejected any thoroughgoing effort to limit the population, refusing a fair test to the doubtful proposition that mass birth control was actually possible in China. From 1962 to 1966 the population increased rapidly, reaching a total between 700 and 750 million by 1967.

Mao was not moved by willful perversity to seek to destroy precisely those elements that had preserved the vigorous Chinese civilization: the family system, the ideographic script, a dispersed handicraft industry, intellectual tolerance, and laissez-faire administration. Holding *all* the old ways responsible for China's weakness in the world, he was determined to destroy them all. Confucian society was obviously his chief enemy, for it was inimical to change. By 1964, when the Maoists had been uprooting traditional institutions for more than a decade, they could still not pause in their attacks. Mao had discovered a hidden vitality in the old culture; he had learned the extent of popular opposition when, for a few months in 1957, he permitted free speech. He drew the

obvious conclusion. If the people were given a protracted breathing spell, a recurrence of traditional Chinese civilization might
well destroy all his accomplishments, like the tropical jungle
creeping over an abandoned clearing.

Beset by the sheer number of Chinese and by their stubborn
preference for the old ways, Mao Tse-tung was convinced that he
must whip the exhausted masses to ever greater prodigies of toil—
and conformity. He apparently believed that he could exact tremendous sacrifices because he had already given China power, for
which his generation yearned above all else. Though their grand-
parents told them that the Central Kingdom was the world's supreme civilization, Mao's generation grew up in a disintegrating
nation that was constantly humiliated by the physical power of
foreign nations. Mao was the creature of an overwhelming compulsion to return China to her rightful place among the nations—
at their head. Determined to restore the proper order of mankind,
he apparently felt that the Chinese masses, who partook of his
vision, would accept almost any sacrifice required to force other
nations to their knees.

The immediate goal had been attained by 1965. China, for
decades a source of amusement or an object of greed, was
counted in the scales of power, for she was becoming *the* counter-
poise between East and West. It was undoubtedly with great satisfaction that Mao felt his hand to be on the balance between an
uneasy peace and the nuclear war which, he proclaimed, China
does not fear.

"The Nationalists, who felt China's degradation as keenly as
do the Communists, used to hold 'National Humiliation Days' to
mark the indignities imposed upon China by the West," an American scholar once remarked. "The Communists hold 'National Retaliation Days'!"

China no longer suffered foreign humiliation. For the first
time in two centuries foreigners did not ask: "What *will* we do
about China?" The question was: "What *can* we do about China?"
But those substantial accomplishments were not enough for the
Maoists. They wanted nothing less than total domination.

Because Mao Tse-tung's most effective appeal was directed to the semi-mystical nationalism of the Chinese, belief in an anti-Chinese devil dominated his lay theology. The United States served him well in that role. A sense of wrongs redressed—and of great wrongs still endured—inspired the pathologically self-confident Maoist hierarchy to further assertion. The sheer magnitude of China made her assertiveness a major force in the world for there is *virtus* in size alone. No one could ignore a nation of 750 million persons, occupying more than 4 million square miles, when it was bent upon revenge.

Driven by ambitions and fears so profound that they became ingrained compulsions, a talented and industrious people was embarked upon a course new in human history. The United States insisted that Communist China was a maverick nation—and the United States was right. China was a maverick, though not necessarily an incorrigible rogue bull, which could only be destroyed, as the new American folklore maintained. The Maoist regime had rejected so many of the common principles of international behavior and domestic administration that it was hardly describable in the conventional terms of political science—either bourgeois or Marxist. At the heart of an experiment in the control of men that was unique in both magnitude and intensity lay a unique conviction of superiority—racial, cultural, moral, and physical. Harnessed by a messianic political party, the Chinese spirit was dedicated to creating another unique society that would be the center of world power, just as Imperial China was the Central Kingdom.

The unique Chinese spirit, which found its expression in Maoism, was bred by a unique civilization, which developed in substantial isolation from the other great civilizations. It was not remarkable that the Chinese should have adopted an inflexible conviction of superiority when the little they saw of the outside world was, for millennia, manifestly inferior to what they possessed within China. The Chinese leadership selected Marxism-Leninism as the vehicle that would carry it to the traditional goals, and Communism in China today must therefore be considered as much an outgrowth of the ancient mind of China as a branch of the international Communist movement. The Communist leaders themselves have always displayed curiously alternating attitudes of revulsion and attraction toward the traditional Chinese civilization. They hated it because it prevented change, but they loved it because it was the essence of China's greatness.

It is, therefore, impossible to understand contemporary China unless one examines the historical basis of modern Chinese habits of mind. However, it will be possible in this book to elide the process by starting not with the dim origins of Chinese civilization, but with the West's intrusion upon China in modern times. Coming at the end of the sixteenth century just as the Ming Dynasty was perishing of traditional ills, the advent of the West revealed the technological weaknesses of the old society and forced intelligent Chinese to examine the sources of their national and their individual identities. The West came in cassocks and soutanes, preaching Christianity and, incidentally, displaying the marvels of Western science. The Jesuits, who were its vanguard, never succeeded in converting China to Christianity, but they did change the nation's soul beyond restoration.

This book, which attempts a certain comprehensiveness because it is intended for the general reader rather than the specialist, follows an unusual plan. After two general chapters (of which this is the second) dealing with the present state of China and the major reasons for that state, two Parts, comprising six chapters in all, take the reader chronologically through vital events from 1600 to 1967. Although this is not a history, a knowledge of those events appears to me essential to understanding the influences which have shaped the minds of the Communist leaders and their responses. Part Two, which follows immediately after the present chapter, therefore deals with the arrival of the first Westerners to reside in modern China, with the economic disasters produced by overpopulation, with the reaction of the Westerners to China in the nineteenth century, and with the Chinese reaction to the West during that same period. Part Three describes, in Chapter 7, the collapse of the Manchu Empire and the establishment of the Republic of China, touching on the intellectual currents of the time. The following chapter begins with the establishment of the People's Republic of China in 1949, concluding with a chronology of the chief events between that date and the present.

Thereafter the emphasis shifts from the chronological to the particular. Part Four, in two chapters, attempts to set forth the intellectual bases of the regime. Chapter 9 therein outlines the traditional Chinese political and social philosophy. Chapter 10 describes the influences that acted upon Mao Tse-tung and the manner in which he adapted traditional Chinese thought to his own interpretation of Marxism-Leninism.

Part Five, in four chapters, tells of the organs and the methods by which the Communists rule China: the Communist Party, the People's Government, the recurrent campaigns that are the Chinese Communist contribution to modern political techniques, and the methods developed to "reform" the thinking of the Chinese people. Part Six is concerned with the results produced. Chapter 15 therein relates the first culmination of Communist thinking and ambitions in the creation of the People's Communes. The next two chapters are concerned respectively with China's relations with the outside world, including the Sino-Soviet quarrel, and with the state to which China was reduced by the Maoist excesses. Chapter 18 describes the Grand Climacteric of the Red Guards, called the Great Proletarian Cultural Revolution. The Epilogue offers some tentative conclusions and suggestions based upon the evidence presented throughout the book.

The central motif is what I consider the single most important theme in modern Chinese history—the nation's alternating attempts and refusals to adjust to the West. China has never succeeded in reconciling herself to living on the terms of the outside world, nor has she been able to attain the power to force the world to live on her terms. During somewhat more than a century of intimate contact with the West the Chinese have attempted to gain their ends by a variety of means. The adoption of Communism was the culminating device, which the zealots were convinced would solve all China's problems—economic, social, spiritual, and military. They were understandably dismayed when they discovered that Moscow was subtly recasting the doctrine into a shape which would make it impossible for them to attain their most cherished objectives. They had, therefore, no alternative but to fight for the preservation of orthodoxy, even at the risk of splitting the Communist world. Finally, the great catharsis of the Cultural Revolution forced realistic Communists to try to come to terms with the reality of a world China could not dominate.

The entrance hall of the School of Medicine at Wuhan University is flanked by two portraits, each considerably larger than life. On the right is the mythical Emperor Shen Nung, the "Divine Farmer," who taught the Chinese race husbandry and the principles of medicine. On the left is I. P. Pavlov, the Russian physiologist, whose researches provide the basis for Peking's conviction that man's internal life and moral responses can both be determined in advance by external manipulation. China pays no other foreign scientist a fraction of the homage she renders Pavlov, for his doctrines are, as much as Marxism, the basic canons of the regime. While democracy must believe in the infinite perfectibility of the human individual, Maoist Communism is based upon a conviction of his infinite malleability.

The incandescent intensity of the Maoists' zeal impelled them to excess. A singleminded impatience is, contrary to the common Western belief, characteristic of the modern Chinese. Because the Maoists' ambitions were so sweeping and their means so limited, it was almost impossible to distinguish those excesses forced by necessity from those other excesses, which were the product of sheer fanaticism. Besides, the hierarchy suffered from a confusion of purposes and means because of the complex sources of their actions. The Maoists sought deliberately, above all else, to make China a great power. They were almost as strongly impelled to attempt the creation of a uniform, reborn Chinese personality because of the manner of the persistent seeking after Utopia which characterized the traditional Chinese state ideology. Even less than most statesmen were the Maoist prophets of Peking—their Maoism Leninist and Confucianist in nearly equal parts—either consistent or aware of why they acted as they did.

Some Maoist pronouncements and some Maoist policies were so extreme that the liberal Western mind instinctively refused belief that they actually existed. Mao Tse-tung himself declared: "Atomic weapons are [powerless] paper tigers . . . nuclear war would be a good thing, since it would lead to the worldwide triumph of Communism." Western-trained psychologists affirmed the Party's dictum: "There is no such thing as universal human nature; there is only class nature, differing widely." The Communists actually did seek to create a new earthly realm based upon the new Communist individual, purified of bourgeois dross; and they did enjoin everyone from farmers to physicists to put complete faith in the inspired guidance of the Party, disregarding the limitations upon their potential achievement taught by previous experience.

It is almost incredible to Westerners that such pronouncements can be wholly earnest—and mean exactly what they appear to mean. Nor does it much help understanding to note that those excesses arose from overreaching self-confidence, profound lack of knowledge of the outside world, and overwhelming compulsions. Within the framework of their own assumptions and the limitations of their knowledge, the Maoists were wholly logical. Of course, great divergences gaped between their proposals and their achievements. Even before the Cultural Revolution, the corps of middle and lower cadres, who dealt with reality, had by its resistance often saved the leadership from the consequences of the worst excesses. But those excesses continued to proliferate because the leaders were, in a most immediate sense, at war with themselves; they were seeking the destruction of the institutions which had made them. Attempting to affirm one's legacy by destroying its parts is a schizophrenic occupation at best. This elemental contradiction was the chief source of the enormities which confounded the Western mind—and the nearly incredible irrationality of the Cultural Revolution.

The course upon which Red China was embarked raised profound questions in all human souls. The Chinese experiment was of enormous portent in a world in which population is swelling, belief is dying, and self-aggrandizement has been exalted to a moral imperative. The Maoist People's Republic posed not only the practical problem of countering a new danger from the East, but a searching moral and intellectual challenge as well. The Chinese Maoists, impelled by their historical passions and the pseudologic of Marxism, were a wholly new moral force. After almost two decades in power, they stood opposed to most of the world—

and frightened even their allies. The final rejection of Maoism by the great majority of Mao's own cadres was a decision of enormous significance which extended far beyond China. Deplorable as the loss of the moral and revolutionary fervor of the People's Republic may be to the Marxist-Maoist purists of the world, the courage and recognition of human limitations displayed by the anti-Maoists in their determined resistance to visionary excess was an affirmation that the human animal remained ultimately a brave and rational animal.

Part Two

THE OUTER DARKNESS
(1600–1900)

*Western Aggressiveness Penetrates
the Glorious Isolation of Imperial China*

*China has moved through time much like a gigantic jellyfish
in the twenty-two hundred years since she became a political entity by the consolidation of her independent feudal states into an
empire. Vast in bulk at the outset, she has constantly expanded.
The process has, from time to time, been checked or reversed,
sometimes for centuries, but the instinctive outward growth has
always been resumed. China has changed her internal organization—or become conscious of her own character—only in response to external stimuli. Her reaction has sometimes been a
shrinking into herself, sometimes an unhurried ingestion of the
intruder, and sometimes a violent striking out. China, like a Portuguese Man-of-War, has always possessed stinging tentacles
whose embrace could maim or kill the adversary.*

3

The West's First Contact with an Affluent Chinese Empire

On the 16th of October in the year 1552 Matteo Ricci was born amid the hills of northern Italy. Macerata, his birthplace, was about two hundred and fifty miles from the city of Genoa, which had ninety-nine years earlier produced the sea captain Christopher Columbus, who discovered the New World to Europe. As a priest of the dedicated and aggressive Society of Jesus, Matteo Ricci was to explore a world more ancient than Europe and teeming with more wonders than America. It was fabled Cathay, which had first burst on the consciousness of Europe through the tales of another Italian, Marco Polo.

Columbus, like all the venturesome sailors of his era, was seeking Cathay when he found his New World. Avidity for the incalculable wealth of the Orient and curiosity regarding its strange ways dominated sixteenth-century Europe as the quest for the Holy Grail had ruled the Knights of the Round Table. If the vision of Cathay had not kindled the spirits of the bold and stirred the avarice of princes, it is more than likely that the present shape of the Western world would be quite different.

The missionary priest Matteo Ricci was not primarily an explorer, but a scholar and a great reporter. An eminent astronomer and mathematician, he served China by introducing Euclid and Copernicus to the few intellectuals of that self-satisfied country who would condescend to new knowledge. The Chinese were later to find themselves forced to a desperate interest in European science—and the power that knowledge provided. Ricci, who came to preach a universal doctrine and universal love, instead stirred the Chinese to a jealous consciousness of their own unique character. He initiated the process which continues to the present day. China still searches for a fomula that will enable her to rise above the distasteful necessity for living with other nations—a formula that will force them to live on Chinese terms.

Father Ricci was a meticulous reporter. He did not minimize China's accomplishments, despite his continuing irritation at the self-centered complacence that characterized the Chinese he knew. His dispatches and journals drew for Europeans a picture of China, flesh and blood, marble and silk, that was even more wonderful than the tales Marco Polo had told of Cathay under Mongol rule. During the four hundred-odd years that elapsed between the accounts of the two Italians, China had grown even richer than the fairy-tale realm of the Great Khan that Marco Polo described, for she had known three centuries of relative stability and rapid economic growth. Princes and bureaucrats continued to live in splendor, but the commonalty also passed their days in comfort and ease unknown to the great masses of Europe. China was rich in natural resources, richer than all the other civilized realms combined. She was even more fortunate in the possession of political and social institutions, already eighteen hundred years old, which endowed her with the most equitable and stable government in the world. The teachings of the social and political philosopher Confucius, who was in his prime about 500 B.C., had provided the framework for those enduring institutions. Only human frailty could mar the glittering fabric of prosperity and justice.

The missionary was almost lost to his mission before it began. Although the youth attended a Jesuit college, where he felt a strong sense of vocation, he went to Rome at seventeen to study law in obedience to his father's wishes. Two years later, in 1571, he was admitted to the Society of Jesus as a novice and wrote to ask his father's blessing. The elder Ricci, a true man of the secularist Renaissance, set out for Rome to withdraw his son from the novitiate. But he was forced to halt midway when stricken by a fever. A true man of the age of superstition, he became convinced that the fever was a sign from heaven. After a long convalescence, he returned home to bestow the long deferred blessing by letter. Matteo Ricci was thus preserved to the Society of Jesus and the Apostolate to the East.

In 1577, just as Ricci was completing his studies, the Procurator of the East India Mission came to Rome, seeking recruits for his arduous service. After receiving the blessing of Pope Gregory XIII, a handful of newly ordained priests, including Father Ricci, traveled overland to Lisbon to sail with the Portuguese trading fleet on its annual voyage to India. Portugal was then the chief European power in Asia, and King Sebastian, receiving the group, sighed: "How can I ever be sufficiently grateful to the Father General of the [Jesuit] order for so much help for the Indies?"

Sebastian's pious exclamation alluded to the cooperation between church and state in opening the Orient to Christian civilization—and providing a lucrative trade for Europe. Chinese scholars have taken it as evidence that religion was in the service of imperialism.

China presented a unique challenge. Here were no befeathered and painted savages to be converted, but men and women of a highly complex civilization. The Jesuits' response was flexible and subtle. Ricci, who mastered written classical Chinese during his twenty-seven years in the country, was one of the first missionaries who "decided to turn Chinese, rather than attempt to convert the Celestial Kingdom by changing its millions into Portuguese and Italians," in the judgment of a great modern churchman.[1] For the first time, the Roman Catholic Church was called upon to prove that its universality did not rest upon the imposition of European social, cultural, and material forms, but was truly spiritual.

Despite the Jesuits' adaptability, they were soon enmeshed in the first of those psychological and physical clashes which have ever since characterized relations between China and the West.

[1] Archbishop (now Cardinal) Richard J. Cushing of Boston in Louis J. Gallagher's translation *China in the 16th Century: The Journals of Matthew Ricci 1583–1610* (New York: Random House, 1953), p. ix.

To this day, neither artifice nor compromise has ever convinced the Chinese—who are, perhaps, the most stubbornly nationalistic people on earth—that embracing Christianity will not alter their essential character. Missionaries have had their greatest success with the Chinese only during the past decade and only in Hong Kong, where the vast refugee population has been involuntarily denationalized. Christianity has always found a somewhat warmer welcome among the overseas Chinese, because they too were cast out of the mainstream of national life and because it was often commercially advantageous to adopt the religion of their European patrons. Before the Communist conquest, converts generally came from the educated classes of China's coastal cities, who were already partially Westernized by other forces, while the masses held to the ways of their fathers. But the great mass of the Chinese, whether peasants or scholars, have displayed great resistance to conversion since Ricci's day.

Since that time, China's reaction to both the West and Christianity has been dominated by apprehension. The Chinese have felt that Christianity, in the service of adventurous merchants and politicians, wished, at its most beneficent, to transform them into something they were not. At its most malignant, they have feared that it sought to convert them into the slaves of foreigners. The history of modern China has been shaped by such fears and by the determination to resist enforced change.

The Jesuits established their first mission house at Hsiaoching on the West River some hundred miles from Canton in 1583. Their efforts to preach their gospel in peace were, time and time again, frustrated by the instinctive suspicion and wilful obstruction they encountered. Ricci himself concluded early that the Chinese "fear and distrust all foreigners." [2]

Even the Jesuits' most altruistic deeds provoked violent resentment. Soon after their arrival, they gave shelter to a dying man who, shortly before his death, became the first convert made by the modern Christian Church in China. The Cantonese whispered that the foreigners really wanted to dig out a precious jewel concealed within the convert's skull. The incident was an uncanny

[2] Ricci, p. 160.

precursor of the charges made against missionaries during succeeding centuries, culminating in 1951 in the tumultuous "public
trial" in Canton of Canadian Sisters of Mercy for "murdering" the
orphans under their charge. It was also a classic demonstration of
the suspicion with which the Chinese, like all human beings, look
upon an action that is inexplicable in terms of their own logic.
Since they could not comprehend the missionaries' compulsion to
save souls, they concluded that the motivation was evil.

Other difficulties were of the Jesuits' own making. They were
nearly expelled by the Chinese because they assisted the King of
Spain in his efforts to breach the Portuguese monopoly of the lucrative China trade. Although they were constantly seeking to extend their influence, the Jesuits were forced to close their outlying
mission houses or were actually expelled on five separate occasions during their first decade in China. Not until 1595, eighteen
years after he came to Asia, did Ricci himself finally penetrate as
far as the southern capital at Nanking.

The upper classes of Nanking, who argued philosophy as
avidly as other men discussed race horses, were attracted by the
priest's doctrines—and even more by the mechanical contri-
vances, the maps, and the astronomical charts he carried. Ricci
converted a few men of influence who secured permission for him
to visit the northern capital at Peking, where the Ming Dynasty
kept its Court. His first attempt to open a mission house in the
capital failed. It was not until 1602, twenty-four years after he left
Rome, that Matteo Ricci finally came to Peking to stay. Yet China
felt herself sufficiently secure to be hospitable to foreigners and
their ideas. Despite the unremitting opposition of the conservatives, Father Ricci was to become the Court Astronomer, to intro-
duce Western mathematics and science to China, to found a line
of Jesuit advisers to the Emperor of China, and, on his death in
Peking in 1610, to be honored by a state funeral at the Emperor's
expense.

The savant from the mysterious Occident was a revelation to
a nation that venerated knowledge but had lost its vigor under a
perfected intellectual system that was subject to almost no
external stimuli. The Ming Empire was an even greater revelation
to Father Ricci. His writing breathes wonder at a nation that was

greater in extent and richer in material goods than all the nations of Europe—and more equitably governed than any of them.

Coming as an emissary of revealed truth from a continent accustomed to think of itself as the source of all civilization, Ricci was ill-prepared to discover a nation that believed that it encompassed the civilized world and was itself the sole repository of knowledge. After explaining in his journal that the term Cathay, given currency by Marco Polo, was simply another name for China, one of the innumerable variants by which her neighbors call the Great Empire, Ricci added:

"Today we usually call this country Ciumquo or Ciumhoa, the first [suffixed] word signifying 'kingdom,' and the second, 'garden.' When put together the words are translated, 'To be at the center.' . . . He whose authority extends over this immense kingdom is called Lord of the Universe, because the Chinese are of the opinion that the extent of their vast dominion is to all intents and purposes coterminous with the borders of the universe. The few kingdoms contiguous to their state, of which they had any knowledge before they learned of the existence of Europe, were, in their estimation, hardly worthy of consideration. . . . With such a limited knowledge, it is evident why they boasted of their kingdom as being the whole world, and why they called it Thienhia, meaning 'everything under the heavens.' " [3]

The cultured Italian, whose professional humility was not undiluted by pride in his intellectual attainments, was appalled at the Chinese attitude toward the learning he represented. "The Chinese," he wrote, "look upon all foreigners as illiterate and barbarous, and refer to them in just these terms. They even disdain to learn anything from the books of outsiders because they believe that all true science and knowledge belongs to them alone. . . . Even the written characters by which they express the word 'foreigner' are those that are applied to beasts, and scarcely ever do they give them a title more honorable than they would assign to their demons. One would scarcely believe how suspicious they are of a legate or an ambassador of a neighboring country, sent in to pay respect to the King, to settle a tributary tax, or to conduct any sort of business. The fact that China may have been on friendly

[3] *Ibid.*, pp. 7, 166.

terms with the kingdom of the visiting legates, from time immemorial, does not exempt the visiting dignitaries from being conducted along their entire route within the realm as captives or prisoners and permitted to see nothing in the course of their journey." [4]

Accustomed to the relative freedom of Europe, Ricci was shocked by the discovery that unofficial travelers from neighboring lands were never permitted to leave China and that *no* foreigner might travel freely within the country for fear that he might later tell unsuitable tales abroad.

The Italian was personally distressed at being ranked no higher than the beasts. He knew constant frustration in his endeavors to open a way for his true faith into the hearts of a people who were convinced that their own philosophers had already explored the realm of knowledge to its outermost boundaries. An eminent Ming authority had written: "Ever since the time of the philosopher Chu [Hsi, A.D. 1130–1200] the truth has been made manifest to the world; no more writing is necessary; what is left to us is practice." [5] Ricci was, in short, faced with the utter self-satisfaction of a society which believed itself complete.

Yet Ricci was not only a European and a Jesuit but a child of the age of wonder, and the Cathay he had rediscovered in the guise of China was truly a realm of wonders. His conscientiously factual description of Ming Dynasty China is almost as startling to one who is familiar with the state of present-day China, pinched and brawling, as it was to his own contemporaries.

If Father Ricci had been a joyous pagan, he might have declared that he had found the Elysian Fields. In no other region of the world did nature yield her bounty to man's needs in such abundance and variety. "Everything which the people need for their well-being and sustenance," he wrote, "whether it be for food or clothing or even delicacies and superfluities, is abundantly produced within the borders." [6] His list comprehended all. Grains of every kind, fruits, vegetables, herbs, and even flowers grew in

[4] *Ibid.*, pp. 88–89.
[5] Quoted in K. S. Latourette, *The Chinese, Their History and Culture* (New York: Macmillan, 1946), p. 300.
[6] Ricci, p. 10.

innumerable shapes and immeasurable quantities. China was no less blessed in her profusion of useful animals: cattle, lambs, and pigs; hens, ducks, and geese; deer, hares—and fish "so numerous that a fisherman never casts a line without making a catch." [7]

The Chinese clothed themselves in silk, which was available at reasonable prices in every corner of the Empire, or wore cotton, which had been introduced only half a century earlier but was already thriving so that "enough cotton could be grown in China to supply the whole world." [8] By the standards of their own abundance the Chinese were deficient in wool and linen. But they made garments padded with cotton which were as warm as woolen fabrics, and they were plentifully supplied with the fur of weasels and foxes. Coal was found in plenty, as were "all the known metals without exception." [9] Gazing upon China's naked hills and plains today, it is astonishing that Ricci found it "difficult to express how great is the quantity of lumber and how vast are the forests in which practically every species of wood known in Europe is to be found." [10] To supplement vast herds of draft animals, the Chinese had constructed so many river craft from their plentiful timber that "there are as many boats in this kingdom as can be counted up in all the rest of the world." [11]

Matteo Ricci was overcome at the contrast between China and Europe, even though the Europeans had already begun to drain the wealth of the Indies and the Americas. It was not only the material abundance that transfixed him, but the richness of intellectual life and the perfection of public administration. He felt almost that he had discovered the kingdom of the philosophers envisioned by Plato. The dominant aristocracy of the Chinese Empire, to whom even the Emperor deferred, was chosen on the basis of intelligence and classical learning, as demonstrated in rigorous examinations.[12] "Only such as have earned a doctor's de-

[7] *Ibid.*, p. 12.
[8] *Ibid.*, p. 13.
[9] *Ibid.*, p. 14.
[10] *Ibid.*, p. 15.
[11] *Ibid.*, p. 13.
[12] Westerners were much impressed by the Civil Service Examination System through which the Chinese selected their officials. Particularly during the eighteenth century's craze for *Chinoiserie* did Europe draw extensively upon

gree or that of a licentiate," Ricci recorded, "are admitted to take part in the government of the kingdom. . . . Every public office is therefore fortified with and dependent upon the attested science, prudence, and diplomacy of the person assigned to it. . . ." [13]

China had passed beyond feudalism, which still tormented Europe. No petty despots sacrificed thousands in contention for titles whose resonance proved their hollowness. Princes did not fight for strips of land to enlarge their domains, nor did they contend for gold and jewels. A united nation, greater in extent than the Europe of a hundred sovereign princes, was ruled from a single center under a uniform code of law. The burden of government rested lightly upon the people, who said, with truth and complacency: "Heaven is high and the Emperor is far, far away!" Men of many races, professing many religions, lived in amity in a society without marked class divisions, aside from the scholar-officials and a nobility whose successive generations descended one step in rank, finally to become commoners again. Only the heirs of the Sage Confucius retained their noble ranks in perpetuity. Landed magnates held their domains at the Emperor's pleasure, and not even great wealth conferred exalted status. Gold could buy luxury but not dignity, since contempt for the trader tarnished every ounce.

The social and political systems that characterized the Ming Dynasty were consciously cultivated growths, the most tenacious examples of successful planning in man's history. Confucianism, the official ideology, which shaped both institutions and men's behavior, was fixed early in China's history. The feudal state of Chin had imposed its hegemony on its neighbors from 251 to 221 B.C., enabling its ruler to assume the title *Shih Huang Ti*, literally, the First Yellow Emperor, actually, the First *Chinese* Emperor, yellow being the Imperial color. Although the Chin had been

---

Chinese aesthetic and administrative models. The English ruling class was disciplined by studying the Greek and Roman classics, as China's mandarins were drilled in the Confucian classics, and the United States later adopted the Civil Service Examination System *en bloc*. But the West has never been willing to follow the Chinese example to the logical conclusion of requiring even the highest officials to qualify by examinations.

[13] Ricci, p. 45.

a tight totalitarianism, complete even to thought control and secret police, its successor state, the Han Dynasty, which ruled from 203 B.C. until A.D. 220, had cast about for a more liberal form of government. The Han found its model in the teachings of the Sage Confucius, who had lived from approximately 551 to 479 B.C.

Confucius had expounded a minutely detailed morality whose practice, he contended, could re-create the golden age that Chinese mythology assigned to the era of the Duke of Chou at the beginning of the second millennium B.C. Between 200 and 150 B.C. the Han Dynasty adopted the teachings of Confucius as the basis for the organization of government, the philosophy of politics, the structure of society, and even the emotions of the individual. Not sentimentality but recognition of reality has impelled the Chinese to call themselves "men of Han" ever since that dynasty created a centralized nation by extending its sway over a good part of the territory that is today China and by employing the generalized principles of Confucius as the framework on which to erect the practical institutions of government. Those institutions and those principles were adopted with little change by all subsequent major dynasties, whether the rulers were non-Chinese by race, like the Mongols of the Yuan Dynasty (1274–1368) and the Manchus of the Ching Dynasty (1644–1911), or Chinese, like the Sui and Tang (589–907), the Sung (960–1279), and the Ming itself (1368–1644).

Since Confucius, like Socrates, never wrote down his precepts, his wisdom has survived in a series of disjointed dialogues with his disciples. Those collected dialogues, called *The Analects,* are the chief of the Confucian classics; other classics include fragmentary histories, collections of ancient poems, books on divination, and legendary accounts of the vanished Golden Age. After the death of Confucius his followers began the process of enlarging those classics, a process which did not end until the Confucian system was destroyed with the collapse of the Ching Dynasty in 1911. The first official commentaries, produced by the scholars of the Han, began the process of institutionalizing Confucianism. Those classics and the commentaries thereto, together with the minutely detailed chronicles of the successive dynasties, became the foundation of the longest-lived political system in the life of mankind.

With the same pardonable self-approbation displayed by Socrates and Plato, Confucius had declared that the highest expression of mankind was the cultivated, moral scholar. His ethical and administrative systems rested upon the example and the dominance of that superior individual. Seeking to build functioning political institutions around the philosopher-king, the Han Dynasty devised the Civil Service Examination System as a means of selecting men qualified to fill that role. The examinations tested the candidate's knowledge of the Confucian classics and his ability to write in the elided, polished style in which the classics were couched. The examination system became the heart of practical Confucianism, providing a system under which proven scholarship—and the moral qualities that presumably derived from that scholarship—led directly to political power. All education, therefore, concentrated upon inculcation of the Confucian classics, while independent thought, original speculation, and scientific inquiry were discouraged.

From 150 B.C. until A.D. 1580, when the Jesuits began to study Confucianism, neither the structure of government nor its intellectual basis had altered fundamentally—nor was either to alter in essence until the Confucian empire was destroyed in 1911. For two thousand years the best minds of China concentrated their energies upon refining and utilizing the ideology of Confucius. The social order created by the Confucians was hierarchical socially and absolutist politically. It was devoid of an absolute standard of morality, since the good example of one's superiors, rather than any moral imperative, was the basis of proper behavior. The ethical content of actions depended largely upon the relationship between the persons concerned. A highly organized catalogue of social and individual virtues was the theoretical basis of a system that ideally did not employ rewards and punishment to ensure compliance, but rather depended upon reactions already instilled in the individual. Society was made perfect by making mankind perfectly and automatically responsive to the tacit will of the ruler. There was no need to make that will explicit since the compulsion to obedience was not external but lay in the heart of the individual.

The cardinal Confucian virtue was filial piety, expressed in observance of the social distinctions that the mythical Sage Kings of the Golden Age had decreed for mankind. The five relationships that encompassed all others were: ruler and subject, father and son, husband and wife, elder brother and younger brother, friend and friend. Only the last was a relationship of equals. The others strictly defined the manner in which the inferior must render obedience and service to his superior—and the superior's corollary responsibilities to his inferior. Knowing his precise position within the state and the family, the individual knew all he needed to know about his personal behavior. Once his position was defined, protocol told him exactly how to act in any conceivable situation.

Although China knew other great currents of thought, which will be examined later, the official ideology was supreme. By 1600, under the Ming, it had produced a formal social structure that changed little. Art, literature, and political thought were sluggish, deadened by the same ballast of custom which assured stability. The Ming Dynasty, having fulfilled itself, looked neither toward perils to avoid them nor toward goals to attain them. Men were convinced that the Great Wall, thrown up by the First Chin Emperor in the third century B.C., still made China absolutely secure by containing the ambitious barbarians of the northern steppes who had sought to conquer the rich southland as long as history had been recorded. The little wars on the marches of the Empire were far away, and they did, after all, provide employment for generals and artisans. Life was, above all, abundantly comfortable, for that most useful of all the arts—the art of living—flourished. Chinese architects, painters, cooks, and potters produced some of their finest works, infinitely refined in technique if hardly original in conception. The government's Board of Rites maintained sixteen perfumed and silken brothels, called Halls of Learning, where courtesans proficient in literature and music entertained. But tired businessmen were not permitted entry; only officials might enjoy these delights. Though the commonalty was denied some refinements, life was pleasant for all.

Despite the universal pressure for sated complacency, a few spirits retained their curiosity. The desire to learn survived even the institutionalized disapproval of the bureaucrats, who held power because they were versed in the state ideology, which already comprehended all *worthy* knowledge. The scientific and mathematical techniques introduced by Ricci and his Jesuit successors fascinated successive Emperors and their Courts. But the Western devices appeared to the cultivated Chinese to be little more than toys. Chiming timepieces and clockwork music boxes were highly valued for their naïve ingenuity. Devices of broader usefulness contrived by the Jesuits were considered practical, if somewhat distasteful, gadgets, like the reformed calendar, which actually accorded with the movement of the heavenly bodies, or the brazen cannon cast for the Imperial bodyguard. Nor was there any reason for the mandarins to realize that Europe's box of tricks was eventually to alter the nature of China by awakening the Chinese to their scientific and industrial deficiencies, and by making them conscious of themselves as a part of the great world—rather than the world itself.

The Jesuits' spiritual message aroused little interest. The great majority of the cultivated Chinese with whom the missionaries mingled were simply not susceptible; they were neither discontented with their earthly lot nor fearful of the hereafter.

But the Jesuits themselves became aware of gross flaws in the Mings' political and ethical systems when they progressed from theoretical study of the Confucian texts to intimate acquaintance with the daily life of the Court and the people. Enchanted by the living principle of an aristocracy of intellect, Ricci was distressed to find that the ideal had been corrupted. Instead of harmonious affection, he discovered mutual suspicion so intense that the Emperor himself trusted neither his advisers nor the masses. The later Ming Emperors rarely left the "royal enclosure" in Peking, having abandoned their ancestors' practice of appearing among the people in state. But even earlier Emperors, noted Ricci, ". . . would never dare to do so without a thousand preliminary precautions. . . . Secret service men were placed along the route over which the King was to travel and on all roads leading to it . . . the public never knew in which of the many palanquins of his cortege he was actually riding. One would think he was making a journey through enemy country rather than through multitudes of his own subjects and clients." [14]

The Jesuit had come upon a society on the verge of dissolution, all its grandeur faintly overripe. The plight of the Ming Dynasty, which had ruled for more than two hundred years when the Jesuits arrived, was the normal culmination of each new dynasty that ruled the traditional Confucian state. The Mongols, the first aliens to rule all China, had utilized the Confucian administrative machinery, although ruling somewhat more intrusively than had previous native dynasties. As the dedicated *Chinese* successors of the alien Mongols, the conservative Ming had restored all the old institutions. The dynasty consciously sought to return to the older, purer form of Confucianism which was itself an attempt to re-create the simplicity of a protohistorical era of ideal happiness. Instead of drawing toward that goal, the Ming, like all its predecessors, became the victim of encrusted interests and institutionalized corruption.

Confucian government radiated from an elaborately organized capital with the Emperor at its heart. His representatives went out to the mountains and the plains, to the snow-covered steppes and the glowing green tropics, to the cliff-hung shores and the deserts of the great winds. Viceroys, governors, prefects, and, finally, the district magistrates, who were called "father and mother officials," noted all affairs, but were charged to interfere with customary village self-rule only to the extent necessary to preserve order and to collect taxes. Each official was reasonably free of interference as long as he discharged those two functions—or appeared to do so.

In the springtime at each successive dynasty, the system operated efficiently and beneficently. But with the passage of time, the autonomy granted officials presented irresistible temptations to the avaricious and the ambitious. Largely devoid of effective safeguards against excess or any objective criteria for the administration of justice, the system depended ultimately upon the individual official's efficient and disinterested discharge of the

[14] *Ibid.*, p. 88.

duties assigned to him. When a dynasty was young and the Emperor vigorous, his personal example and the Court's loose surveillance were enough to keep most men honest. But inbreeding and intrigue produced an inevitable decline in the powers of successive Emperors, while isolating them from the people behind an ever larger and ever more self-seeking Court.

Although it depended absolutely upon the honesty of the individual for its operation, the system subtly if inadvertently encouraged him to be corrupt. It not only lacked an effective independent judiciary, but also placed a premium upon the appearance —rather than the reality—of rectitude. Manners rather than morals were all-important. Moreover, the overriding emphasis upon the family as the nucleus of the social structure provided both justification and incentive for individuals' stealing from the state for the benefit of their private clans. Once corruption bubbled forth, no safeguard was adequate to prevent its slow seepage into every crevice of the administrative structure. The universal, unspoken conspiracy defied the regulation that no official might remain in the same area for more than three years or govern his native district. "So great is the lust for domination on the part of the magistrates," wrote Ricci, "that scarcely anyone can be said to possess his belongings in security, and everyone lives in continual fear of being deprived of what he has by a false accusation." [15] The familiar phrase *Tan-kuan Wu-li* (corrupt officials and grafting councilors) fell often from the lips of aggrieved citizens at the beginning of the seventeenth century. "There was always corruption in China, but it was never so virulent as during the Ming era," the German historian Wolfram Eberhard remarks.[16] He contends that the introduction of cheap printing made it possible for a new group of *arriviste* adventurers, who were without the ingrained morality passed from generation to generation of the old ruling class, to acquire learning and thus become officials by passing the Civil Service Examinations.[17]

[15] *Ibid.*, p. 88.
[16] *Chinas Geschichte* (A. Francke AG-Verlag, 1948), pp. 280–281.
[17] The habits of mind and the systematically amoral code of behavior encouraged by Confucianism were to play a major role in the Chinese adoption of communism. Particularly significant were the absence of almost all spiritual

The Ming Dynasty, devoutly Confucian, was on the point of the final dissolution that had brought all preceding dynasties to an end at just that moment when the Jesuit's keen observation provided the Western world with its first thorough examination of China. Systematically misinformed by its representatives in the provinces, Peking was wholly detached from the country. The Court shrank into an isolated and self-contained world that was dominated by vicious perversion and self-seeking frivolity. Its decrees were as little pertinent to the condition of China as they were to the Western Cloudland, where the Heavenly Mother Goddess held court. Successive Emperors, deliberately denied adequate education and knowledge of the true state of the Empire, busied themselves with their harems, with hunting, or with carpentry—according to their individual inclinations—while cabals of corrupt ministers and rapacious eunuchs feuded for power and promulgated laws intended solely to enrich themselves. Since such a capital could hardly choose proper men for the provincial service, the process of decay inevitably spread downward and outward into an administrative inferno.

In the early decades of the seventeenth century the Ming needed an effective army as never before, for the nomads of the northern steppes and forests had been welded into a mighty weapon by the Manchu tribes under their leader Nurhachi. The marches of the Empire became a bloody playground for the hungry barbarians. Nurhachi proclaimed himself First Emperor of the Ching Dynasty in 1616, franking his proclamation with the Imperial Seal, which his ancestors had captured from the fugitive Mongol pretender centuries earlier. In 1625 the Manchus took Mukden, sealing their conquest of the area now called Manchuria. Thirteen years later the Manchus, under Nurhachi's successor Abahai, invested Peking itself, but the Prince rejected his advisers' counsel that he take the city while it lay between his palms.

"We have as yet established no terror in the heart of China itself," he said. "Let us return to our own lands and prepare for

---

or moral absolutes and the positive discouragement of independent thought. The intimate relationship of those attributes to the development of the doctrines of Mao Tse-tung will be discussed at length in later chapters.

the sounding of the horn of destiny, when God will deliver the entire Empire into our hands."

At the moment troops were needed most, internal rot had transformed the Chinese army into disorganized bands of gaily costumed adventurerers, fierce only when prying open the money boxes of good burghers or breaking the waistbands of honest wives and daughters. Even cavalry chargers, infected by their poltroon masters, stampeded in terror when they heard the neighing of the Manchus' horses across the empty steppes. Any general who won a significant victory was destroyed by the suspicious Court, lest he become a contender for supreme power. Taxes and prices soared—taxes to support the depraved luxury of the Court, prices because the population was pressing hard on the land and the government sought neither to develop resources nor to insure equitable distribution of goods. Great estates were granted outright to Court favorites or accumulated by corrupt officials in league with usurers. Small peasant proprietors, their holdings swallowed by great estates, became first sharecroppers and then outlaws. The brigands united under pressure to become in fact what officials had long called them—rebels.

While the Manchus awaited the summons of fate beyond the Great Wall, small bands of Chinese rebels grew into large armies. The most successful generalissimo was Li Tzu-cheng, whom the Communists exalt today as the leader of a peasant revolt like their own.

Upon his father's death Li had inherited both his land and his position as village headman. He thus possessed an assured position atop the ancient structure of paternalistic and often hereditary local self-rule which was distinct from the official hierarchy, that qualified by examination, but was, nonetheless, the foundation of that hierarchy—and the Empire. During Li Tzu-cheng's first year in office, drought parched the North China Plain. Though the farmers of the village were starving, the district magistrate insisted that taxes, properly assessed, must be promptly remitted. He, after all, had an obligation to his family. Held personally responsible for payment, the one-eyed village headman sold his own property, but neither the proceeds of the sale nor further sums he borrowed satisfied the tax collectors. Pressed be-

tween officials and usurers, Li fled to the hills. In the land of out-
law his education and his dominant personality brought him into
the head of a band of fugitives who were similarly dispossessed,
similarly impoverished—and masterless until his advent.

Unremitting government oppression raised recruits for Li's
brigands, while the absence of effective authority allowed them to
pillage at will. Li swaggered across Shensi Province, followed by
his army of desperate men. Ambition feeding upon success, he
determined to make himself Emperor. He promised retribution
upon oppressive officials and bloodsucking usurers, whose lands
would be distributed to the oppressed. His slogan was: "Support
the New King and Pay No Grain Taxes!" Heaven, he declared,
had shown by a rain of calamities that the Ming was no longer its
faithful servant.

In a country where the mystique of noble blood and legiti-
macy had been abandoned millennia earlier, Li saw no need to
establish a legal claim to the throne. He was, in any event, better
born than the first Ming Emperor, a lapsed monk turned
carpenter, who had ruled by right of conquest—as Li proposed to
do. The Ming conquest had, in any event, been attained by proclaiming the same slogans Li broadcast, just as the Communists
were to make identical promises three centuries later.

He was short and swarthy and delighted in brutality, but Li
was a compelling leader to men in rebellion, for he won all his
battles. Even his deformity was an advantage, since soothsayers
had prophesied that a one-eyed man would topple the Ming.
Though he could read the simpler classics and was a connoisseur
of painting, Li was no less superstitious than his troops. When a
sudden snowstorm forced him to camp in the open, he plunged an
arrow into the ground, promising that the flurry would cover the
nock as an omen that he would become Emperor. The snow piled
higher than the shaft, and he was content.

Li Tzu-cheng, like William of Normandy, manipulated his
own omens, assuring their accuracy by his ruthlessness. In 1644,
the sixteenth year of the reign of the Ming Emperor Tsung Chen,
Li's armies appeared before Peking in a torrent of dust. The few
troops still loyal to the Ming were campaigning against the Manchus north of the Great Wall. Within the silk-hung palace the

Emperor, who had ignored affairs of state while he played at carpentry, was alone except for one faithful eunuch. The heir-apparent, smuggled out of the city in the guise of a peasant boy, had been captured by Li's forces. Accepting the end, the Emperor stabbed his daughters and the Empress hanged herself. Clothed in the somber garments of a penitent, Tsung Chen climbed the eminence within the Imperial City known as Coal Hill. His eyes fixed on the banners and turmoil of the rebel camp, so different from the silence within Peking, the Emperor hanged himself from a stunted locust tree. From his breast hung a scroll reading"Deficient in virtue and contemptible in character, I have incurred the wrath of God on high. . . . Do not harm a single one of my people!"

A triumphant Li Tzu-cheng led his rejoicing rabble into the deserted capital. When he came to the Gate of Heavenly Peace (*Tien An Men*), the southern entrance of the Imperial City, the rebel generalissimo rose in his stirrups under the unseeing eyes of the dead Emperor and unslung his bow. Li bawled out that Providence would guide his arrow to the character *Tien* ("heaven") above the gate as a token of the decree of Heaven that he should reign over all China. This time Li could not force the omen: his arrow missed the easy mark. But his followers dispelled their gloom in a frenzy of looting.

Among the spoils was the young concubine of Wu San-kuei, the last loyal general of the Ming, who was off campaigning against the Manchus with the only effective troops left to the Dynasty. When Wu heard that his Emperor was dead and his concubine bedded by Li Tzu-cheng, he struck a truce with the Manchus and marched on Peking at the head of his own troops and seven thousand Tartar horsemen. Although the rebel Emperor offered to return the concubine and proposed an alliance, Wu refused, convinced that he could control the Tartar wolves he had enlisted to protect the Chinese sheep. Li Tzu-cheng's rabble melted away before the barbarian cavalry, and Li himself fled into the limbo of history. His brief reign was over, the reign of the last Emperor of Chinese blood to sit on the Dragon Throne, first reared in 221 B.C. His final arrow had missed its mark, but the impact destroyed traditional Chinese civilization.

＊　＊

Burdened by no convention of magnanimity in victory, the Manchus rejected Wu San-kuei's hopeful request that they return to the steppes, happy in the satisfaction of a mission accomplished. They courteously reminded General Wu that Nurhachi had proclaimed himself Emperor three decades earlier, his title and powers descending by right to his young grandson, who had already taken the reign name Shun Chih. Wu acquiesced with so much grace that he was created viceroy of the southwest. But he was soon in rebellion himself, joined by a shifting group that included unhappy yeomen, fearful officials, and Ming pretenders to the Dragon Throne.

The turmoil attendant upon the establishment of a new dynasty rent the peace of China for a generation, the struggle quite like that which was to accompany the rise of a non-Confucian dynasty three centuries later. Kang Hsi, Nurhachi's great-grandson, who became Emperor in 1662, finally pacified China with fire and the sword. He slaughtered the entire population of rebellious cities. To prevent their aiding the great pirate-patriot Cheng Cheng-kung, whom the West called Koxinga, the Emperor ordered all civilians removed from a zone extending ten miles inland from the coast in breadth and from Shanghai in the north to Canton in the south. The order was actually enforced in Fukien Province, directly opposite the island of Formosa, which Koxinga ruled.

In 1683, with their conquest of Formosa, full control of China passed into the hands of the Manchus. Minor local disturbances inevitably flared from time to time among a heterogeneous population that was linked to the administrative center only by the most unreliable communications. Men continued to die on the borders of the Empire, but they died in small numbers since they were on the offensive. Kang Hsi was securing his frontiers by carrying the fight to the disorganized tribes of the high mountains and the steppes, rather than waiting for them to ravage the foothills and the areas immediately south of the Great Wall. The year 1684 began an era of peace, moderate government, and material abundance which was to endure for a century and a half.

Like all China's conquerors, the Manchus were awed by the

grandeur of the civilization they had inherited by right of the sword. Promising to rule in the traditional manner, they won the support of the majority of the scholar-officials, whose loyalty was given not to the ruling house but to the Confucian ethos. Since Kang Hsi maintained the Confucian forms—and did not curtail their own privileges—the professional civil servants were prepared to ignore both his barbarian origins and his determination to rule more rigorously than they thought quite fitting. It was not the mandarins' purpose to thwart Kang Hsi's desire to carry the perfected Confucian system as far into the future as men's minds could see. The bureaucrats were well content with the Emperor, since they knew that the only flux in history was the disorder attendant upon the change of dynasties. All men looked forward to a future of illimitable millennia dominated by Emperors who were seated upon the Dragon Throne and sustained by their Confucian ministers.

Kang Hsi reigned for sixty years, from 1661 through 1722, a full cycle of Cathay. He cleared the Empire of rebels, Chinese and Moslem; he extended Imperial rule to Tibet and Turkestan, which he called Sinkiang, the New Dominion; he forced every adult Chinese male to wear the queue; he received numerous embassies from abroad; and he brought traditional Chinese civilization to a peak of technological accomplishment and material prosperity. His inquisitive mind turned to the Jesuits for instruction in elementary physics and astronomy, as well as to the Confucians for instruction in philosophy, literature, and statecraft. He was a great Emperor.

Perhaps because he sprang from the northern tribes the Chinese called barbarians, Kang Hsi was more deeply devoted to the Confucian ethos and more assertive of his power than had been any Emperor of the Ming Dynasty. Since the highest expression of Chinese civilization was literary composition in the classical style, Kang Hsi was determined to be not merely a patron of letters, but a writer of note. He sponsored publication of four massive encyclopedic dictionaries, comprising 1,718 volumes in all, and he composed much prose and verse in his own hand. The tragedy of his life was that his calligraphy was undistinguished and his inspiration weak, even by the petrified standards of the Confucian *lite-rati*. Nonetheless, the aura of universal authority conferred by absolute power sustained Kang Hsi's literary reputation.

In 1670, the Emperor, who was distressed by the moral laxity of his subjects, promulgated an edict of sixteen maxims, one for each year of his age. There was, in Chinese eyes certainly nothing wrong with his injunctions, which are typified by the seventh: "Discard strange doctrines in order to glorify the orthodox [Confucian] teaching." There was nothing particularly distinguished about them either. Nonetheless, the Emperor Yung Cheng, Kang Hsi's son and successor, later invited a hundred eminent scholars to submit essays commenting on his father's Sacred Edict. He thereafter ordered that the Sacred Edict and the sixteen best commentaries thereto be read to the assembled people on the first and fifteenth of each month in every metropolis and hamlet of the Empire. Mao Tse-tung, whose literary reputation rests upon his interpretation of new classics, is even more verbosely honored today.

No more than the Communists' was the Manchus' ideological fervor satisfied by providing orthodox literature—and insuring its currency by fiat. The Emperor Chien Lung, Kang Hsi's grandson, undertook to purify the nation's literary and philosophical heritage. He examined the entire body of Chinese literature, first destroying the Imperial Libraries' copies of works he judged unsuitable and then proscribing their publication—or even possession—anywhere within the Empire. Living writers who transgressed the Emperor's exacting standards found violent correction directed not only to their works, but to their persons.

During the hundred-and-thirty-four-year period encompassed by the long reigns of Kang Hsi and Chien Lung and the brief interregnum of Yung Cheng, the men from the steppes created a faithful replica of Ming Dynasty China at the height of its glory. The Ming had also sought to reproduce the characteristics of preceding dynasties—each dynasty shaping itself after its predecessors back to the original model of the mythical Golden Age hallowed by Confucius. Except where barbaric vigor and the fervor of converts strengthened the structure, the *Ta Ching* (Great Pure) Dynasty was identical in its institutions with the *Ta Ming*

(Great Bright) Dynasty. Although minor modifications were unavoidable, the ideal was a magnificent vessel, manned by the best of mankind, swinging forever at her fixed moorings in the tides of time.

For practical dynastic reasons the Imperial family preferred to preserve the purity of its Manchu blood, and the Manchu legions, which were called Banners after their distinctively colored guidons (the flags that distinguished individual units), were not permitted to marry the Chinese of the cities they garrisoned. But Chinese troops, enrolled under the green banner, were an integral part of the military establishment, and Chinese officials administered the Empire for their Manchu rulers. Except for its gauche tendency to be more orthodox than Confucius himself, the dynasty which called itself pure appeared utterly serene as well.

4

The Rich Impoverished, the Poor Starving

The New Dynasty's Magnanimity Produces Overpopulation, Hardship, and Revolt

One habit of mind approaches universality, manifesting itself among modern nationalists and Communists, as well as among medieval Christians and nineteenth-century industrialists. Modern men tend to measure the virtue of a people by the degree of suffering it has innocently endured. By this standard the Chinese are among the most virtuous of peoples.

For the past sixty years Chinese patriots have counted the memories of past oppression, perverse misers glorying in their hoards of virtue. Yet few Chinese historians, drawing their indictments of the *Ta Ching*, have marked the gravest sin of the Manchus. It is nevertheless true that during the hundred and thirty-four miraculous years from the accession of Kang Hsi to the death of Chien Lung, the Manchus inflicted upon the Chinese the greatest indignity rulers can put on their subjects. They contrived the most grievous suffering the Chinese people have known— suffering that continues to this day. They altered forever the basic character of Chinese society and even changed the contours of the land.

As is so often the case, the Manchus sought the opposite of what they accomplished; they thought to demonstrate their own magnificence within the orthodox Confucian structure by a display of benevolence that would make the Chinese people happier and more prosperous than they had been under any previous dynasty. It was, however, the very liberality of the great Ching Emperors which allowed the Chinese population to outpace the productivity of the land and produce starvation, disease, rebellion, and permanent exhaustion of the abundant natural resources Matteo Ricci had seen during the Ming Dynasty.

The converted barbarians displayed their disastrous magnanimity as soon as they came to power. Nurhachi, who forged the feuding tribes of the steppes into the weapon that conquered China, had used terror as his chief tactic. His grandson, the first Ching Emperor, Shun Chih, who ruled for eighteen years and fathered the great Kang Hsi, sought to win by love the people his father had mastered by fear. In 1644 he took Peking and, with the unaccustomed weight of his ceremonial regalia still irksome on his shoulders, he ordered remission of the staggering superstructure of surtaxes the Ming had imposed to finance its excesses and its last frenzied efforts to maintain its sway. However, the need to consolidate their conquest somewhat restrained the Manchus' proclivities toward excessive benevolence until Kang Hsi completed the pacification of China in 1683.

Approaching the fiftieth anniversary of his accession in 1711, Kang Hsi looked upon his achievements with satisfaction. He had remitted annual taxes amounting to 100 million taels, about $120 million,[1] a staggering sum in an economy that was only in part monetary. Scholars and philosophers busily classified the past in order to insure contemporary orthodoxy; agriculture and handicrafts flourished; officials were just; and the people were content. Having grasped the thread with the decision to make the Empire secure by persistent offensive action against the barbarians on the frontiers, Kang Hsi was led ever outward to new conquests. The Empire attained its greatest expanse, comprehending Tibet, Nepal, Burma, Laos, northern Vietnam, Sinkiang (Kang Hsi's

[1] Since it is almost impossible to arrive at exact modern values for Chinese monetary units, which, even then, varied not only from province to province, but from city to city as well, all dollar figures in this chapter are approximations. They can, at best, convey an impression of the values involved—if one remembers that money was worth incalculably more in a pastoral, barter society than it is in a modern, monetary economy. In modern American terms 100 million taels would be more of the magnitude of $50 billion than the formally assigned value of $120 million.

New Dominion and the West's Chinese Turkestan), the maritime provinces of Siberia, Korea, most of Sakhalin Island, much of Russian Turkestan, and parts of Kashmir. The Ching also assessed tribute on feudatory states running eastward from Bhutan through Sikkim, northern Thailand, and Cambodia, while asserting a looser suzerainty over most of the nations of southern Asia.

The Emperor Kang Hsi, who had always been too fully occupied to survey his realm, marked his golden anniversary by an extended journey through his dominions. The triumphal tour of inspection, which lasted five months, left Kang Hsi well content with his life's work. He felt that only one thing was lacking. The number of China's people, he concluded, was too small for the span of the Empire, the abundance of its natural resources, and its glorious prospects. The growth of the Empire's population had not kept pace with its territorial and economic expansion.[2] In 1500, there had been 130 million Chinese, their number expanding slowly during the century of the Ming Dynasty's overripeness to about 160 million in 1600. War, disease, natural disaster, and famine scourged China between 1600 and 1683, and the population fell well below its level at the beginning of the century. The years from 1683 to 1700 were a period of slow recovery which brought the population back to about 160 million and, according to one authority, were "a prelude to the unique chapter of population growth that did not end until the outbreak of the Taiping Rebellion in 1851."[3]

Returning from his grand tour, Kang Hsi promulgated the most important single decree of his reign. He froze in perpetuity the *ting* tax, the basic Imperial levy collected in labor, produce, and precious metal, assessed upon each county according to the estimated number of its inhabitants. Although the *ting* was a complex growth, its social effects were those of a head tax. Freezing— and later abolishing—the *ting* was the capstone of the oppressive

---

[2] Generally accurate in describing the trends of China's population, though they do not claim absolute precision for individual figures, modern demographers agree that war and natural calamities had checked natural growth. Cf. Ping-ti Ho, *Studies on the Population of China, 1368–1952* (Cambridge, Mass.: Harvard University Press, 1959).

[3] *Ibid.*, pp. 266–67.

structure of benevolence the Emperor erected, since those measures removed the economic reasons for limiting the size of families. Secure in the conviction that there would be food—and even dowries—for all, the Chinese began to abandon abortion and female infanticide. Peace and prosperity, enhanced by more effective control of floods and droughts, prevented the normal depletion of population through slaughter, starvation, disease, and catastrophe.

With a population of approximately 160 million in 1700 China had fewer persons to each acre of cultivated land than did the United States in 1930. By 1779, however, the population had grown to 275 million, and by 1794 there were 313 million subjects of the Manchu Empire. The increase continued unchecked until 1850, when the population reached 430 million.[4]

Increased population appeared at first to be the final contribution to the new Golden Age which those devout Confucians, the Ching Emperors, sought to create. Although no new Matteo Ricci arrived to discover a new world with the rapture of Archimedes, the contrast between China and Europe was more marked at the beginning of the eighteenth century than it had been at the beginning of the seventeenth. Even contemporary Chinese writers were dazzled by the Empire's wealth. Kang Hsi and his successors had apparently discovered a new phenomenon: the infinitely expanding economy, fed by an ever growing population, whose constant expansion automatically increased the wealth available to the individual.

Throughout the Empire, men rejoiced in abundance. In seagirt Shantung, with its inhospitable climate and harsh soil, farmers were amply provided with grain, meat, vegetables, fowl, eggs—and more than enough earthenware jugs of the home brew

[4] *Ibid., passim.* The century of continuous disorder and natural catastrophes which extended from 1850 until the Communist regime's establishment in 1949 checked this dizzy rate of growth. But the first Communist census in 1953 claimed a population of 583 million, a figure almost certainly, if unconsciously, inflated by the conviction, both Chinese and Marxist, that large numbers are a source of strength. Although Communist excesses between 1957 and 1961 reduced the rate of expansion briefly, there were in 1967 not fewer than 700 million and perhaps as many as 750 million Chinese. Their number was increasing by somewhere between 10 and 20 million annually.

called *bygar,* "white and dry." Families could consume only a portion of their overflowing abundance during the wasteful feasts which marked the Lunar New Year. Even in Shensi Province—mountainous, rocky, and parched—a chronicler wrote in 1762: "Our old local history [1557 edition] said that the people were so frugal sometimes they failed to comply with the customary standards of propriety. Previously, even at a banquet, there were but few courses, now people vie with each other in offering more. Wine, silk, and meat have become common articles of local consumption. . . ." [5] Land values in the hinterland of Hunan Province doubled, trebled, and then increased ten times in a single decade. Fortunes of ten thousand taels (say $12,000) were common in Hupei, and everyone knew at least one family which was worth more than a million taels ($1.2 million). Two cities in central China became synonymous with luxury, and the Chinese said: "*Shang yu tien-tang, hsia yu Su Hang!* [Above there is Heaven, below Suchow and Hangchow!]" To these cities aging silk merchants, their fortunes bloated by prosperity and their bellies by indulgence, came to revive their jaded palates with piquant delicacies—and to renew their flagging ardor with skillful singing girls.

Until the eighteenth century had moved well into its final quarter, it was impossible for any reasonably optimistic Chinese to doubt that the Manchus had indeed discovered a new law of nature. As the number of consumers increased and their standard of living became more lavish, production would automatically rise to meet demand—and exceed it by a constantly increasing margin. It seemed that the self-generating and self-satisfying process would never end.

There had been early signs, which few cared to read, that the spiral of prosperity might not rise forever. Despite bumper harvests, the price of rice doubled during the brief reign of the Emperor Yung Cheng (1723-36). In 1748 the governor of Hunan Province, responding to the Emperor Chien Lung's urgent enquiry, reported several reasons for spiraling prices: a constantly rising standard of living everywhere in China, growing extrava-

[5] Quoted in *ibid.,* p. 269.

gance among all classes, great public purchases of rice, hoarding and manipulation of prices by traders, and the constant increase in the size of the population. By 1750 even traditional surplus areas were buying rice from provinces where population was less dense.

Chinese agriculture expanded to meet the challenge. The Emperors advised farmers to improve both their techniques and the quality of their crops, while planting more grain and fewer money crops like tobacco. The potato, the peanut, and other new crops were introduced under government sponsorship, while marginal farmland was fully exploited. Swamps were filled and mountains terraced; millions of farmers migrated to new territories, where forests were hacked down to create farmland.[6]

But expansion brought its own problems. By 1800 the hills and mountainsides had been so intensively cultivated that widespread erosion resulted in diminished crop yields. Nature lashed out violently, as if seeking to redress the balance between her own capacity and humanity's demands. Chingchou Prefecture,[7] comprising several counties in Hupei Province, suffered a disastrous three years. Massive floods rolled over one county in 1830, drowning hundred of thousands and befouling the rice fields with sand. The dikes restraining the Yangtze River collapsed in a neighboring county in 1831, and half the population starved to death. In 1832 the prefectural capital suffered a severe famine, while elsewhere in Chingchou cholera struck down tens of thousands, and the normal autumnal floods were unprecedentedly severe. Food was so scarce and so expensive that many survived only by cannibalism. The same year, 1832, brought famines and

[6] The same phenomena, enormously accelerated by modern techniques, occurred during the first ten years of Communist rule, the first period of strong central rule and stability China had known since the Ching began to decline about 1800. The Communists attempted to apply much the same remedies the Ching Emperors had devised. Although results were limited, the Communists' greater administrative efficiency checked outright famine.

[7] Under the old organization of the Empire the administration units, reading down from the nation, were: vice-royalties, provinces, prefectures, counties, and districts. Their administrators, qualified by possession of specific academic degrees, were all appointed by Peking.

epidemics to every county of the prefecture.[8] Chingchou's tribulations were not unique, but representative.

Hung Liang-chi, an economist now called "the Chinese Malthus," had warned as early as 1793 that his country's population ". . . within a hundred years or so can increase from fivefold to twentyfold, while the means of subsistence, due to the limitations of the land area, could increase only from three to five times." [9] Since most men would be unable to find work, he added, there would be an inevitable and disastrous confrontation of cheap labor and expensive goods. By 1820 his predictions were becoming reality: half the population of China had become parasitic—engaging neither in scholarship, husbandry, commerce, nor manufacturing—because there were no opportunities for employment.

Another contemporary commentator urged the Dynasty "to relax the prohibition against female infanticide or rather to encourage such a practice en masse, to establish more nunneries and to forbid the remarriage of widows, to propagate the use of drugs that would sterilize adult women, to postpone the age of marriage for both sexes; to impose heavy taxation on families having more than one or two children; and to drown all surplus infants of both sexes except the physically fittest." [10]

Thus, a few men foresaw the calamities toward which the Dynasty rushed, and they proposed harsh remedies. But they were generally considered malcontents whose judgment was soured by disappointment or by antagonistic humors. Their voices died in the vast vacuum of disregard created by the conviction that a beneficent nature would somehow continue to provide abundance for her chosen people.

By 1825 the Ching Dynasty had passed the point where more equitable distribution of food might have provided a subsistence diet for all. Millions of Chinese were fated to die because there was not enough food for them. The exhausted earth could no longer bear the burden of humanity laid upon it by the Manchus' benevolence.

Most Chinese were stunned by the abrupt transition from

8 Ho, p. 270.
9 *Ibid.*, p. 271.
10 *Ibid.*, pp. 274–75.

lavish abundance to grinding deprivation. China had one night gone to bed plump and content; she had awakened emaciated and hungry. Officials who encouraged popular belief in a sentient providence but considered themselves enlightened agnostics, wondered themselves if the Dynasty had not, somehow, actually displeased Heaven.

By following the traditional Chinese road to glory, the Manchus had also chosen the traditional mode of immolation, though they had added their own unique burden of massive overpopulation. When the nineteenth century began, the Manchus' barbaric vigor had been exhausted by two centuries spent among a subject race which enslaved its conquerors by its complaisance. Their decadence was on display throughout the Empire, for slothful Manchu Bannermen garrisoned every large town. The lethargic descendants of the horsemen who had swept out of the north like a tidal wave lived in magnificent idleness. They were cosseted like prize bulls, but they were without useful employment, and their chief martial attribute was the brave slogans embroidered on their tunics. Even their weapons were burnished by Chinese servants. The Chinese bureaucracy, through which the Manchus ruled, had also become corrupt. The age-old pattern was repeating itself; extortionate maladministration made the effects of nature's unkindness more severe.

The Chinese quite naturally blamed their alien rulers for their suffering. Large groups united in anti-Manchu societies, which soon developed into a highly organized political and criminal underworld. Brought together by the instinct for survival, they were bound together by religious rituals pledging loyalty to the *Chinese* Ming Dynasty against the *barbarian* Ching. Since no man knew the fate of the Ming's legitimate heirs, pretenders to the Dragon Throne appeared in great numbers, particularly in the restive south. They were sponsored by secret societies like the Three Harmonies, whose very structure commemorated the underground formed by loyalist monks immediately after the Manchu conquest. The primary function of the secret societies in a disintegrating society was mutual protection against rapacious officials and marauding outlaws. This function, even more than their political pretensions, inevitably brought them into conflict with the weakened government whose proper functions they usurped.

The societies found natural allies in the tens of thousands of the dispossessed who sought refuge in the mountains, the swamps, and the forests. Powerful bands took control of entire counties and some prefectures. Local officials were reluctant to reveal their own impotence to their superiors by making honest reports of the brigands' activities, and, in any event, administrative fragmentation prevented effective cooperation between provinces. But the outlaws' growing strength led them in time to pitched battles against Imperial troops. The transition from spontaneous brigandry to organized insurrection was gradual—and inexorable. No fewer than a hundred distinct rebellions occurred between 1841 and 1849, with twenty-six crowded into the single year 1847. During the decade of the 1850s six major insurrections against the Manchus tormented China.

Chinese dynasties were like living organisms, for their mortality was implicit in their birth. Each dynasty shaped its own end, contriving the manner of its destruction. Economic distress, growing out of degeneracy and perversion of Confucian institutions, had summoned Li Tzu-cheng to administer the *coup de grâce* to the Ming. Amid similar anguish, intensified by overpopulation, the Ching brought forth its own nemesis. He was Hung Hsiu-chuan, the God-intoxicated son of the headman of a small farming village near the metropolis of Canton.

Unlike Li Tzu-cheng, Hung never took Peking, but the duration of his reign and the extent of his power justified his proclaiming his own dynasty while the Ching still endured. Riding a tide of bloodshed unique in Chinese history, he called his realm the *Taiping Tien Kuo*—the Heavenly Kingdom of Great Peace. Crowned *Tien Wang*, Heavenly King, Hung was a great eagle among the flocks of lesser bandit chieftains who harried the Manchus.

The *Tien Wang*'s revolution, now glorified by the Communists as "the greatest peasant revolt in China's history," also represented the first major impact of Western ideas upon the Chinese masses, for Hung possessed a unifying and inspiring ideology in his own version of Protestant Christianity. But the Taiping's grotesque Christian heresy was finally destroyed by the West's armed intervention. An excessively literal interpretation of their own words gravely embarrassed the envoys of Western culture—as it sometimes does today.

The great storm that shook China and almost destroyed the Ching Dynasty began with a personal revelation in 1837. Hung Hsiu-chuan had been carried home raving and insensible after again failing the examination that would have qualified him for appointment to the lowest rank in the official hierarchy.

Since the unsuccessful candidate was finally beginning to convalesce after weeks of delirium, his father, the village headman, was setting out a blackwood chair for him. The old man fussed with the chair like a mother placing her firstborn's cradle. The invalid must be placed so that he was shaded from the glare of the early morning sun on the flooded rice paddies but could still benefit from the healing rays.

The elder Hung reflected that it was time to find the boy a wife, who might allay the soul-searing knowledge that he was an utter failure at twenty-four. The distraction might also destroy the son's elaborate delusion that the Heavenly Emperor had, in personal audience, chosen him to rule China as Heaven's regent on earth. Besides, it was past time for the youth to fulfill his duties to the family by begetting sons who would attain official rank and thus bring honor to all their ancestors, including even their unsuccessful father.

A sheet of paper tucked into the gatepost caught the headman's eye. He shook his head sadly as he puzzled out the message. Inscribed in bold characters in vermillion, the color reserved for the Emperor's brush, was the heading: "The Noble Principles of the Heavenly King, the Sovereign King, Hsiu-chuan." The calligraphy was unmistakably his son's.

When he had returned from Canton early in April, Hsiu-chuan knew that he had failed not because of his lack of merit, but because of his lack of silver to bribe the examiners. He had fallen at his parents' feet, sobbing deliriously: "How badly have I returned the favor of your love! I shall never attain a name to reflect luster upon you."

During weeks of delirium, while priests and physicians hovered helpless about his bed, the young man had dreamed that he journeyed to another world, where an old crone washed him clean of his sins. An assembly of the great men of history cut out his troubled heart and implanted a bold new heart. He was borne up to the Thirty-third Heaven, where the Heavenly Emperor charged him to destroy the demons who walked on the earth and called him by a new name, Hsiu-chuan, meaning "perfectly accomplished." As he departed the eldest son of the Supreme Ruler gave him a magical sword to slay the demons. He then returned to earth, treasuring the Heavenly Emperor's words: "You too are my son!" [11]

The visions lasted full forty days. Thereafter, Hung appeared calmer. But he still insisted that he was the chosen Emperor because the Mandate of Heaven had passed from the Manchus to himself. It remained only to make the divine decree effective on earth.

Since he could conceive of no route to power other than the official examinations, Hsiu-chuan returned to Canton for the third time in the summer of 1843. Failing once more, he realized that he must carry out the Will of Heaven by force. He refused to join a secret society because the ritual did not accord with his visions and because he refused to pledge fealty to the Ming. He was the Emperor, not some Ming pretender. His will was firm and the way to power was clear, but he lacked the means.

It required another revelation, which rose in the West.

The Reverend Robert Morrison had come from Scotland in 1807, the first Protestant missionary to China. He saw that the Catholics had acquired privileges and a familiarity with the people and the language so great that the Protestants would seek to compete in vain on the same ground. Morrison therefore deter-

[11] The story of Hung's visions has been most graphically told in Flavia Anderson's *The Rebel Emperor* (London, 1958), pp. 50–59. Contemporary foreign and Chinese sources support her version. For a scholarly appraisal, see Vincent Y. C. Shih, *The Taiping Ideology, Its Sources, Interpretations, and Influences* (Seattle: University of Washington Press, 1967).

mined to spread the Gospel in print, exploiting popular reverence for the written word. Helped by devoted Chinese assistants, he translated and published a series of tracts; they were naturally written in the codelike style of the Confucian classics, the only mode of written expression acceptable to educated Chinese. Assiduous in distributing their booklets, the Protestants had pressed a set into the hands of candidate Hung when he first took the Civil Service Examination in 1835.

Almost nine years later, after his third failure, the future Taiping Emperor found the tracts again. Reading the Christian texts in the light of his personal revelation, Hung Hsiu-chuan realized that the Emperor of Heaven and his own Heavenly Elder Brother were once more communicating with him directly. All he read confirmed his previous solitary vision—and expanded its meaning.

The Protestants translated God as *Shang-ti*, literally the "Emperor Above," though the Catholics used the term *Tien-chu*, meaning the "Heavenly Lord." The Emperor Above, Hung said, was obviously the Heavenly Emperor who had appeared in his own visions. It was equally clear that Jesus Christ was the Heavenly Elder Brother who had given him a sword to slay the demons. He read the words of the Heavenly Emperor as translated by Dr. Morrison, finding in them exhortations to action—and promises of success.[12]

The elided classical style contributed to Hsiu-chuan's conviction. The word *chuan*, meaning "all" or "whole," occurs often in classical Chinese. Since that word was half the name bestowed upon him by the Heavenly Father, the future Emperor knew the timeless texts were addressing him personally. One began: "The heavens declare the glory of God." It continued: "Their voice has gone out to all the nations. . . ." The phrase "all the nations" Hung read as "the country of Chuan." [13] Later he found in the forty-fifth chapter of Isaiah: "I am the Lord and there is none

[12] *Ibid.*, pp. 78–79.

[13] For the curious it might be noted that classical Chinese has no specific plural form. The phrase *chuan-kuo* (全國) can, therefore, mean "the entire nation," "all the nations," or, as Hung interpreted it, "the country of [Hung Hsiu-] Chuan," just as *Chung-kuo* (中國) means "the country of the center" or China.

else, there is no God beside me. I girded thee, though thou hast not known me. . . . Thus saith the Lord, my hands have stretched out the heavens and Chuan's host have I commanded."

During the next decade, Hung created a complete private theology. Its basis was Christianity, derived from a full translation of the Bible which later came into his hands and from a series of Jesuit manuscripts which he found in a pawnshop in Canton—another revelation of Heaven's concern for him. His only formal instruction in Christianity was three months under the grim tutelage of the fundamentalist Reverend Issachar Roberts, a self-appointed missionary from Sumner County, Tennessee. Hung's politico-theology and the plan of the Heavenly Empire of Great Peace were a mélange of fundamentalist Christian fervor, Confucian models, and Hung's own visions.

Hung Hsiu-chuan preached his new doctrine in his isolated home village and later in the back country of mountainous Kwangsi Province, winning many adherents in those times of turmoil and uncertainty. He attacked idolatry; he proclaimed the equality of man; and he bound his converts to his new morality. Only Hung and his intimates knew that he had received the Mandate of Heaven. But his followers, now counted by the thousands and armed with spears and swords, soon fought a pitched battle against the Imperial militia. The bureaucracy could not abide Hung's attacks upon the established order, expressed in his injunctions to ignore Imperial ordinances—and to refuse to pay Imperial taxes. Pledging blood brotherhood with an effeminate Ming pretender, Hung made alliances with the secret societies, which were sworn to restore the Ming. In 1851 he donned the Imperial yellow and, as sunrise turned his army's fifty thousand torches pale, proclaimed his dynasty.

Hung never reached Peking. But he established a brief suzerainty over at least 100 million Chinese and ruled ten populous provinces of southern and central China. The Taiping Empire lasted just thirteen years. Its capital at Nanking fell in 1864 to the Imperial armies, which were assisted by the Ever Victorious Army organized by the English Colonel Charles George Gordon and the American adventurer Frederick Townsend Ward. Hung felt that he would have prevailed if his "co-religionists," the Europeans, had supported him. Instead, British warships struck a mortal blow at his Empire when they shelled his strongpoints on the Yangtze River. Hung himself died in the flames of Nanking, which he had held for eleven years, and the head of his last surviving general, the Loyal King, was displayed in Peking in August 1864.

Hung Hsiu-chuan, though defeated, had destroyed a dynasty. The Manchus dragged out their tenure through 1911, but never regained the power thay had held before 1850.

The Taiping Emperor did more than raise the greatest *jacquerie* China had known—an uprising exceeded in military might only by the Communists' millions of peasants in arms. He further created a new kind of Chinese army which served as the inspiration, if not the immediate model, for the indoctrinated divisions of Mao Tse-tung, another Chinese rebel who would elaborate a foreign doctrine into peculiarly Chinese fanaticism. Hung's troops were, like Mao's later, told that their commander-in-chief spoke from transcendent knowledge, though the Taiping Emperor claimed divine communication, while the Communist Chairman maintained only that he commanded all worldly knowledge by his mastery of scientific Marxism-Leninism. The Taipings, too, were instructed: "You should not go into the villages to seize people's goods. When you go into battle, you must not retreat. When you have money, you must make it public, and not consider it as belonging to one or another. If, after being instructed, you should still break Heaven's commands, do not be surprised if I, your exalted Elder Brother, issue orders to have you put to death." [14]

Discipline was ruthless. A soldier forced into service knew that his entire family would either be mustered into the Taiping armies or slaughtered. (Hung, who had led a crusade, not a conquest, razed cities rather than garrison them—until he came to Nanking.) The recruit's mother, sisters, and wife were enrolled in the Women's Legion under the command of female officers. Although the Emperor kept a harem of hundreds, the common soldier might not speak to women nor even see his mother and sisters, except at a distance.

Rewarded with martial titles for valorous deeds, the recruits

[14] Anderson, p. 167.

passed their days in military exercises. Like Mao Tse-tung's be-medaled Labor Heroes at their evening political indoctrination courses, the Taiping soldiers spent many of the hours of darkness in religious training. Since women were so strictly segregated, there was little opportunity to break the Sixth Commandment. Rape, prostitution, opium smoking, and desertion were expiated by death, while adulterers were burnt alive. Drinking, smoking, gambling, or looting for personal enrichment were somewhat less severely punished. Aside from the Emperor, his princes, and high-ranking officers, all the Taipings addressed each other as brother and sister. The parallels run close.

The Chinese compulsion toward tidy self-justification showed itself in the confessions that both the Taipings and the Manchus required prisoners to compose before their execution. The slaughter that followed almost reduced Genghis Khan and Tamerlane to the level of boys pulling wings off flies. In Kwangtung Province alone a million persons were executed by a single Imperial vice-roy. Throughout China 20 to 30 millions perished as offerings to the stern deity Hung Hsiu-chuan had seen in his visions.

Nonetheless, a Jesuit visiting the Taipings wrote: "One cannot deny that there is something in their relationships with each other which justifies these long-haired rebels' calling each other brothers. They give the impression of being of one family." There was little question that the Heavenly Emperor sincerely sought to succor the oppressed and to provide land for the dispossessed; it was unfortunate that he believed he could best attain those ends by slaying millions of demons. Above all, he strove to create a new society shaped by the absolute virtue of a new human being purged of all his inbred faults.

Instead of attaining that recurrent Chinese ideal, Hung Hsiu-chuan destroyed the functioning Confucian ethos that had inspired so much of his visions. The excessive benevolence of the Manchus and the terrible apocalypse of the Taipings made China pitifully vulnerable at a time when the Ching was entering the period of normal dynastic decay. When the European powers began to probe the Empire in force during the nineteenth century, the contrast between Chinese feebleness and Chinese pretensions made China ridiculous in their eyes. The West was not reticent in revealing its attitude—in words and deeds.

5

Salesmen with Muskets

The West's Militant Approach to China in the Nineteenth Century

The Chinese were not people, and China was not a country—or so it appeared from most foreign accounts during the century and a half before the Communist victory.

In most Western minds Chinese individuals were laundrymen or mandarins, master criminals or coolies, deluded pagans or natural philosophers. China herself meant unbearable suffering or a fairy-tale empire, a bottomless market or the missionaries' despair, little yellow brethren or evil hordes. A novel with a Chinese hero was rarely successful in the West, unless he was an acceptable stereotype—a simple victim of oppression like Lao Shaw's *Richshaw Boy* or a quaint Celestial like Ernest Bramah's *Kai Lung*. From marked physiognomical differences and antipathetic habits of mind to antipodal customs—social, political, religious, and even culinary—innumerable obstacles prevented Westerners' attaining emotional communion with Chinese.

Western attitudes toward China have at different times been compounded of diverse elements, including, among others, condescension, awe, greed, and a self-imposed sense of responsibility. Through their diplomatic or military agents, Western sovereigns have dealt with China as a problem—not as a nation.

Tormented, like the Spaniards, by the hypersensitivity that proceeds from pride, the Chinese have deeply resented Western attitudes that coincided only in considering the Chinese curious natural phenomena rather than men. Since at the time of the West's incursion they were barely aware of China herself as a discrete entity, the Chinese could hardly be expected to understand other nations. Resentment has subsequently dominated China's response to the West, just as Westerners have been stalked by frustration at their inability to comprehend the mind of China. Constant tension has, therefore, underlaid relations between China and the West, although few countries have a greater number of ardent foreign aficionados.

Many foreigners have studied Chinese institutions, often with greater objectivity than the Chinese themselves. Some have attained broad understanding, though many have concentrated upon the relics of the past, like scholars attempting to explain present-day England largely in terms of *Piers Plowman* or the *Morte d' Arthur*. Chinese aloofness—psychological and economic, inherent and intentional—has challenged the curious West, stirring both men of affairs and men of the mind. It has been difficult to believe that that aloofness was primarily based upon little more than infinite self-satisfaction. Even her detractors have, therefore, expressed great—if sometimes misdirected—respect for the vanished wonders of traditional Chinese civilization.

In the latter half of the nineteenth century, after the Taiping Rebellion, the West considered the Chinese largely deluded, faintly comical, and wholly ineffective. In the latter half of the twentieth the West—particularly the United States—seems to see the Chinese as brutal, ruthless, and overwhelmingly dangerous. It is unlikely that a nation of comic-opera characters has suddenly been transformed into a semi-mechanized reincarnation of the hordes of Attila. Yet mystery continues to evoke stereotypes. Knowing little of China, the West has tended to seize upon the most obtrusive appearance of the moment as the essential quality of the nation.

Western stereotypes all touch reality at some point, but none comes close to *the* truth about China. It is unlikely that the simple truth about the Chinese—or any other nation—is neatly tucked away in some Platonic treasure house. Yet men continue to seek a refined formula that will express the essence of a nation, a formula like the single equation describing the physical universe whose pursuit the physicists periodically abandon.

China herself knows hardly more of her essential character than does the West. Although they may appear self-obsessed, the Chinese are not really introspective; their conviction of superiority, still based in part upon complacent ignorance, is not conducive to self-examination. They are still inclined to shun analysis in favor of authoritative pronouncements. The Confucian extirpation of original thought is a major source of the Chinese mind's affinity for the certainties of Marxism.

More than a century elapsed between 1793, when Great Britain dispatched her first Ambassador, Lord Macartney, to seek normal diplomatic and commercial relations with the China of Chien Lung, and Bertrand Russell's visiting professorship at Peking University in 1919. It was a century of intense conflict of ideas—and weapons. Not until the end of the period did the British begin to realize that the Chinese simply could not understand the meaning of normal trade, since a supreme empire which did not acknowledge the existence of other, equal nations could hardly trade with them on commercial terms. It was, on the other hand, almost as difficult for Britain to appreciate that China was not simply an enlarged version of a European nation as it was for the Chinese to grasp the concept of nationhood.

The failure of communication with the West is central to the development of present-day China—and her future course. Each party has yielded too often to the temptation to believe that it has found a key—or a series of keys—explaining the character of the other. Yet in neither case has contempt bred true familiarity.

Matteo Ricci had contrived to live in some intimacy with the Ming Court. Later missionaries contracted guarded friendships with individual Chinese, but most foreigners living in China in the nineteenth century were isolated from all except formal contact with Chinese. In the twentieth century, before the Communist "liberation," liberal foreigners lived in the major cities on terms of friendship with individual Chinese. But a Westerner's attempt to understand China through knowledge of one—or even ten—Chinese was much like a Frenchman's interpreting American civilization solely through his friendship with a Texas cowpuncher, a Southern lawyer, or a New England professor.

Europe approached a China beset by internal difficulties in the frame of mind suggested by C. Wingrove Cooke, correspondent of *The Times* of London. Writing when Britain had already fought two successful wars against the Manchus, Cooke noted that lying was the "public pastime" of the Chinese. They did not, he wrote, possess the spirit—evinced even by Greeks, Jews, and Italians—to resent being called liars.[1]

"Much has been said and written about Chinese politeness. There is no nation in which in public places you see habitually so little of it," he added, apparently unaware that his own experience had been limited to the Cantonese, who, even today, display remarkable variations from the accepted standards of Chinese behavior. "The Chinese peasant has no notion of courtesy. He never makes you a salutation in passing; he never moves out of your way, or even deflects from his straight course, without looking to see whether you will get out of his way. . . . Humanity, self-denial, and that true courtesy which teaches Western nations that it is a part of personal dignity to respect the feelings of others, is in China dead in fact, and alive only in pantomime. The life and state papers of a Chinese statesman . . . abound in the finest sentiments and the foulest deeds. . . . They will put you to death if you innocently cause a death, yet they will not draw a struggling man out of the water, because it would spoil such a capital joke. A Chinese laughs when he tells you of the death of his most intimate friend—I mean acquaintance, for John Chinaman does not know what friendship means." [2]

If the Europeans were infuriated by Chinese behavior, the Chinese were dismayed by European manners. Commenting on the unwelcome arrival in 1816 of Britain's envoy Lord Amherst, a Chinese commentator wrote: "In the twentieth year of Kia King, an envoy, with tribute from England, arrived at T'ientsin. . . . When he reached the capital, Hoshiht'ai was commanded to exercise him in the ceremony [of prostration, the kowtow]; but the

[1] *China and Lower Bengal* (London, 1861), p. x.
[2] *Ibid.*, pp. x–xi.

envoy said he was quite perfect in it and when presented would be sure to perform it according to the rite. . . . But when the day came on which the Emperor desired him to appear, the envoy made no obeisance, but departed. . . . He was pursued to Kwangtung, and there escorted on board his ship in which he returned to his country.

"Now the Emperor of China is the common ruler of the Empire: England is a single, small barbarian state: and was it the form of things that should be, that when the envoy of the latter gave himself such airs as these, the government of China, so far from being able to punish his crime, should actually go the length of escorting him home? Herein we find the origin of the pride and intractability of the barbarians of the seas." [3]

China's first response to the importuning of foreign merchants and their governments had been favorable, even generous, from Peking's viewpoint. The Chinese, avidly commercial for all the Confucian ideology's formal disapproval of the trader, were graciously prepared to accept these new, red-faced barbarian merchants on the same terms they had always accorded neighboring Asian barbarians. All the Empire required was an occasional ceremonial obeisance, the discreet cloaking of trade as tribute that would evoke reciprocal gifts from the Emperor, and above all, the formal acceptance of the Chinese Emperor's pre-eminent position. Although China did not need foreign manufacturers, because she produced all that men could reasonably desire, the benevolent Court was prepared to admit limited quantities of foreign goods and to bestow Chinese goods in return. What other relationship, the Chinese asked, was possible? On the one hand there were distant barbarian territories, and on the other there was civilization, supreme in mechanics and philosophy—civilization endowed with suzerainty over all men, although, in its benevolence, it often refrained from imposing its will.

The contest between two ways of thought which began in the 1790s appeared pitifully unequal to China, sequestered behind her deep seas, her broad deserts, her massive mountains, and her pre-eminent culture. Only politeness required that the barbarians

[3] Quoted in *ibid.,* pp. xvii–xviii.

of the seas be granted audience, for they were obviously no threat. China under Chien Lung was governed in accordance with Confucian orthodoxy and was buttressed by unassailable virtue. Her wealth was the greatest in her history, as was her territorial expanse—stretching north almost to the Arctic Circle and south through "tribute states" to the Gulf of Siam and India; reaching from Korea and Sakhalin Island in the east to deep Central Asia on the west, including vast areas that are now part of the U.S.S.R. Against these grand proportions the West could show only Portuguese Macao; a tolerated enclave, five square miles of leased territory occupied by the "factories" at Canton; and scattered Russian trading posts in the northern wilderness. What China did not see did not concern China, for she enjoyed "the repose of indolence and seclusion when she looked down on the nations in her overwhelming pride . . . ," as the great American Sinologue S. Wells Williams observed.[4]

At the end of the eighteenth century, even men with greater geographical knowledge could argue that the Chinese assumption of superiority was justified. China's influence upon the West was much stronger than the West's upon China. The Age of Reason took the serene rationalism of the Confucian ideology as a model for its own secular creed. Liberal Europeans seized upon that calcified political philosophy as a rationale for their own revolutionary doctrines, maintaining the Western tradition of exalted misunderstanding of Chinese thought. Alexander Pope built a Chinese garden, complete with tile-roofed pavilion, on the grounds of his villa at Twickenham-on-Thames. Fashionable ladies decorated their drawing rooms with wallpaper in Chinese motifs, while Chinese porcelains, silks, and lacquerware were the rage of Europe. At masquerade balls the courtiers of Europe disguised themselves as Chinese mandarins, and their ladies dressed as Chinese concubines. China could indeed feel superior, for Chinese gentlemen did not pretend to be European feudal lords, nor did they walk the public streets wearing stovepipe hats, clutching spindly black umbrellas, or ostentatiously consulting pocket watches as big as dinner plates. When they were later forced to throw open their islands, the Japanese did just those things, but that is an-

[4] In *The Middle Kingdom* (New York, 1883).

other story, the story of a wholly different response to the West.

All her intercourse with the West had fed China's sense of secure supremacy. Admitted to China to preach their religion, the Jesuits were expelled because the Vatican insisted that converts must give up certain Chinese practices, including the rites honoring Confucius and their ancestors. Nonetheless, the Empire felt itself so strong that other Catholic missionaries had again been tolerated, though they were closely watched. In 1689 China had signed her first formal agreement with a European nation in the hope of ending clashes with Russian pioneers in the valley of the Amur River. The Treaty of Nerchinsk, establishing definite borders and laying down conditions of trade, was, from the Russian point of view, an agreement between equal sovereigns. To the Chinese it was no different from the treaties that puissant Chinese Emperors had concluded with weak but annoying northern barbarians for more than two millennia.

The West was not prepared to accept the relationship the Chinese offered after it saw the Empire's weakness in the nineteenth century. His Britannic Majesty's emissaries would not play the role of tribute-bearing ambassadors, knocking their heads on the floor in humiliating obeisances. Besides, the Chinese offered highly restricted terms of trade which were not commercially practicable because they could be altered radically at the Court's pleasure. Portuguese and Dutch merchants had already discovered that the wealth they expected eluded them, although they conformed to Chinese etiquette, presumably abasing themselves before Mammon rather than the Ching Emperor. The scope of trade under the Manchus' galling terms could not satisfy the visionary merchant-adventurers who believed, as one British envoy declared, that in China ". . . a new world was open to their trade, so vast that all the mills in Lancashire could not make stocking stuff sufficient for one of its provinces. . . ." [5]

Only on terms of equality—or better still, outright superiority—could Western commerce properly exploit the fabulous wealth of Cathay. Besides, British merchants came to feel that it would be easy to bring China under domination. Their purpose, they declared in a formal submission to a British plenipotentiary in 1858,

[5] Lord Elgin quoted in Cooke, p. xxii.

was always "more fully to develop the vast resources of China, and to extend among the people the elevating influences of a higher civilization." The noble lord said in reply: "Christian civilization will have to win its way among a sceptical and ingenious people, by making it manifest that a faith which reaches to heaven furnishes better guarantees for public and private morality than one which does not rise above the earth. At the same time the machina-facturing [*sic*] West will be in the presence of a population the most universally and laboriously manufacturing of any on the earth. It can achieve victories in the contest in which it will have to engage only by proving that physical knowledge and mechanical skill applied to the arts of production are more than a match for the most persevering efforts of unscientific industry." [6]

The language of conflict was quite appropriate in the mid-1800s, for Britain had already mounted military assaults upon the Chinese Empire. Their purpose was to change the Chinese conventions which prevented normal trade. But the continued use of force merely hardened China's basic attitudes, though altering their outward appearance—as pressure and heat create diamonds from carbon, leaving the chemical structure little changed.

The pressure was applied so frequently and so variously that a chronology can best give an impression of the rush of events:

1793: Lord Macartney and his retinue arrived in Peking beneath Chinese banners declaring them: "Envoys bearing tribute from the country of England!" They carried back only a humiliating Imperial Mandate from Chien Lung to his "vassal" George III:

> You, O King, live beyond the confines of many seas. Nevertheless, impelled by your humble desire to partake of the benefits of our civilization, you have dispatched a mission respectfully bearing your memorial. . . .
>
> If I have commanded that the tribute offerings sent by you, O King, are to be accepted, this was solely in consideration for the spirit which prompted you to dispatch them from afar. Our dynasty's majestic virtue has penetrated unto every

[6] *Ibid.*, p. xxiii.

country under Heaven, and Kings of all nations have offered their costly tribute by land and sea. As your Ambassador can see for himself, we possess all things. I set no value on objects strange or ingenious, and have no use for your country's manufactures.

This then is my answer to your request to appoint a representative at my Court, a request contrary to our dynastic usage, which would only result in inconvenience to yourself. . . . By perpetual submission to our Throne, you may secure peace and prosperity for your country hereafter.

1795: A Dutch Embassy, treated with even less consideration, was even less successful than the British had been.

1806: A Russian Embassy was turned back before it arrived in Peking because the Ambassador refused to perform the ceremonial prostration before the Emperor.

1816: Lord Amherst, on another mission for England, was forced to flee Peking as previously recounted, when he refused to kowtow.

1839: The Chinese Empire fought the first Opium War. The cause was Britain's insistence upon importing opium freely into China. The drug had long been used by the Chinese, but social disapproval and high cost had limited addiction. British merchants, hoping that trade's vast profits would halt the drain upon their bullion reserves produced by a highly unfavorable balance of trade with China, wished to import into the Empire unlimited quantities of cheap opium from India and the Middle East. It appeared to the Chinese that the merchants sought to create millions of addicts—and evade Imperial taxes. The conflict began with a clash between British frigates and Chinese war junks near Canton, after Chinese confiscation of opium shipments. The British fought a naval war, before which the Chinese were powerless.

1841–44: The Treaty of Nanking, which ended the Opium War, opened five southern ports to residence and trade by Britons. Hong Kong was ceded to Britain and intercourse between British and Chinese officials on terms of equality was guaranteed. China promised "fair and regular tariffs," paid an indemnity, and permitted British merchants to use their own agents, bypassing the licensed merchants of the *Co-hong*, who had previously been the only nonofficial Chinese authorized to deal with foreigners.

1843: A supplementary treaty fixed tariff rates, promised Britain that she would automatically enjoy any concessions that might be granted to any other nation in the future (the "most-favored-nation clause"), and made the first concessions of "extra-territoriality," the independence of foreign subjects on Chinese soil from Chinese law.

1844: China's sovereignty had been heavily eroded by this forced abdication of her rights, and the erosion became worse when first the United States and later France forced the Empire to sign treaties granting them privileges similar to those the British enjoyed.

1845–51: Belgium, Norway, Sweden, and Russia secured treaties granting their subjects special privileges.

1852: The British annexed the Chinese protectorate of Lower Burma.

1856–60: With Britain and France in the lead, the Western powers fought the second Opium War against the Manchus. Their pretext was the defense of national sovereignty and freedom of the seas, but their purpose was to secure further concessions. The immediate cause was the merchantman *Arrow*. China-built, the vessel was of the type called a *lorcha*, carrying a Chinese junk-rig on a Western-style hull. Her legal position was equally confused: a British captain and a Chinese crew sailed under the British flag, though her British registration had expired. When the Chinese authorities in Canton seized the vessel on charges of piracy and hauled down the British flag, the British consul ignored the murky legal position to champion the *Arrow*'s cause. The British argued that the Chinese had no right to seize a British-flag vessel, even if its British registry had actually expired, because "they did not know" that the *Arrow* was no longer a British ship.

The British and French fought another naval war against China, capturing Canton in 1857 and seizing in 1858 the Taku Forts that commanded the harbor of Tientsin and the sea approaches to Peking. (The United States, invited to participate in this war, declined; Washington was content to shell the forts at Canton in retaliation for an insult to the American flag.) When the Taku Forts fell, the Manchus capitulated and signed the Treaty of Tientsin, which granted new privileges not only to Britain and France, but to Russia and the United States as well. The war was renewed when foreign envoys met obstacles to securing proper ratification of the treaties. In 1860, British and French forces took Peking and burnt the Emperor's Summer Palace in retaliation for a massacre of foreign prisoners.

The second Treaty of Peking, ratified in 1860, confirmed the privileges of foreigners, making China, in effect, a dependent nation. By refusing to deal equally with the importunate West, China had ensured that she would deal unequally. Fifteen "treaty ports," some of them lying far inland, were open to residence by foreigners, whose extraterritorial privileges made the cities in effect enclaves on Chinese soil ruled by foreigners. The Chinese paid the first of the indemnities that were to become a regular consequence of defeats by the West. Control of the Chinese Customs and a number of inland waterways passed to foreigners. Britain secured cession of Kowloon, opposite Hong Kong Island on the mainland of China.

During the same period Russia took all of the Asiatic mainland north of Korea and Manchuria.

1862: France was granted southern Indo-China.

1867: Portugal was confirmed in her possession of Macao.

1868: Russia completed her campaign to take control of a large part of Sinkiang (Chinese Turkestan).

1881: Nepal became nominally independent, but actually passed under British control.

1885: France took all of Indo-China.

1886: Britain completed her conquest of Burma.

1895: China's war with Japan ended with the disastrous Treaty of Shimonoseki that gave Japan sovereignty over Formosa and paramount status in Korea.

1898: The French took the port of Kuangchou Wan, opposite Hainan Island; the Germans were granted Kiaochow on the Shantung Peninsula; and the British secured a naval base at Weihaiwei in Shantung.

1899–1900: A quasi-religious patriotic society called the Yi Ho Tuan (literally the "Righteous Harmonious Society," but commonly referred to as the "Boxers") laid siege to the legation quarter of Peking with the encouragement of the Court, which finally ordered Imperial troops to join them. Missionaries were slaughtered in the inland provinces. After a long summer of blundering, an allied expedition drawn from the forces of eight nations took Peking, and the final settlement forced China to further self-abasement.

The century, which began with Chinese pride and arrogance rampant, ended with total Chinese humiliation. Foreign envoys, who had been scorned, dictated terms in the Imperial City itself. Foreign missionaries, who had barely been tolerated, ranged everywhere to subvert the people from their proper duties to the Emperor. In violation of Peking's express decrees, hundreds of thousands of Chinese emigrated to serve the imperialists abroad—and to create the overseas Chinese problem that vexes Southeast Asia today.[7] Western merchants, who had refused to deal with the special class of Co-hong merchants appointed by the Manchus, created a special, privileged class of compradores to serve as their commercial and linguistic agents under the protection of extraterritoriality. Some Chinese—and many foreigners—accumulated fortunes through the trade won by arms. They planned great schemes to exploit the country even more exhaustively.

Yet the final yield never equaled the expectations foreign merchants had entertained since Macartney's first mission. The adventurous began to talk of increasing profits by cutting China up "like a melon" and substituting colonial rule for the mélange of extraterritoriality, treaty ports, and special privileges they enjoyed. China's sovereignty was maintained only by conflict among her conquerors. She was divided into spheres of influence by the powers, whose mutual jealousy prevented outright colonization.

[7] The Chinese of Southeast Asia have grown rich in their countries of residence, but they have encountered neither coercion nor persuasion which could effectively induce them to abandon their primary loyalty to China. They therefore remain an indigestible lump in the body politic, all the more troublesome because of the power their wealth confers upon them. They can be expelled or suppressed by native government, but only at the sacrifice of their technical, professional, and financial expertise.

The United States, which had no territorial possessions on the mainland of China, formalized the precarious *status quo* toward the end of the century by proclaiming the Open Door Policy, which guaranteed equality of commercial opportunity and enjoined against further territorial seizures.

The Manchu Dynasty had been degraded. The old relationship had been reversed, and the West was dominant. A new, Western-oriented city had been created in Shanghai, while the imposing homes of foreign consuls, missionaries, and merchants rose in the principal trading cities of the interior. Foreign gunboats patrolled the great rivers, puffing past steamships carrying foreign goods to inland cities.

Yet the physical impact of these legal and financial changes was still superficial at the beginning of the twentieth century. Most Chinese lived in small towns much as their ancestors had lived for two thousand years, although they might light their new kerosene lamps with patent matches, called "foreign fire." The life of the hundreds of millions of peasants, who *are* China, had hardly been altered by the advent of the West.

No more than the West had changed the fundamental life of China were Western goods and Western guns the chief force that overthrew the Manchus, whose protracted decadence was to be ended by revolution in 1911. But for decades most Chinese believed—almost beyond the possibility of discussion—that the West had actually destroyed the Ching Dynasty. If they had not exaggerated the West's impact and power, they would have been forced to concede that China was actually inferior to Europe in certain essential qualities. If the West had not really brought overwhelming force to bear, China's inability to resist and the collapse of her ancient institutions could only be interpreted as demonstrations of fundamental weaknesses. Because it was unthinkable to admit such quintessential inferiority, most Chinese ignored the obvious.

It was, however, not China's reluctance—or even her inability—to use force which allowed the West to dominate. The true cause of the Manchus' collapse and the nation's subjugation was China's inability to recognize, until it was much too late, that the

West was truly a powerful adversary. The flaw lay deep in the traditional Chinese intellect, not merely in failures to utilize superficial techniques of weaponry and strategy.

It was the degenerate state of the Ching that permitted the West such easy inroads, rather than the West that broke the Ching. The advent of the West did, however, break the chain of new Confucian dynasties succeeding worn-out Confucian dynasties—a chain whose first link was forged in 207 B.C. Other Western-oriented revolutionaries were to finish the task begun by the Taipings under the inspiration of their own version of Christianity. At the same time, the West woke the spirit of a nation whose culture had been stirred by no deep-running creative currents for seven centuries. Its chief impact was on the mind of China, not on her physical or political institutions. The Chinese themselves changed China after Westerners had changed Chinese minds.

Cannon, Science, and Democracy

China Adopts Various Means from the West to Meet the Challenge of Western Material Supremacy

At sunrise on October 18, 1870, sixteen men dressed in the coarse white smocks of condemned criminals marched to the public execution grounds in the port city of Tientsin in North China. The warders carried themselves like a guard of honor, and voices from the throng cried: "Well done. . . . Be brave. . . . You are virtuous!" Despite the autumnal chill, most of the crowd carried large fans of bamboo and paper which bore pictures of the condemned men pillaging the city's Roman Catholic cathedral and attacking French Sisters of Charity. Each man in turn strode proudly to the block, heartened by the shouts of the crowd and the groups of admiring friends who surrounded him until the moment the executioner flipped his queue forward and swung the great two-handed sword.

The sixteen men of Tientsin, who went to their death applauded by their executioners, were paying for their deeds of the day in June 1870, when mobs killed forty foreigners and Chinese Christians. Still, even the senior officials who ordered the unavoidable executions could hardly forbear hailing the murderers as heroes who died for China.

The riots sprang from resentment and from superstitious terror of the manner in which the Sisters of Charity had bestowed their kindness upon the pagans. Superficially, it appeared that the slaughter might have been avoided if the French Consul

81

had cooperated with the Chinese authorities—or if either side had sincerely sought to understand the other. But in retrospect the massacre appears predestined by the manner in which the Europeans dealt with the Chinese. By the same token, the modern reader can almost hear the tread of inevitable tragedy behind the spirit in which the Chinese approached the foreigners.

Chinese attitudes toward foreigners in their midst—and toward the entire world outside China—underwent a kaleidoscopic series of changes during the nineteenth century. It is impossible to describe those changes categorically since each phase displayed some of the characteristics of both its predecessor and its successor.

The transition can be sketched roughly: from complacent contempt until the second Opium War; through irrational fear until the 1880s; to determined, albeit grudging, emulation of the West thereafter. The two constants, manifested throughout the century by men of different classes and temperaments whose reactions otherwise varied widely, were an instinctive revulsion from the intruders and a determination that they must eventually be expelled from China. Revulsion, so deep it was beyond reason, led to grotesque incidents of which the Tientsin massacre was typical.

During the second Opium War European warships had bombarded the Taku Forts near Tientsin, and the allied expedition had later marched on Peking from that city. In 1860 the foreigners moved with gusto into Tientsin, their first enclave in north China won by that war. The French Sisters of Charity established an orphanage and foundling hospital, paying a bounty for each child, ". . . it being understood that a child, once in their asylum, no parent, relative, or guardian could claim or exercise any control over it," as the American Consul, F.F. Low, reported. The rewards encouraged kidnaping, perhaps unintentionally, as did the payments offered for mortally ill children, who might be baptized. "All these acts, together with the secrecy and seclusion . . . ," added Consul Low, "have created suspicion in the minds of the Chinese . . . and intense hatred against the Sisters. . . . Any rumor concerning the Sisters or their acts, however improbable or absurd, found thousands of willing and honest believers among the ignorant and superstitious people." [1]

At the beginning of June 1870 an epidemic of fever swept the orphanage. The rumors which had swirled around the orphanage thereupon hardened into the conviction that the nuns were slaughtering their charges in order to grind their eyes and hearts into medicines which commanded fabulous prices in Europe. The next day, mobs stormed the orphanage, the French Consulate, and the cathedral, determined to rescue the children. They killed all the nuns—and the French Consul, who had refused to heed the warnings of Chinese officials. Three Russians, mistaken for Frenchmen, were torn apart. Chinese Christians were struck down, and a number of buildings were burned.

Although Peking ordered the arrest of both the ringleaders and the responsible local officials, the Western powers assembled their fleets, their imaginations inflamed by fragmentary reports. Some contemporary foreign writers scoffed at fears of a slaughter of all the foreign innocents in China, but the powers felt they had cause for alarm. The bloody eighteenth of June in Tientsin was the last and the worst in a series of incidents, and men remembered well the massacre of millions during the Taiping Rebellion. No man's life was sacred in China, and the Europeans were pitifully few among the Chinese masses. Like lion tamers, their only security lay in intimidation, since the aroused Chinese could smother them by weight alone if they attacked.

When the fleets arrived, the cowed Chinese government ordered the execution of the sixteen and offered the Russian Minister four more lives in recompense for the three dead Russians.[2] Peking tendered formal apologies, accompanied by an indemnity of 400,000 taels of gold, worth about $17.5 million. The French were, however, not satisfied until they had won from Peking addi-

---

[1] Quoted in Williams, p. 700.

[2] Two were executed, after the Russians had satisfied themselves that they were indeed guilty. Convinced that the remaining two were, at worst, only accomplices, the Russians requested that their sentences be commuted to banishment. The Chinese authorities, startled at a demonstration of humanity so much in contrast to the vindictiveness they had come to expect, happily agreed.

tional privileges for their missionaries—and further commercial concessions. Righteous indignation had again proved highly profitable.

The Europeans had been frightened, but they were still contemptuous of their involuntary hosts. The Chinese were appalled by the executions, but they were still complacent when they reflected upon their demonstrable superiority to the intruders. The crude behavior that seemed characteristic of all Europeans, when it did not defy logical analysis, tended to support the Chinese belief that these fierce new barbarians would eventually be overwhelmed by the prowess and culture of the Central Kingdom. In 1870 the Chinese were still confident of the future. Their perceptions had hardly progressed beyond the state of mind typified by the then Emperor's conclusion that his defeat in the first Opium War of 1839–42 was due not to any innate superiority of European arms or tactics, but merely to his own failure to employ experienced generals.[3] China had simply been incapable of considering the possibility that the West might prove a serious intellectual or material rival until she was defeated in the second Opium War in 1860 and Peking itself was occupied.

Even those catastrophes at first awakened but the faint fluttering feeling that something serious might be amiss, though by that time it was not only the vulgar who from time to time felt the stabbing of superstitious fears aroused by the West's power and purposes. Some men began to suspect that more might be required than a happier choice of generals, if they were to cope with the "oceanic barbarians."

A few years later the spectacle of Chinese troops successfully fighting the Taipings under foreign generals offered a new vision of hope. Chinese optimism was strengthened by Japan's metamorphosis during the 1870s under the "modern men" of the Meiji Restoration who had cast off almost all the old ways in order to make their country an industrial and military power. A handful of Chinese thinkers saw that the East could, indeed, learn from the West. Yet their first endeavors resembled a treasure hunt rather than a serious investigation. They searched for the Philosopher's

[3] Arthur Waley, The Opium War Through Chinese Eyes (London: George Allen and Unwin, 1958), pp. 184–185.

Stone, which would miraculously transmute China's weakness into strength—without altering the traditional social and intellectual structure. Just as the citizens of Tientsin were convinced that the Sisters of Charity boiled babies to extract priceless potions, the few liberal mandarins believed that the West possessed a single, simple secret. When they uncovered that secret, they felt, the proper order among the nations would automatically be restored by China's ethical and intellectual superiority.

A few Chinese believed that China must systematically learn material techniques from the West. But even in the 1870s, a decade after their defeat in the second Opium War, most Chinese still felt a scornful abhorrence of the West. All Chinese who dealt with foreigners were called *han-chien*, "traitors" or, literally, "Chinese evildoers." *Han-chien* might be compradores or interpreters, pilots or artisans, servants or teachers—in short, any Chinese who worked for foreigners or any Chinese who learned a foreign language. Traditionalists felt that the spirit of evil was incarnate in the West's ships, watches, cannon—and, even music boxes. The perfection of those devices merely demonstrated the Europeans' obsession with nasty toys. Although the Jesuit Adam Schaal had cast two hundred cannon for Kang Hsi himself, the Chinese had, after all, invented both gunpowder and missiles, firing cannon and war rockets at the Mongols at the battle of Kaifeng in 1227. Some of the orthodox contended that European weapons were abominations, unworthy of use by good Chinese, who could prevail by their valiant deeds alone.

More practical men felt the Chinese could make good use of the new weapons—as long as it was understood that they were merely useful devices. Few understood that the power of modern weapons sprang from modern industry, based upon systems of thought and social organization which were antithetical to Confucian China. The Japanese, accustomed to adapting themselves to foreign cultures, could with little strain alter their society sufficiently to accept Western industrial and military institutions. But the Chinese social order, which was firmly based upon the primacy of the Confucian learning and the scholar-bureaucrats, simply could not accommodate those Western institutions. Even the initial step was beyond Chinese capacity, since it would have required supplanting petrified Confucian wisdom with the spirit of free inquiry. Assuming that it was psychologically possible, such a change would, in the first instance, have destroyed the dominant position of the *literati* and cast the intellectual, spiritual, and social bases of the Chinese Empire into complete confusion. Even if the bureaucracy had been capable of contemplating such class suicide, the stratified Chinese state provided no openings for the institutions the Japanese had accepted so easily —a generally intelligible literary style, universal education, military conscription, investment and ownership in the modern capitalist pattern, equal terms of trade, and the like. It would have required no less than a revolution, and there were as yet no men prepared to make a revolution.

Modern men may wonder at China's fumbling response to the massive challenge of the West. But history is not clear to those who live it, and contemporary episodes do not fall into the clear categories so deceptively obvious a century later. Events which tower in retrospect are merely scattered incidents to those whose lives they shape. Besides, the true aspect of Western civilization was invisible to the Chinese, who saw only a few adventurers and a handful of commercial or military artifacts.

The basic patterns of thought of the dominant scholar-bureaucrats, the mandarin class, had not been altered by Li Tzu-cheng's capture of Peking in 1644 nor by the subsequent Manchu conquest of all China. There was no reason for the Mandarins to feel that the allied forces' capture of Peking in 1860 revealed a fundamental disorder in the pattern of their days or the state of their souls. They were armored by historically demonstrated truth —the eternal continuity of the predominant Chinese race under the eternally wise and virtuous Confucian system.

The Chinese Empire, therefore, suffered an absolute psychological incapacity to appreciate the true nature of the challenges hurled by the West. Other great civilizations have displayed the same inability to discern the obvious meaning of events or to recognize the scope of threats that finally destroy them. This inability to appreciate one's peril, even more than the lack of will to fight for self-preservation, evidences deep decay.

The more successful a civilization, the greater is the likelihood that it will dismiss Nemesis as an annoying cat burglar.

Insular Japan, a heretical offshoot of the great Confucian civilization, was sufficiently flexible to adopt Western technological and political methods without passing through a mortal psychological crisis. She had few deep-rooted institutions to supplant. Since massive Imperial China could not adapt herself, she was destroyed.

In the Dynasty's early days, the intellectual climate of the Ching actually appeared even more hospitable to Western knowledge than the Ming had been. The Manchu Emperors, intrigued by Western devices, patronized the Jesuit savants and encouraged them to apply their technological knowledge in China. But the Ching was finally constrained to prohibit all original investigation in order to preserve a political structure built upon an ideology that shrank from investigation or discovery. The Emperor Chien Lung remarked severely that scholars must not consider it "their duty to govern the nation" [4] and ordered an inquisition to enforce orthodoxy.

Fearful of provoking Imperial wrath, Chinese scholars of the middle-Ching period turned to what they called "empirical research." Since close examination of either the nature of man or the nature of things might prove hazardous to their personal security, they did no more in reality than restate the past. They prided themselves on their "concrete studies" of the artifacts of the Chou Dynasty (c. 1100–500 B.C.): the design of sacrificial halls and royal sleeping chambers, the shape of hats, and the mechanism of carts. Since neither the objects themselves nor exact descriptions existed, the scholars were actually engaged in an elaborate process of self-delusion. Since it was based upon almost no concrete evidence, textual or archaeological, their empirical research degenerated into an elaborate mechanism of busywork. The worst intellectual effects stemmed from their sincere self-delusion, their

[4] Quoted in Liang Ch'i-ch'ao, *Intellectual Trends in the Ch'ing Period,* Immanuel C. Y. Hsü, trans. (Cambridge, Mass.: Harvard University Press, 1959), p. 85.

honest belief that they were actually engaged in scientific investigation. That smug self-assurance effectively closed their minds to pressingly immediate problems which desperately needed independent investigation. They invented an archaeology when they should have been studying political science and ballistics.

The West's aggressive superiority finally forced the *literati* to overcome their repugnance for the concrete and the unprecedented. Practical administrators, facing constant, humiliating demonstrations of China's inadequacy, goaded the scholars into a serious search for the secret of Western material supremacy. China finally recognized that she must learn to make—and employ—her own rifles, cannon, and gunboats.

Li Hung-chang and Chang Chih-tung, the two outstanding Chinese statesmen of the later nineteenth century, urged intelligent, traditional China to deal with the West realistically. Both were men of remarkable talent and ability by any standards—Chinese or Western, traditional or modern. But they themselves embodied the moral and intellectual traits that made it impossible for traditional China to cope with the West. Their hands—and the wings of their imaginations—were fettered by the degenerate Manchu Dynasty.

The Viceroy Li Hung-chang of the north won the highest appointment at the disposal of the Empire by his services against the Taipings. His campaigns against the rebels also gave him a greater knowledge of the Westerners than was possessed by any other ranking official. He learned that the foreigner might be as weak and corrupt as the series of adventurers employed against the Taipings—or as sternly dedicated as the Puritan British Colonel Charles George Gordon. Li further saw that even the weak adventurer could be highly effective militarily because of the techniques at his disposal, while the Bible-reading Gordon could conquer tens of thousands with a disciplined Chinese force of not more than three thousand. But Li could never understand why Gordon sulked for weeks after the authorities executed a few hundred Taipings who had surrendered on his promise of their lives—or why he refused the handsome bounty the Court proffered to allay his inexplicable shame.

In 1861 the Emperor received from Li Hung-chang a long

Memorial.[5] In response to a secret appeal for advice on dealing with the "oceanic barbarians," Li flatly declared China's unreadiness to try issues with the West. He wrote: "The truth is that at present the foreigners are powerful and the Chinese feeble. And whence arises the power of the former? It certainly is not innate in them. But it depends upon the fact that 'the requisites of government are sufficiency of food, sufficiency of military equipment, and the competence of the people and their ruler.' [Confucius] And how is the weakness of China to be accounted for? This also is not innate, but as a result of the above axiom not being sufficiently realized." [6]

It was the edge of heresy for Li Hung-chang to suggest that Chinese study the Westerner. "The memorialist, however, has had several years' experience in conducting business with foreigners, and is thoroughly familiar with their character . . . ," he wrote, skirting the issue. Advising compromise for the moment, he struck the keynote of Chinese feelings toward the West: it would be necessary, sooner or later, to destroy the foreigners' arrogance by force of arms. But he counseled: "It will be necessary to wait until—with large armies and abundant supplies, with no rebel or Mohammedan outbreaks in the provinces, and no difficulties in the Capital—we can cope with them without hesitation. We shall be a match *then* for all adversaries." [7]

Li's rival for official preferment, the Viceroy Chang Chih-tung of central China, looked deeper for the sources of China's weakness in his tract called "An Exhortation to Learning." He excoriated the ruling class as "befuddled, indolent, aimless, braggart, useless, ignorant [men who] continue hopelessly proud, overbearing, sitting complacently in their places while the country is going to pieces and the Holy Religion is being eradicated. . . . [They hide] in the regalia of Confucius, and quote long and elegantly from the Classics. . . ." Chang felt there was only one solution. "In order to render China powerful, and at the same

[5] The formal report of a senior official to the Emperor was called a Memorial; the portentous term was wholly justified by the rigidly prescribed forms in which the document was couched.
[6] Quoted in J. O. P. Bland, *Li Hung-chang* (London, 1909), pp. 82–83.
[7] *Ibid.*, p. 86.

time preserve our own institutions, it is absolutely necessary that we should utilize Western knowledge," he wrote. "But unless Chinese learning is made the basis of education, and a Chinese direction given to thought, the strong will become anarchists, and the weak, slaves. . . . Chinese learning is moral, Western learning is practical. Chinese learning concerns itself with moral conduct, Western learning with the affairs of the world. . . ." [8]

Chang Chih-tung's message was summed up in the maxim: "Chinese learning as the foundation for all things; Western learning for practical use!" That maxim was to dominate the thinking of China's rulers until 1949. Chang saw that there was no single Philosopher's Stone. Instead, he sought a series of formulae, never thinking that China might find it impossible to use Western techniques if she rejected their intellectual and moral bases. Nor did he ask why China, which was morally and intellectually far in advance of the West by his definition, had never developed the technology she now so desperately sought to learn from the West.

Li Hung-chang and Chang Chih-tung cajoled the demoralized Manchu Dynasty into adopting some Western techniques. The modern Kiangnan Arsenal was established in Shanghai with its own language school to train technical translators. Paper mills, railroads, cotton mills, and a general interpreters' college in Peking sprang from the new spirit. The Ching created the *Tsung-li Yamen*[9] to treat with foreigners, and more than one hundred students were sent to study in the United States. Under duress the Chinese had already appointed foreigners to administer the Maritime Customs, and other foreigners were voluntarily employed as fiscal, technical, and military experts. However, their careers usually ended in violent disagreement with their Chinese superiors, since, as one contemporary Chinese wrote, "The men of that time positively would not admit that the Europeans and Americans, apart from their ability to make [guns], explore [terrain],

[8] J. R. Levenson, *Liang Ch'i-ch'ao and the Mind of Modern China* (London: Thames and Hudson, 1959), pp. 6–7n.
[9] Literally, the "Bureau of General Affairs." This organization was the closest the Dynasty came to creating a Foreign Office. The Ching never established a modern diplomatic service.

sail [ships], and drill [troops], had any other kinds of knowledge." [10]

Despite occasional difficulties, the Chinese felt a sense of real accomplishment by 1890. Most Chinese and a good many foreigners as well believed that China was rising successfully to the challenge of the West. Intelligent Chinese did not deny that the Empire faced major problems, which stemmed as much from cyclical dynastic decay as from foreign intrusion. But most saw no need to remake the nation. It might be advisable to adjust, but there was, they felt, no reason to stoop to equality with the West, since China could obviously work out her problems within the traditional framework.

Complacent officials boasted that China, unlike Japan, had not surrendered to the West by recasting her government and her philosophy, nor had she been colonized like her former tribute territories in Southeast Asia. China's reasoned response to the challenge of the West restored confidence in her immutable superiority. Besides, she was building a formidable army and navy. Some thinkers in 1890 compared their own era with the Renaissance in Europe, for the Empire's eternal strength was re-established, based upon the moral and political values bequeathed by antiquity. All it had needed, the Chinese felt, was a little change, and they could face down the West without altering their own essential nature.

In 1894, China's dreams of eternal vigor were brutally dispelled. The humiliating disillusionment was contrived by the Japanese, a rather ludicrous nation whose previous role had always been to add luster to the Empire by aping its ways. The Japanese had, however, also proved brilliant pupils under the enforced tuition of the West. They had learned not only how to remake their own society, but how to enlarge their domains by force of arms—the root technique of Western civilization. Having built a powerful navy and a conscript army, Tokyo employed them to further traditional ambitions and to resolve old quarrels in its own favor. Unsure of their new strength, the Japanese first sparred with China over her offshore islands, the Ryukyus and Formosa. The

[10] Hsii, p. 113.

denouement came in the tortured Korean Peninsula, the land which had carried Confucian civilization to Japan and had for centuries been the arena where China and Japan fought for hegemony over Northeast Asia.

The Korean King had made ceremonial submission to Peking for centuries and was invested by his Imperial overlord, the Son of Heaven, as the Holy Roman Emperor was invested by the Pope. In 1893 the King, on the advice of the Chinese Resident in Seoul, requested the assistance of Chinese troops in suppressing the rebellious Tong Hak secret society. The Japanese, uninvited, sent troops to assist the "liberal" faction, which looked to Tokyo as the "conservatives" looked to Peking.

Neither Tokyo nor Peking would withdraw its troops after Korean forces put down the rebellion by themselves. The war that broke the impasse brought glory to Japan, which sacrificed few lives while China suffered a series of costly defeats.

China had entered the war wholly confident of victory. The coastal defenses of the north were Li Hung-chang's personal responsibility in his role as Viceroy of the Metropolitan Territories, since China possessed only provincial forces and no national army or navy. In 1893 Li had made a triumphal tour of the forts and schools, the railways and dockyards, the ships and arsenals whose creation crowned his life's work. His viceregal navy, the North Seas Squadron, mustered two battleships, six cruisers, and dozens of patrol and supply craft. Its corps of officers was stiffened by foreign advisers. Li's viceregal army was hardly less imposing, with its rapid-fire rifles and heavy artillery. In gratitude for the shield he had forged, the Empress Dowager bestowed upon the Viceroy the Triple-eyed Peacock's Feather, the Empire's highest honor. The world press echoed the Court's approbation. No one, including the Japanese, who hastily accelerated the pace of their naval construction, doubted that the old Empire once more possessed formidable forces.

The trial of arms that followed revealed that Li's great dreadnaughts and swift cruisers were no more effective than the gaudy war-junks that had sounded drums and clashed cymbals to frighten British frigates in the Pearl River in the first Opium War, fifty-five years earlier. At the Battle of the Yalu in September

1894, the Chinese ships' magazines held no more than fourteen rounds for each gun. Most of those shells were loaded with light practice charges, and some were empty. The two battleships carried three high-explosive shells for all their ten-inch guns. When the Japanese fleet besieged Weihaiwei a month later, only a hundred and four rounds lay in the magazines feeding the eight-inch Armstrong coastal defense rifles, and only four rounds were charged—one with powder and three with sand. The sighting mirrors of the guns could not be found, and their breechblocks were in need of repair.

Behind its Western façade Li Hung-chang's army proved no more effective than the Imperial forces which had sought to defeat the Taipings by raising fierce chants, donning hideous masks, and blowing discords upon their bugles. Foreign military advisers had been systematically thwarted or suborned by their Chinese colleagues and superiors.[11]

Li Hung-chang was justly held responsible for the debacle. His career—and his life—were preserved only because the Empress Dowager, who dominated the Court, remembered his earlier services gratefully and because he was still considered the only man who could deal with foreigners. The defeat eclipsed China's military pretensions until 1950. It also made possible open discussion of the facts everyone from the Empress Dowager to the lowliest official messenger had known—and condoned.

Li's clansmen and fellow Anhwei provincials had managed the forces which were the shield of the Empire as a commercial enterprise, systematically discrediting those officers who sought to create an effective army and navy. "Li's *yamen* at Tientsin became, like that of Prince Ching at Peking, a market place for the sale of jobs, offices and honors," observed his biographer.[12] His brother was commonly called the "Bottomless Purse." His sons and sons-in-law ordered equipment with but one consideration in mind: the profit it would yield the purchasing officer. Salesmen of the great European armament firms were pleased to cooperate,

---

[11] The continuing inability of the Chinese military to cooperate with foreign advisers has been amply demonstrated, first by the Nationalists with the Americans and later by the Communists with the Russians.

[12] Bland, p. 221.

since bribes enabled them to dispose of rifles, guns, and ammunition of innumerable patterns and great age which they could sell nowhere else. The navy and the army were staffed by officers who had purchased their commissions at great expense and, therefore, bore a sacred obligation to their families to recoup the purchase price—plus a justified profit of many thousand per cent.

The most enlightened—and wealthiest—of the mandarins had obviously failed to grasp the lessons he had been vouchsafed during the Taiping Rebellion. Li Hung-chang had found his Philosopher's Stone in European military forms. He believed that the forms alone would work their magic, regardless of his own behavior or the behavior of his subordinates. He did not suspect that the essence was more important than the name or that power yields herself to work, not to proclamations.

In 1895 the Treaty of Shimonoseki stripped China of her pretenses as well as her territories. She recognized Korea as an independent country, and she ceded to Japan the island of Formosa with its satellite islets, the Pescadores, as well as the Liaotung Peninsula in Manchuria with its naval base at Port Arthur. China also agreed to pay an indemnity, to open four new ports to trade, and to grant the Japanese extraterritorial rights under a new commercial treaty. She was further humiliated when France and Russia, fearful of competition, combined to force Japan to vacate the Liaotung Peninsula in return for an additional indemnity from the Empire. To her ultimate degradation, China saw that only her great size and her enemies' inability to agree on division of the spoils prevented the Empire's reduction to the status of Burma or Indo-China.

The Japanese War engendered divergent attitudes among small groups of ardent, thinking Chinese. One group believed that a return to fundamental Confucian virtues would revitalize the Manchu Dynasty. Another insisted that the Manchus must be replaced by a new dynasty, since Heaven had demonstrated its displeasure by a rain of calamities. A third contended that the monarchy must give way to a republic. All three, however, agreed that China must overcome her difficulties by sweeping internal changes, since the ruling dynasty was rotten with decay.

The would-be reformers found unexpected allies from the West. The vast Christian missionary establishment in China was one of the most successful efforts by one culture to influence another. If the missionaries produced few Christians, they encouraged many skeptics; if they did not establish Christian morality, they engendered discontent; if they did not turn men's minds to contemplation of eternity or awaken the desire for spiritual enlightenment, they made known the material benefits enjoyed by Christian nations. Above all, the missionaries encouraged intellectual communication with the West, though that was not their chief purpose.

Moving with the new intellectual currents, two professional translators introduced those abstract ideas—as distinguished from material techniques—which destroyed the spiritual basis of the Confucian state. Although the traditional mind considered fiction a divertissement fit only for women and the half-educated, forcing scholar-officials to publish their novels under pseudonyms, Lin Shu translated about a hundred and fifty foreign novels into polished classical Chinese. The first lesson his multitude of readers learned was that the West was a true civilization made up of educated human beings. It was a wholly new concept to the Chinese.

Yen Fu translated scientific and philosophical works, revealing economic and political systems as astounding to the Chinese as were Jonathan Swift's imaginary realms to the English in his day. It was shocking enough to realize that the existence of other fully developed systems meant that China was not the sole civilized realm. But it was shattering to read Charles Darwin's *On the Origin of Species* and Julian Huxley's *Evolution and Ethics*. The eternal continuity of the generations of mankind, without beginning and without end, underlay the Chinese certainty that the Confucian system would itself endure forever. Adjustment might be necessary, the Chinese believed, but never radical change, which was at variance with the purposes of nature. China's deepest spiritual and political foundations were shaken by the theory of evolution's revelation of the brief span—and possible impermanence—of humanity's tenure upon the earth.

The Protestant missionaries had involuntarily stimulated the

flow of secular knowledge from the West, though many of the
new concepts were as abhorrent to them as they were to orthodox
Confucians. The Protestants, beginning with Robert Morrison's
tracts which inspired the Taiping Emperor, had introduced periodical journalism as a channel for disseminating the Gospel.
About 1870 a swarm of gifted malcontents began issuing China's
first secular newspapers, usually from the refuge of the treaty ports
where the Imperial law did not run. Since editors were almost
invariably members of the mandarin class who had fallen out with
the regime—through principle or through thwarted ambition—
the press championed reform. Journalism was an occupation less
hazardous than open revolt, which had theretofore been the only
major channel of protest available to the commonalty. It was also
more effective than the Memorials so often addressed in vain to
the Throne by the dedicated Censors, who were the Confucian
regime's equivalent of Rome's Tribunes of the People.

After the "National Humiliation Treaty" of Shimonoseki in
1895, Chinese journalism produced a figure who was to dominate
it until 1921, when, coincidentally, the Communist Party was
founded.

Liang Chi-chao was an intellectual agitator, political reformer, tract novelist, and journalist. But he underwent an orthodox education in preparation for success in the three stages of the
Civil Service Examination, which would successively win him academic degrees approximate to the A.B., M.A., and Ph.D. and
qualify him for successively higher official appointments. In 1889
he passed the provincial examinations for the second academic
degree, at sixteen the youngest candidate and fifth in standing.
The chief examiner was so impressed by the young man's promise
that he offered his younger sister in marriage to the brilliant youth
in a gesture out of a typical Chinese success story. Despite the
influence of his new relations by marriage, Liang failed the doctoral examination in Peking in 1890.

Nonetheless, he found his true vocation in 1890. Passing
through Shanghai on his return home, he saw for the first time the
Western books translated by the new Kiangnan Arsenal as part of
the enlightened madarinate's attempt to master Western indus-

trial and military techniques. After reading an outline of geography that contradicted all traditional teaching on the shape of the earth, he awakened to a sense of the great world and to China's degraded place in the world. "Since my seventeenth year," he later wrote, "I have known much anxiety over the signs of strength and the signs of weakness among foreigners and Chinese." [13]

In the same year, Liang Chi-chao first met another scholar who was dismayed by the nation's weakness and the foreigners' strength. When the Court rejected his proposals for reform, the Cantonese Kang Yu-wei had established a private school where he taught the classics, stressing always that China must find her salvation by returning to the original Confucian virtues. He also offered a course on the outside world called *I-wu*, or "barbarian affairs." His own dream was *Ta Tung*, the "Great Commonwealth," a Utopian vision of the entire world under one government. *Ta Tung*, the term itself Confucian, was largely an echo of the traditional concept of *Tien Hsia*—all that is under heaven—for humanity would be governed in accordance with Confucian principles administered by a refurbished Confucian bureaucracy.

For the moment, however, Kang and his followers, with Liang Chi-chao chief among them, sought to rule neither the world nor even China. Instead, they studied the West, disseminating their findings through the *Chiang Hsueh Hui*, which Europeans called the Reform Club or the Mutual Improvement Society, though the name literally meant the "Association To Study Power." The "liberal" mandarins who financed the Association would have been horrified at its secret aims. Their ardent young protégés proposed not merely to broadcast the secrets that made the West powerful, but to take power themselves in order to reshape China into a powerful nation.

It was obviously heretical to champion general education under the slogan: "It is better to share learning with a group than to have learning by oneself, and it is better to share this learning with the millions of the masses—than to share it with a [small]

[13] Quoted in Levenson, p. 17.

group." [14] Despite their egalitarian fervor, the first journal published by Kang and Liang addressed itself to that one audience
which could produce immediate results, China's thousand or so
ranking officials. Aroused by the reformist tone of Liang's articles
and by his impartial coverage of world affairs, the conservatives
soon proscribed the Association To Study Power and banned its
journal.

Although the reformers seemed further from political power
than ever, Liang Chi-chao was entranced by the power of the pen.
Reaffirming his preoccupation with the "fundamental sources of
national power," [15] he published *Current Affairs* from the sanctu-
ary of Shanghai at intervals of ten days for a two-year period that
began on August 9, 1896. In a style midway between the classical
and the vernacular, the magazine discussed the arts and sciences,
as well as domestic and international politics—and published
the texts of Mandates and Memorials, which were of professional
interest to officials. Liang's editorials avocated: "industrialization,
widespread education in new schools with Sino-Western curricula,
translation of books, [and] constitutional government." [16] Articles
ranged from a biography of George Washington to a history of
British railways, all seeking to make China strong by teaching her
modern ways. Even the serialized *Adventures of Sherlock Holmes,*
while undoubtedly attracting readership, taught the scientific
method and the daily life of Victorian England. The magazine
was dubbed *The Chinese Progress* by the foreign community,
which was gratified by the voluminous translations of Western
literature. It was also patronized by a number of high-ranking
officials. The inspiration of *Current Affairs* created similar provincial journals and societies for technical study. Those organizations sponsored campaigns against social evils like foot binding,
indentured slavery, and opium smoking.

The fairy-tale quality of Liang's life, a Horatio Alger story
with an inconclusive ending, reasserted itself after his brief period

[14] Lin Yu-tang, *History of the Press and Public Opinion in China* (Chicago,
1936), p. 95.
[15] Roswell Britton, *The Chinese Periodical Press, 1800–1912* (Shanghai,
1933), p. 18.
[16] Levenson, p. 23.

in the wilderness. Liang Chi-chao and his mentor Kang Yu-wei were finally granted the opportunity to remake the structure of government—in part because Liang's brother-in-law had attained high rank and in part because of conflicts within the Court. For a hundred days in the summer of 1898 the reformers controlled the machinery of the state, even sitting familiarly beside the Emperor Kuang Hsu while their three heads bent over the drafts of Mandates. It was as if Warren Harding had summoned Norman Thomas and the editor of *The New Republic* to Washington to act as his chief advisers and executive officers. But the debacle toward which the reformers hastened arose not so much from the essential incongruity of the alliance as from the conflict between the Emperor Kuang Hsu and China's real ruler, the Empress Dowager.

Her name was Yehonala, and her reign name was Tzu Hsi, which means "motherly and auspicious." The Empress Dowager's array of titles increased as she grew in power, but behind her back the Court called her the Old Buddha. She came from the Yeho tribe of the Manchus; her father was an obscure military officer; and she had been introduced to Court with a hundred other maidens of pure Manchu blood, all aspirant concubines. Although tales of her life are rich in legend and deficient in fact, it is clear that she did not wait for fate to bestow the Emperor Hsien Feng's favor upon her. When she bore the son who was to become the Emperor Tung Chih, Kuang Hsu's father, she was raised to the rank of Imperial Concubine. Thus began a career which later Chinese historians have characterized as one of unbridled sexual license and uncontrolled bloodletting. Blaming Tzu Hsi for all the evils which beset China, they have deliberately overlooked the fact that her strength of character and her ability to inspire loyalty actually served as unifying forces within a disintegrating dynasty. The Ching Dynasty was, in any event, doomed. If it was, in truth, preserved beyond its normal term by Tzu Hsi's leadership, it also died harder and in greater anguish because of her obduracy.

When the Emperor died in 1862, she seized supreme power as regent for her infant son. She did not relinquish final control over China until her death. She slew her rivals, including the senior Empress Dowager and perhaps even her husband, the Emperor himself; she ennobled and enriched her favorites; and she fought with all her ruthless wiles any reform that might weaken her power. Brought up as a sheltered Manchu lady, a fit bride for an Emperor, and struggling to mature years within the walls of the Forbidden City, Yehonala knew little of either China or the world. But she possessed a sensitive instinct for the slightest threat to her position and, unlike many princesses, both charm and gratitude.

Weary or complacent, Tzu Hsi gave up direct control of the government in the late 1890s, content to demand long accountings of the Emperor Kuang Hsu, her grandson. Though she retained the ultimate power of approving appointments to the higher official posts, the Emperor was nominally ruler of the nation, for the imprint of his seal alone was enough to enact a law. Inevitably weak because his world was the Court dominated by women and eunuchs, Kuang Hsu was nonetheless conscious of his responsibilities. When Tzu Hsi retired, the Emperor sought to change China. He knew that the world had changed, though not quite how.

Despite the suppression of their political movement, the propaganda of the reformers Kang Yu-wei and Liang Chi-chao had influenced the mandarins who were the personal advisers of the twenty-seven-year-old Emperor. On June 11, 1898, Kuang Hsu issued an Imperial Mandate that was more homily than fiat. He stressed the necessity for reform in education and the military services and the need for an effective diplomatic establishment. The response was favorable, for many loyal mandarins had come to feel that some changes were essential. Liberal officials, including Liang Chi-chao's brother-in-law, pointed out that the Meiji Restoration in Japan had ignored all precedent in its search for talent and urged that Kang and Liang be offered employment. Kang became a chief adviser to the Emperor, preaching his slogan: "Reform and Be Strengthened! Guard the Old and Die!" [17] Liang Chi-chao immersed himself in the new Translation Bureau. As if determined to wring the secrets of supremacy from the West by sheer industry, he ordered translations of thousands of books. Decrees signed by Kuang Hsu established a national university in

[17] *Ibid.*, p. 300.

Peking,[18] purged the bureaucracy, and reorganized government departments.

The Reform Movement, the last effort of intelligent, traditional China to come to terms with the West, momentarily appeared to be moving toward success. But the reformers went too fast. Their failure was insured when they abolished sinecures and perquisites in the hope of cleansing the troughs of corruption in which the Court wallowed content. Tzu Hsi left her seclusion to champion old China by humbling the Emperor and exacting vengeance on the reformers who were his collaborators.

Liang and Kang fled sentences of death, while Kuang Hsu was imprisoned in a lonely pavilion within the Imperial City. His room was heated only by a noisome charcoal brazier, and he slept on a rough pallet. He was stripped of every comfort which should have enhanced his state. Ten years later the Empress Dowager, realizing that she was dying, sent her grandson some spice cakes, probably with a few grains of poison baked into them. Kuang Hsu died just one day before Tzu Hsi.

But the grand public tragedy was not yet played out when the hapless Emperor was thrust into the shadows from which he passed directly into the final night. Relentless as an early Elizabethan drama, a great bloodletting preceded the death of China. It was an ignoble end to two thousand years of high heroism and malignant self-seeking in an atmosphere compounded of profound philosophical speculation and the rote mumble of fossilized inanities.

During the last two years of the nineteenth century China was convulsed by the folk movement which styled itself the Association of Righteous Harmony. Foreigners called them the Boxers because they practiced the old Chinese exercise of shadow-boxing. The rituals of the Boxers owed much to the old secret socie-

---

[18] The uncanny cyclical reversions noted by Chinese historians have appeared again. Peking University has been a storm center of the Great Proletarian Cultural Revolution. In their death throes the Maoists have, with approbation, compared themselves to the Boxers. Their denial that Mao Tse-tung was like the Empress Dowager defending the pure tradition against traitors was expected but lacking in conviction.

ties and more to Tantric Buddhism. They were possessed by spirits in orgiastic trance dances and preached a confused theology whose main tenets were their divine mission and their invulnerability. Their purpose, however, was clear: all foreigners must be expelled from China and the officious missionaries must die.

When the Empress Dowager gave her tacit assent, hundreds of missionaries were slaughtered in the hinterlands. Under the bombardment of Chinese siege guns, the legation quarter of Peking fought with rifles to maintain the extraterritorial privileges it had won with cannon. Troops of eight nations finally lifted the siege and forced the Empress Dowager and Kuang Hsu, united in misfortune, to flee Peking. The allied troops' behavior and the diplomats' exactions confirmed the Chinese traditionalists' hatred for the West. No less did hatred animate those Chinese who were determined to destroy all traditions.

After its last wild outbreak, old China was obviously dying, though her death agonies convulsed another decade. The Ching Dynasty somehow endured, though its pulse almost stopped when the Civil Service Examinations were abolished in 1905. There was no real government in China during the Ching's last decade, but there was great inertia in traditional Chinese civilization.

The new men who came to the fore were determined to destroy the Confucian system. They were even ready to adopt democracy if it would help them use science in turning the cannon against their makers. The Chinese felt they had finally learned the true secret of Western culture: Confucius, Buddha, and Christ might console old ladies or inspire fanatics, but there was no morality in the affairs of this world and no god greater than power.

Part Three

SHAPING THE WEAPON
(1900–1963)

*Twentieth-Century China Experiments
with Sweeping Internal Changes,
Determined to Confront the West on
Terms of Equality—or Supremacy*

*A dreamer sat in the chair of the Minister of Transportation
of the new Republic of China in 1912. He had acquired even more
than the usual Chinese profusion of names during his revolutionary career. He was known to the West as Sun Yat-sen, though he
signed himself Sun Wen and most Chinese would remember him
as Sun Chung-shan, the father of Republican China. His contemporaries dubbed him "Big Gun" because of the vast scope of his
ambitions for the country, expressed in one respect in his grandiose plans for expanding China's few thousand miles of railroad.*

*The Minister's most fantastic vision was a railroad from
Chengtu in Szechwan Province to Lhasa, the capital of Tibet. The
distance on the map was seven hundred miles westward, but for
railroad tracks more than twice that extent through the highest*

*peaks in the world. The unsurveyed territory was sparsely inhab-
ited by hostile tribes; it was covered with ice and snow for nine
months of the year; and it was made hazardous by sudden ava-
lanches and the abrupt appearance of great crevasses. The nearest
existing railhead to Chengtu itself was at Hankow, six hundred
miles due east—and at least a thousand track miles.*

"Big Gun" Sun went on to greater achievements, but he never
built the Chengtu-Lhasa Railroad. That line is today still projected. It was not until 1952 that the railroad came creeping to
Chengtu from the east.

Yet the nationalistic ambitions that impelled Sun Yat-sen to
plan the Chengtu-Lhasa Railroad were realized in good part by
the People's Republic. The Communists built three motor roads
from western China through rebellious Tibet to Lhasa. They laid
roads from Lhasa south to the frontiers of Nepal, Bhutan, and
Sikkim, the speed of construction mocking the Indians' snail-pace
construction of a sixty-five mile road from their border north to
the Nepalese capital of Katmandu. Along those roads moved the
troops and supplies that overwhelmed Indian border defenses in
the autumn of 1962.

Although airliners bearing the five golden stars of the People's Republic of China can now make regular flights to Lhasa, the
Communists still hope to build the Chengtu-Lhasa Railroad. Its
completion would not only link China's least developed border
territory with the nation proper, but would complete the transformation of the world's highest plateau into a powerful Chinese
base on the brink of the Indian and Middle Eastern worlds.

The power vacuum in Tibet, which insulated China from
clashes with those worlds, has already been filled. That extension
of Chinese power, consistently sought by the Communists, was
Sun Yat-sen's chief purpose as well.

7

The Blade Shatters

A Republican Revolution Destroys the Empire, But Parliamentary Democracy Fails

The most powerful and most direct stimulus to fundamental change, as the Manchu Dynasty passed through the agony of its last decade, was not new ideas but the energy of Western businessmen. Although the great masses of China remained as they had always been, peasants as well as townfolk found their lives altered considerably if their homes lay in areas where the foreigners thought there was money to be made.

In his memoirs[1] Chang Kuo-tao, the Leon Trotsky of the Chinese revolution, recalled the German mechanization of the coal mines at Anyuan in inland Kiangsi Province in 1898. The railroad built to serve the mines was extended to the county seat of Pinghsiang in 1905 and, shortly thereafter, to Changsha in Hunan Province, completely changing the face of the county by the time Chang Kuo-tao entered the "modern" Pinghsiang Primary School in 1908. A tiny shop specializing in foreign goods which was originally no more than a stall had become the city's largest emporium. Travelers from Shanghai brought back fountain pens, clocks, and drafting instruments, as well as tawdry ornaments and lithographs, each article a direct blow to the traditional culture and traditional handicrafts. Cheap imported cloth made the town dwellers' garments, and oil lamps lit their houses; even farmers

[1] A manuscript in Chinese and English prepared with the assistance of Prof. Robert A. Burton of the University of Kansas, to be published soon.

used the foreigners' iron pots, steel knives, and thermos jugs. For the first time in thousands of years there occurred sweeping changes in everyday life. Gentry or peasant, the Chinese of 1808 had been almost indistinguishable from his ancestors of 808 in his manner of life and thought. His great-grandsons of 1908 were wholly different.

The older generation of Pinghsiang hated the intrusion of the West. The railroad deprived chairbearers, boatmen, and coolies of their jobs, breaking their rice bowls, as the conservatives bitterly said. It also warped the *Feng Shui*,[2] the proper balance of nature, releasing tormented spirits to prey upon mankind from roiled rivers and desecrated graves. Men whispered darkly that the locomotive would not operate unless a living child was fed into its funnel each day.

"Grandfather was outraged when I arrived home one day dressed in a gown of foreign cloth . . . ," Chang Kuo-tao remembered. "The large-flowered Suchow and Hangchow silks and satins were, he felt, still the only civilized garb." The elders felt that abandoning traditional goods, no less than forswearing traditional learning, meant surrendering Chinese virtue to Western gimcrackery—and presaged utter damnation.

The primary school young Chang attended had been established to teach "Western learning" after abolition of the Civil Service Examinations destroyed the foundation of Chinese civilization. But it was controlled by old-style scholars who were unable to "utter a sentence without quoting Confucius" and still tried instinctively to instill the classics because they knew nothing else. The students preferred the courses in the natural sciences, which were taught by young teachers who asserted that education should impart new ideas, not merely preserve old ones.

Each hour brought fresh revelations. Students learned that the earth was not a flat dish with China in the center, but a "round, ball-like thing." They learned that the West, too, had produced sages and great men who were fit to rank with China's own heroes. Mr. Wang, the geography teacher, told them that foreign

[2] The words mean, literally, "wind water." The term, usually translated "geomancy," is the old Chinese science of situating buildings, farms, and graves so as to avoid evil influences—and invite good spirits.

goods and foreign methods had undoubtedly hurt the Chinese people, but hatred, maledictions, and their elders' determination to preserve the old ways unchanged would merely make the nation suffer more. Since she could no longer live in self-suffient isolation, he said, China must utilize the new techniques. Chinese could build their own machines and compete successfully with the foreigners in running business enterprises. "Daily," recalled Chang, "we became more enamored of Mr. Wang's position."

The boys were shaken by constant demonstrations of China's inability to withstand Western incursions. They were infuriated by the corruption, brutality, and inefficiency that marked the last days of the Manchu Dynasty. They were therefore convinced that China could live through the storm only if she jettisoned her old ways. Young students made violent scenes when their sisters' feet were bound and they burned the opium pipes treasured by their elders. They stormed temples to smash idols and denounced the mumbling monks. They even taunted minor officials, whom they hated for their bullying and extortion.

"To fight all that is old, rotten, and senseless, to make China powerful, to stop Chinese from being the sick men of East Asia became the goals of aspiring young men," Chang Kuo-tao wrote, summing up the spirit of an age when resentment sought political outlets. Older men who felt as the boys did were already directing discontent into the rebellions whose backwash swept over isolated Pinghsiang—though they were never as violent as the revolts of the mid-nineteenth century. The new rebels were nevertheless to administer the *coup de grâce* to the tormented Ching Dynasty.

The liberal reforms of Liang Chi-chao and the vindictive reaction of the Boxers had both proved themselves incapable of arresting normal dynastic disintegration or checking Western intervention, when Sun Yat-sen, a doctor of medicine of Queen's College in Hong Kong, proclaimed new slogans. Only a sweeping political revolution could make China strong, he asserted. Since not only the Manchus but the Imperial system itself had failed, China must adopt Western political institutions—as well as Western material techniques. Sun chose much modified forms of parliamentary democracy and socialist economics as the means to restore China's greatness. Since no modern nation could be truly strong and respected if the common people were poor, it was also necessary to create a prosperous citizenry.

The despised Manchus were still too deeply entrenched to fall before haphazard internal revolts. Since only the free Chinese, living outside China, could provide the force he required, Sun built his revolutionary movement abroad.

The Ching had created its own nemesis. Seeking the perfect closed system, the Empire had restricted the export of its human resources as well as its material wealth. Like Chinese goods, Chinese subjects might venture abroad only on the Emperor's business—to open new lands to Chinese hegemony or to accept the tribute of vassal states. Yet in the nineteenth century neither legal strictures nor patriotic sentiments could withstand the thunders of the European's guns and the lure of his gold. Hundreds of thousands of Chinese left their impoverished native places in the southeastern coastal provinces during each decade after 1870 to open plantations, to build railroads, and to staff trading posts. By 1900 nearly four million Chinese lived abroad and pursued the industrious and speculative ways that earned them a commanding economic position in Southeast Asia. Though they were formally outlaws, they were still Chinese. Anxious to assert their distinction against both the aloof Europeans and the lackadaisical southerners whom they lived among and exploited, the younger overseas Chinese sought to renew the ties with the motherland their parents had evaded. They claimed their heritage: the ancient, glorious culture of China.

They found that their identification with the Chinese tradition provoked greater scorn than admiration. Foreigners felt no awe of a nation so weak it had become the prey of half the world. The overseas Chinese decided, with almost a single will, that they could win respect only through a resurgence of the Chinese nation itself. The emotional need was usually explained as a quest for practical benefits. Men argued that a strong China would marshal her military and diplomatic power to protect them from slights and injustices. Chinese in exile wove a dream against the toil and outrages of their daily lives. The smiling laundryman, the sweating coolie on the railroad work-gang, and the silk-robed magnate —each comforted himself in adversity and rejoiced with greater zest in his seasons of joy because he was a Chinese, born of a race set far above the rest of mankind. The determination that this superiority must be universally acknowledged led the overseas Chinese into radical political movements.

Sun Yat-sen was the greatest of the political adventurers who exploited the discontent of the wealthy overseas Chinese. Drawing financial support from the Chinese of Southeast Asia and the Americas, the conspirators of Sun's *Chung-kuo Ko-ming Tang*[3] were themselves refugees or students in the foreign concessions and Japan. Westerners and Japanese alike encouraged the movement toward a modern Republic of China, which, they believed, would welcome normal diplomatic and commercial relations—unlike the stubborn Empire. The foreign aficionados happily disregarded Sun's strident appeals to Chinese racism—an emphasis dictated by his personal emotional needs, as well as his followers'.

Born in 1866 to a prosperous family of farmers in the district near Canton which today bears his name, Sun Yat-sen was entirely a modern man. He was cut off by his education from traditional China, unlike the great journalist Liang Chi-chao, his junior by five years, who performed the normal *cursus honorem* of the Civil Service Examinations. After studying at the village grammar school, Sun lived with his elder brother in Honolulu, where he attended an American high school. Half-converted to Christianity, he desecrated the images in the village temple upon his return to China. But in the early 1880s idol-smashing had not yet become the national sport of ardent young Chinese. Sun fled the villagers' indignation, fetching up in Hong Kong, where he completed his secondary schooling and received his medical degree in 1892. Angered by the Court's disregard of his formal proposals for reform after the Sino-Japanese War, Sun Yat-sen led his first revolt in 1895. When that inept rising was suppressed, he began his long hegira, sixteen years of wandering among the overseas Chinese which were to end with the successful revolution of 1911.

Liang Chi-chao was a man of traditional China, a reformer with compromise in his bones. Sun Yat-sen was a Westernized

---

[3] The "Chinese Revolutionary Party." *Ko-ming*, the modern word for "revolution," literally means "to change the Mandate [of Heaven]," wresting it from an unworthy dynasty.

revolutionary whom his critics called "deracinated." Converted to Christianity, Sun founded the Kuomintang, the National People's Party, which in exile on Formosa still honors his picture with daily veneration like that tendered images of Confucius under the Empire. His second wife, Madame Sun Soong Ching-ling, preserves the living connection as one of two vice-chairmen of the People's Republic of China, which also pays lip service to the father of the nation.

Sun's personal motto was: "Action is easy, understanding difficult!" He undoubtedly wished to be remembered as a modern sage rather than an implacable revolutionary in a high-buttoned tunic. But his great achievements were as an agitator. In 1905 he founded an active revolutionary league in Tokyo. The *Tung Meng Hui*, literally the "Sworn-together League," which finally became the Kuomintang, attracted most men who despaired of the Confucian system. Its purpose was clear: to overthrow the Manchus by force of arms. The League's first task was to fan dissatisfaction into violent action; the obvious means was the propaganda press.

During the next five years the *Tung Meng Hui* issued dozens of newspapers and magazines that incited revolution. The Court's attempts to suppress the journals merely forced the publishers to greater ingenuity in distribution and increased the papers' circulation by bestowing upon them the lure of the forbidden. *The Democrat*, which was the most professional of the revolutionary journals, printed dispatches from a network of correspondents abroad and was distributed by a host of secret sympathizers within China. Its news services surpassed the commercial newspapers', and it was selling twenty thousand copies of each issue by 1910. Since the popularity of the revolutionary press forced the commercial press to follow its opinions, the Court was soon surrounded by clamoring Chinese, all determined that the Manchus must go.

The din of discontent mocked the Manchus' eleventh-hour attempts to reform under a drumfire of small rebellions. Angry youths, the future leaders of the Communist Party among them, smashed idols in village temples; they snipped off their queues, those symbols of Chinese subjugation; and they joined the Imperial

Army to learn to use arms—against the Manchus. Secret agents of the *Tung Meng Hui* traversed the face of China, seeking alliances with the secret societies whose Ming loyalism was transmuted into pure anti-Manchu fervor. As one rebellion was suppressed, two others rose, for popular anger was heightened by the misdeeds of the Imperial soldiery. Despite local officials' reluctance to report the true extent of disorder, even the Court at Peking could not remain unaware that its existence was threatened. Upon the Empress Dowager's death in 1908 the Court expanded the piecemeal reforms she had proclaimed reluctantly since 1900. But it was too late—decades too late—to save the Ching Dynasty or the civilization it represented.

The loyalty of a few Chinese bureaucrats could not preserve the Ching imperium. The local gentry repudiated the Manchus, though the gentry had been the mainstay that supported the towering Court. The clumsy machinery of Chinese society no longer responded to the Manchus' will, for all its parts were adrift—clan associations and temples; merchants' and artisans' guilds; peasants and boatmen; even the local militia and the police. Amid this disintegration an accident precipitated the revolution that swept away the institutions of two thousand years in less than two months.

Rising like the Yangtze River itself in Szechwan Province in the west, a torrent of resistance swept the entire Yangtze Valley when Peking revealed its plans to nationalize the country's railways with a loan from foreign bankers. Chinese capital had already built a fragmentary rail system. Peking now proposed to make it state property, arguing with justified logic that the railways could be operated more efficiently as a single unit. But, the opposition pointed out, the decision had been made under foreign pressure. A state railway system dependent upon Western capital would, in the eyes of most patriots, be simply another device for Western exploitation of China.

The protestants therefore denounced the move as selling out China to the West. Heavy-handed suppression of the Save the Railways Movement led to armed clashes throughout Szechwan. When the Manchus transferred troops to the west, the revolutionists decided to strike in Wuhan, the triplet industrial cities of east-central China—Wuchang, Hanyang, and Hankow.[4] Early in October 1911 a small group of revolutionaries in Wuhan were busily manufacturing bombs. More familiar with couplets than explosives, they managed to blow themselves up. But even the somnolent Ching was convinced that a major plot was afoot.

The authorities' untypically successful attempt to discover the culprits brought on revolution. The captured membership rolls of the conspiracy listed so many names that the government was puzzled as to where to begin suppressing the movement. Fearful conspirators in the army struck first. On October 9, 1911, an Imperial brigade in Wuchang mutinied, forcing its commanding general, Li Yuan-hung, who was only half-reluctant, to lead them against arsenals and communications centers. On October 10th the rebels proclaimed the Republic of China, and shortly thereafter they took Hankow and Hanyang.

The issue was still in doubt when the Court placed its fate in the hands of the Viceroy Yuan Shih-kai, who had betrayed the reformers in 1898. Yuan appealed to the Court not only because of his impeccable record of conservatism, but also because he commanded, in the armies of North China, the only effective military force that had not been corrupted by the revolutionaries. The Viceroy bargained with both the Court and the rebels, but finally joined the rebels. He was not moved primarily by the promises he won, but by his own vision of emerging from a tumultuous interregnum as the founder of a new dynasty.

Their last support withdrawn, the Manchus were powerless. There had been no real fighting, except the confused street skirmishing of the first few days in Wuhan, but the Manchu power was completely destroyed as province after province proclaimed its allegiance to the new Republic of China. In December 1911 a provisional National Council assembled in Peking to elect Sun Yat-sen President of the Republic. To mark the new era, the National

---

[4] Again the uncanny parallel: Szechwan was an anti-Maoist bastion from the time the Great Proletarian Cultural Revolution began to go awry. An incident in Wuhan in July 1967 precipitated the latter stage of the anti-Maoist movement, and the Yangtze Valley provided the opposition with a broad base.

Council decreed that all calendars would begin anew from 1912—"Year One of the Republic of China."

The Republic started life in an atmosphere of reasonableness. In February 1912 the young Emperor Hsuan Tung abdicated.[5] A few days later, Sun Yat-sen resigned the presidency in favor of Yuan Shih-kai, who, men contended, could rally conservatives to the support of the new Republic and thus create a unified nation. In 1913 a Parliament was elected, its members mostly young radicals. But sweet reason vanished when Yuan took all power into his own hands, first dismissing Parliament and finally proclaiming himself Emperor of the Great Constitutional Dynasty in 1915. After an unsuccessful rising against Yuan in 1913, Sun Yat-sen and his followers returned to their accustomed state of exile and began plotting to restore the Republic. Until his death in 1925, such was to be Sun's occupation, either in exile or at the head of a rump republican government in the south of China. When Yuan Shih-kai died in 1916, the capital of Peking, which the foreign powers recognized as the seat of the legitimate government, became a shuttlecock tossed back and forth between contending warlords.

The former Emperor Hsuan Tung, later and better known as Henry Pu-yi, was allowed to remain in his palace, where faithful Manchu officials clothed in traditional court robes continued to perform the traditional obeisances. He later fled Peking to become ruler of Manchukuo, reigning over the land of the Manchus under the aegis of the Japanese invaders. After "reform through labor," he was released by the Communists to tell Field Marshal Viscount Montgomery in 1960: "I am a new man, I am the new Pu-yi. I am much happier today as a gardener than I ever was before." So ended the intercourse between British peers and Manchu princes that Macartney and Chien Lung had begun.

No more than the West did Sun Yat-sen's revolutionaries destroy the Ching Dynasty. The long-lived Ching, paralyzed by dissension and corruption, had been on the verge of spontaneous

[5] His reign had been as unhappy as it was brief; he had been only two years old when he was designated to succeed his childless uncle, Kuang Hsu, on that Emperor's death in 1908. He died in 1967.

disintegration. Sun's new political concepts did, however, prevent the Ching's being succeeded by a replica of itself. The chain of Imperial dynasties was broken, and the Confucian ideology was dethroned. With the proclamation of a modern republic, it appeared, China was finally about to come to terms with the world. Nonetheless, one of the first official acts of the new Republic of China was to order the compilation of the dynastic history of the Ching Dynasty, just as each Confucian dynasty had published the history of its predecessor.

Sun Yat-sen, like the journalist Liang Chi-chao, had sought in Western books the devices which would bring about a renascence of the Chinese race. Sun's gleanings were concentrated in his master work *San Min Chu Yi* (*The Three People's Principles*) whose purpose, he declared, was to "elevate China to an equal position among the nations, in international affairs, in government, and in economic life. . . . The *San Min* principles are the principles for our nation's salvation. . . ." [6]

The first and predominant doctrine was the "principle of nationalism," expressed as *Min-tsu Chu-yi*—quite literally, "People's Stock Chief Doctrine," although it is normally translated as the "Principle of Nationalism." The term conveniently means both "nationalism" and "racialism." Sun intended the double meaning. China, he declared in the final version of his magnum opus, was the only nation where "state and race" were a single entity, because "China, since the Ch'in and Han [221 B.C.–A.D. 220] Dynasties, has been developing a single state out of a single race, while foreign countries have developed many states from one race, and have included many nationalities within one state." [7] The two additional principles, "popular welfare" and "popular rule," were secondary to revitalizing the Chinese race, for "the greatest force is common blood." [8] Sun affirmed the superiority of the yellow race, noting that all European empires had been greatly inferior to the Mongol Empire. "Never before," he wrote, "had a nation's

[6] Sun Yat-sen, *San Min Chu Yi, The Three Principles of the People*, F. W. Price, trans. (Chungking, 1941), p. 4.

[7] *Ibid.*, p. 6.

[8] *Ibid.*, p. 9.

armed forces occupied the two continents of Europe and Asia as did the Mongol armies of the Yuan dynasty in their prime." [9]

But, asked Sun, what has happened to the race which can proudly say: "In comparison with other nations we have the greatest population and the oldest culture, of four thousand years' duration"? He answered: "We are the poorest and weakest state in the world, occupying the lowest position in international affairs; the rest of mankind is the carving knife and the serving dish, while we are the fish and the meat. Our position now is extremely perilous; if we do not earnestly promote nationalism and weld together our four hundred millions into a strong nation, we face a tragedy—the loss of our country and the destruction of our race." [10]

The consistent theme in a life marked by incongruous alliances and adolescent eclecticism was the crusade for Chinese nationalism. Sun wrote with full justification in his political testament: "For forty years I have devoted myself to the cause of the people's revolution with but one end in view, the elevation of China to a position of freedom and equality among the nations. . . . To attain this goal we must bring about a thorough awakening of our own people. . . ." [11]

All other purposes yielded to the one cardinal purpose. Recognizing that "the world is already suffering from overpopulation," [12] Sun nonetheless urged the Chinese to increase their numbers at a constantly accelerating rate. Although the statistics on which he based his conclusions were characteristically erroneous, Sun told his followers: "When I compare their [the European and American powers] increase with China's I tremble." [13] Likening the Chinese nation to "a sheet of sand" because it was vast, numerous, and fragmented, he attacked the doctrines of "internationalism and cosmopolitanism" as cultural tricks devised by the imperialists to sap China's nationalism.

Although he never lost his ardent confidence, the noble goal

[9] *Ibid.*, p. 10.
[10] *Ibid.*, p. 12.
[11] *Ibid.*, p. 11.
[12] *Ibid.*, p. 27.
[13] *Ibid.*, p. 25.

must often have appeared infinitely distant to Sun Yat-sen, who died just three years before his party entered the promised land—a unified China under its own control. Casting heroically Platonic plans for the perfect system, he never considered how his ideal organism was to conduct itself in the world. Re-creating a mighty China was goal enough for any man.

His dedicated spirit—the first functioning blend of China and the West—was refreshed by taking not only money, but temporary wives from among the overseas Chinese, and he evolved a system of thought the irreverent call "intellectual chop suey." But the implication that Sun Yat-sen brewed nothing more than a mess of pottage is unfair. Although he was never able to test them in practical administration, his theories displayed some brilliant insights. They were based on ideas borrowed equally from China's past and from Western political philosophers.

Sun rejected the West's "mystical" insistence upon the equality of all men under divine law as superfluous to a culture which had abolished institutionalized inequality with the end of feudalism two thousand years earlier. Since China had not believed in the divine right of kings for millennia, there was no need to displace that principle by asserting the divine right of the people. He conceded certain advantages to parliamentary democracy, but proposed for China a form of government based upon recognition of the natural *inequality* of men.

The Sage and the Superior Man, those *beaux idéal* of the Confucians, he felt, might best discharge their responsibilities to their inferiors through a five-part administrative apparatus. In addition to the Executive, the Legislature, and the Judiciary, two coequal branches would respectively administer the new Civil Service Examinations and serve as Censors (the Tribunes of the People), criticizing the government from within. Both concepts obviously came directly from the Empire. Although his followers did finally create this apparatus, they never used it as Sun had directed. It would, therefore, be wholly unfair to condemn the concept of a five-branch government. The verdict must remain "not proven." But the Nationalists' failure to put Sun's plan into effect certainly did demonstrate that his scheme, like the Confucians', made no allowance for imperfect human nature. Both had created intricately organized systems which depended ultimately upon the good will and perfect honesty of the administrators, rather than upon the exercise of the popular will or a legal apparatus which would be self-enforcing in any sense.

Nor have the Nationalists ever attempted to realize Sun's economic ideal, which was a blend of moderate socialism with Henry James's single tax upon land. Although he borrowed certain Marxist techniques, Sun rejected the thesis that labor was the ultimate measure of economic value. Henry Ford and twentieth-century mass production, he declared in the final version of his magnum opus, had disproved that nineteenth-century concept of Karl Marx. Quite original in his adaptation, Sun Yat-sen might stand forth today as a greater political thinker if his heirs had truly understood his doctrines beyond the stark principle of nationalism.

Only hostility to the Manchus had united China. With the Dynasty's passing, the nation splintered into contending factions. Instead of the Golden Age, the first revolution re-created the Period of the Warring States. Semiliterate generals in gorgeous uniforms scrambled for the material rewards of power, wooing foreign support by means as diverse as economic concessions and baptizing entire divisions with fire hoses. Between 1913 and 1927, when the Nationalists established their regime, the successive pretenses of functioning central governments were never convincing. Warlords like Chang Tso-lin of Manchuria and Yen Hsi-shan of Shansi split the nation into private domains. Shifting coalitions of warlords dominated the capital at Peking, and a succession of powerless "presidents" represented China in the eyes of the world. Not in the worst days of the Ching had the nation been so utterly demoralized, disorganized, and disunited.

The formal political picture was exceedingly intricate between February 1912, when Yuan Shih-kai became President of the Republic of China, and July 1921, when the Communist Party was established.[14] The Western reader, already confused by the

[14] From 1921 on, events become somewhat easier to follow because the coincident rise of the Kuomintang's power made for clear polarization between the modern men who sought to unite the nation and the conservative warlords who were primarily interested in self-aggrandizement. Since the period

rapid succession of unfamiliar monosyllabic names, is likely to be even more troubled in an examination of the period from 1912 to 1921 because of the wide disparity between formal titles and actual power. At any given moment the President of China might be a puppet, while his military adviser exercised actual power—in North China alone. Developments of the period are, however, worth surveying briefly so that the reader may have a notion of the shifting background against which were played the critical psychological and cultural dramas that led to the formation of the Communist Party of China. For clarity's sake it would be well to remember that not one of the men who held the office of President or Premier ever ruled all of China. Each politician's authority ended at the last outpost of his personal army, and those armies were themselves usually for sale to the highest bidder.

Becoming President in February 1912, Yuan Shih-kai was seriously disturbed in March, when the Provisional Assembly adopted a constitution making the presidency a largely ceremonial post. The first Chinese Parliament, elected under the new constitution and composed largely of the more radical revolutionaries, soon clashed with the autocratic Yuan Shih-kai. In 1913 Yuan negotiated a large loan from a consortium of foreign bankers, ignoring so soon the fact that the Revolution of 1911 had been provoked by the prospect of just such a sweeping loan to the Manchus. When it emerged that Yuan had pledged the salt tax as security for the loan and placed the collection of that tax in foreign hands, the Kuomintang rose in the Second Revolution. Yuan Shih-kai brushed the revolt aside, forcing Sun Yat-sen into exile. He arranged his own election as lifetime President with sweeping powers, and in January 1914 he dismissed Parliament. His power grew until 1915, when he felt sufficiently secure to proclaim the establishment of the Great Constitutional Dynasty with himself as the first Emperor. Although his tailors prepared the Court regalia, Yuan Shih-kai was constrained by a wave of resistance to postpone his coronation. A revolution against his rule broke out in Yunnan Province in the far southwest and spread rapidly. As his

---

from 1921 until the establishment of the Nationalist government in 1927 also encompasses the early years of the Communist Party, it can best be recounted in the next chapter.

power dwindled, Yuan developed toxic uremia. So violent in his case were the mental aberrations characteristic of the disease that, persistent reports relate, he hacked his favorite concubine into bits in a fit of rage. In June 1916 Yuan Shih-kai died.

His death precipitated a continuing state of chaos. Li Yuanhung, who had been a reluctant leader of the Wuhan revolt in 1911, became President of China. His purpose, as always, was to please all factions. His Vice-President was a leader of the southern faction, which was also pleased by his recalling Parliament and restoring the constitution of 1912, while his Premier, Tuan Chi-jui, was a former protégé of Yuan Shih-kai. The ill-matched alliance lasted until the spring of 1917, when President Li Yuan-hung was forced to dismiss Premier Tuan Chi-jui. Tuan in turn united with a group of like-minded generals to march on Peking and depose Li Yuan-hung. After much maneuvering, Tuan again became Premier under a powerless President at the head of what the Chinese called the *tuchun* (warlord) government. This government in Peking was, appropriately enough, overthrown in 1920 by a new alliance of China's three most powerful warlords—Chang Tsolin (who ruled Manchuria), Tsao Kun, and Wu Pei-fu. That group was to control Peking until 1927, although its internal balance was often altered, and it was occasionally displaced by other warlords. During the entire period, real power outside the immediate neighborhood of Peking was in the hands of a constantly shifting band of local warlords, each ruling one or two provinces quite independently of the capital and of each other.

Meanwhile, the radicals had set up a rival government at Canton under Sun Yat-sen. Although it was weak and disunited and did not enjoy the recognition of the foreign powers, the Canton Government was finally to triumph. While the warlords contended for the possession of the city of Peking as the center of "legitimate" power, the Kuomintang would build up its strength until it was powerful enough to take Peking in 1927, as the next chapter will relate. But the only orderly government in China during the entire period was that imposed by foreigners in their various treaty ports. Those ports also continued to serve as effective bases for the economic exploitation of China.

Continuing chaos had sweeping psychological effects. It was

neither pleasant nor a source of pride to be a Chinese. The wealth
of China was the prey of foreigners, while cultured Chinese had
been reduced by their own folly from the masters of the world's
oldest civilization to infants playing with tools they did not understand.

In Westernized treaty ports and in inland hamlets each new
day added new weight to oppressive reality. The young Chinese
tended to scorn other Chinese—and himself—for their degradation. The chief clubs of China's major cities either excluded Chinese or admitted a few as historical curiosities. The Christian missionary enjoyed extraordinary privileges amounting to immunity
from the law and paternalistically extended his own prerogatives
to his converts. Foreign warships patrolled the coasts and rivers of
China to maintain commercial order and to enforce payment of
taxes for the foreigners' benefit. Along the riverfront of Shanghai great skyscrapers housed the offices of foreign firms, which,
Chinese felt, were the true center of power in the nation. Despising his compatriots who served the foreigners, the young irreconcilable told himself, with bitter satisfaction, that they too bore the
stripe of enforced inferiority. No more than he, could the Westerners' wealthy lackeys enter the public park in Shanghai's International Settlement, which, a persistent story said, bore on its
gates a placard stating: "No dogs or Chinese allowed!" There was
actually no such notice, but it was not necessary, since practice
barred Chinese from the park.

The irreconcilable's character was shaped by thousands of
imaginary slights—and hundreds of real indignities. The most
idealistic and talented youth of China grew to maturity in a
miasma of hatred. Modern Chinese patriotism was born of adversity. No longer the smug heirs of a predominant culture that transcended nationality, youths began to give their loyalty to the reality of the tortured nation called China. Shaken out of their
complacency by the guns and railroads of the West, young Chinese felt that their purpose must be to make China a powerful
nation in her own right. The image of the nation called China
displaced the concept of the supra-national Confucian civilization.

It was a bitter patriotism. Nothing but vengeance upon those who humiliated him could ultimately appease the irreconcilable's sense of outrage.

The utter distress of ardent youth in the decade between 1910 and 1920 bred not only hatred of the overbearing West, but also disgust with the ancient institutions that barred the road to progress. The generation just a few years older than the century was determined to destroy all the forces that had shaped the land they loved. They did not distinguish the virtues, which had insured continuity and endurance, from the flaws, which had led to degeneration. The Gordian solution appeared the only remedy for China's decadence: the good was to be destroyed with the bad to make way for the new.

Driven more by instinct than by logic, young Chinese directed their reformist desperation to the soul of traditional China: her language and literature. Reforming the Chinese language was, nonetheless, a logical approach to remaking society. The reformers knew that the homogeneous bureaucracy that had governed China for two millennia had been selected through examinations in a vast body of literature in a dead language. It was as if the English administrative class, educated *solely* in the Greek and Roman classics, had been required: to communicate with each other in Augustan Latin; always to cite Latin quotations to prove that their personal and public lives accorded with those canons; and to demonstrate the wholesome balance of their souls by gracefully inscribing the archaic letters. Young intellectuals felt with good reason that China could never struggle out of the slough of degradation as long as she bore upon her back the burden of the classical literary style.

Japan's experience after the Meiji Restoration had proved that universal education to provide literate conscripts for a modern army was a *sine qua non* of modern power. Equally avid for military power, Chinese theorists knew that universal education was impossible without a simplified written language. If an elided, codelike style limited knowledge to a small group of initiates, the written word could neither inspire nor instruct the common people for the nation's service. An easier style must impart new knowledge wholesale.

The first man who sought to use imaginative writing as an instrument of social reform was the great publicist Liang Chi-chao. Presenting his thesis that China's salvation depended upon developing "new men suited to a new age," he advocated widespread education to produce those new men. The novel, he added, was an ideal instrument of education. "The function of literature lies in conveying meaning," wrote Hu Shih, who was later Chinese Ambassador to the United States, "and in the sphere of conveying meaning, communication with the greatest number may be considered the attainment of greatest success." [15]

The rebels were delighted to discover an antagonistic literary tradition in the language of the people. They championed *pai-hua*, the plain style, praising it as a vigorous growth which had survived official displeasure. They argued that *pai-hua* offered an ideal vehicle for works of the imagination, for scientific reports, and even for government documents.

Change was, however, hampered by many factors. The written and spoken styles appeared to be mere variations of the same language, but were actually two distinct tongues. The static ideographs tended to fossilize the language, and *pai-hua* carried an ancient social stigma. The older generation reacted much as a Tory Cabinet today would respond to the proposal that not only novels and odes, but state papers and royal proclamations should adopt a style epitomized by the speech of London taxi drivers. Though it was finally to triumph, the New Literature Movement appeared in the beginning to be no more than the plaything of a coterie.

One man was paramount in initiating the literary revolution; in bringing it to limited success; in directing the new energy thus released into political channels; and finally, as first Secretary-General of the Communist Party of China, in initiating the radical political action the times apparently demanded. He was Chen Tu-hsiu, the rebellious son of a prosperous family of minor mandarins from Anhwei Province in Central China, who was only thirty-six

[15] Hu Shih (ed.), *Chien-she Li-lun Chi* (*Collected Essays on Reconstruction*) (Shanghai, 1935), p. 4. Most of the material in this section is drawn from a manuscript on "The Chinese Literary Revolution and Chinese Politics" written by the present author in 1949.

when he began reshaping the Chinese nation in 1915. The spirit of a tormented age expressed itself with much intensity in his career.

Liang Chi-chao had embodied the noble—and, ultimately, in-effectual—reaction of intelligent traditionalists to the tumult of the late nineteenth century. Sun Yat-sen, virtually uneducated in the classics, had sought to blend Chinese folk culture with an admixture of Western concepts so heavy that his most loyal followers misunderstood his ideas as thoroughly as they revered his person. Chen Tu-hsiu, though more radical by far than either Liang or Sun, was truly cosmopolitan in his outlook, for he was versed in both the Confucian and the Western traditions. His sophisticated breadth of vision contrasts with the myopic xenophobia of his disciples, who elevated themselves by casting him out and finally became the Maoist rulers of China.

At the age of six Chen Tu-hsiu was consecrated to the mandarinate by his mother's determination that he fulfill the promise of his deceased father. Under his grandfather's harsh tutelage young Tu-hsiu developed an early distaste for the intellectual and aesthetic rigidity of the Confucian curriculum. He was also inspired with a loathing for authority by the old man's automatic discipline: a bad recitation was followed by a severe whipping, the willow wand whistling down on his upturned palms. If his grandfather's sensitive ear did not detect sincere repentance in the boy's cries, another whipping followed.

When Tu-hsiu was nine, his grandfather died and a succession of hired tutors passed through the prosperous household. Bored by the arid curriculum and the long hours of memorization, the boy still bent over his paperbound textbooks to placate his mother. He also gave periodic reports of his progress to the wraithlike figure of his grandmother, who lay on her couch clutching her long opium pipe.

When he was nineteen, Chen was almost reconciled to classical education, for he passed first in the county examinations for the bachelor's degree. In obedience to his elated mother's urging, he entered his name for the master's examination to be held at Nanking in 1899.

Chen traveled to Nanking, but halted at the door of the examination hall. During his brief journey to the viceregal capital, he had learned that the Civil Service Examination system was meaningless because the dynasty it served was dying. He realized that his years of application had procured him neither worldly advancement nor intellectual benefit. Finding in Liang Chi-chao's injunctions to study Western scientific techniques a bright thread in the maze of frustration, the disillusioned Chen enrolled in a course in naval architecture. But he found his true vocation only when he entered Tokyo Normal School at the age of twenty-one in 1900. He was to be an inspired teacher until he died.

At Tokyo Normal School and later at Waseda, Japan's great private university, Chen Tu-hsiu's Chinese classmates were dedicated to the revolution of Sun Yat-sen. Although he had already espoused a non-doctrinaire social democracy, Chen refused to join the revolutionists. He was repelled by their crude chauvinism, which was exemplified by Sun's slogan: "Exalt the Chinese race, destroy the Manchu race!" In 1907 he left Japan for France, still pursuing his own vision of civilized learning—and still sustained by the revenues from the family landholdings.

The atmosphere of France before the deluge of 1914 was the most congenial Chen was ever to know. He became an ardent Francophile, a connoisseur of French literature, and a convert to the belief that Western parliamentarianism as exemplified by France could save China.

He preached that there could be no compromise between the senile Orient and the vigorous Occident. China must adopt the institutions of the West, casting out every remnant of decadent Orientalism—lest she perish. He rejected the slogan: "Western learning for practical purposes, Chinese learning as the moral basis!" Any attempt to blend the two cultures, he felt, would invite disaster, since the essence of Orientalism was a static conservatism that made it impossible to utilize Western material knowledge. Those chief qualities of Western civilization, concluded Chen, which must be transplanted entire to the East were: dynamic science, respect for the individual, and equality before the law. Those precepts once rooted in China, a moral revolution and a consequent political renascence would follow spontaneously.

The proposition was as practical as telling the survivors of a typhoon on a devasted atoll that all they needed was coconuts and palm trees would spontaneously appear to bear them. Nonetheless, Chen had attained knowledge beyond all his predecessors, beyond most of his contemporaries—and beyond almost all his successors. He knew that China's survival could not be insured by seeking the nonexistent Philosopher's Stone. He understood that the material attributes of Western civilization, which all Chinese coveted, were a direct outgrowth of Western political and social institutions, which most Chinese despised.

Although he later blamed himself severely, it was hardly Chen's fault that he thought he had seen a vision when he had actually been gazing upon a mirage: France, a nation in which men lived in harmonious prosperity, their actions guided by respect for the dignity of their fellow men and their thoughts disciplined by absolute logic.

Returning in 1910 to a China in metamorphosis, Chen Tuhsiu found a market for his talents and an audience for his ideas—political and pedagogical. Too fastidious to join Sun Yat-sen's *Tung Meng Hui*, although he too wanted a parliamentary republic, his true passion was concentrated upon educating the youths who would shape the future. He was appointed principal of a middle school in his native Anhwei Province immediately upon his return, but he soon resigned to become private secretary to the Imperial Governor of the Province. Chen became Provincial Commissioner of Education when the same official was abruptly transformed into the Republican Governor of Anhwei by the Revolution of 1911. China's greatest modern teacher had returned to his vocation.

But the Second Revolution of 1913, directed against Yuan Shih-kai's usurpation, once more deflected Chen from his course. Espousing the Republican cause, he fled to Japan when Yuan suppressed the revolt and made himself a dictator.

In the summer of 1915, with Yuan Shih-kai's star falling in the eastern sky, Chen again returned to China. But he was still in exile, immured in the refuge of the French Concession of Shanghai. In September he took the path that was to make him the grand impresario of the New Literature Movement, founding a new literary journal. In the beginning his magazine, *New Youth*, seemed just another one of the journals which bright young men,

temporarily barred from political activity, published to give themselves the illusion of meaningful activity. But it was wholly different in essence. Chen Tu-hsiu had, finally and reluctantly, come
into harmony with the times. His questing spirit, which was entranced by sweeping theoretical solutions, was the spirit of the
age—and his readers cried out for ever more radical concepts.

Chen's bold generalizations appeared to provide the answers
for which China's "new youth" yearned, the answers to social,
political, and above all, personal problems. What better slogan
than "Change everything!"? Each issue of the magazine sold out
on the day of publication, and the first, reprinted again and again,
sold more than two hundred thousand copies in all. Its readership
was probably ten times that number.

With the Gallic clarity he loved and the vivid metaphors that
were his own riposte to the fossilized classical style, Chen introduced two new men to his eager Chinese audience. *Sai-yin-ssu
Hsien-sheng* and *Te-mo-ko-la-hsi Hsien Sheng*—Mr. Science and
Mr. Democracy—would save the nation if the fetters of archaic
thought and feudal institutions were struck from their wrists, he
promised. To unshackle the new forces, Chen asserted, was the
paramount task of young China.

Intellectuals were inflamed by the prophet who promised a
revolution in politics—if only morality and culture were remade
first. The method was certainly more attractive than a direct attempt to impose order on the chaos of Chinese politics. Besides,
there was traditional precedent for the view that the fate of nations rested upon the self-cultivation of the superior individual,
who might be distinguished by his good manners and his polished
style.

It was, therefore, a most receptive audience which read the
first advocacy for literary reform in *New Youth* for January 1917.
The author, Hu Shih, called his article "Some Tentative Suggestions for the Reform of Chinese Literature," but Chen Tu-hsiu's
own article in the next issue demanded "A Revolution in Chinese
Literature." The "tentative proposal" of the scholarly reformer
was inflamed by the ardor of the revolutionary. Chen wrote:

A movement for a literary revolution pioneered by my friend Hu Shih is now in progress. I am willing to brave the enmity of all the pedants to assist in hoisting the great and glorious banner of the army of the literary revolution. On the banner's face we shall inscribe in bold characters the three great principles of the revolutionary army: (1) to destroy the painted, powdered, and obsequious literature of the aristocratic few and to create the plain, simple, and expressive literature of the masses; (2) to destroy the stereotyped and monotonous writings of classicism and to create the fresh and sincere literature of realism; (3) to destroy the pedantic, unintelligible, and obscurantist literature of the hermit and the recluse and to create the plain-speaking and popular literature of the masses.

Chen's sponsorship kindled afresh the ardor of men like the critic who had written in 1915:

As to fundamental [national] salvation, I believe its beginning must be sought in the promotion of a new literature. In short, we must endeavor to bring Chinese thought into direct contact with the thought of the world, thereby to accelerate its radical awakening. And we must see to it that basic ideals of world thought are related to the life of the average man. The method seems to consist in using simple and simplified language and literature for wide dissemination of ideas among the people. Have we not seen that historians regard the Renaissance as the foundation of the overthrow of medievalism in Europe? [16]

The New Literature Movement was born of the first wholly honest despair felt by modern China. It developed amid the desperate recognition that half-measures, such as adopting Western technology or political systems unchanged, could *not* solve the nation's problems. Yet the New Literature itself found immediate acceptance only among men professionally concerned with words.

[16] Hu, quoted, *loc. cit.*

As teachers and writers they nurtured a generation that considered plain language the norm and the literary style the exception. Since the pioneers were unable to convince the mass of their non-literary contemporaries that they must adopt the new style, *pai-hua* in itself proved ineffective. The New Literature Movement's failure to achieve the social objectives that were its chief purpose bred the conviction that only direct political action could effect the radical social and political changes required to redeem the nation. The literary movement led directly to political action.

Chen Tu-hsiu himself had actually offered no concrete proposals for political action in the *New Youth*. He had, however, stirred youth to awareness of its own potential for effective action. At the National Peking University, which was established during the reform movement of 1898, more students opposed Chen's literary and political ideas than espoused them, but all students talked about them.[17] Approving his fervor, the old radical journalist who was Chancellor of the University asked Chen to become Dean of the College of Letters. Among a dozen men who became the paladins of the new culture movement, the brilliant faculty included Li Ta-chao, who, even more persuasive than Chen himself, converted scores of students to Marxism. Peking University became not only the chief recruiting center for the soldiers of the left, but the forward outpost from which they rallied for the first telling assaults against the old order. Finally united in support of the Literary Revolution sponsored by Chen Tu-hsiu, students discovered with exuberant delight that their united action could affect not only internal events but the nation's foreign policy as well.

The revelation that agitators could effectively mobilize the popular will against politicians and generals was a consequence of the First World War.

Despite its name and unlike its successor, that war's major actions were confined to Europe and the Middle East. Both weak, divided China and united, powerful Japan, lying far from the chief theaters, carefully calculated the advantages they might seize from the conflict. Chinese hopes were simple and essentially passive. Individual warlords sought to play the belligerents against each other in order to enhance their own power, while the

17 According to Chang Kuo-tao's memoirs.

impotent intelligentsia hoped China might avoid further encroachment on her sovereignty because the great powers were fully engaged elsewhere. Japan, growing ever more ambitious, saw her great opportunity in the preoccupation of the same powers, which had previously pre-empted the exploitation of China. The Japanese began to give their imperial ambitions practical form. They cast those grandiose plans of conquest which were finally to fail amid the agony of hundreds of thousands of Japanese and Allied fighting men on Pacific islets and in the sunless jungles of Southeast Asia. In 1915 Count Shigenobu Okuma, the Japanese statesman and strategist of conquest who for his own reasons encouraged Chinese revolutionaries, had declared: "In the middle of the twentieth century, Japan will meet Europe on the plains of Asia and wrest from her the mastery of the world."

In the same year, Japan had sought to lay the basis of her later conquests by serving the "Twenty-one Demands" on China. Although his power was waning, Yuan Shih-kai remained President. But even he could not accede to Japan's ultimatum, since acquiescence would have meant the end of Chinese sovereignty. Yet the Chinese knew that a flat rejection would have brought a Japanese invasion of a defenseless China "to fulfill her obligations" as one of the Allied Powers. She had already used that pretext to take over Germany's prerogatives and territories on the China coast. None of the Allies could spare forces to restrain Japan's ambition, and none wished to shake the delicate balance of the alliance by thwarting her. The United States, still formally neutral in the World War, had long sponsored the Open Door Policy, which guaranteed equal opportunity to all to exploit the Chinese market. Washington was not prepared to use force to prevent Japanese expansion. But the State Department did dispatch a sharply worded note to both Peking and Tokyo, declaring that the United States would not countenance any agreements that curtailed American rights or the political and territorial integrity of China. The combination of American protests and Chinese maneuvering was sufficient to thwart the more outrageous Japanese demands for the moment.

But the pressure was unrelenting; and Tuan Chi-jui, the warlord who was dominant in north China, drew his chief support from Japan in return for manifold concessions.[18] China was, therefore, forced to agree to limited concessions. It was no idle fear that China might, at any moment, disappear as an independent country—to reappear as a Japanese "protectorate." Although Peking had not acceded to the demand that Japan control the Chinese police force "in order to ensure civil security," her armies were passing under the command of the Japanese officers who served as "training advisers." The end was in plain sight.

Except for some warlords, all politically conscious Chinese, regardless of their economic or doctrinal interests, hated Japan's growing power. The new class of native capitalists flourished in the vacuum of competition created when the European powers concentrated their energies elsewhere. The capitalists were not interested in politics, but they feared that Japanese hegemony would blight the growth of their new enterprises. Students had immersed themselves in the New Literature Movement in protest against the futility of politics, castigating as "just another warlord coalition" [19] even Sun Yat-sen's Kuomintang. But the patriotic appeal rallied intellectuals from their paper towers of refuge. The nation was in danger! China must be preserved!

The common purpose was clear, but the means were, as usual, confused. The students of Peking University debated the issues over bowls of noodles in cubbyhole restaurants. A large group contended that it was frivolous to talk about students' taking action, since there could be no hope for China until patriots came to power through democratic elections. Others argued that students must not turn aside from the New Literature Movement, the only means by which they could effectively seek to save the nation. The radicals said flatly that only violent revolution could destroy the pro-Japanese regime.

Most, however, finally agreed. The terms of agreement, as recorded by Chang Kuo-tao, who was a participant, seem at first

[18] It was the practice of foreign governments—and even foreign firms—to support one of the numerous contenders for power in return for economic favors—and promises of additional favors. The pattern, familiar in Latin America, reached its most ludicrous extreme when Americans urged support of Field Marshal Feng Yu-hsiang largely because he was a Christian convert who baptized his troops with fire hoses.

[19] Chang Kuo-tao's memoirs.

glance merely to restate the problem without offering a solution: "The whole student body should take part in the Save the Country Movement. Saving the country is more important than anything else. From the deepest conservatives to the anarchists, everyone [must] rise up and unite to save the country. 'Save the country first!' "

The students had ringingly agreed on the obvious necessity to "save the country." But, significantly, they had also agreed on the necessity for *united action*. That was progress—even if no one knew what action to take.

Chen Tu-hsiu and Li Ta-chao had begun to publish *The Weekly Critic,* a frankly political rather than cultural journal. Following their lead, the students created a nucleus of political leadership in the hundred-odd youths who founded the monthly *National Magazine* in January 1919. The group was split into conservative, moderate, and radical factions, but all were agreed upon the need to resist Japan's glacierlike encroachment upon China's sovereignty. Offshoots appeared, their members devoted to arousing the masses by speeches and broadsides. Although the student groups, disunited and feuding, did not know where they were going, they had begun to move.

The Versailles Conference aroused the angry intellectuals to fury by conceding almost all of Japan's demands upon China. Chen Tu-hsiu, no less than Adolf Hitler, though for different reasons, railed against the "betrayal" at Versailles. It was the death of Chen's Francophilia—and the birth of his political extremism. In his bitterness Chen could still see no way to prevent Japan's slow ingestion of China.

Less inhibited by political sophistication, the *National Magazine* group, meeting with its sister organizations on May 2, 1919, grandiosely resolved to prevent the government's signing the Versailles Treaty. On May 4th students from all Peking's universities assembled before the massive Gate of Heavenly Peace, ignoring their teachers' advice to refrain from demonstrations. Three thousand marched through the capital, chanting slogans and carrying banners exhorting: "China for the Chinese!" "Punish the Traitors!" When armed guards kept them from entering the Legation Quarter to demonstrate before the Japanese Legation, they sacked the home of the pro-Japanese Minister of Communications and pummeled the Japanese envoy, whom they found there. In the light of the Minister's burning home, police arrested thirty-two students.

The government ordered the students to halt their disorders, but they rioted again to demand the release of their schoolmates. After five days, part of which the ringleaders spent under siege in the Law School, the University made its peace with the government. The government bowed to the popular will and promised to reject the Versailles Treaty. In recompense, the Chancellor of the University resigned and Chen Tu-hsiu was imprisoned for eighty-three days for "distributing pamphlets." His colleague Hu Shih many years later observed [20] that the charge was not only obscure, but wholly unjustified. Chen, he said, had actually been quietly correcting proofs at home, unaware of the events of May 4, 1919, until late in the day.

The May Fourth Incident, now exalted by Chinese historians, was itself trifling—a house burned, a few slogans proclaimed, a few students arrested. But its consequences were enormous. Groups of students, intellectuals, and workers throughout China rallied around the leadership provided by the students of Peking. An explosion of popular resentment made it impossible for the government to give in to Japan's demands and forced several ministers to resign.

The intellectuals, traditional leaders in thought and action, had found a new lever—the popular will. Their energies were thenceforth directed toward shaping that will. For the first time, the natural leaders of modern China had discovered that the people could influence the course of public events. At the time it did not seem terribly important that the discovery had come about through mob action.

[20] In conversation with author.

8

The Sword of Wrath

The Communist Party of China:
Its Birth, Struggles, Victory, and a
Brief Account of Its Conduct in Power

Though the Shanghai night was hot and close on July 8, 1921, twelve tired men in their late twenties and early thirties sat behind drawn curtains in a study in the French Concession. For the past week they had been meeting in the nearby Po Wen Girls' School, shaping a policy in the mold of compromise.

Their discussions were often heated. Only constant self-reminders that "doctrinal disagreements must not affect personal relationships" had kept the Communist Party of China from dissolving into factions before it was formally established. Despite conciliatory smiles and ruthless suppression of disagreement, bitter differences were already apparent among the delegates. Those differences were to give rise to defections before many years had passed—and to hamper the Party throughout its life.

Depressed by the absence of their leader, Chen Tu-hsiu, the delegates also struggled against a sense of unreality. The twelve young men—a number of them still students—representing some sixty members of provisional Party branches and three hundred fifty members of the Socialist Youth League, were gathered as the First Party Congress to inaugurate the Communist Party of China. They possessed neither the organization nor the funds to contend seriously for political power; nor did most believe that the Party would actively seek power until many years had passed. Their meeting was largely an institutionalized affirmation of the need for action and a formal recognition of the forces that were stirring the world as Karl Marx had predicted. The evening session was not an integral proceeding of the Congress, but, specifically, a formal obeisance to the principle of international solidarity.

That principle was represented by the two Europeans present. The extraordinary evening session had been convened so that they might speak, though they were excluded from the working sessions. The Dutchman Hendricus Sneevliet, who called himself Maring, and his Russian assistant were representatives of the Communist International. Maring had already offended the ardent young Chinese by his superior manner, which they unhesitatingly ascribed to racial arrogance, rather than to a consciousness of superior skill in making revolution. He was to irritate them further by demanding, against the general inclination, that the new Party must immediately begin to play a violent revolutionary role.

Maring was the first of the triumvirate of Comintern representatives who sought to dominate the Communist Party of China from 1920 to 1927.[1] Like great ocean liners roiling the sea with their multiple screws, the trio momentarily altered the set of the waves. But their passage did not affect the deep-running currents. The Chinese Communist movement was to flow in courses determined by Chinese leaders and by Chinese history, rising to high water regardless of the Communist International. Independent even at the very beginning, the CPC would have come into existence in much the same form if the Comintern had taken no direct interest in its creation.

On that evening in July 1921 the leaders of the Party which was not yet a Party were cool to the men from the Comintern. Determined that they would not be forced into premature political action, the young Chinese were braced to reject an offer of financial assistance. They had invited Maring to the evening dis-

[1] Moscow sent many envoys to China during the period, but three were outstanding: Maring, Adolf Joffe, who negotiated an alliance with Sun Yat-sen's Kuomintang in 1923, and Michael Borodin, who organized the Kuomintang after the pattern of the totalitarian Communist Party of the Soviet Union (CPSU).

cussion only on his direct—and, they felt, self-demeaning—request.

As the acting chairman, twenty-four-year-old Chang Kuo-tao, raised his hand to hush the anticipatory hum of talk, a Chinese in a traditional long gown drew aside the curtain at the door and peered at the startled group.

"Oh," he said, "I must have come to the wrong house!"

The curtain fell, and he vanished.

The infant Communists were fearful. As the chairman began giving low-voiced instructions to disperse, Maring jumped up and, banging the table with his fist, made his sole formal contribution to the deliberations: "I propose that the meeting adjourn immediately, and that everyone leave by separate ways."

Led by the two foreigners, the First Congress of the Communist Party of China rushed into the night, leaving only two of its number behind. Three minutes later a squad of Chinese policemen under a French officer threw a cordon around the house. The curious stranger had been a spy sent to investigate the house after the authorities' interest had been aroused by so much coming and going in a normally quiet neighborhood. The French Concession, foremost among the foreign enclaves of Shanghai, offered free refuge to political fugitives. Though even the French banned meetings of Bolshevik conspirators, the young Communists had hoped they would be overlooked in the general atmosphere of tolerance.

When the police painstakingly interrogated the remaining pair on the meeting's nature and the foreigners' presence, they did not learn that they had interrupted a Bolshevik Congress. Nonetheless, the Communists felt that it would be foolhardy to hold their final session anywhere in the French Concession.

A few days later, just before eight in the morning, the delegates slipped singly onto a local train of the Shanghai-Hangchow railway. The foreigners were not invited. Alighting at Kasing in Chekiang Province, about two hours' ride away, the young men fell into a holiday mood as their rented houseboat floated on the still waters of the South Lake. All that day the nucleus of the Communist Party of China drifted, occasionally dropping anchor, but for the most part content to let the boat go where it would.

The formal purpose of the final session was to ratify the Party Constitution, which had been worked out completely by the earlier sessions. After the creative frenzy and the quarrels, the discussion amid the rushes considered the actions the Party must take if it were to be more than a debating society. Despite the conflicting opinions of activist extremists on the left and passive liberals on the right, the moderates secured general agreement on a minimal policy. The Party would concentrate upon the industrial proletariat by organizing militant labor unions. Though the purists objected, the Congress agreed to accept aspirant proletarians into the Party, even if they had no knowledge of theoretical Marxism. The Communists did not consider the revolutionary role of the peasantry, nor did they consider how the labor unions, once organized, would proceed to political action.

As the glaring lanterns of the fishing sampans skittered in irregular arcs through the darkness gathering over the lake, the Congress hastily elected the absent Chen Tu-hsiu Secretary-General. The title conformed to Chen's own wish that they choose not an all-powerful chairman, but a secretary who would merely carry out the Party's will. Li Ta, a gifted writer, was put in charge of propaganda, and Chang Kuo-tao was elected to head the Organization Bureau.[2] Chang then spoke briefly to conclude the First Congress of the Communist Party of China.

Twelve young men had created the political organism that was ultimately to rule a greater number of human beings, more ruthlessly and more intimately, than any other group in history. The founders were divided by temperament and by purpose. Although some soon began organizing industrial workers, most felt that they themselves must first make a thorough study of Marxist doctrines. They really knew little of their new classics. While seeking intellectual unity with international Communism, they were

[2] Of the three, only Li Ta remained in favor until the Great Proletarian Cultural Revolution disgraced him in 1966. Chen Tu-hsiu was expelled for Trotskyite deviationism in 1929 and died in 1942. Chang Kuo-tao, after unsuccessfully challenging Mao Tse-tung's power in 1938, in 1968 lived in penurious exile in Hong Kong.

jealous of their independence of action, and they condescended to accept a small subsidy from the Comintern only after prolonged haggling.

They were, above all, a Chinese movement that was utterly dedicated to Chinese goals. Chang Kuo-tao recalls in his memoirs the remark with which Chen Tu-hsiu prefaced his personal espousal of Communism:

> The militarists and politicians of Japan are unbearably arrogant. They look down on China, with her history of five thousand years and her four hundred million descendants of the Yellow Emperor. They think only of scheming with her old warlords, her corrupt bureaucrats, her smugglers, her drug peddlers, her gangsters, and the scum of China. They see only the queues and the bound feet of China, and the people who spit about them, and everything corrupt. Consciously or unconsciously, they belittle the new thoughts and the new influences that are rising in China. But there will come a day when they will crush their heads against the wall of their own misconceptions.

Although he delighted in the cut and thrust of argument—as long as he triumphed—the delegate from Hunan Province, young Mao Tse-tung, had little to say on basic issues. His theoretical knowledge was rudimentary. But he had already begun to organize the peasants of his native province. He was not concerned with the urban proletariat who, the Congress decided, must be the spearhead of the revolution.[3]

The wonder was not that the Communist Party of China began so quietly in the hands of amateur revolutionaries. The wonder was that a dozen avowed Marxists existed in China in mid-1921 to dedicate themselves to political action in concert with the Communist International. It was only two years since the May

[3] I owe much of the detail and analysis in this section to the manuscript of Chang Kuo-tao's memoirs already cited. The Chen Tu-hsiu remark appears on p. 333.

Fourth Movement had taught the intelligentsia that they could essay effective political action. The Chinese were cut off from the intellectual currents of Europe by breakwaters of distance and language and, above all, by the unique culture that had evolved into decadence without ever confronting the challenges of science and industrialization. Few of the basic theoretical works on socialism or Marxism had been translated into the Chinese language. The Chinese were just beginning to learn of the controversies that had agitated European thinkers fifty to a hundred years earlier.

Still largely isolated from the radical thought of the West, the Chinese embraced Marxism because it boasted that it possessed solutions to dilemmas elsewhere that were superficially like the dilemmas they themselves then faced in China. But few Chinese comprehended the historical and philosophical essence of the doctrines they espoused—and the present leaders of the Communist Party of China were not among those few. When they took power in 1917, the Russian Marxists were direct heirs to a great body of organized radical thought. They had an intimate acquaintance not only with the fertile later commentators on Marx and Engels and the two masters themselves, but could look back to the early socialists and anarchists. They were sustained by a tradition of organized political action nearly a century old. In China even anarchism, the most elemental and most idealistic modern doctrine of social protest, was unknown before 1912.

The Chinese persistently searched for radical solutions to their knotted problems, once more seeking the Philosopher's Stone, as they skipped across rather than traversing a hundred years of European political development in two years' time. They were impelled by disgust at the failure of liberal devices and by the shock of discovering that "liberal nations" sought national and class advantages, rather than behaving as the incarnate agents of abstract principle. The infant Marxists were driven by their need for a simple political formula whose application would solve all problems. Marxism's promise of an eventual, self-operating Utopia *sans* rulers and *sans* ruled, evoked tribal memories of the Golden Age idealized by Confucius. The Marxists' predilection for achieving social justice by violent retribution for past injustice awakened a harmonic resonance in the nerves of young Chinese, whose humiliation by the West could be assuaged only by violent revenge.

Their vision clouded by ignorance and frustration, the Chinese fledglings understood even less than most revolutionaries the nature of the forces to which they joined themselves. Chen Tu-hsiu's was the most original and the most honest mind among the activists. But even Chen, whose experience of practical politics was slight, could hardly comprehend that men are shaped by the political weapons they take up—as surely as the carpenter's right hand grows larger than his left from grasping the hammer, as surely as the coolie walks with shoulders awry, a pad of callus on his right shoulder where the bamboo carrying-pole rests. Neither mentors nor experience told him that professional revolutionaries tend to become debased intellectually and brutalized emotionally by alternately cajoling the masses with impossible promises or sacrificing thousands for the theoretical ultimate benefit of millions. In the bright dawn of 1921 men could hardly realize that the jealous mistress they were taking would ultimately force them to choose between their personal integrity and their political lives.

Chen Tu-hsiu himself adhered to Marxism in violent reaction against his previous belief in parliamentary democracy, just as he had come to that faith in reaction against the strictures of traditional Chinese civilization. Versailles began his conversion to Communism, but he still professed faith in democracy as late as the autumn of 1919. His chief complaint was that democracy had as yet been achieved nowhere, and his chief fear was that democracy could not be achieved anywhere.

Chen had come to a halfway house of vague Utopianism with Marxist trimmings. "We must," he wrote, "break down the barriers between the governors and the governed," so that the people, participating directly in government, become both the rulers and the ruled. He proposed the establishment of governing organs whose "total membership" would include all adults subject to their direction, with officials chosen from among the members for short, fixed terms. Industries and trades, as well as localities, would be represented in the corporate bodies of his minutely charted Utopia.[4]

By the end of 1919 Chen Tu-hsiu had put aside these dreams for Marxism. Until he came to know them better, he used the tactics of conspiratorial Communism with great enthusiasm. But he was always suspicious of the Communist Utopia, a major deviation on his part. The voluminous Marxist writings, otherwise painstakingly categorical, offered no guide to its creation, but promised only a spontaneous birth when certain social and economic conditions had been created. Chen's final doctrinal break with the Party came over his denial that true Communism could ever be attained by the state's withering away.[5]

Chang Kuo-tao summed up tellingly: "Chen Tu-hsiu did not accept Marxism without reservations. Often he stressed the need to use it only as a blueprint applied to the special conditions in China." [6]

The young Chang Kuo-tao was by inclination and by circumstances a professional revolutionary, rather than an intellectual. Yet the tactician Chang also came to Communism through his dreams of a world where China occupied the pre-eminent position that was her birthright. He has noted in his revealing autobiography that the ideals of Woodrow Wilson first inspired him and that he turned to Moscow because "as the West cast away its visions, it seemed, Soviet Russia picked them up." [7]

Chang's first knowledge of Russian foreign policy came early in the summer of 1919, when he read in a Peking newspaper the text of the Decree on Peace passed by the Second All-Russian

[4] Chen, "Build the Foundation for Popular Rule." The Utopia based upon the model of the Paris Commune of 1871, which the Maoists attempted to create through the Cultural Revolution, not only embodied many of those features, but was also the ultimate expression of the Chinese Communists' compulsion to create a perfect, new Golden Age.

[5] The nature of the Communist Utopia—and the manner of its attainment—were central to the quarrel between Peking and Moscow, for those issues remained overwhelmingly important to the Communist Party of China in its Maoist phase.

[6] Chang, p. 238.

[7] *Ibid.*, p. 214.

Congress of Workers', Soldiers', and Peasants' Deputies in 1917. The Decree, which was actually Lenin's declaration of war on all established authority, Chang considered attractive because "it enjoined both allied and central powers to end the war on essentially Wilsonian terms." [8] His first favorable impression was heightened by the unilateral declaration of July 1919, when Deputy People's Commissar for Foreign Affairs Leo Karakhan surrendered all Russia's special privileges in China and renounced further payment of the Boxer Indemnity. Chang turned for guidance in Marxist thought to Li Ta-chao, the librarian of Peking University, who was also Mao Tse-tung's occasional mentor. He read all available Marxist writings and "soon came to believe that Socialism offered the only solution to China's problems." [9]

Other conversions occurred in a similar manner, including the impetuous Mao Tse-tung's. Although the material available to them was most limited, young Chinese glimpsed a celestial vision in a few translated books and in occasional newspaper dispatches. It was all the more dazzling because they viewed it from the depths of despair. The revelation led different men into different paths. A small group, which included Chou En-lai and Chen Yi, later the Prime Minister and the Foreign Minister of the People's Government respectively, joined the Worker-Student Movement which took them to France. Others, like Liu Shao-chi, later Chairman of the People's Republic, were sent to Moscow by the Communist International. Lacking either financial support or international connections, some tried to study Marxism in China, while Mao Tse-tung immersed himself in the life of the peasants—to preach the new doctrine and to test it. Chang Kuo-tao organized schools and unions among the railroad workers of the Peking area. Small branch organizations sprang up in scattered localities. They were formally dedicated to Marxism, but they included social democrats, anarchists, and simple men of good will.

Scenting opportunity, the Communist International began to interest itself in the fledgling Chinese Marxist movement in 1920. Although they expected the welcome accorded to prophets bear-

[8] *Ibid.*
[9] *Ibid.*

ing divine revelations, the emissaries of the Comintern aroused suspicion. They inflamed young China's hypersensitivity by their obvious assumption of superiority and their equally obvious anticipation of grateful obedience. Russian diplomats later disillusioned Chinese converts by behaving like bourgeois diplomats and seeking immediate national advantage even to the point of sacrificing fraternal solidarity. Most disheartening was Moscow's compelling the Communist Party of China to unite with Sun Yatsen's Kuomintang in the cause of bourgeois revolution—particularly since the Chinese Communists felt that the money and the organizational support Moscow gave to the Kuomintang directly deprived them of the patronage they needed. The Chinese were not moved from their devotion to Marxism by the demonstration that the Mother Church was itself imperfect, but they did become ever more wary of putting their fate in Moscow's hands.

Soon after its creation the Communist Party of China was forced to descend from the lofty theoretical peaks it favored to the sordid haggling of everyday politics. The first crucial decision that faced the Chinese Communists was whether to join the Kuomintang or to develop independently. Most of the Party's leaders favored an independent course, but the Comintern insisted that they must "immediately join the struggle against imperialism and reaction." The Kremlin's strategy held that the Chinese Communists could best achieve their ultimate aim of seizing power for themselves by operating through an existing political force of demonstrated strength. The chosen instrument was Sun Yat-sen's Kuomintang.

Yuan Shih-kai had driven Sun from the formal seat of power in Peking in 1913. While China's ancient capital was held by a succession of warlords, Sun and his Kuomintang could not return. Instead, the man and the party who had overthrown the Empire laid their plots from places of refuge in the foreign concessions or abroad. But in 1921, the same year the Communist Party of China was founded, their long, frustrating exile came to an end. The original Parliament of 1913 had by then reassembled in the south. Occasionally meeting in Shanghai, where the authorities were sometimes friendly, but usually in Canton, where its welcome was more certain, the Parliament reaffirmed its claim to be the only legal government and elected Sun Yat-sen President of the Republic of China.

It was a republic with few of the normal trappings beloved of governments—except for the well-founded legal claim and the determined high hopes. The only effective administration in China was exercised by the foreign powers in their treaty port enclaves, many of them far inland, and through the Chinese Maritime Customs, which they controlled and which carried out its appointed tasks along the country's navigable rivers. Elsewhere local warlords held sway, some actually ruling one or two provinces, others little more than bandit chieftains who claimed authority over a few counties. The alliances and understandings among the warlords were so impermanent and so confused that it is literally impossible to re-create the events of the period. It would, in any event, require a dozen volumes merely to recount the more obtrusive events. Of supreme importance, however, was the fact that there was no real government of China. Where they wished, the foreign powers enjoyed *de facto* rule, exercising their will through the rights granted them by the "unequal treaties" and gaining their economic ends through collaboration with local warlords.

Contemplating the inglorious confusion, later historians, both Chinese and Western, have tended to concentrate upon the government at Peking. Because it suited their convenience, the foreign powers gave legal recognition to that regime at the time. It was, nonetheless, impossible for the warlords to maintain even the semblance of a stable regime in Peking, much less extend their influence to the rest of the country. The warlords' scrabbling for possession of the seat of the "legitimate" government, therefore, increased the amused contempt with which the rest of the world contemplated China. The catalogue of events and the names of the participants are not terribly important in themselves, but the detail serves, as could no amount of circumlocution, to display the state to which China had fallen.

In the summer of 1920, as has been noted in the previous chapter, a new clique deposed the warlord Tuan Chi-jui. In 1922 the two most powerful members of the new group fell out. They were Chang Tso-lin, the ruler of Manchuria, and Wu Pei-fu, lord of north China. The latter, finally victorious after a mock trial of arms, attempted to legitimize his position by summoning the Parliament of 1913 to Peking and restoring to the presidency Li Yuan-hung, once the reluctant leader of the 1911 rising in Wuhan, later successively Vice-President and President. Since Sun Yat-sen was opposed, only a portion of the Parliament went to Peking, where it sat uncomfortably while Chang Tso-lin glowered from Manchuria to the north. In 1923 a subordinate of Wu Pei-fu named Feng Yu-hsiang—famous as the "Christian General"—moved against Li Yuan-hung, who left the presidency and withdrew to the safety of his home in the foreign concession of Tientsin. In September 1923 Tsao Kun, the nominal superior of both Wu Pei-fu and Feng Yu-hsiang, intimidated the rump of the 1913 Parliament into electing him President.

The reader's confusion at this point is probably no greater than was that of the Chinese people, whose lives often depended upon those heavily armed but singularly bloodless bouts of musical chairs. It may, nonetheless, be worthwhile to cap the confusion by quoting a paragraph from a historian who did comprehend the process, Kenneth Scott Latourette: "By this time the recurrence of civil war had become almost as regular an annual event as the return of spring, and in 1924 the major generals were once more moving against each other. This year Chang Tso-lin was victorious, due chiefly to the sudden defection of Fêng Yü-hsiang from Wu P'ei-fu. Ts'ao Kun was deprived of his office and imprisoned, and Fêng and Chang placed Tuan Ch'i-jui at the head of the Peking Government. Tuan, however, did not have the title of President, but was denominated what may be translated as Provisional Chief Executive. Moreover, he had under him only the skeleton of a national government. In 1925 the inevitable falling out between Fêng and Chang resulted in the withdrawal of the latter, thanks to the disloyalty of some subordinates. The following year (1926) however, Wu P'ei-fu and Chang Tso-lin ignored their differences for the moment and joined in driving Fêng Yü-hsiang's forces out of Peking and into the Northwest. A few weeks afterward, Tuan Ch'i-jui retired into the convenient haven of Tientsin. Not even a 'Provisional Chief Executive' was left in the capital." [10]

Although these events were but in embryo in 1921 when the Communist Party of China was formally created, it required no particular gift to foresee the course of their development. The key features of the situation were clear to the men who wished to put their own stamp on the future, whether they were dedicated Chinese, striving to "save the nation," or the conspirators of the Comintern, determined to claim China for the international proletarian revolution. There could be no hope of creating a truly nationalistic force from among the feckless warlords, who were in any event in league with the country's foreign exploiters. Nonetheless, only a political group that commanded its own armies could possibly end the sway of the warlords and take power for itself. The Chinese Communists, barely hatched as a political force, had no program of their own. The impatient Comintern rejected the faint promise of the Communist Party of China and decided that Sun Yat-sen's Kuomintang, which was explicitly anti-imperialist, could become the nucleus of a "national bourgeois revolution." Moscow felt it would be time enough for the Communists to take over once the nationalist revolution had been successful. The Comintern therefore promised assistance to the Kuomintang and ordered the CPC to cooperate with that party. Moscow continued to insist upon the CPC's cooperating with the Kuomintang even after Sun Yat-sen had lost his territorial base at Canton in 1922, when he quarreled with his chief warlord adherent and was driven into exile in the French Concession of Shanghai.

Despite their own misgivings, the Chinese Communists surrendered their independence. Its penchant for lakes persisting, the Party held an "extraordinary plenum" in August 1922 beside the West Lake at Hangchow. The Chinese Communists—yielding to Moscow's greater experience, and relentless pressure—agreed

[10] Latourette, p. 406. (Latourette uses the diacritical marks of the Wade-Giles system of transliteration which I have omitted throughout this book since it seems to me they would only serve to confuse the uninitiated reader.)

to work with the Kuomintang. But Chen Tu-hsiu, writing in the Party organ *The Guide*, revealed the Chinese aversion to the proposed alliance. Arguing passionately that the CPC must not submerge itself in the KMT,[11] he drew a sharp distinction between those bourgeois elements with whom Marxists might make common cause and those who were the implacable enemy of the proletariat. He also adjured his followers to remember that their ultimate mission was to lead the true proletarian revolution. Since the peasantry was too diffused to provide an effective popular base, he wrote, only the self-conscious industrial proletariat could serve as the nucleus of revolution. But the Communists, Chen continued, could not achieve their aims while China was held in semicolonial subjugation by Western imperialism. The Party would, therefore, temporarily make common cause with the Kuomintang to expel the imperialists by depriving their Chinese lackeys of power.

When the CPC had made its intellectual submission, a new man came from Moscow, Adolf Joffe, the Soviet Government's special emissary to the nations of the Far East. After protracted discussions, Sun Yat-sen and Joffe issued a joint public statement in January 1923. They formally declared that China was "not suited to Communism," and announced the Soviet Union's support of the Nationalist revolution. The Chinese Communists resented the Soviet Government's denouncing Communism, fearful that they were to be sacrificed to Moscow's plans for the rapid creation of a Chinese government it could dominate. The Chinese Party, nonetheless, adhered to the enforced decision to collaborate with the Nationalists.

Neither side envisioned an equal alliance, though fifty-three Communists and Nationalists had met in November 1922 to draw plans for reorganizing the Kuomintang. A year passed before the Kuomintang was prepared to entertain applications for admission from individual Communists. The two Parties were not to merge, but Sun Yat-sen did waive the normal prohibition against KMT members' belonging to another political party because he hoped

[11] For convenience, I shall continue to use the initials CPC for Communist Party of China and KMT for Kuomintang, the latter alternating with the term Nationalists.

to strengthen his hand greatly through the new agreement. He was not primarily interested in the support of the minuscule native Communist forces, who were merely the pawns, but in Moscow's financial and organizational assistance.

The collaboration began harmoniously, though neither Party really desired association with the other. Michael Borodin, a professional agitator who had been deported from the United States, came to China as the Comintern's representative. He was to teach Sun Yat-sen how to organize and control an authoritarian political party. The former librarian of Peking University, Li Ta-chao, and Sun Yat-sen were elected co-chairmen of the Kuomintang Congress, which met in Shanghai in January 1924. Chen Tu-hsiu joined the KMT's Central Executive Committee, and still another Communist became chairman of the Nationalists' Organization Bureau. Chou En-lai was appointed chairman of the Political Training Section of the Whampoa Military Academy; Chiang Kai-shek was commandant. Chiang was recommended not only by his graduation from a Japanese military academy, but because he had toured Russia as Sun's personal representative in 1923. He was soon to become an honorary member of the Comintern's Executive Committee.

As relations became more intimate, both the Kuomintang's right wing and the Communists grew more wary. Each of the natural rivals suspected, with total justification, that the other wished only to exploit its strength before destroying it. Chen Tu-hsiu late claimed that he had constantly fought concessions to the Kuomintang which Borodin had urged in the Comintern's name. But in 1925, with Soviet support offering the first real hope of the revolution's success, these disputes were merely portents. Kuomintang armies were increasing in size and fire power, while Communist-dominated labor unions were for the first time a significant element in the balance of power.

It was also in 1925 that the Comintern, conspiring against the alliance it had created, instructed the Communist Party of China: "Fight against the right wing of the Kuomintang; organize the left in unity; and criticize the center." The Communists expanded their independent strength. In May 1925 the All-China Labor Federation was born in Canton as a branch of the Communist

Trade Union International. The Federation publicly affirmed that Leninism, combined with the doctrine of Sun Yat-sen, would "insure China's salvation." Communist Party membership grew from fifteen hundred on January 1, 1925, to three thousand on May 30, 1925. Late in the same year British Hong Kong was paralyzed by a merchant seamen's strike directed by the new Federation.

The Kuomintang became increasingly wary of its ally after Dr. Sun Yat-sen's death in 1925. Meeting in November 1925 in the Western hills near Peking, the KMT's right wing expressed alarm at the ease with which the Communists were winning control of industrial and transport workers. The Whampoa Academy, despite Chiang Kai-shek's formal control, was turning out many ardent Marxists, since the faculty knew no other militant political doctrine.

With the alliance's growing strength promising quick victory over its disorganized enemies, a power struggle convulsed the movement. In March 1926 the KMT right wing, under Chiang Kai-shek, seized the city of Canton, slaughtering Communists and liberals. Under the leadership of Wang Ching-wei, the intellectual heir of Sun Yat-sen, the moderate left wing fled. Chen Tu-hsiu's demand that the CPC withdraw from the Kuomintang was overruled by the Comintern bloc in the CPC's Central Committee. In May 1926, the Kuomintang's Central Committee ejected Communists from executive positions and restricted their representation in deliberative organs.

The Communists' response was more Christian than Marxist: the CPC's Fifth Party Congress expressed its sincere desire to continue its cooperation with the Kuomintang. On June 4, 1926, Chen Tu-hsiu composed an open letter to Chiang Kai-shek affirming the CPC's loyalty to the "national revolution" and denying any intention to sabotage the joint cause.[12] For the moment all factions were formally reconciled.

Military victory delayed the inevitable split. On July 9, 1926, the Nationalist armies under Chiang Kai-shek marched out of Canton on the first leg of the Northern Expedition, which would destroy the power of the warlords and unify China. Chou En-lai

[12] Chen was later to claim that the letter was not an expression of his true feelings, but had been written to the Comintern's order.

was political commissar of the First Division, and every unit incorporated a political and propaganda section staffed largely by Communists. By September the Northern Expedition had taken Hankow, the great industrial city of central China. By December, a provisional government for all China was established in that city by the victorious Kuomintang and its Communist allies. More adroit politically and better endowed with administrative talent than the conservatives, the moderate left wing of the Kuomintang and the Communists dominated the Hankow government. The pro-Communist Hankow General Labor Union was the government's mainstay and was also the headquarters for Communist agitation throughout central China.

Chen Tu-hsiu himself went to Shanghai to join Chou En-lai in rallying the militant unions in the Chinese sections of that international city. There, among the largest proletarian concentration in the Orient, the pair trained militia units which were to mobilize when the time came to take the city. The rising came in the spring of 1927 as Chiang's armies approached the richest prize in China. The workers disarmed the defending warlord's armies and held Shanghai until the Nationalist armies arrived. The Shanghai rising was to be the Communists' only successful use of the classic weapon of the urban proletariat during nearly three decades of revolution.

During the first days of April 1927 the workers patrolled the city, brave in the dignity of their armbands and rifles. The regulars encamped outside the city limits, while Chiang Kai-shek conferred with the leaders of the commune—and with bankers and secret society chieftains in the French Concession. He knew that the Communists and their left-wing allies were rapidly seizing all the vital centers of power. They already controlled the government at Hankow and the propaganda machinery, as well as the unions, while major units of the Kuomintang's army were already infiltrated. Feeling that he must strike back then or be swallowed later, Chiang sought allies where he could find them. He found them among the capitalists who were the Communists' greatest enemies.

At four in the morning of April 12th secret-society toughs dressed as workingmen joined the Kwangsi Division to attack the workers' strongholds. The men from rural Kwangsi, who did not particularly like the slick Shanghailanders, gleefully obeyed Chiang's orders to disarm the workers without excessive gentleness. By noon the Shanghai workers, who had expected victory celebrations, were fleeing through the narrow streets. They were pursued by Kuomintang regulars firing rifles and submachine guns. The headquarters of the Shanghai Federation of Labor Unions was their last citadel, where stubborn militia units held out for several hours under Chou En-lai until they were slaughtered.

Chiang Kai-shek had made his peace with the bourgeoisie, whom the Communists denounced as lackeys of imperialism. He was soon to make his peace with the Western capitalists and begin his thirty-six-year war against the Communists. As Chou En-lai and Chen Tu-hsiu fled from the stricken city toward their separate destinies, the break between the left—both Communists and moderate members of the KMT—and the increasingly conservative Chiang Kai-shek was still not quite complete.

The Comintern was still intoxicated by the prospect of seizing power in China through the Nationalist Party, which Moscow considered its own creature. For several years Borodin had been not merely an adviser, but actually the most powerful of the triumvirs who controlled the Kuomintang. Stalin was not merely vainglorious when he bragged to his cronies in 1927 that he would use Chiang Kai-shek and then "cast him aside like a squeezed lemon." But the Chinese Communists felt that it was they who had been squeezed. Moscow's insistence that the Chinese must cooperate with the Nationalists sowed seeds of lasting bitterness —and immediate confusion.

Even after the Shanghai rising, the Comintern insisted that the CPC must continue to work through the moderates of the Kuomintang. Stalin himself directed the Chinese Communists to maintain the alliance, although Moscow had by that time lost control of even the left wing of the KMT. In mid-1927 the Hankow government, still the official instrument of the Kuomintang though it had almost broken with Chiang, suppressed peasant risings amid great bloodshed. Though he declared in a telegram to his agents: "Without an agrarian revolution, victory is impossible!" Stalin ordered the peasants sacrificed on the altar of CPC-KMT cooperation. He parted completely with any realistic appraisal of the Communists' capabilities when he instructed them in the same telegram to cooperate with the Kuomintang as long as necessary—and then destroy it. Since Stalin had troubled to draw a light veil of ambiguous language over his purpose, an Indian representative of the Comintern, M. N. Roy, felt he could reassure the Kuomintang's left wing of Communist constancy by showing the telegram to Wang Ching-wei, who headed the Hankow government. Wang's reaction was, quite logically, the reverse of the reaction Roy had expected. As Roy himself later recounted,[13] Wang was shocked. The split between the Communists and the left wing of the Kuomintang became inevitable.

It was a summer of dreadful confusion. Chiang Kai-shek marched on Nanking to force the outraged Western commercial community to come to terms, while Moscow fulminated and the Chinese Communists led peasant revolts and urban riots throughout the central China plain. Their fury was now directed not against the reactionary Chiang, but against the liberal Hankow government. The Communists' curious approach to the task of salvaging a center of conventional revolutionary power in the Wuhan industrial area insured the destruction of the moderate Hankow government. Thus the Communists laid the basis for twenty-two years of supremacy by Chiang Kai-shek's right wing. The leaders of the non-Communist left fled to Moscow to take refuge in the arms of the Comintern that had broken their power. Conventional Leninist tactics had disastrously failed to bring the Communists to power in China.

The heart-stirring days were over, the days when the Chinese Communist revolution had appeared to follow the classical European pattern. Yet victory had appeared tantalizingly close, and the continuing political confusion invited direct action by the troops the Communists still controlled. They hazarded one more blow for victory by conventional means.

On August 1, 1927, cadets of the Whampoa Academy's branch rose in revolt in the city of Nanchang in Kiangsi Province. Their commandant was Chu Teh, a secret Communist who had once been a powerful warlord. The rebels were joined by two regular

[13] *Revolution and Counter-revolution in China* (Calcutta, 1946).

divisions of the Kuomintang army and by scattered companies and battalions under men like Lin Piao, a young major fresh from the Socialist Youth League and the Whampoa Academy. For all their fervor, the Communist troops had no clear purpose. They were driven from Nanchang to straggle aimlessly across southern China. The final triumph of unreason came on December 10, 1927, when a small group of extremists, encouraged by the Comintern, seized the city of Canton and held it for three days. The Communists were deeply disappointed in the response of the hundred fifty thousand members of their own labor unions. Only ten thousand rose when the tocsin sounded, although they were joined by military units dispersed after the Nanchang rising. But the local Kuomintang commander soon recaptured the city, annihilating the Red battalions and killing thousands of workers.

The Canton Commune was but a gory aftermath, for the Communist Party's leadership and ranks were already fragmented. When the Kuomintang and its army expelled all known Communists in July 1927, it had finally become clear to all but the Comintern's most bemused puppets that the Communists required a new strategy for China. Conventionally enough, the bewildered, adolescent Party turned on its mentor. Just a week after the Nanchang Rising the Central Committee, meeting in an "extraordinary session" of dubious legality under Mao Tse-tung's control, removed Chen Tu-hsiu from the secretary-generalship. Castigated for "rightist opportunism," Chen was further charged with violating the Comintern's orders. He was assigned full blame for the debacle.

The Communist Party of China was sharply divided for a number of years thereafter. A clandestine Central Committee in Shanghai, still subservient to the Comintern, continued to strive for a proletarian revolution by conventional means. At the same time Mao Tse-tung's slow-burning revolution began to smolder in the countryside, far from the normal centers of power. The Central Committee had ordered him to unfamiliar Szechwan, but Mao returned to his native Hunan to organize the Autumn Crop Rising of 1927. When it failed, he fled to the hills alone.

Mao was captured by local militia, but escaped by feigning lameness and bribing the soldier assigned to watch over his hobbling progress. A lone fugitive in the green hills, dressed in cast-off clothing given him by a friendly farmer, Mao fell in with a band of refugees near the Kiangsi border. They were not Communists, but simple farm people who had followed the Red flag and now found themselves broken, dispirited, and leaderless. Their nominal chief, a peasant who was somewhat less frightened than his men, asked Mao to address them.

The tall, awkward rebel rose to stand among the lesser rebels who lay sprawling on the ground around him. Though he was normally plump, the month just passed had shrunk the flesh from under his skin, which stretched loose and unhealthy. He tossed back his lank black hair and emphasized his points with angular gestures.

"Comrades," he declaimed, "we have evaded the enemy and he can only fire random shots behind us—where he thinks we *may* be. And how can that harm us? We are all born of woman. The enemy soldier has but two legs and each of us has also two legs. . . . When Comrade Ho Lung first rose in revolt, his entire arsenal was but two kitchen knives. Today he is a general, a true soldier. We have here much more than two kitchen knives; we have nearly two battalions. Why should you fear that we will not succeed?"

The tired rebels rose to the practiced ardor Mao had learned in seven years as a professional agitator. Their lives were forfeit if they were captured; a leader and a cause might give them another chance at life. Those two ragged "battalions," totaling no more than two hundred men, became the core of the force Mao led to the mountain called Chingkang Shan in southern Kiangsi Province.

In May 1928 Chu Teh, the leader of the Nanchang Rising, joined Mao Tse-tung on Chingkang Shan. After fleeing Nanchang, Chu had gone to earth in northern Kwangtung Province, where he joined a local warlord. Chu's ragged, ill-armed troops were not quite a thousand strong, including walking wounded. During the winter of 1927–28 he had built up his forces and expanded the area under his control to include several counties in Hunan to the north and Kiangsi to the northeast. When he was strong enough, Chu had broken with his sponsor to build China's first

secure Soviet military base and to recruit the nucleus of the Workers' and Peasants' Red Army. In the secure highlands, Chu developed the tactics that were to bring ultimate victory to Communist arms. Instead of striving to create an army independent of
the people, he determined to knit the two into one force. Mao and
Chu shaped the organization and tactics of the Red Army together,
working in such close harmony that the local peasants called the
force the Chu-Mao Army. Within the next three years they carved
out of the hills the Communist Party's first territorial base, the
Kiangsi Soviet Area. While the pair, effectively cut off from the
rest of the world, charted their own laborious course to power,
the Communist Party of China was passing through its days of
reconstruction after the debacle of 1927.

When Mao Tse-tung, as a naïve schoolboy, ran a newspaper
advertisement requesting men of sympathetic political views to
communicate with him, one of two replies came from a youth
named Li Li-san. The pair disliked each other at sight, but Li also
followed his own road to Communism. He went to France with
the Worker-Students, who were the nucleus of the French branch
of the CPC, and was later admitted to the inner mysteries in the
Soviet Union. Li Li-san maneuvered himself into power in late
1927, when many eminent Communists had sought refuge in the
Soviet Union and formal leadership had passed to a weak Secretary-General who was distinguished chiefly by his refined literary
style and his subservience to Moscow. The official seat of the clandestine Central Committee was in the international sections of
Shanghai, insofar as the broken Party can be said to have possessed a fixed site. Although it was in touch with Moscow, the
Central Committee had little communication with the Chu-Mao
group.

Li's doctrines were paramount in the official Party Center
until 1931. He scoffed at the conservatism of Mao's rural faction
and advocated immediate assaults against China's cities to take
advantage of the incipent worldwide collapse of capitalism he discerned. He argued that the worldwide economic catastrophes that
had followed the American stock-market crash of October 1929

were not merely a Great Depression but the death throes of capitalism—and many in the West agreed with him. China, Li maintained, was particularly ripe for revolt because her reactionary masters were utterly dependent upon the support of foreign imperialist capital. With the home bases of imperialism weakened by economic crisis, a series of strong blows, Li concluded, could give the Communists complete control of China. Then the world would fall.

Having demonstrated to his own satisfaction that China was ripe for revolt, Li audaciously went on to argue that the Communist victory in China would precipitate the final worldwide crisis of capitalism. China, not Russia, he implied, was the pivot of the world liberation movement because her continuing economic exploitation was vital to the survival of international imperialism and because her vast population was an invincible weapon. Li thus anticipated the line his rival Mao Tse-tung was to adopt three decades later, when he proposed to "liberate" the entire world by waging triumphant "people's wars" in the underdeveloped nations, thus isolating capitalism and forcing its collapse.

"We have arrived," he wrote, "at the moment for the total destruction of imperialism, with the destruction of the chief international imperialists—England, the United States, and Japan—coming first . . . the Chinese revolution must seize victory in this final battle and, in the same battle, the proletariat of the entire world can attain final victory. . . . The victory of our revolution will fix irrevocably the victory of the worldwide revolution."

The Comintern, still dismayed by the debacle in China, was weakened by the struggle against Leon Trotsky and preoccupied by the grave internal crisis in the Soviet Union. Moscow looked upon Li without enthusiasm, but did not oppose the only man in China who appeared to offer a positive policy, any more than it disowned Mao's rural faction completely. After a time, however, the Kremlin began to regard Li as a threat, even discerning symptoms of incipient Trotskyism in his doctrines.

Obviously no inspired theoretician, Li Li-san was a proficient conspirator. In 1929 his maneuvers captured the Political Bureau, which had become the center of power within the Chinese Communist Party. The new Secretary-General was Li's man, as was the Chairman of the Military Affairs Bureau. Liu Shao-chi headed the Labor Bureau, while Chou En-lai, returned from a second quick visit to Moscow, was Chairman of the Organization Bureau, a post second in power only to the secretary-generalship. Liu and Chou generally voted with Li, their support tempered somewhat by consideration for the future when he might go down before the "rural faction" of Mao Tse-tung. Li Li-san, a kingmaker because he had aroused too much personal antagonism to be king himself, headed the Propaganda Bureau. The cabal held complete power from November 1929, when Chen Tu-hsiu was formally read out of the Party, until January 1931, when they themselves barely escaped excommunication.

The Red Army had expanded greatly around the small nucleus of the original Chu-Mao force, and local adherents of the Shanghai Central Committee had been able to establish areas of military power in scattered pockets throughout China. In July 1929 a force made up primarily of such local units attacked Changsha, the center of communications and commerce for south-central China, establishing a commune that endured for ten days with Li Li-san at its head. Citing the raid's "success" as proof of his sweeping thesis, Li forced a resolution through the Chinese Politburo on "the new revolutionary high tide and the question of prior victory in one province or a multiprovincial offensive." The Party Center committed itself to an all-out offensive to snatch quick victory while the enemy was weak. Its first action was another attack on Changsha in July 1930. The Red Army was thrown back at the city's walls by the forces of the local warlord, who gave nominal allegiance to Chiang Kai-shek.*

A third group in the Party had begun to protest against Li Li-san's recklessness. They were the "Russian faction," diffident in decision and capable of action only when Moscow pulled the leading strings. Wang Ming, spokesman for a group of about two dozen Chinese who had just returned from Russia,[14] was backed

---

* As late as February 1968 the Maoists were horrified by the Viet Cong's "Spring Offensive" against the cities of South Vietnam because it repeated Li Li-san's error.

[14] Wang still holds minor positions, but is employed chiefly as a horrible ex-

by Pavel Mif, the Comintern's resident representative in Shanghai. Li Li-san's follower, Chou En-lai, scurrying to Moscow to plead his leader's case after the defeat at Changsha, was anticipated by a telegram from Mif in Shanghai to the Comintern in Moscow violently denouncing "the Li Li-san line."

Though the matter was still under consideration, the supple Chou En-lai hurried back to China in late September 1930 to attend the Central Committee's Third Plenary Session at Lushan, once a favorite summer resort of foreigners. With him came the weak second Secretary-General, who had become the Party's representative in Moscow. Together the pair beat down the swords leveled at Li Li-san by the Russian faction of Pavel Mif and Wang Ming, but they could not prevent passage of a resolution mildly critical of Li's tactics. The Comintern was still officially silent, and Li continued in authority, though his prestige was tarnished.

On November 12, 1930, the Russian faction presented a fresh resolution that repudiated Li Li-san and all his works. On November 16th the long-awaited telegram arrived from Moscow. The Kremlin ordered the Chinese to abandon insurrectionism. From the Mount had come a wholly unsatisfactory solution: the Kremlin condemned a policy discredited in action, but offered no new policy.

On November 25, 1930, the Chinese came to heel. The Politburo formally accepted the Comintern's directive and reprimanded Li Li-san for theoretical errors amounting *in toto* to "unprincipled opportunism." A plenary session of the Central Committee on January 1, 1931, stripped an abjectly repentant Li Li-san of his offices, but rewarded his belated cooperation in true Chinese fashion by appointment to the Party's delegation in Moscow.[15] With Li pigeonholed, the Party was then cleared of his followers. Among the chief advocates of the Li Li-san line, only Chou En-lai, with his uncanny instinct for survival, emerged unscathed, moving laterally from the Organization Bureau to be-

---

ample, since he suffered successively from left-wing and right-wing extremism.

[15] Li Li-san remained in exile for sixteen years, returning to Manchuria with the Russian armies in 1945. But his political eclipse was total.

come head of the Military Affairs Bureau. Wang Ming was re-warded for his constancy by the secretary-generalship.

In late 1931 Chou En-lai and Wang Ming arrived in the First —and only—Soviet Area in the mountains of Kiangsi Province to mend fences with Mao Tse-tung and Chu Teh. Their "rural faction," building its strength in isolation, had become the only group in the Party that commanded significant popular support, armed forces, and material resources. The representatives of the Shanghai Central Committee came to Juichin, the small mountain village that had become the capital of an independent regime, to attend the first Congress of Soviet Representatives. Having carved out a domain that seemed reasonably secure, Mao had determined to create a functioning apparatus of government. Ignoring Chou En-lai and Wang Ming, the Congress elected Mao Chairman of the Soviet Government and Chu Teh Chairman of the People's Military Affairs Committee.

The power of the Chinese "rural faction" was firmly established within the Communist movement in China, though the Comintern withheld its formal recognition. Wang Ming soon returned to Moscow, although he was not removed as the nominal head of the Party in favor of Mao Tse-tung until much later. The formal seat of the Central Committee of the Communist Party of China remained in Shanghai, but the quarrel with the Comintern had ended in apparent victory for the Chinese faction, since Moscow, despite its manifest ill grace, gave partial endorsement to Mao's strategy of building a peasant army. Thereafter, Mao quarreled with the Comintern from time to time and struggled with Chang Kuo-tao. But his power was established in 1931, and his pre-eminent position remained beyond serious challenge until the debacle of the Great Leap Forward in 1958.

The secret of Mao's ascendancy was a simple one, though its execution had required him to defy both the Comintern and the formal leaders of the CPC. Rather than dissipate his energies in the Byzantine intrigues of the Party Center, Mao had gone to the peasantry, whose support alone could provide an enduring base for his own power within the Party—and for the Party's campaign to seize the machinery of the state. Since the great masses of China were farmers, his limited success changed the emphasis of the revolution from the proletariat to the peasantry. The "rural faction" forced even the Comintern to grant its halfhearted approval of Mao's strategy, though Moscow provided almost no practical assistance for years to come.

When the Comintern abdicated direct control over the Communist Party of China, Mao Tse-tung was free to pursue the course that would bring him to victory within two decades. He expanded the First Soviet Area and developed pockets of resistance elsewhere by dispatching his agents to woo discontented peasants and the secret societies. Chiang Kai-shek, consolidating his own power by dealing with local warlords through the traditional techniques of strife, negotiation, conciliation, and bribery, did not seriously challenge the Kiangsi Soviet Area for a time. Besides, the mountains were so steep and the inhabitants so poor that the area was a most unattractive target. It was, therefore, easy for the Communists to remain undisturbed and in their isolation to turn the impoverished peasants against the gentry undisturbed. The slightest benefit, perhaps an additional bowl of rice each week, was a major change in the peasants' lives, while the call to struggle gave excitement and dignity to men and women whose previous existence had been shrouded by a gray mist of hopelessness. The First Soviet Area proved an ideal laboratory. There Mao developed the special techniques of his revolution: distributing land to the tillers; directing special appeals to the oppressed women; conducting popular indoctrination by permitting the people to participate in their own affairs; employing itinerant propagandists and theatrical troupes; rigorously disciplining his troops to respect the rights of civilians; and waging campaigns of calculated terror against "class enemies."

Mao's success within his limited sphere was so great that Chiang Kai-shek finally mounted a series of "extermination campaigns" against the Soviet Area. Although the Nationalist forces were relatively well armed and were tutored by foreign generals, the Communists held out for several years. Their tactics were simple. When the enemy threatened their strongholds, the Communist leaders and soldiers simply dispersed into the hills. Finally yielding to intensified Nationalist pressure in 1934, the Communists began the epic Long March, which was both their Anabasis and their Valley Forge. Armed units totaling more than a hundred thousand men—with all their worldly wealth, their women, and even their printing presses—began a march of six to eight thousand miles toward the remote northwest, where the Central Government's power attenuated to the point of impotence by the vast, empty spaces and the prevalence of local warlords. The area around Paochi in Shensi Province was also recommended by its proximity to the Soviet Union's Central Asian territories and by the existence of a powerful and active Communist underground in the territory around the city.

The Long March was actually a mass migration rather than a military campaign, though the Communists had to fight their way to safety. Becoming aliens as soon as they crossed the Kiangsi border, the Communist troops were plagued not only by national and provincial troops, but also by the resistance of the minority peoples through whose lands they passed. The Lolos of the high mountains of Szechwan and Yunnan fought the Red Army in pitched battles, and Khampas on hairy ponies harassed the column that traversed the high eastern steppes of Tibet.

Tales of the Long March forcibly recall the confused nature of war. The private soldier hardly knew where his squad marched, and even his officers did not know where other large units fought. The lines of march formed an intricate web on the great wall map of China. The commander of each column, briefed on the over-all plan and his own responsibilities, was released to make his own way to the rendezvous in the northwest by a route corresponding to a trek from Tennessee to Nebraska by way of Colorado. Because Nationalist resistance was even more diffused than their own effort by faulty communications and local political rivalries, the Red Army reached its goal, though its killed and missing amounted to more than half its numbers.

The common peril did not halt internal quarrels. Chang Kuo-tao, Mao Tse-tung's rival since the First Congress when he was named to head the Organization Bureau, became increasingly disaffected. He actually held General Chu Teh prisoner for a few days, demanding that Chu transfer his allegiance or face execution. But he was finally forced to release Chu Teh, who refused to

betray Mao Tse-tung, because his own soldiers would have mutinied if he had put Chu to death.

In January 1935 the Red Army occupied Tsunyi, a small city
in the north of Kweichow Province. While his column was out of
touch with the outside world and the Central Committee members present lay wholly in his hands, Mao Tse-tung chose to make
his bid for supreme power. He prefaced the election with a bitter
attack on the Russian faction for its constant errors. With his chief
rival Chang Kuo-tao in communication only by uncertain tele-
graph, Mao Tse-tung was formally elected First Secretary of the
Communist Party of China. Thereafter, the internal affairs of the
Party become easier to follow, for they center upon Mao Tse-
tung.

In 1937 the Japanese, emboldened by their piecemeal conquest of north China, staged the mass attacks that led to the Sino-
Japanese War. The Communists' chief concern remained the ultimate conquest of power and Mao's own concern to consolidate his
control of the Party machinery. Chang Kuo-tao, still influential,
contended that the Communists must concentrate all their energies upon defeating the Japanese. He even argued that they must
abandon for the moment the struggle to destroy Chiang Kai-shek.
But Mao replied that the battle against the Japanese must engage
no more energy than the battle against the Kuomintang. The
new period of internal disruption, he maintained, was the Communists' great opportunity to sabotage their new ally, the Nationalists. Chang Kuo-tao declared in his memoirs that in 1938 Mao
overruled the decision of a formal conference that favored a policy of honest cooperation and forced Chang himself out of the
Party.

Mao was committed to the proposition that conspiracy and
betrayal of allies were not merely justified by the ends sought, but
were actually desirable tactics in themselves, since they developed
proletarian ruthlessness. Both men favored a temporary alliance
with the KMT against the Japanese, and both agreed that such an
arrangement would facilitate the CPC's conquest of power. But
Chang Kuo-tao argued that the internecine struggle must be sus-

pended for the moment because the Japanese posed an immediate and total threat to the nation's existence. Mao Tse-tung contended that the Communists must continue to direct their chief barrages against the Nationalists under the cover of cooperation against the Japanese.

The basis for the new KMT-CPC collaboration had been laid at Christmas of 1936 in the city of Sian near the new Soviet Area when the Communists conspired in the kidnaping of Chiang Kai-shek. Although Chiang had, under duress, agreed in principle to a truce so that all Chinese might unite against the invader, the formal entente was not formed until the end of 1937. It was a most uneasy alliance, for it was troubled by the Communists' single-minded efforts to expand the Soviet Area and by Chiang's desultory attempts to blockade the Communists. Neither side, consequently, directed its chief efforts to the struggle against Japan. The Communists sought primarily to create a basis for future power by recruiting guerrillas and by expanding their conventional armies, while the Nationalists, despite prodding by their American allies after 1941, were reluctant to risk their best forces against the Japanese. Regardless of their leaders' duplicity, the Chinese people themselves and the Chinese rank and file wrote a new chapter in the record of human glory by their mass resistance to the Japanese.

Neither the heroic deeds of those days nor the struggle between the KMT and the CPC is immediately pertinent to this narrative, since the character of both the Communist Party of China and its leaders was formed by 1938. The end of the war in the Pacific found vastly enlarged Communist armies opposing a Kuomintang which had actually been weakened by the struggle. The Nationalists had also conspired toward their own ineffectiveness. Chiang Kai-shek's favorite American soldier, Major General Clare Chennault, had urged the Nationalists to concentrate upon air power, rather than building the powerful ground forces the abrasive General Joseph Stilwell argued they needed—for political as well as military purposes. Despite infusions of gold and arms from the United States, the Kuomintang's position deteriorated rapidly, while the Communists' power increased. The CCP was reinforced mightily when Manchuria was given into its hands as a firm territorial base by the withdrawing Russian armies.

Foreign intervention did not, however, decide the issue. Chiang Kai-shek wrought his own defeat by relying upon the corrupt old power structure, though it had been all but shattered by the war. From his victory in 1927 to his final defeat in 1949, Chiang's greatest failure lay in his inability to break the old balance of power in China, in part because he was plagued by the Communists and the Japanese. He tolerated the continuing sway of local warlords bolstered by foreign support, though the KMT's original purpose had been to destroy such regional authority and such alliances. Ruling by juggling opposing interests, Chiang was never able to create the strong central government China needed. He was, therefore, never able to stamp out abuses or exploitation, and he failed to improve the lot of the Chinese masses. Mao Tse-tung was carried to victory by the peasantry, which was aroused by his promises of material abundance and individual dignity. After two years of half-war and half-peace, interspersed by armistice talks sponsored by an American truce mission under General George C. Marshall, the Communists struck. From 1947 through 1949 the massive People's Liberation Army rolled the Kuomintang forces south toward their final exile on Formosa. The battle for conquest of power had ended—and the Chinese Communists began to build their promised paradise.

An elided chronology may indicate how they discharged the responsibilities of absolute power:

1949: The People's Liberation Army takes Nanking, Shanghai, Canton, and Chungking, gaining effective control of China. The People's Republic of China is established on October 1, ruled by a "coalition" government of the left under the CPC's leadership. Internationally, Mao Tse-tung declares China "will lean to one side"—the Russian side; he proclaims November 1949 Sino-Soviet Friendship Month; and in December he makes his first journey abroad, going to Moscow.

1950: After a series of threats, the Chinese People's Volunteers enter the Korean War on October 25, backed by the Sino-Soviet Treaty of Friendship and Mutual Defense signed in February. The United Nations Armies are forced back. Tibet is invaded. Internally, Mao proclaims land reform; the campaign for suppression of "counter-revolutionaries"; "rationalization" of commerce and industry (read: initial expropriation to be followed by later nationalization); and the New Marriage Law, abolishing polygamy and providing for easy divorce. (The last measure aims not only to win the support of women, but to accelerate the breakdown of the old social order.)

1951: The Korean War continues, with peace talks starting in July and China charging the United States with using germ warfare. The conquest of Tibet is completed. Widespread executions accompany land reform and the campaign against counter-revolutionaries. The Aid Korea-Resist America Movement is in full swing, the first of innumerable campaigns to sweep up the labor and wealth the Peking regime requires.

1952: The Three-Antis Campaign, against "waste, corruption, and bureaucracy" within the Communist ranks, reaches crescendo. It is followed by the Five-Antis Campaign against individual businessmen through which Peking extorts vast sums and breaks the back of private commerce and industry. Land reform's completion is announced. Public trials condemn foreign missionaries for horrible crimes. The educational system is revamped to provide "practical" courses that will aid in reconstruction.

1953: Truce is signed in Korea, and Peking hails a great victory, while Peng Teh-huai, commander of the "Volunteers," publicly reveals plans for the "liberation" of Southeast Asia. More than fourteen thousand Communist soldiers captured in Korea choose to abandon the mainland and go to Formosa. The First Five-Year Plan begins.

1954: The Sino-American talks on repatriation of their respective nationals begin, after China participates in the Geneva Conference "settling" the fate of Indo-China, but reaching no agreement on Korea. Chou En-lai and Jawaharlal Nehru issue a joint proclamation of adherence to *panch sheel*—the "five principles" of peaceful coexistence. A Sino-Soviet communiqué announces a 520-million ruble credit to China and extends Russian use of north China naval bases like Port Arthur. Peking adopts a new constitution, establishing the Central People's Government with Mao Tse-tung as its Chairman. Peking reduces the power of generals who had previously ruled semiautonomous Military and Administrative Areas. The Chairmen of the Manchurian and the East China Regions are purged for separatism. The first collective farm is established, joining a few existing cooperatives and state mechanized farms.

1955: Dag Hammarskjöld visits Peking. Chou En-lai dominates the Afro-Asian Conference at Bandung. Sino-American ambassadorial talks begin at Geneva, and the first Chinese trade delegation visits Tokyo. The Tibet Autonomous Region Preparatory Committee is set up with the Dalai Lama at its head. Ten People's Marshals are created. Communist forces occupy tiny Yichiangshan Island near Formosa, and the Nationalists evacuate the Ta Chen Islands on America's urging and with American assistance. Mao Tse-tung proclaims the "high tide of Socialism in the countryside," calling for the establishment of "cooperative farms" across the nation. Grain rationing begins in the cities—and later in the countryside. "Thought reform" of intellectuals is intensified. A trade offensive against Southeast Asia begins. This year is a high-water mark of Peking's prestige—internal and international.

1956: Socialization of the cities begins, with the abolition of private business and its replacement by "joint public-private enterprises." Pressure on intellectuals increases until suddenly, at the year's end, the relaxation of the Hundred Flowers Movement is proclaimed. Agricultural cooperatives are reorganized, and most individual holdings are abolished. The Tibetan revolt begins. Prime Minister Chou En-lai tours Southeast Asia at the end of 1956 and Eastern Europe early in 1957.

1957: Mao Tse-tung reveals his thesis on "Internal Contradictions." The first original Marxist thinking in a decade justifies his difficulties by asserting that "non-antagonistic contradictions" can flare up between a Socialist government and its citizens. The Hundred Flowers Movement, permitting free speech, blossoms into open denunciation of Communist rule and the Russian alliance; university and high school students stage demonstrations and riots against the regime. At mid-year relaxation ends, and a new purge begins. The first deviationist cadres and intellectuals are sent to the countryside for reform. (Their number will reach ten million by the end of 1958.) The rate of economic expansion is cut back, because excessive capital investment in 1956 has produced major dislocations.

1958: The year of the "Great Leap Forward." People's Communes are established throughout rural China. A hundred million Chinese work at backyard blast furnaces that are fed primarily with scrap metal to produce an inferior grade of steel. By the year's end popular discontent, food shortages, transportation snarls, and exhaustion force reconsideration of basic policies in a meeting of the Central Committee at Wuhan. Mao's resignation as Chairman of Chinese People's Republic is announced, but he remains at the head of the Party. "Tidying up" of the Communes is ordered, with the Army assuming major responsibility; urban communalization is postponed indefinitely. The Army leadership is shaken up. The Communists bombard Nationalist-held Quemoy. Khrushchev visits Peking. The trade offensive halts for lack of goods. Mao Tse-tung proclaims his crusade to "liberate" the oppressed of all the world and "crush" capitalism through "people's wars."

1959: Liu Shao-chi is named Mao's successor in April. The tidying up of Communes continues. Intellectuals begin returning from the countryside. In August a Central Committee communiqué reveals that production figures for 1958 were overstated and sets new, modified targets. Defense Minister Peng Teh-huai is relieved of all his offices for leading a Russian-oriented opposition group within the Central Committee, which denounces Mao's economic excesses and failures, his adventurous foreign policy, and his emphasis upon politics, rather than professional competence within the People's Liberation Army. The internal fight is bitter, and Mao Tse-tung prevails only after threatening to go into opposition. The Army leadership is shaken up again, and Lin Piao becomes Defense Minister. A new campaign begins against "rightists" allied with Peng Teh-huai. The Tibetan revolt is suppressed, and the Dalai Lama flees. The Viet Minh, with Chinese backing, begin to infiltrate Laos, and the Indian government reveals Chinese incursions on its northern frontiers.

1960: China endures famine, brought on by "the worst natural calamities in a century," according to the Communists. The People's Communes begin to decay. Economic emphasis switches to agriculture, at the expense of industrialization. The smoldering Sino-Soviet dispute on tactics and goals, domestic and international, becomes public. The Party is purged, and a new thought-reform campaign begins.

1961: The first of two years dedicated to "consolidation and tidying up." China retrenches, concentrating upon agriculture to the exclusion of new industrial construction. Industrial production drops radically, but the Chinese people eat a little better for a brief time. The People's Communes and their "collectivized life and economy" cease to exist in practice, though the names and the slogans are retained. Peasants are permitted to farm their own garden plots and sell the produce in "free markets." The authority of the People's Government is seriously eroded, though its position is still secure. The opponents of Mao's extremist policies begin to assume effective control of the Party and state machinery. They ignore his more imaginative directives. The quarrel with Russia becomes more intense, and Viet Minh guerrillas begin to attack South Vietnam in force.

1962: The Communists continue to struggle with the internal problems produced by the excesses of the Great Leap Forward. Although the formal structure of the Communes is retained, Chinese agriculture reverts to precollectivization forms, with the individual farmer primarily responsible for tilling a small plot of ground and permitted to retain a larger share of his own produce. Nonetheless, the Commune structure is useful administratively for insuring that the state continues to extract the lion's share of a harvest that has increased somewhat, in part because natural conditions are better, but largely because the new laissez-faire policy acts as an incentive to greater production, while avoiding the maladministration characteristic of previous years. Even the obsessive goal of mechanizing agriculture is largely shelved. The moderates begin a period of effective liberalization which will improve economic conditions and allay popular discontent.

In the autumn Chinese armies attack Indian units all along their disputed northern border, routing them in the course of a few days. The Chinese then withdraw and settle down for protracted negotiations, having demonstrated their military superiority and having humiliated the Indians.

1963: The Sino-Soviet quarrel carries the Communist world to the point of an open break. After a series of European Party congresses during the latter half of 1962 in which the Chinese are ignored, the breaking point is reached at the congress of the East German Party in East Berlin in January 1963. Wu Hsiu-chuan, the Chinese delegate, is shouted down by the audience and Peking soon reacts by publicizing all the steps that have led to the schism, arguing always that the Chinese have sincerely tried to compromise. In the summer, the quarrel becomes public, explicit, and virulent as a last-minute attempt at reconciliation fails when a Chinese ideological delegation to Moscow proves completely obdurate. The Chinese attack Nikita Khrushchev by name, and the Russians retaliate. The steps that led to the break are revealed in a series of Chinese publications. The struggle for the allegiance of the Communist Parties of the underdeveloped world is intensified.

At home continuing relaxation brings increases in agricultural production and a marked improvement in living conditions from the miserable days following the Great Leap Forward. China seeks to expand her trade with the Western world, but has little to offer except promises. The Chinese people are urged to develop their self-sufficiency, and the dominant slogan of the year is: "We shall triumph by our own unaided efforts!"

1964: Continuing their attacks upon the Russians, the Chinese bend every effort to increase their influence in the underdeveloped world. Premier Chou En-lai devotes six weeks to a tour of Africa, behaving most circumspectly, but announcing on direct orders from Peking just before his departure that the continent is "ripe for revolution." Chinese influence in uncommitted Africa is stricken by Chou's enforced candor. Shortly thereafter, he carries the flag to Cambodia and Burma in Southeast Asia. Simultaneously, Peking's campaign for diplomatic respectability wins a major victory by French recognition, which the French follow with maneuvers that force the Nationalists to break their diplomatic ties with Paris. Curiously, the former French African territories do not follow suit.

Despite continuing negotiations over minor matters, involving in certain cases other Communist Parties as well, the Sino-Soviet quarrel remains irreconcilable. But the Chinese are doing very well in their drive toward conquest of Southeast Asia, with the military and political situations in South Vietnam deteriorating day by day. Peking's chief efforts are now concentrated upon exporting the revolution to Africa, Asia, and Latin America.

China explodes her first atomic bomb.

1965: Massive American intervention in South Vietnam shakes the basis of Maoist foreign policy. Instead of crumpling before the attacks of the Viet Cong, who are sustained by men, matériel, and inspiration from the north, the United States elects to fight to maintain a non-Communist state in South Vietnam—and, perhaps most significantly, to demonstrate to the Maoist leadership that "people's war" is no quick road to universal hegemony. The "liberation struggle" in South Vietnam, which appeared all but won at the beginning of the year, is experiencing severe difficulties by the end of 1965.

Defense Minister Lin Piao, Mao Tse-tung's chosen successor, reacts in September with the first major article attributed to him since the 1930s. The critical statement of policy—entitled "Hail the Victory of People's War!"—affirms the "inevitable victory" of the Maoist revolution throughout the world and notes that the focus of that movement is at present fixed in Vietnam. At the same time Lin Piao cautions both the Viet Cong and their sponsors in the Democratic Republic of (North) Vietnam that the struggle will be long and arduous. He advises the Viet Cong that, essentially, they must win their victory by their own efforts. Despite the ardent support of the Chinese people, he adds, the Vietnamese, like all oppressed peoples everywhere, must "liberate" themselves.

Within China, there are curious omens. Mao Tse-tung disappears from sight in early November, in part because he is shaping a major new policy and, it appears, in part because he is ill. A series of articles by obscure critics attacks established writers who, the Maoists say, have ridiculed Mao Tse-tung in veiled language. On the pretext of composing historical dramas, those writers have assailed the innermost citadels of Maoism. The relatively pleasant state of economic and ideological relaxation is, it appears, inimical to the Maoists.

1966: The Great Climacteric of the People's Republic of China begins with the new year in an allusive attack by the Political Commissar of the People's Liberation Army on "men entrenched in power within the Communist Party and bourgeois academic savants" who have turned against Maoism. The Commissar declares that all areas of life must undergo sweeping reform; those areas include: military affairs, the economy, the Party, the People's Government, all organs of publicity, and the entire academic community. Talk becomes action in the early summer, when the entire Peking Municipal Committee of the Chinese Communist Party is removed from office. Chief object of the attack in this first phase is Peng Chen, First Party Secretary and Mayor of Peking, who stands sixth in the national hierarchy.

Revelations accompanying the purge reveal that there has been in progress within the hierarchy since 1960 a massive—if ill-coordinated—campaign of effective resistance to the extreme policies of Mao Tse-tung and his intimates. Despite Lin Piao's "cleansing campaign," significant segments of the People's Liberation Army are still tainted by professionalism. Economists argue that material incentives and local initiative are essential to the proper functioning—and growth—of the Chinese economy. In practice, the peasants farm private plots and sell their private produce in free markets; almost all economic entities, from brickworks to bicycle factories, have been granted a fair degree of autonomy. Thought control, proclaimed with ever increasing intensity, has become more a token than a reality, and the obsessive concentration upon creation of the "perfect new Communist man" has receded. Conventional academic subjects have been given greater emphasis, and more lip service than devotion is paid to the sacrosanct Thought of Mao Tse-tung. Local cadres have guided their actions by immediate and generally practical considerations, rather than by rigid adherence to the extremist tenets of the

Thought. They have been encouraged in their pragmatism by powerful men in Peking.

Determined to make an end to all such backsliding and to restore the eroded authority of Mao Tse-tung, the Maoists proclaim the Great Proletarian Cultural Revolution. "All the old ways" are to be destroyed, including those "bourgeois-tainted customs" produced after "liberation" in 1949. The Maoists warn that China will become a capitalist country, "changing color from white to red," unless the evil new growths are "completely uprooted." It soon becomes apparent that all but the small group of Maoists themselves are to be purged. The great majority of the cadres at all levels are attacked for backsliding. The Political Bureau is reorganized by a rump Central Committee meeting acting under duress. Lin Piao is elevated to second place in the hierarchy, and Chairman (President) of the People's Republic Liu Shao-chi is dropped to eighth place. The Red Guards, millions of fanatical adolescents, swarm into the streets to enforce the Maoists' will. In the process they become for a time the virtual government of a nation in which all conventional structures of power are paralyzed.

But the intensity of the attack produces a reaction of corresponding intensity. The mass of cadres unites with the mass of the people to resist Maoist attacks. The quick victory envisaged by the Maoists recedes ever further, and the hard core of Maoists dwindles as practical politicians perceive the total threat of the Cultural Revolution. By the year's end the nation is close to chaos.

1967: The entire year sees a shifting battle that reduces China to a state of virtual anarchy. The Maoists concede almost all their major policy objectives, including the creation of a totally new structure of power. They seek to woo back the mass of the cadres, whom they have alienated, and they call upon the Liberation Army to preserve a minimum of order while backing their campaign to "seize power." But the Army, itself divided by the struggle, chooses to remain aloof from the power struggle wherever it can do so.

The Maoists' ideological defeat is signaled by their retreat from their chief objectives. By late 1967 they have repudiated the two chief purposes of the Cultural Revolution: the creation of a new form of "perfectly non-exploitive government" based upon the model of the Paris Commune of 1871; and "extensive democracy," an attempt to provide for direct rule by the masses. The Maoists seek frantically to control the forces they have set in motion, but the fundamental resentments of the Chinese masses are too powerful. Maoists and anti-Maoists fight in the streets of China's major cities, and armed military units clash from time to time. A new China is being shaped, though it will probably take several years before it comes into coherent existence. It is likely to be a much more realistic nation in both its internal and external policies. The era of Mao Tse-tung is ending amid utter turmoil which could prove to be a great catharsis of the Chinese spirit.

China's foreign relations enter a disastrous new period. The Maoists offend and attack almost every nation in the world except Albania—their single ally. Relations with other Communist countries have never been so strained. The American effort in Vietnam gains momentum, further frustrating the Maoists—and giving fresh ideological ammunition to the anti-Maoists, who attack the extremists for their impractical, ineffectual, and hazardous foreign policies. Nonetheless, China explodes her first hydrogen bomb in June 1967, and rocketry development proceeds at a good pace. Despite the severe economic dislocation worked by the Cultural Revolution, the core military programs continue. But the sweeping changes in the Chinese mystique significantly decrease the danger of a nuclear confrontation between China and other powers.

In 1968 the internal struggle continues, with the Maoists' failing to re-establish their authority. Revolutionary Committees are established, supplanting previous government and Party organs. Theoretically Maoists and mouthing Maoist slogans, they are actually alliances of generals and old-line cadres. Their purpose is to impose order and restore economic life. They are frustrated by the intransigence of Maoist "revolutionary rebels" and by "economism," the rise of a form of primitive, local free enterprise. Disorder, even to open armed clashes, spreads. China is "like a radish, red outside and white inside" as all men quote

Mao Tse-tung for their own purposes. Industry and transport are severely hampered, but agricultural production increases, for the farmers are encouraged by lack of state interference and by the opportunity to retain much of their own produce. Regionalism intensifies.

The Viet Cong launch their "Spring Offensive," spreading almost as much dismay in Peking and Washington. The catharsis of the Cultural Revolution, stimulated by the failure of "people's war" in Vietnam, is probably irreversible. Nonetheless, there is danger that a failure of American resolution in the new, largely military phase of the war may yet confirm China's crusade of "world-wide liberation." Nuclear and rocketry development, though hampered by the turmoil of the Cultural Revolution, proceeds effectively.

Mao Tse-tung, his ambition feeding on his success, was confronted for the first time in 1957 with an enemy he could not conquer by the tactics that had carried him to power after nearly three decades of struggle. His purpose remained constant: to make China the paramount nation of the world. But he was thwarted by China's limited natural resources and by her minuscule industrial establishment. He therefore proclaimed the Great Leap Forward to conquer both man and nature. When the Great Leap failed, he directed his followers to "liberate" the world by the tactics of a "people's war." Subversion, propaganda, and guerrilla campaigns were to sweep Peking-oriented Communists into power throughout the underdeveloped world. Then the capitalist world was to perish because it had been deprived of both its markets and its sources of raw materials in the underdeveloped world. The concept was as sweeping as the Great People's Communes—and as futile. Turning again to internal problems in 1966, Mao determined to remake China first in order to remake the world afterward. The final goal remained Chinese tutelage of all mankind.

Mao Tse-tung is the creature of his own past and China's past. The events that occurred from Matteo Ricci's arrival in China in the late sixteenth century until 1949 shaped a nation, determining its emotional and intellectual responses. The chronological framework having been displayed in the foregoing sections, it is now possible to examine in detail the psychological pattern of the Communists, the measures they adopted, and the results they achieved.

Part Four

THE MYSTIQUE

The Sinocentricity, Authoritarianism, And Utopianism Evident in Traditional And Communist Patterns of Thought

Since that protracted moment in pre-eternity when he over-took the great apes, man has been oppressed by a longing for certainty in a world where the moods of nature and the vagaries of his own emotions have confounded his understanding and menaced his existence. During the dark centuries before recorded time began, infant humanity created black magic to treat with the powers of the deep and the spirits of the hills. Folk wisdom everywhere still clings to original superstition, handed down in the unconscious of all mankind.

The central tradition of the Western world, after the dawn of sophistication, pursued certainty on at least two distinct planes. Systematic theology sought to illuminate the mysteries of the supernatural by the exercise of intelligence. Scientific investigation sought to measure the ways of nature. Both approaches proceeded from the underlying assumption that greater knowledge—of the spirit of man and the will of nature—would assist man in controlling both nature and himself.

The central tradition born when the Chinese world transcended universal superstition favored neither of the methods employed by the West. Instead, China sought certainty by imposing a man-made order on the face of things. The Chinese assumed that both man and nature could be controlled by decreeing the proper emotions for the one and categorizing the functions of the other. Free analysis, proceeding from one discovery to the next, was not the Chinese way.

The official Chinese tradition, therefore, developed an obsession with categories. The ancients spoke of the five relationships that governed human intercourse; of the six domestic animals; of the five elements; and of the eight trigrams employed in divination. Today, the People's Liberation Army is governed by the three principles of discipline and the eight basic regulations.

Recently, new canons have been added to the welter of numerical categories that shape the life of Communist China. A People's Commune in Hopei Province has decreed "Four-Togetherness and Five-Love Inspection Day." In Shensi Province the "three-three system of leadership is now universally enforced." It is not to be confused with either the "two-five system" or the "three-seven system."

There is magic in numbers—Socialist magic, if not black magic.

9

What Is a Man?

The Confucian State-Ideology that Shaped the Chinese Mind

"What is a man?"

The question's form displays its Western origin. The Chinese normally ask: "What is man?" or "What is an individual?" It is more than a linguistic quirk that there is so often no middle ground between the grand generalization and the minute particularization in Chinese.

Yet the traditional Chinese answer was clear, comprehending all three forms of the question. A man or an individual was nothing unless he was that rare figure, the hero or the great man—the Princely Man or the Sage. Even then, he was a member of a precisely defined category, owing his greatness to his conformity to the standards of that category, rather than to his wholly individual qualities. Mankind was all, transcending the supernatural and the individual in the same degree. Manners were mankind, for a sanctified code of etiquette determined exactly how men were to behave—and to feel—in all conceivable situations, so that they might function as cogwheels in the great machine of society. The ideal pattern made no provision for emergencies that were not already anticipated. Unexpected situations simply did not arise in the well-ordered society, any more than the minute polyps in a coral atoll were ever forced to a conscious choice.

Manners were called *li*, and the *Li Chi*, the *Record of Rites*, which was compiled from earlier texts in the second century B.C., was a fundamental canon of traditional Chinese society. The *li* prescribed correct behavior in a hierarchical society upon the assumption that proper conduct toward the external world would result in the proper internal reactions. "The man who possesses manners [*li*] is at peace," declared the *Li Chi*, "while, without manners, all else is imperiled. Therefore it is said: We must emulate him who possesses manners." [1] It was not only the Chinese compulsion to avoid conflict that made *li* essential. The definitive passage in the canon asserted specifically that manners made society function properly in all its aspects.

"The ways of truth, morality, compassion, and righteousness —all the things by which men live are meaningless without *li*," declared the *Li Chi*. "Duty, endeavor, discussion, and the processes of law—without *li*, they are uncertain. The prince and the minister, the high and the low, parents and children, elder and younger brothers, one friend and another—without *li*, their positions are not firmly fixed. Without *li*, students and masters cannot achieve understanding. Administration, military campaigns, executive decisions, and law enforcement—none can be accomplished without the sanction of *li*. The sacrifices and devotions to spirits and gods are insincere and ineffective without *li*. The prince must, therefore, above all else glorify [and exemplify] *li*." [2]

Such passages warned against the evils that followed disregard of the fundamental *li*. The practical Chinese were so concerned with the hortatory effect of their words that they even stated the Golden Rule in inverse form: "Do not do unto others what you would not have them do unto you." But the *Li Chi* unbent to the extent of promising Utopia if only all men practiced *li* and thus imposed order upon the universe. It even described the mythical Golden Age when *li* prevailed:

"When the Great Way was followed, all under heaven was regulated for the benefit of all the people. The ruler chose ministers of virtue and ability who dealt with their fellow men in righteous sincerity and harmony. Men, therefore, did not love only their own parents, nor nurture only their own children. The aged were cherished until their deaths; those in their prime had em-

[1] *Li Chi*, Vol. 6, my translation.—R. E.
[2] *Ibid.*

ployment suitable to their talents; and children grew up in fitting circumstances. The people gave loving kindness to orphans, to widows, to the [aged] childless, and to those stricken by disabling diseases. All human beings received proper care. Men had their work, and women had their homes.

"There was an abundance of wealth, since it was not good to leave wealth unproductive as if it were buried in the ground. But the individual did not accumulate goods solely for his personal gratification. Realizing that it was wrong not to do so, everyone worked with all his strength. But he did not exert his energies solely for his own benefit. There was, therefore, no reason for men to scheme or plot, and men did not contend against each other. . . . There were neither thieves, nor rebels pillaging the land, for each man had his proper place. When men threw open their front gates and did not ever feel the need to close them again, that was the time of what we call the Great Commonwealth." [3]

This Chinese Utopia was the *Ta Tung*, the Great Commonwealth which was the ideal of Kang Yu-wei among the reformers of 1898. Its chief characteristic was the absence of all conflict in a realm of harmonious order. The fruition of individual talent was a secondary concern. The great majority of Chinese philosophers and statesmen dedicated themselves to the description and the attainment of the Great Commonwealth from the time Confucius flourished in the sixth century B.C. until the Communist conquest in A.D. 1949.

The West often described the ideal society, but only rarely—and then within the most narrow scope—did it attempt to create the Utopias of the philosophers' and humanitarians' dreams. Robert Owen's experiments in the Midlands, Brook Farm, the Oneida Colony, and even Brigham Young's theocracy were among the number of isolated Anglo-Saxon Utopias which soon perished—or conformed. Yet many of the principles, if not the practical measures, that obsessed those reformers have now become part of the normal fabric of Western society.

The Chinese have not only yearned after the ideal for millennia. They have actually attempted time after time to create an ab-

[3] *Ibid.*

solute and universal Utopia. This pursuit owes as much to their unique secular theology as to their passion for a perfect mundane order. Because the central tradition of China has been agnostic since 200 B.C., the Chinese have sought spiritual satisfaction not from the supernatural but from the eternal ebb and flow of the generations of mankind. Sustained by no vision of another world, but discerning the actual lineaments of divinity in the face of humanity, the Chinese have naturally sought to create their paradises in this world.

China has always yearned after the perfect earthly system that utilizes individuals as its building blocks but is above personal interests. It has, therefore, always been necessary to convince both the builders and their animate bricks that they possessed *no* personal interests. The consequent conflict between what a man is expected to do and what he wants to do, infinitely more intense than similar conflicts in the West, has dominated the development of the Chinese individual. The tension has been manifest in the continuing protestant tradition; in the persistence of heresies from the official philosophy; in the popularity of plays and novels that were licentious by the orthodox standard; and even in official Memorials and Mandates. The struggle to impose conformity by fiat has consistently disturbed a society based upon the premise that the creation of the official Utopia was its own reward. The system has not only disregarded the happiness of the individual, but has actually regarded individual fulfillment as an evil ambition that must be thwarted.

Mao Tse-tung's heroic striving after the Utopia he envisions is, therefore, neither unique nor even novel. Nor does Mao, whose imported creed promises the transcendent Utopia, disdain to seek popular support by recalling the mythical Golden Age which Confucius sought to re-create. China's present convulsion is merely the latest—and by no means the ultimate—stage in a process that began about 900 B.C., when annals described the Edenlike abundance and order that had once prevailed in China, not by the dispensation of God, but through the wisdom of the protohistorical Duke of Chou.

Confucius was the first to impose order on the traditional legends of Utopia. But his works were often amended within the orthodox dispensation. His greatest successor, Mencius, who lived about two hundred years after him, somewhat untidily provided for the essential relief from oppression. Since the Prince ruled for the benefit of the people under the Mandate of Heaven, Mencius argued that the people might employ the remedy of revolution when oppression or neglect offered *prima facie* proof that the Mandate had been withdrawn. Later, Hsun Tzu, last of the great triumvirate, attacked Mencius for his idealism. He insisted that there was *never* a justification for disobeying authority or for altering the absolute precepts laid down by Confucius. "There is no way of human living," he wrote, "which does not have its distinctions; no distinctions are greater than the rules of proper conduct [*li*]; there are no rules of proper conduct greater than the Sage-kings'." [4]

Even its heretics affirmed the authority of the tradition by the manner of their deviation. Wang Mang, the "Socialist Emperor" who ruled from 6 B.C., to A.D. 23, actually sought to create a new system. Wang An-shih, the social-democratic statesman who lived in the twelfth century A.D., was a New Dealer. He was concerned with administrative and intellectual adjustments that would preserve the fundamentals of the old order, rather than with altering basic principles. The central tradition of Chinese thought, therefore, descended in direct line to Kang Yu-wei, who envisioned a new Great Commonwealth—and to Mao Tse-tung himself. Because it has always sought categorized solutions, the Chinese mind is quite hospitable to the visions of the Marxists. Conditioned by a history of occasional dissent which failed to shake the central tradition, the Chinese are not daunted by intra-Communist controversies, which may appear to Westerners to impair the doctrine's transcendent authority. Above all, they are accustomed to submitting themselves to intellectual authority as enunciated by the temporal rulers.

The mind developed by the central tradition of Chinese history is hyperlogical yet utterly dependent upon recorded precedent. Because its literalness is effectively tempered neither by a sense of humor nor a sense of awe, it is inclined to hurl itself into

[4] Fung Yu-lan, *A History of Chinese Philosophy*, Derk Bodde, trans. (Peking, 1937), Vol. I., p. 282.

vast excesses in obedience to logic. This tendency is aggravated by the Chinese language, which is at once highly concrete and grandly imprecise. The literal, concrete form in which abstract ideas are expressed in speech often convinces disputants that they are dealing with hard reality when they are actually playing with verbal shuttlecocks that have no defined meaning. The classical written language, at the other extreme, is so elided syntactically and so poor in vocabulary that the reader can choose at his pleasure from a wide range of meanings for each of the actual words employed. The result has been a sweeping imprecision of thought and the proliferation of a vast body of commentary on the original classics. When the origin of words became more important than the meaning they attempted to express, battalions of lexicographers warred with squadrons of exegetes, trampling reality into the dust of the battlefield.[5]

There is an inescapable—and perhaps overworked—parallel between the Chinese mind and the Talmudic mind, which developed among the Jews of the Diaspora. In both cases the obsession with linguistic subtlety and recorded authority rendered the thinker's contact with reality extremely tenuous, although the Jewish scholar was withdrawing from oppressive reality, while the Confucian was convinced that he had attained ascendancy over reality. Despite the differences in their actual circumstances, the Chinese *literatus* and the Talmudic scholar both displayed great arrogance. Each had the utmost confidence in the scope of his powers and in the conviction that intellect had established primacy over material reality. Each lived in an inverted world in which his energies were directed to examination of neither nature nor himself but to the incessant turning over of commentaries on doctrine. Both the orthodox Confucians and the orthodox Jews

[5] None of these observations means that modern Chinese is not a suitable language for the study of the natural sciences or that the Chinese mind is not adapted to those studies. On the contrary, the language's concrete nature makes it a good vehicle for expressing concepts relating to concrete phenomena, no matter how abstruse they may be, while Chinese scientists abroad are foremost in theoretical physics. But Chinese is not a good instrument for political study, since concrete expression of an abstraction—which may or may not be valid—often leads the investigator to believe that he is dealing with reality when he is actually discussing a mirage.

were truly people of the book, more concerned with the name than the essence. They were, further, people of the doctrine, obsessed with appearance rather than reality. Neither tradition experienced the equivalent of the Renaissance, which freed the Western mind from scholasticism.

Convinced that Utopia could be attained through the minds of men, the Confucians were rarely distracted from their political purposes by either the natural or the supernatural. Men believed that they themselves were not only the measure but the masters of all phenomena.

Many Chinese still possess overwhelming confidence—which survives every disproof—that they can finally enforce their will upon men and events. This touch of madness preserves them from the grosser forms of insanity, for they do not often collapse emotionally when their worlds collapse. It also leads them to defy the fates. Chiang Kai-shek may appear somewhat ridiculous in his infinite confidence that he will reconquer the mainland of China. But he is sustained by historical precedent in the Ching Dynasty's final suppression of the Taiping Rebellion, which appeared for almost two decades about to destroy the Empire. He conveniently ignores the closer parallel of the Ming loyalists who were themselves destroyed after holding Formosa against the Manchus for nearly fifty years. Mao Tse-tung, contemplating the grand panorama of Chinese history and his own victories over impossible odds, has displayed infinite confidence in his capacity to reshape not only China but the entire world.

Both leaders owe not only their habits of mind but also the social material with which they work to an unsuccessful politician who was born about five hundred and fifty years before Christ in the feudal State of Lu, which is now part of Shantung Province. His surname was Kung; his personal name was Chiu; and his courtesy name was Chung-ni. But the Chinese have known him for two and a half millennia as Kung Fu-tze, which means the Master Kung, while the West calls him Confucius, after the early Jesuits' Latinization. He was the single most influential figure the world has known in the political, intellectual, and spiritual realms. His effect upon the beliefs, the manners, the institutions, and the intellectual processes of that considerable portion of humanity which inhabits East Asia has been as great in scope and as lasting in practice as the joint influence exerted upon the West by Jesus Christ, Aristotle, and Julius Caesar.

The essential temper of China is revealed by the fact that this man, who shaped a civilization, did not consider himself a creator, but merely the transmitter of truths previously revealed and the champion of institutions which were once perfect.

Like so many of the men who have shaped our world, Confucius was born into the depressed middle classes, according to imperfect tradition in 551 B.C. He was reared in shabby gentility, rendered at once more poignant and more bearable by memories of past glory. He was descended from the princely house of the feudal State of Sung, his great-grandfather having migrated to the neighboring principality of Lu when the family fell into disfavor and poverty. His father, who was an army officer, died when the boy was three, and Confucius was brought up by his mother. At nineteen he married and started his official career at the lowest level, first as a keeper of the stores of grain and later as warden of the public lands. Tradition relates that he became Prime Minister of the State of Lu in 501 B.C., after spending two decades as a wandering official who hired his services to any prince who would employ him. Confucius was so successful in the stewardship of his native State of Lu that a rival prince who feared Lu's growing strength diverted the ruler from his strict attention to Confucius' teaching with presents of female dancers and musicians. Ashamed of his feudal lord's neglect, the apocryphal tale ends, Confucius resigned his office to live as a wandering teacher from 497 B.C. until he died in 479 B.C.

Unlike other officials when they fell from power, the impecunious Confucius neither tended his ancestral estates nor earned his bread through commerce, but lived instead upon the tuition fees paid in kind by his disciples. The first professional teacher and thinker in Chinese history—indeed, the first intellectual— Confucius disdained the homely virtues of husbandry and toil for his disciples, as well as for himself. Seeking his ideal, the Princely Man, he created a new class of administrative technicians and established the tradition that the nonproductive bureaucrat, the philosopher-minister, was the highest expression of humanity.

To a disciple who wished to learn agriculture and market gardening, Confucius replied: "What a small-minded man are you!" Since they neither traded in goods nor produced them, but lived by selling their knowledge of the ancient rites and their verbal skill, the disciples of Confucius were attacked as parasites. Said a text of the Taoist school:[6] "You are a mere word-monger, who talks nonsense about Kings Wen and Wu [mythical founders of the Chou Dynasty]. . . . You do not sow and yet are you clothed. Your lips patter and your tongue wags, and you produce your own rights and wrongs, with which to mislead the rulers of the world and prevent scholars from reverting to the fundamentals of things."[7]

Although contemporary detractors attacked him as a radical who plotted to create a new order of society, Confucius professed only a desire to re-create the Golden Age. His inspiration was the sparse written records of the past, which he used as guides to action and as textbooks for his disciples. Some of his texts were undoubtedly genuine, but the Confucians edited them all heavily. On the authority of the past, he created a state-ideology which was to serve both as a moral standard and a handbook of administration for more than two millennia. Knowledge of the Confucian texts and a felicitous literary style inscribed in graceful ideographs where the sole qualifications for public office from 150 B.C., when the Han Dynasty made Confucianism its official ideology, until A.D. 1905, when the Ching Dynasty abandoned the system of Civil Service Examinations.

Although *li* was the basis of the social order, Confucius somewhat paradoxically insisted that proper behavior was meaningless if it did not proceed from virtue. In a typically homiletic passage from the *Analects,* the work that embodied the doctrines of Confucius in Socratic dialogues, the Master answered a request to explain the following passage from the canonical *Book of Odes:*

[6] The name of the school—incidentally, pronounced Dowist—comes from the *tao,* literally, "a road," but in this sense "the great way [of the universe]," which cannot be explained, but must be perceived by the individual through supralogical inspiration.

[7] Fung, p. 51.

As she artfully smiles,
What dimples appear!
Her bewitching eyes
Show their colors so clear.
Ground spotless and candid
For tracery splendid!

"The painting comes after the groundwork," he said.
"Then manners [li] are secondary?" asked the disciple.
"It is he who unfolds my meaning," replied the Master. "Now indeed, I can begin to discuss the Odes with him."

The authoritative interpretation of this passage, which is, like every Confucian passage, much interpreted, holds: "A man must have a nature of sincere genuineness before he may practice ceremonial and etiquette, just as a beautiful woman must first have a bewitching smile and lovely eyes, before she may make use of powder and rouge." [8]

The Confucians thus boasted that their system, unlike the systems of competing political philosophers, rested upon moral values, rather than upon coercive law codes. In reality, Confucian moral values derived from indoctrination and not from any higher moral sanction within the individual or outside him. It was a morality limited socially as well as in inspiration. The common people were required neither to possess virtue nor to practice the higher protocol, since the example of the virtuous *literati* would insure their good behavior.

The ruling classes, for their part, were inculcated with both protocol and virtue by rigid education and by social pressure. Since it proved possible to teach protocol but not virtue, Confucian morality became a systematic pretense, and the display of proper manners became the final measure of a man's value—in his own eyes, as well as others'. Protocol thus developed into a substitute for personal and political morality. Forms superseded substance. Neither administrative efficiency nor personal honesty was the true measure of a man. It was, however, vitally important that he wear the appropriate robes on ceremonial occasions; that he observe a three-year period of mourning for his parents; that

[8] *Ibid.*, p. 66.

his personal life not be openly offensive; that he be able to compose accurate couplets; and that his decrees accord with precedent.

Under Confucianism the family was the basic unity of society. The microcosm embodied the macrocosm, for the state itself was explicitly a great family,[9] its proper functioning dependent upon the fulfillment of the responsibilities and duties that superiors and inferiors owed to each other, just as concern on the one hand and respect on the other governed the relationship between parents and children. In the ethical muddle of Confucianism, only two strictures were absolute: an individual might never violate protocol nor might he injure either the state or the family, regardless of whether he was driven to rebellious deeds by conscience or by self-interest. Since they assumed that the practice of protocol would prevent conflicts between the interests of the family and those of the state, the Confucian classics implied—rather than stating explicitly—what nature dictated. In the unlikely event of conflict between the welfare of the state and the family, the interests of the smaller group were paramount.

In theory a perfect blending of ethics and empiricism under philosopher-kings who disdained compulsion, the Confucian system was amoral in practice. Since the magnitude of the state transformed it into an abstraction, the only absolute imperatives were obedience and service to the clan. The Duke of She observed to Confucius: "In my part of the country there is a man so upright that when his father appropriated a sheep he bore witness to it." Confucius replied: "The upright people in my part of the country are different from that, for a father will screen his son, and a son his father. In that there lies uprightness." [10] The person who was affected determined whether a deed the West might call a crime was condemned or praised.

[9] Even in modern Chinese, "everyone" is expressed by *ta-chia*, a term made up of individual words meaning "big family."

[10] Fung, p. 67. The Duke did not mean to imply that sons should be encouraged to report their fathers' misdeeds to the authorities in the manner of modern totalitarianists. He was, rather, pointing to an extraordinary example of virtue. Confucius, on the other hand, expressed one of the few absolutes of his ethical system in his sharp rebuttal. The claims of kinship always took precedence over abstract justice.

Eschewing effective legal safeguards and endorsing a wholly relative morality, Confucianism actually encouraged stealing from the body politic. Official corruption—reaching up to the prime minister and down to the lowliest assistant clerk in a junior magistracy—was a consistent characteristic of Confucian civilization, not only in China itself, but in Japan and Southeast Asia as well. From the junior civil servant who administered the government's monopoly of the salt trade in a minor prefecture to the Viceroy Li Hung-chang himself, an official of the Ching Dynasty was expected to enrich himself in the office he had, more often than not, purchased. The machinery of government was not merely oiled by bribes, it actually ran on the daily fuel of graft, favoritism, and nepotism. Men finally owed no absolute duty to society, except observance of the proper forms. Confucian civilization neither imposed moral standards nor evoked patriotic loyalty, but fostered ethical anarchy, since all standards were relative.

The official life of the ideal man of the Confucian ideology, the cultivated official, was a jungle in which contending factions clawed for advantage. But the Prime Minister and his scapegrace nephew seven times removed both found security and comfort within the fortress of the family. As long as a man did not break with his family, he was sure of enjoying food, comfort, and even the glory of his kinsmen's public prestige—hardly less bright for being reflected. Next to death or exile, the most terrible punishment was expulsion from the family, since it left a man almost literally naked in the world. The family was further solidified by external pressure. Each member bore direct responsibility under law for every other member's deeds. If the head of the family were executed for treason, his brothers were also punished and all his male descendants were castrated at the age of sixteen—to drive the example home and to insure that no family would endure "inclined to treason by nature and for revenge." It was therefore essential that each man be not only his brother's keeper, but his tenth cousin's keeper as well.

Offering these benefits and exercising these sanctions, the Chinese family easily imposed its will upon the individual. The enforced loyalty to the clan, with its attendant responsibility, was absolute. Absolute, too, was the individual's claim on the clan.

The injunction to share with all who were kin often made more noble those who knew neither glory nor wealth. Ideally, it taught the masses to be generous not only with those who bore the same name, but also with those who shared the common lot. The doctrine of the educated man's responsibility for those less fortunate also tended to produce a class of responsible local gentry which was generous to its inferiors and devoted to its acres. But the great Court families, often removed from the land and the people for generations, came to consider their own self-interest a law above all else.

The Confucians were little concerned with divine beings. Like Plato, Confucius apparently believed in a supernatural intelligence, but he never described the entity he called Heaven. Like Plato, he felt it socially desirable that men should strive to obey the presumed wishes of the deity. Toward the spirits that inhabited the Chinese pantheon, Confucius preserved a cool and almost disdainful skepticism. "To devote oneself earnestly to one's duty to humanity, and, while respecting the spirits, to keep away from them, may be called wisdom," he said. To a disciple asking for instruction in his duties to the spirits, the Master replied: "When still unable to do your duty to men, how can you do your duty to the spirits?" When the same disciple asked about death, Confucius answered: "Not yet understanding life, how can you understand death?" [11] For the rest, Confucius believed that sacrifices to the spirits were doubtless useful to exalt the spirit of man and to incline him toward proper behavior.

Hsun Tzu, the devoutly orthodox early commentator, explained: "Sacrificial rites . . . represent the height of altruism, faithfulness, love, and reverence . . . the completion of propriety and refinement. . . . The Sage plainly understands it; the scholar and Superior Man accordingly perform it; the official observes it; and among the common people it is considered to be a serving of the spirits . . . with such sorrow and reverence one serves the dead as one serves the living, and serves the departed as one serves those who are present. What is served has neither substance nor shadow, yet this is the completion of refinement." [12]

[11] *Ibid.*, p. 58.

[12] *Ibid.*, p. 351.

Only in one aspect were all classes of society united in a common mystical emotion. Just as a pioneer in the wilderness assisted his neighbor so that he might be similarly served, the Chinese served his ancestors so that he might be remembered by his descendants. A skeptical race found true spiritual exaltation in the grand procession of the generations of mankind through the halls of time. The contemporary philosopher Fung Yu-lan has observed: "The Confucians, as we have seen, held that the function of marriage lies in creating a new self to replace the old. The hope of the old self is that the new one will be able to perpetuate the life and activity of the old self down to 'ten thousand generations,' and the new self, if it can fulfill this aspiration, is a filial offspring."

Since not only the spirit but also the flesh was a sacred bequest from one's ancestors, the Chinese felt a mystical compulsion to preserve the body untouched. To this day many a devoted Chinese husband will try desperately to buy blood for his dying wife, but will rarely offer his own. He will not betray his ancestors by mutilating his body, which is theirs.

"Yo-chang Tzu-chun," declared the *Li Chi*, "injured his foot in coming down from his hall, and for some months was unable to go out. Ever after this he had a look of sorrow. . . . [He said:] When, his parents having given birth to his body whole, he returns it to them whole, this may be called filial piety. When no member of it has been mutilated and no disgrace done to any part of the person, it may be called whole. Hence the Superior Man does not dare to take the slightest step forgetful of his filial duty. But now I forgot the way of filial piety, which is why I wear a look of sorrow. [A son] should not forget his parents in a single lifting of his feet, and therefore he will walk in the highway and not take a by-way: he will use a boat and not attempt to wade through a stream; not daring, with the body left him by his parents, to go into peril." [13]

Thus the sacred continuity of the generations reduced to a sprained ankle and selfishness exalted as the high virtue of self-denying filial piety. A man showed the basest disregard of the spirits of his ancestors by failing to indulge the vessel they had

[13] *Ibid.*, p. 358.

bequeathed him. By the same reasoning, failure to beget sons was a greater tragedy than it would ever be in the *self*-conscious West. The line's ending meant that not only one's self, but all one's ancestors, were cut off from the flow of the generations.

While the everlasting family provided social and spiritual security, the intellectual basis of Confucian civilization was the Doctrine of Rectification of Names. When the Duke of She asked him to outline the principles of government, the Master replied simply: "Let the ruler be ruler, and the minister minister; let the father be father, and the son son." [14] The meaning was clear: the individual should first understand the ideal concept of his role and should then insure the proper functioning of society by emulating the ideal. Anarchy was the outcome of men's failing to understand their allotted roles. Proper definition of concepts—the expression rather than the reality—was more important than the actions of the government. If all men thought in the prescribed manner and the ruler's thoughts were also correct, it would automatically follow that the nation was properly ruled. Superficially idealistic, the stress upon correct terminology created a reverence for mere words, providing opportunities for rulers like Mao Tse-tung who manipulate language for their own convenience.

The *Analects* record: "When Chi Kang Tzu [who had usurped power in Lu] asked Confucius for the way to govern, Confucius replied: "To govern means to rectify.[15] If you, Sir, will lead in the rectification, who will dare not be to rectified?' " Confucius carefully avoided telling the usurper whether he was to resign because he was not a legitimate ruler or was merely to rule correctly in the future. When the same man asked: "How would it do to execute the lawless for the good of the law-abiding?" he replied: "What need, sir, is there of capital punishment in your administration? If your desire is for good, the people will be good.

---

[14] *Ibid.*, p. 60.

[15] The character for rectify or adjust (正) and the character for govern (政) are pronounced alike, and the latter contains the former. Government, therefore, does not consist merely in administering the state, but requires the ruler to impose his own morality upon all men.

The moral character of the ruler is the wind; the moral character of those beneath him is the grass. When the grass has the wind upon it, it assuredly bends."

The Doctrine of Rectification of Names gave sanction to absolutism, since the uneducated masses were merely the substance upon which the autocrat's good example worked. Popular participation in government would violate the doctrine, since it was *not* correct for subjects to behave like rulers.

Although the ideology provided both the philosophical justification and the institutional apparatus for rigid autocracy, the Confucian state was not officious. The ruler was discouraged from exercising his authority intrusively, since the people were to emulate his perfect example, rather than move at his explicit command. The correct ruler tended to great affairs. He provided safeguards against external attack and natural calamities, but interfered as little as possible in the people's daily lives. The ideal was a benevolent laissez faire, based upon authority so secure that it was rarely asserted. Although the government was not intrusive, the best talents were drawn into the bureaucracy, and little function remained for private institutions. The character of the Confucian state is indicated by a list of some of the institutions which, ideally, did *not* exist.

There were no great commercial or industrial organizations pursuing their own purposes, but only scattered small merchants whose greatest ambition—if their wealth was sufficient to permit such aspirations—was that their sons should become officials. There were no private schools or universities, except those institutions which taught the classics in preparation for state-controlled colleges, whose sole purpose was training men to pass the Civil Service Examinations and become scholar-officials. There were no newspapers or magazines except the *Court Gazette*, which promulgated decrees and posted official promotions; no private houses publishing books, except for authorized reprints of the classics; no libraries open to the public; and no private libraries whose contents were not limited by the official Index. There were no lawyers to defend private citizens under the voluminous law codes necessitated by the Empire's size; the district magistrate was, in himself, detective-in-chief, prosecuting attorney, defense counsel, judge, jury, and court of appeals. There were, in the beginning, no churches except the state church, whose pontiff, the Emperor, performed the Confucian rites, though the Taoists early and the Buddhists later founded rival temples and monasteries. Since there was not even a distinct military caste, all things derived from the Emperor and flowed through the bureaucracy.

The ideal human being was a social unit. His thoughts and his emotions were prescribed by the Confucian state-ideology, and his actions were controlled by the family. It was, quite simply, bad to be outstanding in any manner not specifically sanctioned by the official ideology. Although they were tolerated and sometimes even patronized by the Court, artists were formally abhorred. The hardworking official might win renown by writing verse in the conventional pattern, but the professional writer was outside the pale. The constant emphasis lay upon conformity rather than individuality, and upon the perfect functioning of a system rather than the development of the individual's powers. Perfect harmony was not to be marred by either original thought or flights of the creative imagination. Compromise and expediency were exalted, since all things were relative. The truly unforgivable deed was to take an absolute or an irreversible position.

Such, in broad outline, was the ideal organism called the Central Kingdom. Such was the picture official historians, all deliberately more orthodox than Confucius himself, drew for posterity. Such was the dominant tradition, more powerful and more enduring than any other tradition the world has known.

Yet China, like other great civilizations, developed traditions of culture and thought outside the chief school. The official tradition did *not* encompass all China, and China was *not* a static civilization, intellectually or socially. A number of nonconformist forces were at work from the beginning, even modifying the Confucian ideology in its formative days.

As much because it denied the persistently heterodox yearnings of human nature as because of its inherent departures from reality, the Confucian ideology never created the perfect closed order it sought. China simply could not be sealed off from outside influences, despite occasional cruel persecution of religious and intellectual heretics and a predilection for burning heterodox books. A country so vast, inhabited by peoples so diverse, was actually hospitable to new religions, new intellectual concepts, and new artistic forms. The administrative system itself was altered from time to time to accommodate concepts or material devices coming from outside. If China absorbed her conquerors, she inevitably absorbed some of their customs too. From trousers for equestrians to the after-life promised by Mahayana Buddhism, mystery and diversity from abroad enlivened the rational and featureless Utopia of the Confucians. There was change and the Confucians mourned, for the nation was constantly moving away from the practices of antiquity.

Even the *literati* occasionally rebelled, writing plays that entertained rather than moralized or satirizing the sacred tradition in essays and novels. Han Yu, the Chesterton of Confucianism, whose essays were perfect examples of the classical style, actually issued a decree ordering the crocodiles of the southern rivers to cease preying upon the people of his magistracy. Of course, such a divertissement was secondary to his serious pursuits, like offering a Memorial urging the Emperor to prohibit enshrinement of a relic of the Buddha. And he did address his exhortations to "the senior official of the crocodiles."

It was, moreover, not easy for an ordinary human being to be an exemplary Confucian, and the only traditional institution that survived without major modifications was the family system. It has often been said of both Emperors and Ministers that they were officially Confucian and personally Taoist, while depending in crises upon the system of rewards and punishment devised by the Legalist Philosophers.

China had always known lively protestants who touched men's hearts more deeply than Confucianism. The humanists of China were the Taoists—with their refusal to define their terms, in contrast to Confucian categorizing; with their joy in joy for its own sake; and with their political doctrine of *wu wei*, inaction. When public affairs grew burdensome or problems seemed beyond solution, the staunchest scholar-official might retire with his cronies, a few gallons of wine, and a covey of dancing girls—to allow events to find their own solution. That was *wu wei*.

The spirits, disdained by Confucius, claimed devotion of common mankind. Buddhism, entering China in the first century A.D., provided the spiritual excitement and the aesthetic satisfaction the austere Confucian tradition lacked. A minor Confucian warrior-sage underwent metamorphosis into Kwan Yin, the Madonna of the East. A dynasty of hereditary Taoist popes maintained their somewhat scandalous state for more than ten centuries. The humanistic folk traditions running beneath the astringent Confucian tradition endured because they appealed to common humanity.

Confucianism, nonetheless, shaped the public character of the Chinese, while China lived in greater isolation from external influences than any other major civilization. It was, therefore, the Confucian mind that dominated China's development—and bore the shock of Western knowledge in the nineteenth century. Because the tradition placed mankind so high, Charles Darwin's relegating biological man to the same plane as the other animals upset Chinese even more than it did devout Christians. Worship of eternal humanity was a mockery if man were merely another animal whose origins could be fixed in time and whose future evolution into another form of life was not unlikely. Nor could the Chinese argue, with some Western rationalizers, that man's body might be an animal vessel, but the soul therein enshrined was a spark of divinity. Body and spirit were united in their mystique, which virtually ignored any divinity beyond man. For the Confucian mind, man was all—or he was nothing.

Later, the passionate urgings of romantic individualism destroyed the last theoretical restraints upon men's behavior. Recognizing few restrictions upon gratification of their desires, the new Westernized bourgeoisie became that licentious, self-seeking class against whom the Communists rail. Found in some aspects in almost every educated Chinese over thirty, and in all its aspects in none, the modern Chinese character blends great pride with hypersensitivity and extreme selfishness with a sense of guilt for failing the nation. When the Confucian strictures were removed, the ideal of serving the clan became callousness toward all persons outside the family.

The old virtues of the old beliefs often lingered in the countryside and the interior. Besides, the Confucian influence was still universally powerful in family relationships before the Communist conquest. A group of university students gathered in the temporary capital of Chungking during World War II conducted an intensive if informal debate on the question: "If your mother and your fiancée were trapped in the same burning house and time allowed you to rescue only one, whom would you rescue?" The solution that was generally accepted recognized the absolute claim of filial piety but acknowledged the new duties of romantic love: "You must rescue your mother first and then return to perish in the flames with your fiancée." To that extent was the body freed from the ancestors' tyranny.

"The basic doctrine of filial duty," explained a Westernized editor, "simply could not be violated. Even Western-educated university students still consider their duty to their parents an absolute imperative. Youngsters still do not argue with their parents—except sometimes on big issues such as patriotism, marriage, or careers."

The editor added: "A Western-educated Christian is not strict about religious rules when they come into conflict with Confucian traditions. Many Christians kneel down before the souls of their ancestors in the rites of ancestral worship, for refusal is nothing less than treachery to national beliefs. A Western-educated girl I know is enthusiastic about Western ways. But she reverted completely when it came to her responsibility to give her parents a home under her husband's roof. She wept at her husband's promise to support her parents comfortably—as long as they lived apart. She said that all her relations would criticize her if her parents did not live with her."

The Communists strive against the persistence of the old ethos. They seek to level every relic of Confucian society in order to clear the ground for their own Utopia. Yet Maoist Communism in China until 1966 was as much a reaffirmation of Confucianism as it was a reaction against the tradition. Only when the Maoists finally recognized, with the proclamation of the Great Proletarian Cultural Revolution, that they must "destroy the entire old civilization" was the past truly confronted. Though the social and ethical institutions of Confucianism were antipathetic to modern Communism, its habits of mind were quite congenial. It was, obviously, necessary for the Communists' bureaucratic hierarchy, which was qualified by its mastery of the Marxist classics, to substitute loyalty to the state for the Confucian loyalty to the family. Once that change in loyalty has been effected, however, the intellectual approach displays many useful affinities—the dedication to the attainment of Utopia, absolute and unimpaired by doubts as to human capabilities; the insistence upon conformity; the reliance upon written authority, variously interpreted to suit political convenience; and the preference for forms, rather than unmalleable reality.

The last great Confucian thinker, Liang Chi-chao's teacher Kang Yu-wei, taking his text from the *Li Chi's* description of the great Commonwealth, offered his own Utopia:

"(1) No nations; the whole world should set up a single government and be divided into several regions. (2) Both the central and regional governments should be popularly elected. (3) No family and clan; a man and a woman should cohabit not more than a year together; upon expiration of this term, there should be a change of mates. (4) Pregnant women should go to an institution for prenatal education, and babies, after birth, should go to nurseries. (5) Children should enter kindergarten and respective schools according to age. (6) Upon coming of age they should be assigned by the government to various duties in agricultural, industrial, and other types of productive enterprise. (7) The sick shall go to hospitals, and the aged to homes for the aged. (8) The establishments for prenatal education, the nurseries, the kindergartens, the hospitals, and the homes for the aged should be the highest institutions within the regional [government]. Those who enter them should obtain the highest satisfaction. (9) Adult men and women should as a rule serve in these establishments for a certain number of years, as they do at present in the military. (10) Establish different classes of public dormitories and dining halls so that each may freely enjoy and use them according to his working income. (11) Reproach for idleness should be the severest form of punishment. (12) Those who make new discoveries in learning and those who serve with special distinction in the five establishments of prenatal education, etc., should receive specific rewards. (13) There should be cremation of the dead, and fertilizer factories in the neighborhood of the crematoria." [16]

Mao Tse-tung's Great People's Communes contained so much of Kang Yu-wei's New Great Commonwealth, even to the grisly final provision, that one may assume a certain direct inspiration. Kang was inspired by the vision of the Utopian Great Commonwealth which would make the entire world one Confucian state, thus partially solving the still vexing problem of reconciling the demands of the modern world with the instinctive insistence upon Chinese superiority. In order to attain that goal, Kang Yu-wei was willing to modify even the all-important article of filial piety. He had seen how much practical harm it could wreak. Mao Tse-tung was similarly prepared to make major modifications in pursuit of the ultimate goal—until he finally recognized that he could attain his goals only by destroying every vestige of the past.

Until the final climacteric of the Cultural Revolution the Communists' frantic efforts to break away from the Confucian tradition indicated how greatly they were still influenced by the old authoritarianism. A hierarchical but otherwise undifferentiated society which allows little deviation from established norms was one of the chief goals of the present Maoist experiment. Their heritage of a monolithic society, at the very least, freed the Chinese Communists from the modifying efforts of the diverse European tradition, which constantly embarrasses the Russians. The dominant Chinese tradition has always resisted external influences, and a benevolent dictatorship has always ruled the Chinese Utopia. The development of Chinese Communism was, therefore, more stringent than Communism's evolution elsewhere.

The Confucian state had the saving grace of tolerating laxity, but the Maoists could permit no exceptions. They therefore came into total conflict with the diversities of human nature.

[16] Hsü, p. 97.

10

The Vision of Mao Tse-tung

*The Communist Chieftain's Thought,
Shaped by Traditional Chinese as Well
As Marxist Influences*

As the great man strode into the Hall of the People, the pale-blue dome, studded with a hundred constellations of lights, echoed the cheers of ten thousand "leading cadres." In the gesture beloved of millions he tossed his massive head, which was high-domed and balding between two great side tufts, and gently raised his right hand as if to protest against the tide of acclamation. Behind him, blinking in the glare, waddled Comrade Nikita Sergeievitch Khrushchev, his pale face shiny with sweat above a collarless Russian blouse. The Chinese accepted his due with a deprecating air, and the Russian clutched his straw hat as a chorus of 540 male voices proclaimed: "The east is red and in China there has appeared: Mao Tse-tung! He toils without let for the welfare of the people! Oh, he is the magnificent saviour of the people. . . . Mao Tse-tung! Mao Tse-tung! Mao Tse-tung! Live ten thousand years!"

The light-gray suit was creased across his protruding paunch, while his prosaic manner and the gaudy medals on his lapel gave Khrushchev the appearance of a boss-plumber from Odessa in the big city for a convention. Mao Tse-tung beside him was an austere Oriental potentate, a Marxist Prester John whose plain, high-necked tunic of fine wool complemented his patrician air. The contrast was even greater when the two supreme leaders of world Communism stood side by side atop the red-brick Gate of Heav-

199

enly Peace on the following day, October 1, 1959, the tenth anniversary of the People's Republic of China. Neither the pinched faces among the spectators nor the first revelations of the great schism between Moscow and Peking detracted from the adulation directed to one man.

Pressed by foreign reporters for details of Khrushchev's program, a Chinese official snapped: "We are celebrating the tenth anniversary of the Chinese People's Republic, not Khrushchev Day!" But the celebrations were, indeed, Mao Tse-tung Day—just as the ten years had been Mao Tse-tung's decade. While the pair stood on the reviewing stand between wings of lesser dignitaries, great waves of sound went up as more than two hundred thousand Young Pioneers again sang: "Mao Tse-tung! Mao Tse-tung! Ten thousand years! Mao Tse-tung! Ten thousand years! Mao Tse-tung!"

The choruses of praise for the Saving Star of the People, Chairman Mao Tse-tung of the Communist Party of China, make Russian adulation of Josef Stalin at its height appear diffident. Never previously has a single individual been so exalted in his own lifetime, for never previously have the mythmakers controlled so efficient an apparatus of publicity directed at such an enormous captive audience. Thousands of poets, painters, songwriters, journalists, and novelists lavish their talents upon Mao's glorification. His benign portrait appears on the walls of every hamlet and city in China, and his image is imprinted on the cover of every issue of most popular magazines to advertise tens of thousands of words from his own pen or the pens of his legion of sycophants. Told that "so-called spontaneous filial love" is a delusion, children are constantly impressed that Chairman Mao Tse-tung's love for them and their love for him are the emotional basis of their lives.

The task of the propagandists is not merely to celebrate the world's greatest revolutionary leader, who is also the heroic chief of the largest state that has ever existed, but to prove that Mao Tse-tung is by far the world's most profound living thinker. Chinese scientists pay homage to the guidance provided by "the scientific principles laid down by Mao Tse-tung." The "artistic *dicta* of Mao Tse-tung" inspire composers, writers, and sculptors, while generals, farmers, engineers, and linguists study handbooks summarizing Mao's directives for their crafts. Above all, the "doctrines of Mao Tse-tung are the highest expression of contemporary political and philosophical thought and a rich creative development of Marxism-Leninism"—the culmination of the endeavors of the keenest and most creative intelligences of all the epochs of human development. A panegyric by the deputy political commissar of the People's Liberation Army declared flatly: "Comrade Mao Tse-tung is the greatest Marxist-Leninist of contemporary times . . . his writings are a treasure-house. . . ." Since Marxism-Leninism is considered the ultimate product of human genius, the assertion was absolute.[1]

Professed materialists though they are, the Chinese mythmakers do not hesitate to invoke the supernatural. Disregarding the irony for a nation tormented by natural catastrophes and tortured by material shortages, an official poet writes:

> When the Chairman walks across the land,
> The hills and many waters dance;
> The Yellow River, tail-wagging, chants;
> And Mount Omei proffers tribute with open hand!

> When the Chairman walks across the land,
> Workers and peasants joyfully arise;
> Hills of grain and cotton split the skies;
> Iron and steel in a mighty stream expand!

There are undoubtedly bitter snickers in Peking, but repetition sanctifies absurdity, and most Chinese today can allow such hyperbole to flash across the surface of their minds without feeling revulsion. The adulation of Mao Tse-tung produced no specific counter-action in China until the vast popular revulsion re-

[1] The cult of Mao Tse-tung was, in large part, a deliberate creation of the ambitious Lin Piao, who had been ordered to purify the People's Liberation Army in 1959 and make the military a model for civilians. By deifying Mao, Lin asserted his own claim to the succession as "Chairman Mao's best pupil and most devoted disciple." The canonical thought of Mao Tse-tung is now acclaimed, simply and definitively, as "The Apogee of Human Wisdom."

leased by the Cultural Revolution. Before that pent resentment burst forth, the chief apparent effect had been stimulating the growing cynicism as to both the regime's objectives and its capabilities.

Although comparisons can often be as misleading as they are presumably odious, a king can be measured only beside other kings. Power imposes its own limitations, but it also offers opportunities that other men do not know. Only Nikita Khrushchev, the wily opportunist who is the son of a Ukrainian miner, occupied a position comparable to that of Mao Tse-tung, the dogmatic mystic who is the son of a Hunan farmer. Khrushchev, who obviously enjoyed the public role of the jovial great man, reversed Stalin's habit of Byzantine seclusion to mingle with the people of Russia and foreign countries. Mao Tse-tung reverted to the practice of the Imperial Court, rarely appearing in public and refusing to travel abroad, except for two unavoidable trips to the Soviet Union before he asserted his absolute superiority. Khrushchev, the practical improviser, was wholly different from the Asian despot, who retreated into the recesses of his own mind. With cynicism and superficiality equally characteristic, a disaffected Chinese remarked: "The only thing the two men have in common is that they are both disgustingly fat. Serving the people must be a good job."

Khrushchev was undoubtedly a devout believer, but his Communism was a more comfortable faith than the compulsive fundamentalism of Mao Tse-tung. The zealot in Khrushchev was normally subordinate to the practical politician, though he did not disguise his confident intention of conquering the world. Khrushchev appeared anxious, above all, to retain power and, secondarily, to guide his country's economic expansion. Case-hardened, but also tempered to flexibility in the heated struggle for power, he made concessions to the Russian people and argued that the world Communist movement must be "principled"—in its tactics as well as its goals. His definition of principle was, of course, not the definition of the Western liberal mind. His violent suppression of the Hungarian Revolt's threat to the integrity of the Communist bloc accorded with his "principled" desire to retain power at all costs, though Chinese pressure was a significant factor in his decision. His increasing "moderation" in foreign policy demonstrated his recognition that the Soviet Union was vulnerable, while a degree of internal relaxation enabled him to exercise power more effectively.

Unlike Khrushchev, Mao Tse-tung never felt himslf engaged in a contest for power with men of equal ability, nor had he ever trembled before a capricious master like Stalin. Mao was never a subordinate after he was thirty-four years old—and he never acknowledged any man as his true master. Mao was unique. He not only dominated his revolution as agitator, generalissimo, propagandist, and administrator; he also justified its course ideologically. The archdeviationist, to his own satisfaction at least, made major theoretical contributions to Marxism-Leninism, though he would not acknowledge that he had materially altered the dogma in the process. He also proved to his own satisfaction that he had never once in his entire political life erred—and had never encountered an equal.

This man at sixty-three swam the broad Yangtze River, not once but thrice—and ordered the widest publicity of his feat. At seventy-two he repeated the performance. This man wrote verses dismissing the great heroes of Chinese history as "brave, perhaps, but lacking culture . . . and so transitory!" He concluded: "To find men truly great and noble-hearted, we must look here in the present time." It was as if former President Dwight Eisenhower, whose talent for painting is only slightly less impressive than Mao Tse-tung's flair for versifying, had composed a vast mural showing himself in the foreground—with Abraham Lincoln, George Washington, Julius Caesar, and Alexander of Macedon standing respectfully around him.

Perhaps overwhelming egotism was essential to a man who dared as much as Mao Tse-tung. Certainly, the inspired cult of Mao Tse-tung was a necessity for a regime that felt that it had within its grasp the greatest attainments ever achieved by a Chinese government. Since all its accomplishments could still be swept from between its fingertips, the regime may well have required the materialist demigod Mao Tse-tung as the focus of all the public and private emotions of the Chinese people. Certainly, Lin Piao required the cult of Mao for his own advancement.

Nonetheless, the soaring self-confidence that made Mao's great achievements possible apparently required constant external confirmation. His refusal to consider ideas that clashed with his own showed itself when he entered a "modern" primary school in the town of Tungshan in 1909 at the age of sixteen.[2] He declared himself an authority on Chinese history because of his intimate knowledge of *The Romance of the Three Kingdoms* and *The Water Margin Tale*, sometimes called *The Hundred Robin Hoods* and most familiar to Western readers in Pearl Buck's translation *All Men Are Brothers*. The two novels of rebellion and power had been the chief sources of instruction and entertainment in his early years, and he had read each dozens of times.

Mao angrily objected to his young history teacher's insistence that *The Romance of the Three Kingdoms* was not an accurate account of the struggle for supremacy among the fragmentary states left when the second Han Dynasty collapsed in A.D. 220. Unpersuaded by historical evidence, he organized a "mass movement" against the teacher. But the headmaster, who had admitted the unqualified youth as a special favor, refused to acknowledge that the pupil was correct and the instructor wrong.

Young Mao harangued his schoolmates and drew up a petition to the Mayor of Tungshan, demanding that the headmaster be replaced. When his fellow students refused to sign, Mao raged: "You are nothing but a bunch of cowards—a lot of useless cowards!"

A boy called Wang, Mao's closest friend, dared to speak up: "I don't see how you can possibly know more about history than the Headmaster. . . . He has a degree and he's written a lot of books on history. . . . I don't think you know more than the Headmaster does!"

"Wang!" shouted Mao. "You don't believe me? But surely you can read my books."

"Tell me, Mao, what books?" asked little Wang.

[2] The tale is told by Siao-yu, the companion of Mao's youth, who later fled China and recalled his friend in *Mao Tse-tung and I Were Beggars* (Syracuse University Press, 1959), pp. 25ff. His brother, Hsiao San, is Mao's authorized Communist biographer.

"*The San Kuo Chih Yen Yi* [*Romance of the Three Kingdoms*]."

"But, Mao, hasn't the Headmaster told you that the *San Kuo Chih Yen Yi* is only a romantic novel? It is based on history but it is not a true account."

"But it is history, I tell you. History!" Mao shouted. "It's just nonsense for you to say it's not true. Of course it's true!" he shouted.

Mao, who couldn't abide contradictions, was furious. He flew into a rage, shouting, "Traitor! Traitor!" and threw a chair at Wang, who quickly moved to one side and escaped harm.

Suddenly, Mao turned his attention away from Wang and toward Chang.

"Little Chang, what a coward you are," he said. "You have often boasted that you were a good friend of mine, but it seems you forgot that you were my friend when Wang was arguing with me just now. Why didn't you back me up? When I threw the chair at him, if you were my friend, you would have thrown another. You are not a true and loyal friend."

"No, no, no, Mao," protested Chang. "I've always been faithful and true to you. I thought what little Wang said was right just now. That's why I didn't say anything against him. But neither did I say anything against you, who are my friend."

"Oh, so you think Wang is right, do you? Good! Now I know whose side you are on. You're a traitor, Chang, and I shall kill you. Just you watch out!"

Mao Tse-tung was forced to leave the Tungshan Primary School after this violent incident. Having frightened and alienated his schoolmates, he felt himself surrounded by "traitors" and determined to seek knowledge elsewhere.

Such secondhand recollections are naturally somewhat suspect after the passage of half a century. But there is sufficient corroborating evidence from both partisans and opponents to justify accepting this incident as indicative of Mao's character. His parallel performance almost sixty years later confirms the insight. Once again Mao Tse-tung discovered that he was surrounded by "traitors" who denied his visions arising from the sacred books of Marxism-Leninism. He ordered the Cultural Revolution to purge these "traitors" and exalt his sycophants.

Once Mao has made an idea his own, any disagreement becomes a personal blow, a direct attack on his self-esteem. He has repeatedly demonstrated that he will kill to impose his version of truth—or to evoke the adulation that is essential to his assumption of omniscience. Truth, for Mao Tse-tung, is what he makes it. Opposition from man or nature has time after time merely intensified his determination to impose his own views. Since each success in forcing his views on others over thirty years has heightened his conviction of infallibility, he is not subject to the restraints of objective reality to the same extent as are most men—regardless of whether reality is expressed through others' opinions or through apparently irrefutable evidence like economic statistics. When events actually force his hand—as China's undeniable economic difficulties have done since 1959—Mao will still not concede the point. Instead, he tends to ascribe his failure to uncooperative natural forces and to malignant human agencies—in this case traitorous counter-revolutionary elements and the jealous Soviet Union. He "chokes back" his righteous indignation in the firm expectation of later proving his omniscience.

Mao regularly triumphs over objective reality—by forcing others to echo his views or by fiats like that directing statistics to become truly "objective" by disregarding "superstitious" Western accounting procedures and reporting production results that would "serve the revolution." In the summer of 1955, when the peasants of China, newly endowed with their own plots, displayed complacent delight at having become landed proprietors, Mao Tse-tung proclaimed that a "new high tide of enthusiasm" for socialist collectivization was sweeping the countryside. When resistance to collectivization prevented his wringing out agricultural surpluses to provide capital for industrialization, Mao invented the Great People's Commune. Constantly lauded for his "intimate knowledge of the affairs of the entire world," Mao cannot admit that the existence of affluent, state-regulated capitalism in the West is not consistent with his philosophy. Instead, he insists from time to time that millions are starving in the streets of

Paris, London, and New York—and that capitalism is in its death throes.

In 1942 the avowedly anti-Confucian materialist implicitly espoused the Doctrine of Rectification of Names. He called the first major campaign to impose ideological conformity upon the Chinese Communist Party the *Cheng Feng Movement,* in obvious reference to *Cheng Ming.*[3] The Doctrine of Rectification of Names, of course, had evolved far beyond the original Confucian assertion that men must behave in accordance with Platonic ideals. But Mao has used it as justification for his own belief that reality may be altered by giving it a new name and forcing all men to behave in accordance with the new formula.

In the early 1960s the professed materialist, pressed by economic dislocations equal in scope to his overriding ambitions, ordered publicists to refute those Chinese who believe that "the material incentive" was essential to industrialization. Material rewards are "given one-sided emphasis by the vulgar materialists," wrote one of Mao's favorites in mid-1960. "If a person lives a wholehearted, Socialist revolutionary life, he can transcend the handicaps of a poor material life. . . ." On Mao's command the publicist was responding to a new Chinese school of economists who stressed material incentives and entrepreneurial autonomy.

Despite his intellectual shortcomings and his frequent ferocity, Mao's complete self-devotion commands not only obedience, but adoration. Mao may not have a first-class mind, but he is a transcendent personality. He is undoubtedly a great man, if greatness can be divorced from morality. Even more than his many virtues are his faults the products of his environment.

Mao's limitations have, in a sense, made his accomplishments possible. His formal education, beginning late, consisted of brief periods of attendance at several schools. He acquired no systematic intellectual discipline, but learned chiefly from brief encounters with a few devoted teachers and by omnivorous reading

---

[3] *Cheng Feng* (正风) literally means "to order the winds [of behavior]"; *Cheng Ming* (正名), "to order or correct the names [by which things are called]." Cf. Chapter 9, p. 191 *passim* and 191n.

of newspapers, traditional novels, revolutionary tracts, and such few translations as happened to come into his hands. A number of his adult associates felt that he was deficient in knowledge of the basic literature of Marxism-Leninism.[4] He is, in short, no intellectual, but the pragmatic man of action who seizes upon an agreeable concept or a convenient fact and stubbornly maintains its truth in the face of all conflicting evidence.

Coupling intimate knowledge of the practical situation with the haziest awareness of the strategic forces arrayed against him, Mao triumphed because he could not see how unlikely was his triumph. His limited knowledge of Marxist theory and Chinese history also gave him strength. Only half-aware of the internal logic that makes Marxism-Leninism a rigorous intellectual system, albeit one founded on absurdity, Mao wielded the dogma like an Excalibur rather than the clumsy flint-axe it is. He was inspired by the word's longest-lived tradition, while exulting in his kinship with rebels against that tradition. Half-contemptuous and half-awed, he used the Confucian culture as both a model and a scapegoat. He fed his arrogance on China's having developed a centralized nation thousands of years before that system appeared in the West and appealed to his compatriots to restore China's ancient glory. But he also characterized the Confucian system as a tool of the corrupt exploiting classes and argued that feudalism endured in China till modern times.

Nonetheless, Mao's grand design—and his actions' immorality in Western eyes—stemmed as much from the central Chinese tradition as they did from his personal experience. The traditional culture—yearning after Utopia, believing wholeheartedly in the possibility of Utopia, and constantly seeking to create Utopia—produced in Chairman Mao Tse-tung its greatest enthusiast, a man drunk with the foretaste of Utopia. The inherent skepticism which had restrained previous Chinese efforts to attain the unattainable was overcome. Hesitation yielded to Marxism's promise of an inevitable Utopia, whose advent could be insured simply by

[4] Notably Chang Kuo-tao in his memoirs; but criticism of Mao's shortcomings as a theoretician were common in the days when such criticism was still possible. With the breakdown of repression under the Cultural Revolution, they are common.

throwing the proper historical switches. A frustrated minor artist, like a number of twentieth-century leaders, Mao Tse-tung took the entire Chinese nation as his medium. He was determined to make the material conform to the vision of the ideal society in his artist's mind. Human beings rather than stone, mortar, and steel were the primary material with which he worked, just as his predecessors in the robes of mandarins had been concerned, above all, with the organization of society rather than with the less malleable matter of economic life.

Only by a process of gradual revelation did the outside world —and the Chinese people—learn the full scope and daring of Mao's transcendent vision of a wholly new Chinese society which would be a compelling model for all humanity. The Great People's Communes, initiated in 1958 and virtually abandoned by 1960, were but the first step toward the attainment of a perfectly seamless and perfectly uniform social order among "new Communist men." Although the Maoists proclaimed in 1958 that all men would be equally soldiers, intellectuals, manual workers, and farmers, distinctions between officials and the commonalty persisted even in the ideal People's Commune, which was, of course, never translated into material reality. In 1966 the Maoists unveiled their total purpose: all men were to become equal in all their functions and all their privileges: all existing institutions and cultures, including the structure through which the Communists exercised power, were to be abolished in order to clear the ground for the first "perfectly non-exploitive system mankind has ever known."

The model for Mao Tse-tung's grand design was the abortive Paris Commune of 1871, which Karl Marx himself had celebrated as the precursor of the perfect proletarian order among mankind. Utterly disillusioned with the Chinese intelligentsia—writers and educators, managers and technicians—Mao determined to create his own totally new intelligentsia from among proletarians who would also be adminstrators, factory hands, and soldiers. All power in China would proceed from the local Revolutionary Committees, chosen from among the proletariat and endowed with legislative, administrative, and judicial functions. No official would remain in office for more than a year or two, and no official would retain office if the universal electorate chose to recall him. All officials would continue to work at their manual trades, and none would enjoy emoluments or compensation greater than those enjoyed by the man at the workbench beside them. Utopia was thus to be enacted. The perfect artistic vision of Mao Tse-tung was thus to be translated into reality.

The dedicated internationalist, who saw himself as the leader of oppressed colored peoples everywhere, vehemently affirmed the old Chinese nationalism in a widely reprinted article in 1960. China, said Mao, must "attain her goals of wealth and strength by her own efforts, not by stretching out her hands in supplication to others!" He complained that China was "bullied and oppressed," but promised that her revenge would come in the future, after redoubled striving. Finally, he exhorted the *Chinese* comrades: "Show the world what kind of people we Chinese really are!"

There was a twofold irony in Mao Tse-tung's exploiting the Confucian tradition for the purposes of Marxism. He was, like so many previous Chinese statesmen, Confucian in his habits of mind and his aspirations, but heterodox in his practices. The techniques of power he employed derived on the Chinese side from Mo Tzu, the philosopher who first developed a rationale for totalitarianism, and from Lord Shang Yang, the practicing politician who created the modern state in China. In contrast to Confucius, who lived two centuries earlier, both were practical men who sought specific ends by direct methods.[5]

Certainly one of the few philosophers who ever possessed a private army, Mo Tzu taught the attainment and exercise of power. The end—which justified his harsh means—was the Doctrine of Universal Love Among All Mankind; the attainment of Universal Love was to make all laws and all coercion unnecessary. An intermediate step toward the attainment of the Mohist Utopia was his Doctrine of Agreement with the Superior, whose ostensible purpose was to insure harmony between the ruler and his subjects. That doctrine maintained that the king's decrees were invariably an expression of the natural law, since the king received divine revelation of the standards of justice. The people's simple duty

[5] The material in this section is drawn largely from a manuscript, "Chinese Jurisprudential Thought," written by the author in 1946.

was to obey. Although his doctrines had a brief vogue, Mohism died as a vital force with Mo Tzu's own death. But he left behind his formula for attaining personal power: terror enforced by fear of human and supernatural power; a highly disciplined, politically conscious army responsive to one man's orders; and vast propaganda campaigns based upon abstruse doctrines most men could not understand. Not only Mo Tzu's theoretical doctrines and goals but his methods as well are so close to Mao Tse-tung's that it is probably superfluous to point out the parallel.

Lord Shang was the apogee of the Legalist School of political philosophy. As its Prime Minister he transformed the feudal State of Chin into the weapon that brought all China under the rule of its first central dynasty barely a hundred years after Shang's own time. The Legalists were cast up by the Period of the Warring States (403–221 B.C.). Feudalism, which had controlled men by strict etiquette and rigidly defined personal relationships, was dying amid violence, but the monarchy had not yet established its supremacy. The Legalists' doctrines reflected a troubled age, which was beginning to look to impersonal rules as the basis of government in place of the disintegrating system of rule by the proper relations among men that Confucius had described. Ironically, the Confucian ethos was already outdated when it was institutionalized about 150 B.C. by the Han Dynasty.

The Legalists were antihistorical. They distrusted sanctified custom, since change was not only unavoidable but was necessary for the state's survival. It was vain, they argued, to depend upon individual morality which derived from personal and historical examples, since those forces could not make the state strong enough to survive in an age of violent competition. The Legalists maintained that only by exercising absolute control over the people through codified law could the state become sufficiently powerful to insure its own survival. Since men were evil by nature, they must be cajoled by propaganda and their disruptive proclivities must be curbed by laws that made no exception for social status or degrees of relationship.

The *Book of Lord Shang*—*The Prince* of this early Chinese political Renaissance—applied those generalizations to the business of government. Shang Yang held each man responsible for his family's and even his neighbor's misdeeds. He believed that the law could make the state strong only if it controlled every aspect of the people's life. One section of his book was called "Elimination of Strength." He deliberately sought to weaken the individual in order to strengthen the state. Other sections, entitled "Discipline of the People" and "Rewards and Punishments," enforced the ruler's absolute control by laying down rigid rules of behavior that were enforced by severe punishments for crime and meager rewards for service.

Lord Shang's concept of law was amoral. He was interested not in divine sanction, but in practical results. He effected a complete breach between ethics and law, with law occupying the primary position. The criminal codes which had originally been intended to buttress Confucian protocol superseded the *li*. Virtue and law became synonymous, but nonethical concepts; both were dominated by the demand for absolute obedience to the ruler.

This austere structure of theory and practice was later hung with a mass of commentary after the manner of the Chinese. Some of those additions are also relevant to the mind of Mao Tse-tung and the manner of government of the Chinese People's Republic. Han Fei-tzu, the most eminent Legalist theoretician, maintained that the law was in itself a perfect imperative and was therefore beyond the necessity for either justification or external sanction. Explanations or appeals to precedent would merely breach the immutable routine that guaranteed the subjects' proper behavior, thus weakening the government's absolute authority. Li Ssu, the Legalist who was the first Prime Minister of the first Chinese nation, was moved by this abhorrence of the past and by the desire to destroy any possible intellectual basis for opposition. He burned all the Confucian classics on which he could lay his hands in a gala ceremony in 215 B.C.[6]

The Legalists present several paradoxes, as does Mao himself.

[6] Li Ssu has been blamed by orthodox historians for the paucity of authoritative classical texts available later. His work of destruction was actually not that efficient, for he preserved copies of all the texts in the closed library at the capital. But that library was burned in 207 B.C., when the founder of the orthodox Han Dynasty took the city. The conflagration was as accidental—and as distressing to historians—as the burning of the library at Alexandria.

Though they were antihistorical, they laid great stress upon the constancy and permanence of the law. *Formally committed since the start of his active political life to destruction of the past, Mao has constantly appealed to the authority and inspiration of China's former greatness.* Advocating law codes sanctioned only by human authority, the Legalists, nonetheless, told the public that the ruler held communion with the divine will. *Mao is an atheist, but he claims transcendent knowledge because of his creative mastery of Marxism-Leninism, the doctrine that reveals the innermost secrets of the universe.* The paradoxes are, of course, explained by the Legalists' recognition that propaganda—appealing to an authority wider and less ephemeral than even the King's —was essential to insure the masses' obedience. The parallels with the present need not be labored.

A full-length comparison between Mao Tse-tung and Sir Winston Churchill would make a fascinating pair of Plutarchian antithetical biographies. The two were exact opposites in all the circumstances of their personal lives, in the societies which bred them, and in their deepest beliefs. But they were alike in the grandeur of their accomplishments and in their stubborn self-confidence, which was actually enlarged by human opposition and the malignity of circumstances.

Churchill, the aristocrat, was fortunate. A democratic electorate removed him from power when the task was no longer suited to his talents, leaving lesser men to preside over the inevitable but still inglorious transformation of a great empire into a comfortable second-class nation. Mao ruled too long for his fame's sake, for he was the prisoner of the authoritarian system he created. Even after he left the chair of government to cultivate his garden of "theoretical leadership," no legal form could relieve him of ultimate responsibility. As Chairman of the Communist Party he still directed China's creeping transition from a fragmented nation of poor farmers into a military and industrial power, where the "new man lives in a new society." The final convulsion of the Proletarian Revolution was taken on his inspiration and with his sanction, though he did not direct its day-to-day tactics.

Mao was inspiring as the leader of a tiny band of guerrillas facing hopeless odds. He was serene as the ruler of a provisional state made up of awakened peasants living in primitive communism on the windblown edges of China. If he had not slaughtered so many millions, Mao would merit sympathy as the architect—and the hard-driving straw-boss—of a fantastically ambitious plan to create a complex scientific power on no firmer basis than the toil, tears, and hunger of those same peasants.

The aging Mao Tse-tung, who lives in the minds of many Orientals as the symbol of a resurgent agrarian Asia, came himself of a long line of farmers. The family was undistinguished, boasting only one degree-holder in all the intricate network recorded in the ancestral tablets. From such families, rooted in the fertile Hunan plain that surrounds the city of Changsha, the Communist Party of China has drawn its most ardent leaders. The Hunanese are famous throughout China for addiction to hot peppers and for fiery dispositions underlaid by granitelike stubbornness. Hunanese obstinacy is so great that three pre-eminent Communists from the area are now in disgrace: Li Li-san, who briefly controlled the course of the Party in the early 1920s; Peng Teh-huai, next to Chu Teh long the most honored Communist general; and Ting Ling, the lady novelist who rose and fell by her persistent individualism. The list was completed in 1966, when the Hunanese Chairman of the People's Republic, Liu Shao-chi, emerged as the leader of the realistic faction opposed to Mao's romantic excesses in politics and economics.

The crucial year in Mao Tse-tung's own career, the year which provided the financial base for his education, passed in the 1880s, a decade before his own birth. His father, Mao Jen-sheng, could not make a living on the family's two-and-a-half-acre farm near Shaoshan Village because the Taiping Rebellion had intensified the general economic disturbances that plagued China during the latter half of the nineteenth century. Two other courses were open to him. Banditry was a profitable business for desperate men, but soldiering could be an even more profitable business since the bandit in uniform enjoyed a certain legal sanction for his looting. Joining the army of an enterprising local general, Mao's father returned to Shaoshan in little more than a year with cash enough to buy an additional acre.

He was soon selling pigs and rice in Changsha and lending money at interest. Before long his capital totaled three thousand Chinese dollars, a considerable sum in an era when a farm laborer could be hired for his keep and twelve dollars a year. Those three thousand dollars set Mao's father as much above his debt-ridden neighbors as possession of $150,000 would have distinguished an American farmer in 1890, when a hired man got $600 a year. Although he did not enjoy the same level of affluence as that American farmer, he was raised in the same degree as the American was above his neighbors. The elder Mao had vaulted from the poor peasant class, over the group the Chinese call middle farmers, into the small company of rich farmers. Although he did not become a landlord, his role as a moneylender made him hardly distinguishable from the class to whose destruction his eldest son was to pledge his life.

When Mao Tse-tung was born in December 1893, Mao Jensheng could provide the rudimentary education his own father's poverty had denied him. After their lessons at a village school run by an unsuccessful candidate for official honors, their father himself continued his sons' training in the evening. The youngest brother, Tse-tan, who was killed in the early 1930s, was too young at the time, but Tse-tung and Tse-min, the middle brother, who died in a Nationalist prison in Sinkiang in 1941, would sit squinting in the moonlight while their father taught them to manipulate the abacus. Mao Jen-sheng was an exacting teacher, since he knew that proficiency in calculating with the polished ebony beads on metal rods would greatly assist his sons in accumulating wealth.

"My father," Mao Tse-tung later recalled, "insisted that we be able to use the abacus with both hands—so that we could figure faster."

Mao Jen-sheng was not only ambitious, but also displayed the Chinese peasant's ingrained stinginess, so intense it makes the frugal French farmer appear openhanded. Young Tse-tung, resentful of his father's parsimony, early developed a contempt for money.

He revenged himself for his father's obsession and acquired a lasting reputation for generosity among the country folk by opening his purse to every plausible beggar. Anecdotes recollected by Siao San, Mao's boyhood friend and official biographer, though intended to celebrate his largesse, reveal also the intensity of Mao's resentment of his father.

Young Mao, returning home with money paid for a pig, gave the strings of cash to a beggar by the roadside. Another time he was sent to collect a hog his father had arranged to purchase ten days earlier. The market price had gone up in the meantime, and the seller refused Mao's money, saying: "The price has jumped, and besides, I fed the animal for ten days. I won't sell at the old price."

"Quite right," Tse-tung replied. "The price has indeed gone up, and you are certainly entitled to something for feeding the animal for ten days. You are quite right in not giving me the animal at the old price."

Some years later his frugal father bought him a new overcoat, a major purchase. On the road back to school Mao fell in with a youth who wore only a thin cotton tunic against the winter cold. Mao gave him the new overcoat and went coatless all through the hard winter to keep his undue generosity from his father's knowledge.

The compulsion to ostentatious generosity endured long after the old man was dead. In 1935 Mao Tse-tung saw an old peasant woman shivering by the roadside as the fugitive Red Army marched through Kweichow Province. He removed his overcoat and threw it over her shoulders. Fortunately for Mao, the contempt for possessions, which would have ruined a businessman, has been useful capital for the leader of a peasant revolt.

Although the elder Mao might have been delighted at the prospect of ridding himself of his profligate son, he set his face in horror when young Tse-tung began to talk of attending the "modern school" at Tungshan. The old man hated losing the labor of the strapping sixteen-year-old. Tse-tung borrowed from a neighbor to launch his educational career. Such a step would have been impossible if his family, like most of its poverty-stricken neighbors, had not been able to endure without his labor. Although he has not liked to talk about it, Mao Tse-tung was obviously sustained by occasional remittances from his father throughout his school years.

As much as Mao Tse-tung hated his father, he loved his mother, a pale woman who found refuge in Buddhist temples from her role as a buffer between her hardheaded husband and her stubborn sons. But his devotion to her memory has not spared the Buddhist clergy from the lash.

Despite his determination to escape it, the farm shaped Mao's life. Millions of farms like it gave him the tools to make his revolution. Unlike Chiang Kai-shek's bourgeois revolution, the Communists' battles were won not on the playing fields of Peking University and the Whampoa Academy, but in the millet fields of north China and the rice paddies of the south. The soldiers and the aspirations of the People's Liberation Army were drawn from the farms of China, from one-acre plots of exhausted soil, whose meager crops were in fee to moneylenders—and only discontent flourished. The revolution was not made by the discontented youth Mao Tse-tung, drifting from middle school to normal school to associations of high-minded young men and women—and even to plans to get rich quick by starting a soap factory. Nor was the revolution made by the pale intellectual Mao, who sat reading in the library of Peking University between checking out newspapers to the intellectual titans who could not find time to speak to him. Not even the unfledged agitator, with his fiery speeches and woolly ideas, led the People's Liberation Army to the conquest of all China. The true victor was Mao Tse-tung of Hunan, the angry farmer's son, who raised up the peasants of China to fling them at the wicked cities of the coast.

China has remained predominantly agricultural throughout the ages; at least 85 per cent of her people have always lived on the land. The banker, the general, and the professor all ride on the gnarled shoulders of the dirt farmer. The same dependence prevails throughout Asia and throughout those portions of the globe which Mao, the farmboy, would now raise against the wicked capitalists of the cities.

Mao knew from the beginning that the farmers were his weapon. At the first Party Congress, his colleagues were annoyed by his long diatribes on the peasantry. But Mao returned to Changsha as chief of the Party's Hunan Committee of about twelve men. There he organized peasant unions, almost ignoring other groups, and began to develop the Maoist heresy.

Later, his colleagues grew cool to the young upstart, for Mao, just twenty-nine in 1922, defied the Comintern's clear edict that the firm base of the revolution must be the urban proletariat. The peasants might assist, declared Moscow, but they could not play a primary revolutionary role. Although Mao had been a frequent contributor to the Party organ, all his contributions were rejected in 1923 because he refused to subordinate his obsession with the peasants to the Party's line. Chastened by the reprimand, Mao later recanted and was restored to the Party's good graces.

Mao Tse-tung was allowed to return to his peasants when the Northern Expedition marched in July 1926. As Chairman of the Hunan Peasant Bureau, he prepared a report, *On the Peasant Movement in Hunan,* which established him as the Party's chief agrarian authority, but again offended the orthodox by its vehemence. He wrote in part: "The present upsurge of the peasant movement constitutes an extremely important phenomenon, since it must in the near future bring about a movement among several hundred million peasants throughout the rest of China. . . . The peasants will break down all that stands in their way and will hasten along the road to emancipation. All revolutionary parties and all revolutionaries will be put to the test by these aroused masses."

After 1927, when he assumed command of his own peasant army, Mao's connections with the Party center were extremely tenuous. Building the base of power in the years from 1927 to 1936, he lived the life of a bandit chieftain out of a traditional novel. Aside from ironbound Party discipline and modern weapons, he might have been an insurgent smallholder of a thousand years earlier, determined to snatch the Mandate of Heaven from its unworthy holder. Neither egalitarian demisocialism nor the *jacquerie* was alien to Chinese tradition.

The peasants of China finally failed their champion. Since circumstances compel inclination, Mao Tse-tung became almost as much a marionette on the strings of fate as the humblest swineherd on a barren Commune. The classic fate of despots overtook the idealistic farmboy. He became a slave to his own delusions. He could not look down to see that the Emperor wore no clothes —but others, good Communists all, finally spoke out to save China from Mao's delusions. The ultimate enthusiast had set out with a will to remake the world. Since he could never accept any possibility but absolute success, he could not acknowledge that his goals were unattainable. Therefore, the final effort either to create a new world or pull the structure of China down around his shoulders—the Great Proletarian Cultural Revolution.

Mao Tse-tung was obviously bewildered by the intractability of the monstrous abstractions that haunt the days of modern rulers—not a mere shortage of food, but the lack of fifty million tons of rice; not a simple need for transportation, but rather railroads that raced forever behind essential schedules; not mere planning for reconstruction, but multitudes of engineers demanding steel when there was no steel. The man who insisted that nuclear bombs are harmless "paper tigers" was adrift in the modern world of computers, automation, and an interlocked international economy. He therefore clung to what he learned so laboriously so long ago: Communism is about to triumph because the capitalist world is crashing into chaos. Imbued with the mystique of struggle and destruction, Mao did not realize that he might well destroy his enemies without gaining his own ends. Nor did he, apparently, realize that certain economic problems are perhaps susceptible to solution by determined efforts—but only when supplemented by the slow, accretive processes of time.

It was the great misfortune of the Chinese peasant masses that Mao Tse-tung, when all else failed him, still believed he could work his miracles through them. Convinced of their infinite capability, he sought to short-circuit the process of development described by Marx. Instead of creating those material conditions which must spontaneously produce ideal human beings in an ideal society, he would first have created the ideal man by direct manipulation of his mind. When he had produced men who felt neither love, nor fear, nor hunger, except as he commanded, he believed he would possess the most powerful instrument in the world. The irrational formula was simple: indoctrination can re-shape any man into the semblance of the ideal; and all things are possible to him who commands the labor of a sufficiently large number of ideal human beings.

The man who set out to exalt common humanity finally de-nied that humanity existed, except as raw material. Man's nature is but the nature of his class, declared Mao's publicists in 1960, implying that what environment has shaped can be reshaped any number of times. At the same time, they returned to the concept of the state as a great family, writing: "As a productive, consum-ing, or educational unit, the small family will no longer function in the future as it did in the past. . . . The laboring masses of our country all understand that it is not the family, but the great Communist Party, and the great revolution which give them ev-erything . . . our big revolutionary family and our fighting fam-ily, which share the fate of life and death with us, are a hundred times warmer than those feudal families of mutual strife, those mutually deceiving bourgeois families, and those quarrelsome old-fashioned rural families." [7]

Determined that no other loyalties should weaken loyalty to the state, the Maoists in 1960 reasserted their conviction that human beings were essentially empty vessels to be filled as the dominant class in each society wished. A series of articles declared that spontaneous affection, emotions, or ideals did not exist, while "to speak of man's thoughts and sentiments in a way which de-grades him from a social being and turns him into a biological being is entirely meaningless. . . ." [8] These ultimate nihilists de-nounced love between individuals as evil, since "the love and affections of proletarians are subordinate to the revolution—and base themselves on Communist morals. . . ." Even the awe the bourgeoisie felt of death was ignoble, since it was not a natural feeling, but stemmed from their "class viewpoint." "From the pro-letarian, revolutionary point of view, the goal of life is the collec-tive, the realization of Communism . . . a true proletarian, there-fore, welcomes his own death if it serves the cause." [9]

[7] *Chung-kuo Ching-nien Pao* [*China Youth*], May 1 and July 16, 1960.
[8] *Ibid.*, June 1, 1960.
[9] *Ibid.*

"Is there such a thing as human nature?" wrote Mao himself. "Certainly there is. But there is only concrete class human nature; there is not an abstract universal human nature."

Mao Tse-tung rushed headlong toward his final personal tragedy, the discovery that he could no more mold human beings than he could control the physical circumstances that shape men's lives. He drafted his own rebuttal to that realization of failure, for he defied his inability to manage his own world of China by seeking to impose his personal vision of revolutionary struggle on the entire world. He rode the maelstrom of his own defeat on the consoling dogma that *no* nation could attain communism until *all* nations had attained communism.

The deep tragedy of Mao Tse-tung's life lay in his constant conflict with objective reality. Idealistic and greatly gifted, he undeniably accomplished prodigies. But he was incapable of setting any limits to his ambitions; and he could not acknowledge that his great work must proceed by measured stages, taking much time for each fulfillment. If he had been content to build China slowly, his work might have been crowned with gratifying success. Instead, he finally committed himself to changing China and the entire world by the direct application of force. Incapable of acknowledging failure, Mao Tse-tung would destroy all men—regardless of faith or class—rather than yield his own belief in himself.

Part Five

PRESSURE, PURGE, AND MENTAL PARALYSIS

The Communist Pattern of Government Before the Cultural Revolution

. . . In the wake of development of production, the living standards of the people have also been greatly improved. . . . In the past, circumstances forced painstaking struggle upon us and we promoted painstaking struggle to make the people look forward into the future and to stimulate the people to remedy their plight and to struggle for a beautiful future. If we, however, constantly emphasize painstaking struggle today, we may well make people lose confidence in the future and actually weaken their longing for a beautiful future. In the past, we promoted painstaking struggle, but, if we do it today and continue to do it in the future, the people will ask: "For what are we persistently waging painstaking struggle?"

HAN CHUN OF KWANGTUNG
China Youth, September 1960

Comrade Han's life philosophy and world outlook are wrong.

Peng Jui-ching of Peking
China Youth, October 1960

. . . since every step forward in our revolutionary cause has been made possible by bitter struggle, so must be every inch we can advance today. . . . Bitter struggle is not just a policy measure of a temporary nature. It is a revolutionary spirit that must be propagated as long as the proletarian class exists.

Chen Kuang of Shanghai
China Youth, October 1960

Our duty is to hold ourselves responsible to the people. Every word, every act and every policy must conform to the people's interests . . .

Mao Tse-tung
The Situation and Our Policy after the Victory of the War of Resistance against Japan, 1945

. . . all our policies and methods are reasonable.

Hsiao Shu and Yang Fu
Red Flag, November 1960

Dare to rebel—and be good at rebelling. Dare to spread disorder —and be skillful at spreading disorder.

Red Guard Motto
Autumn 1966–1968

11

The Structure and Functioning of
The Communist Party of China Before
Its Destruction in 1966

Hard by the time-hallowed Forbidden City, where the temples and pavilions of the ages shone garish in their new paint, the Peking regime built its Red Square—the Plaza of Heavenly Peace.

The regime which promised a violent "liberation" to all the oppressed of the earth retained the old pacific names throughout the district. Looking southward like the Emperors on ceremonial occasions, Mao Tse-tung contemplated his myriad people from a red-brick structure with soaring eaves called the Gate of Heavenly Peace. The Street of Lasting Peace before the Gate of Heavenly Peace was shaken by steel tank-treads, by the ridged tires of artillery pieces, by the hobnailed boots of the armed legions of the people's revolution, and by the padding of the felt slippers of militant workers and peasants. The street was widened to two hundred and sixty feet to accommodate the parades of millions, a major aspect of the secular rites that replaced religious festivals in the new China. Flanking grandstands were erected to accommodate as many as twenty-two thousand distinguished guests recruited from the far reaches of the earth to bear witness to the new splendor.

The Gate of Heavenly Peace testifies to the scope of the regime's overleaping ambition. Its broad lawns are intersected by avenues lined with evergreens and clusters of light globes atop ornamental pillars. Its total area is four hundred and eighty thousand square yards, nearly four times that of Moscow's Red Square. Gazing from his reviewing stand, Mao sees on his right the Hall of the People's Congress and on his left the Revolutionary and Historical Museum of the People of China, each accommodating tens of thousands. Pale-tan walls, showing through forests of marble columns beneath golden pediments, soften somewhat the overwhelming impact of these monumental buildings, which were erected in just ten months by more than a half million laborers. In the center of the Plaza stands the Column of the People's Heroes, a square marble obelisk crowned by curling marble eaves in the traditional manner and inscribed with slogans in Mao Tse-tung's own handwriting. Just a year after its completion, cracks began to appear in the Column's base.

Like the Plaza of Heavenly Peace, the Communist Party of China presented a well-ordered spectacle to the observer. Behind its façade, the Party was as inappropriate a vehicle for the aspirations of the Chinese people—or the will of their masters—as the Edwardian Plaza of Heavenly Peace was incongruous as a symbol of a resurgent Asian race. One was expected to see in the Plaza's vistas a spontaneous declaration in enduring stone that the Chinese people had struck a balance between cooking oil and guns and between steel and rice—in sum, that China had entered upon a new era in which the material strength of the West was finally in harmony with the humanism of the East. But somehow the Plaza's massive grandeur seemed designed primarily to allay the misgivings of its architects. The public face of the Communist Party was intended to convey an impression of seamless unity—an indefatigable group of dedicated men guided by omniscience incarnate. But close examination revealed an unstable equilibrium of the conflicting interests and irreconcilable antagonisms which must arise in a nation of about 750 million whose history began little less than two decades ago. That unstable equilibrium flew apart in 1966, when the Maoists' ruthless Utopianism came into final conflict with the pragmatic approach of a bureaucracy responsible for efficient routine administration.

It was never easy for Mao Tse-tung to impose his inaccurate transcription of an outmoded blueprint of society upon either the Party or the Army, which were the bases of his power. Though personal antagonisms made the task awkwardly difficult from the beginning, it was possible to discipline a small, homogeneous group. But after 1958 the absence of either a workable long-term policy or an integrated intellectual system that could compel obedience was revealed by a vastly enlarged Party's confrontation with reality—and the outside world. The nation challenged the entire world, but its rulers were reduced to two barren themes in their frustrating effort to preserve the nucleus of their power. The first was conformity to the Thought of Mao Tse-tung, whose "creative philosophy" could be reduced to a tactical exhortation to avoid both the rightist extreme of excessive caution and the leftist extreme of excessive enthusiasm. The second theme offered an original strategy for the conquest of power, since Mao's experience in the arena was both profound and original. The final appeal of both themes was not to reason, but to faith: *Mao Tse-tung's doctrines are correct because he is Mao Tse-tung, who has repeatedly demonstrated that he cannot err! If you believe your own senses against his word, you err!* When reality's divergence from the canonical Thought of Mao Tse-tung became overwhelming, the practical men began to ignore his directives. They spontaneously created a new structure of power which was largely free of the hard-line Maoists. To smash that structure, Mao proclaimed the Great Proletarian Cultural Revolution, which finally destroyed his power.

The Maoist hierarchy had already revealed its intellectual poverty in its injunctions to the Communist Party. Activists "must adopt the correct world outlook." But the leadership's world outlook was hardly more than an image of traditional China seen in a Marxist mirror that reflected outlines but reversed both images and color. Because even the most radical innovators must proceed from what they already know, leaders who knew only China sought salvation by inverting the society that had bred them. Since China was weak, she must be strong; since the Empire was based upon clan loyalty, the family must be abolished; since Confucian officials were, in theory, chosen for their knowledge, Maoist officials must, in practice, be qualified by their political piety.

Curious results emerged from the unconscious conviction that he who creates evil's direct opposite produces good. The Maoists

—and, indeed, all modern Chinese thinkers—held explicitly that the old ways were not only impractical, but actually bred social evils. The Confucian ideal was the Princely Man, so moderate that asceticism was as repugnant to him as was debauchery. The ideal Maoist man was the activist. He usually displayed a peasant crudity in his manners because his idolatrous devotion to his Communist Party had allowed him no time to develop social or intellectual graces. Such airs and refinements were, in any event, the beginning of decadence.

"In 1951," confessed a Shanghai girl, "I married Wong Wooming. My love-person[1] comes from a farmer family and is an old Party member . . . after the marriage I felt disgusted at his coarse, vulgar manners, and I was actually ashamed to go out with him on the street. We had nothing in common to talk about."

Exiled from Shanghai to a village in Chekiang Province, the frivolous wife soon realized that the fault lay in her "individualistic bourgeois mind," not in her paragon of a husband. "Work improved me," she finally declared in expiation "and I realized that my love-person was right. He was wise because he had served the Party faithfully for more than ten years."

The Maoist Party was instinctively Know-Nothing; it distrusted all specialized knowledge—and even general culture. It was constantly at war with the scientists, technicians, and engineers whose services it needed so badly. Its most vehement denunciation was directed at the "bourgeois intelligentsia," who are in China merely those persons who have passed beyond grade school. The Maoist hierarchy realized that any knowledge transcending the narrow limits of orthodoxy not only moved men to question their fiats, but also bred an undesirable complexity of emotion and a dangerous richness of thought. The ideal instrument of Maoism possessed neither knowledge nor capability that did not derive from the Party. At least half the works of *belles-lettres* produced in China since 1949 have been devoted to the demonstration that the true heroes and heroines of the modern age must sacrifice all personal inclination to the service of the people, conducting their lives entirely "as the Communist Party di-

[1] The terms "husband" and "wife" are out of fashion.

rects." Local Party Secretaries, the men who ruled China, ideally knew no life outside the life of the Party; even their sexual relations were to respond to the Party's needs rather than to their own. While that perfect servant was in the process of creation, crudeness and vehemence qualified men for power.

When irrational ambition lured the regime ever deeper into the mire of the Great Leap Forward in 1958, the Party turned to its faithful local Secretaries. Those untutored despots "soon became like little emperors," in the phrase of a Chinese merchant who lived in Hong Kong but traveled widely throughout the mainland. Understanding only the uses of repression, the local Secretaries responded to discontent by punishing all dissidents as "landlords, rich farmers, rightists, evil elements, or counter-revolutionaries." Their response to economic difficulties was to falsify statistics—as they had been taught to do.

"Much of the mess in the last few years," observed the same merchant, "has been caused by too much reliance upon Party Secretaries. More and more, they control everything, and they have neither knowledge themselves of the matters with which they deal, nor any staff—except clerks to prepare future quotas and register production figures. Of course, nobody can control those production figures or place any reliance upon them, for they come from other Party Secretaries in factories and Communes and offices."

Perhaps most revealing of the actual "new man" produced by the paradise of People's China were the local Party Secretaries' speeches on the radio. Broadcast throughout the land by the innumerable loudspeakers which have become the symbol of the regime, their voices spoke in accents of absolute authority to hundreds of millions of their countrymen. "When you listen to the speeches of lower Party bosses of counties or Communes or factories, they sound rough and uneducated," commented one professional auditor. "Voices and speech resemble those of sergeants in a peasant army. They speak forcefully, but they stutter and stammer, search for the right word, repeat ad infinitum *che-ko, che-ko* [literally, "this, this," the "uh, uh" of the Chinese language]. When they read a text, they read it laboriously and you can hear them turn the pages with heavy hands. When they speak impromptu, they only repeat well-worn Party slogans, and their I.Q. does not appear to be very high." [2]

Dependent upon such men to perform the complex tasks produced by the meeting of boundless ambition with material and technological poverty, the Party displayed great nostalgia for its pioneer days at Yenan, when guerrilla activists were perfectly adapted to the simple demands of continuous struggle. Basically, the Party was not suited to the tasks it faced. It was still a most efficient machine, given a simple task requiring ruthlessness, single-minded ardor, and destructiveness. It was at its best when it sought to destroy an existing political or social institution. It was at its worst when it sought to create new institutions to replace those it had destroyed. The Communist Party of China was a sword which could not be used as a plowshare or a lathe.

Created amid "constant struggle," the Maoist Party operated efficiently only in emergencies. Perplexed by stability, it continually created new crises. It had to behave aggressively, both internally and externally, and it had to breed revolution, since it could not direct evolutionary progress. Because new men, who might have altered its character with new ideas, were deliberately excluded from influence, the Party was wracked by ever greater tensions.

Just as conflict was the Party's normal relation to the external world, constant flux was its normal internal state. In theory a monolithic structure with an absolute doctrine, the Communist Party of China was, in reality, constantly changing under the impact of inevitable crises. Since the machinery provided no channel for dissent, each new adjustment became a critical internal struggle—and each crisis bred further crises. Finally, the pressure became too intense for even the automata the Maoists felt they had created in the local Party Secretaries. They gratefully followed the lead of the men near the apex who revolted against the impossibility of enforcing Mao's visions. Seeking to create the "new man" by the hundreds of millions, the Maoists were unable to create even a few million "new men" among their closest followers. The force of objective reality was too great.

Sympathetic foreign publicists gave the impression that the

[2] *China News Analysis,* No. 323, p. 1.

Party had never undergone major purges. In truth, the Communist Party of China was free of fierce struggles for power only during the brief period between the confirmation of Mao's absolute authority in 1938 and the moment he began to smell victory in 1942. Mao's unquestioned domination from 1938 to 1959 saved the few dozen men at the pinnacle from fratricidal contention for the Chairman's post. Thereafter, the fight for supreme power was open. It was finally revealed to the world in 1966. Hundreds of thousands of activists, including at least twenty of the demigods called Provincial First Secretaries had been reduced in rank, exiled to the wastelands, or expelled from the Party's ranks between 1957 and 1965. The purges after 1966 caught tens of thousands.

The greatest problem of the Communist Party of China was always its own members, rather than external foes or external circumstances. Difficulties arose from many causes. A nineteenth-century Western European doctrine, modified by the medieval Byzantine atmosphere of Soviet Russia, came into conflict with the Chinese temperament, despite many formal affinities between Confucianism and Maoism. Hope was forever deferred. Challenges that towered like summits, once attained, proved merely pauses on the struggle toward the next peak. Above all, it was extremely difficult to serve as an acolyte of a religion which did not really know its own mind. Most sinners undergoing "thought reform" were not told of the specific sins of which they were required to purge themselves. Instead they were forced to write confession after confession, until they finally dredged their gravest misdeeds from the depths of their own consciences. The faithful Party functionary suffered the same disadvantages in performing his normal duties. He was required to hew without wavering to hazy policies that were precisely defined only in retrospect.

A favored playwright found the Party even more capricious than the sated audiences of bourgeois nations. His short drama, called *Playing the Flageolet Differently*, was produced by almost every dramatic group in China in 1956. It was made into a motion picture and a best-selling novel. Subsequently the same work was condemned as "an attack on the Party, a poisonous weed that must be uprooted." [3]

[3] *Ibid.*, p. 6.

The play itself begins when a veteran of the Chinese People's Volunteers in Korea returns to his village in August 1954. It is the height of the "cooperativization" movement, but his village, having been denied agricultural cooperatives, remains poor, in contrast to the newly prosperous villages all around. The villagers are eager for cooperativization, since they realize that the individual plots they treasured after land reform cannot produce efficiently. But the county's Party Branch insists: "We must concentrate upon important points." The hero's request to organize a cooperative is rejected because "there are no solid bones among the villagers, no Party members." A newly admitted Party member himself, the hero organizes a "secret cooperative." He is denounced by the local authorities, and the conflict is not resolved until the Provincial First Secretary intervenes to endorse the new cooperative, admitting: "The responsibilities for error are the Party's!"

When the period of limited free speech ended in mid-1957, the hierarchy discovered that the drama was a violent attack upon its most cherished principles. Critics violently objected to the representation of the Party's officials as simple men who were overwhelmed by their new authority. Most shocking was the First Secretary's admission that the Party had erred.

The Party simply did not make mistakes. So essential was the appearance of omniscience that it often preferred to persist in error rather than admit error. Nor could anyone who disagreed with the Party Center ever be correct. Writing in the Canton *Nanfang Daily* in 1962, a commentator pointed out: "At the time of guerrilla wars, because the liberated areas were isolated from each other by enemy forces, circumstances compelled us to adopt the *then appropriate* basic principle of allowing different, independent units to exercise a high degree of local autonomy. *This guiding principle later became completely obsolete.* It has been necessary now to curtail the right of different units in different places to autonomy and to centralize the powers which *can and must be centralized* under the Central Committee." [Italics supplied.]

Liu Shao-chi, the architect of the present Party edifice, wrote in 1945 in his *Report on the Revision of the Party Constitution:* "With regard to problems of a nationwide nature, there can be only one kind of attitude and one view; there must not be several different attitudes and several views. Regarding problems which must be considered by the Central Committee, which will itself make its decisions public, local Party organizations *must not* exceed their powers by stating their views in advance of the Central Committee's decision. On problems of a nationwide nature, no spokesman of the Party, not even a member of the Central Committee, may state his views without the consent of the Central Committee. . . . This procedure is essential, since the expression of views or decisions contradicting those of the Central Committee will leave a most unfavorable effect within the Party and among the people in the face of the enemy."

The principle that all initiative must flow downward was described in the ponderous euphemism drawn from Lenin as "democratic centralism." It stemmed historically from a deep fear of corruption, based upon a demonstrated vulnerability to evil external influences. It stemmed immediately from a barren leadership's fear of dissent, which could destroy them. The men in the field felt—often with full justification—that they knew better than the men at the center. Instead of gratefully utilizing the intellectual vigor arising from the clash of ideas, the Maoists ascribed their previous permissiveness solely to difficulties of communication. In the second decade of the People's Republic of China complex problems made free exchange of opinion not merely helpful, but essential to attainment of the regime's goals. The Maoist Party Center, however, insured that only in the bracing air of Peking, where they were stimulated by the divine afflatus of Chairman Mao Tse-tung himself, might Communists think. In practice only a half-dozen men dared offer their opinions, except at the recurring moments of great crisis.

The Maoists' demand for unthinking conformity, enforced by constant repression, produced an ungovernable conflict between the Party Center, which pursued its vision of the ideal, and the provinces, which sought to attain the possible. Attrition destroyed most of the bold spirits and the original minds, leaving the average activist a self-seeking and hypercautious hack. Nonetheless, men moved by fervor or compassion still, from time to time, rose to dispute Peking's fiats. The Party Center's denial that "abstract human nature" existed was, in part, a propitiary invocation against constant difficulties with human nature.

The searing irony in the final conflict arose from the fact that the organization men at the center finally rejected the excesses of Mao Tse-tung's visions. When the organization at length insisted that policy must be shaped by capability rather than the pursuit of ideal and unattainable goals, Mao Tse-tung himself refused to obey the will of the machinery he had created to suppress the individuality of other men. He specifically rejected the principle of "democratic centralism" and he absolutely asserted that his own inspiration was superior to the Party's collective wisdom. Liu Shao-chi, the organization man *par excellence* who had drawn the plans of the repressive machinery, insisted that even Mao Tse-tung must submit his individual will to the Party's decisions. The total conflict was then joined.

The struggle to survive in the chill winds at the pinnacle of the Maoist Party had always been fierce and sanguinary.

Take Chen Yi, a Marshal of the People's Liberation Army, a Vice-Premier, and the Foreign Minister of the People's Republic of China. The Marshal possesses an excellent mind, though his physical appearance belies his stature. Unlike the majestic Mao Tse-tung or Chou En-lai, with his sardonic, actor's good looks, Chen Yi is patterned after Hollywood's idea of a Chinese warlord: plump, self-indulgent cheeks and small, hard eyes usually hidden behind dark glasses. He joined the Communist Party in France and played a minor role in the Nanchang Rising of August 1927, when the Red Army was born. A member of the Szechwan Group, which provided several generals and administrators who stood just beneath the pinnacle, Chen Yi joined Mao Tse-tung and Chu Teh at their first guerrilla base at Chingkang Shan in 1928. By 1930, he was a senior military officer in the Kiangsi Soviet Area, where Mao himself was chairman of the committee which directed military operations.

Mao's drive toward power was opposed by the Central Committee in Shanghai, which was supported by most senior officers, including Chen Yi. This anti-Mao faction followed the Li Li-San line, calling for immediate attacks upon the cities of China. When the second attack on Changsha failed in 1930, the commanders reconsidered, for they feared that their armies would be destroyed in vain assaults on fortified positions. Since the policy of building up strong Soviet Areas promised both a respite for the troops and the prospect that Mao would grow in power while his opponents dissipated their strength, the military's support gradually swung to Mao. By the end of 1930 Mao Tse-tung, secure in their backing, determined to liquidate the persistent opposition within the military establishment.

At Futien in Kiangsi in December 1930 Chen Yi was maneuvered into executing several hundred of his former comrades. Tied to Mao Tse-tung by his role in the slaughter, Chen Yi found his advancement blocked because of resentment in the Central Committee over the role he had played. Although Mao himself prevailed over the "Russian faction" in a series of skirmishes which culminated in his final victory at the Tsunyi Conference in 1935, Chen Yi remained in the second rank of the military. He was left behind with the discards of the rearguard in the New Fourth Army when the Communists left the Kiangsi Soviet Area on the Long March to the northwest in 1934.

Chen Yi was deputy-commander of the New Fourth Army in May 1940, when the unit's political commissar was severely censured for rightist deviationism. A directive from the Central Committee declared that the commissar had "failed to carry out the Central Committee's policy with determination; he was afraid to go all out in mobilizing the masses; he was afraid to extend the liberated areas and enlarge the armed forces of the people within the Japanese-occupied area; he was unable to realize the seriousness of the Kuomintang's reactionary attacks; and thus he lacked the spiritual and organizational preparedness to cope with these attacks."

The political commissar was abandoned to the Kuomintang's executioners, while Chen Yi, who was praised in the same directive, survived to become acting-commander of the New Fourth Army after the commanding general's death in battle.

Chen Yi was thus rewarded for his loyalty to Mao, loyalty to which he had been bound by treachery. Although a number of his personal followers were purged after the conquest of all China, Chen Yi finally emerged triumphant from a new power struggle with his nominal superior in Shanghai. Rumors of Chen's death were abroad for at least a year, but it was finally his opponent who perished.

Jao Shu-shih, briefly political commissar when Chen Yi was commander of the New Fourth Army, was chairman of the East China Military and Administrative Area in 1952. Chen played a subordinate role as commander of the Area's military forces and Mayor of Shanghai. The two were antagonists from the beginning, each invoking the support of his powerful friends. Not only were Chen's friends more powerful, but Jao's own champion was an unfortunate choice.

Kao Kang, a native of the Yenan area who survived the purge of local Party members when the Long March terminated there, was chairman of the Manchurian Military and Administrative Area in the early 1950s. Also First Party Secretary and a favorite of Josef Stalin, Kao Kang set himself up as "independent king" of the area the Russians considered their particular sphere of influence. Manchuria became a unique, semiautonomous area which signed a separate trade agreement with the Russians. Kao Kang initiated major economic and political policies on his own authority, even presuming to suggest that his measures should subsequently be adopted in China proper. It was no coincidence that Kao's new measures were a line-for-line transcription of Russian practices, even to the accounting system used by the railways.

Mao Tse-tung held his hand until a year after Stalin's death, but in February 1954 an extraordinary plenary session of the Central Committee heard Liu Shao-chi excoriate those "leading Communists who disrupt the unity of the Party." Mao himself was conveniently "on holiday" during the meeting. It was not until a year later that a specially convened National Conference of the Party named the dissidents. Kao Kang had already committed suicide, and Jao Shu-shih disappeared into the total, permanent obscurity which only a totalitarian state can conjure. He never emerged. Ironically, again, Liu Shao-chi's attack on Kao Kang was a precursor, albeit a mild precursor, of the vilification the Maoists later directed against himself.

* *

The fabled unity of the Communist Party of China was belied not only by personal conflicts among the titans, but also by the recurring necessity to insure the lower ranks' automatic responsiveness to the Central Committee's orders. Unsatisfactory discipline within a Party at war in 1942 provoked the CPC's first formal ideological purge, the *Cheng Feng* Movement. The lessons taught by the 1942 Rectification Campaign were expressed in several hundred thousand words which can be summed up in four: *obedience, dedication, struggle, conformity!* Its purpose was to establish the primacy of Mao's doctrines in order to complement his control of the Party machinery, which had been established by the defeat of Chang Kuo-tao, his last great rival, in 1938.

But the ideological battle could never be won, for fresh victories merely created new internal strains. When the triumphant cadres, who were the Communists' hard core, marched into the cities in 1949, they had endured two decades of hardship and peril in guerrilla struggle. Men rejoiced at reaching their final goal. Even the most dedicated expected some degree of relaxation and comfort, for they believed that the victors would receive the rewards of victory. Instead, they were enjoined to work harder—and to live as frugally as ever—in order to achieve greater victories. None of the backwoods cadres was enthusiastic over the edicts commanding new self-denial—and some rebelled. During the extended transitional period from private to public ownership, men empowered to issue legal documents or purchase orders encountered innumerable opportunities to enrich themselves. Corruption among cadres became so blatant in 1951 that the Central Committee ordered the Three-Antis Movement to purify the Party. As has been recounted, the campaign was directed against bureaucracy, waste, and graft. Although the onus fell on the bourgeois for corrupting the incorruptibles, the Party itself had sustained a severe shock.

Later crises arose as much from compassion as from self-seeking. Although many cadres fought for their own meager privileges, a greater number rebelled in protest against Peking's exploitation of the masses. Most cadres felt the people were entitled to the fruits of the revolution that had been fought for the people's benefit, but they saw the masses forced to work ever harder on ever decreasing rations.

The Maoists charged that cadres not only shirked and disobeyed, but actually organized themselves in opposition to the Party Center's policies. Rot appeared at that point in the structure where it was least expected and most devastating—in the Provincial Party Committees, the chief agencies of Peking's will. The problem of dissidence in Kwangtung Province was so acute that throughout the latter half of 1957, the Provincial Committee "conducted thorough criticism and resolute struggle against localism," according to the organ of the Kwangtung Provincial Party Committee. The case of the Anti-Party Clique in Kwangtung offers a detailed example of what was happening everywhere in China.

The nation's southernmost province, peopled by a racially distinct group speaking a distinctive language, had always troubled China's rulers. Land reform was repeatedly deferred in Kwangtung to placate the hotheaded Cantonese, while the Party waged an "anti-localism struggle" there as early as 1952. In 1956 a new wave of localism swept the province; on its crest appeared two of the Party's most devout servants. Ku Ta-tsun and Feng Pai-chu were alternate members of the Central Committee, members of the Secretariat of the Kwangtung Provincial Committee, and Vice-Governors of Kwangtung.

Subsequent denunciations revealed that the pair took their stand on a number of concrete issues. They argued that "land reform in Kwangtung was too 'left' and had too wide a scope of attack." They contended that too large a number of persons had been classified as landlords and that "struggles" against those so designated were "too violent." The Maoists noted with sorrow in their own English-language text: "Despite the joy of millions of newly landed [sic] peasants, the pair declared: 'We are like men sitting on a volcano which may explode at any time!'"

The Anti-Party Clique also complained that many southern cadres, after long and loyal service in isolation from the rest of the movement, had been replaced by northerners. They argued that the "foreign cadres," who had become the majority of the Party's functionaries in Kwangtung, "are subjective and do not understand Kwangtung's historical conditions, social characteristics, or production features, and, therefore, make a mess of things."

The Kwangtung Clique's gravest sin was its plea for moderation. In 1955, the indictment explained, a new outbreak of "counter-revolutionary activities" forced the Party to order severe repression of those who "sabotaged, created turmoil—and incited people to beat up cadres and to feud with each other." Yet Vice-Governor Ku Ta-tsun openly contended: "Each person killed during the suppression movement will create a host of additional enemies. This policy will merely force our own men to go over to the enemy side. Therefore, I consider that the movement to suppress counter-revolutionaries will actually have the effect of creating enemies!"

Opposed to the hasty cooperativization program, Ku Ta-tsun and Feng Pai-chu refused to accept Maoist claims of great increases in agricultural production. They not only objected to the brutality of security cadres, but actually dared to charge that the Party's policy "advocates the cult of the individual." The men who helped crush the pair were themselves later to make that charge even stronger and even more explicit. The cult of Mao Tse-tung was to prove the final irritation which drove the faithful into revolt.

Hainan, the large island in the South China Sea where a strong Communist movement flourished for decades behind the enemy's lines, had developed a race of proud and self-reliant native cadres. The Ku-Feng arguments appealed to both the local pride and the reasoned discontent of the Hainanese. In 1956, the Party's indictment charged, Hainan cadres joined the two Vice-Governors in a campaign to change the revolution's course on the tropical island.

Although they were later accused of "large-scale illegal association and secret activities," their activities were quite open in the beginning. With touching faith in the Party Center, the Hainanese wrote a series of letters to the Central Committee. Those letters criticized the mistakes made in Kwangtung and asked Peking's assistance in restoring the revolution to its proper course. When these pleas were not answered, indignant native cadres attacked the "foreign cadres" and their local sycophants. "Everybody was plunged into a state of panic," said the Maoists' later account. In the spring of 1957, having been given no comfort by their superiors, the discontented faithful of one Hainan county actually arose in a miniature Hungarian incident. Not surprisingly, they were joined by the peasants and a few former landlords, whose adherence gave the self-righteous Party Center a pretext for condemning the movement as a "rightist, anti-Party incident."

The Party expelled Ku Ta-tsun and Feng Pai-chu, ordering additional punishments of a nature unspecified. The indictment concluded ominously: "Anyone who tries to reverse the rolling wheels of history essays a foolish task. He will, inevitably, seek to hurl a rock, only to drop it and crush his own feet."

The Communists might have expected trouble in Kwangtung, if only because of historical precedent. There was, however, no reason to expect trouble in Honan Province in the north, where the people were naturally compliant. Yet Honan saw one of the most blatant and closely reasoned revolts against Party discipline. Pan Fu-sheng, First Secretary of the Party's Provincial Committee, not only criticized the Central Committee's policies strenuously and specifically, but actually "attempted to deceive Chairman Mao himself" at a meeting of Provincial First Secretaries at Tsingtao in 1958. Pan drew up a list of "ten contradictions," stressing particularly: "Contradictions between Party people and non-Party people in general, and with democratic parties and intellectuals in particular. And, second, contradictions between centralization and decentralization, between central tasks and particular tasks." Pan trenchantly analyzed the Party's treatment of its own cadres, as well as the masses, treating each aspect separately.

On collectives: "Big cooperatives are nothing better than small cooperatives. In a big cooperative there are more contradictions among more people. Members of the Liulin Cooperative have to walk some ten *li* [about three miles] and queue up before they can talk to the director. . . . Peasants . . . are the same as beasts of burden today. Yellow oxen are tied up in the house and human beings are tied up in the field. Girls and women pull plows and harrows, with their wombs hanging down. Cooperation is transformed into exploitation of human strength."

On the Communist Party: "The peasants see no hope in Socialism. The grain question is grave. . . . Relations are strained between the Party and the masses . . . the masses state that Chairman Mao is not informed of the situation, that the basic-level cadres are hopeless, and traitors are found in the middle strata."

On intellectuals: "The intellectuals are not accustomed to Socialism and between us [Party cadres] and them there are walls and moats. They are right when they criticize us for being conceited and arrogant; for regarding ourselves as meritorious; for not regarding them as equals; for pretending to know what we do not know; and for not giving them authority."

On education: "People say the Communist Party is incompetent and not able to exercise leadership because it does not know its business. I am in favor of setting up as an example several universities in which the school affairs [managing] committees are composed of leftists, rightists, and middle-of-the-roaders."

Pan Fu-sheng was dismissed in the great purge of 1958, when the Central Committee swept the rulers of six provinces from their posts and relegated tens of thousands of "core cadres" to remote villages. He was later restored to grace by realists who sympathized with his position. Again total irony appeared. Pan was one of the few senior provincial officials who allied themselves with the Maoists in the Cultural Revolution. Perhaps he was frightened of being caught on the wrong side again.

The Honan revolt of the cadres and that in Kwantung and Hainan, with its small armed uprisings, were merely examples of an indeterminable number of small risings against the Party leadership that shook China after collectivization began in 1955. Cadres in their hundreds of thousands displayed their discontent by active sabotage or by refusing to drive their people to labor. Even before the threat of starvation turned the mass of the people against the regime in 1959, widespread support for the rebels—and the Party's manifest alarm—demonstrated that the dissidents expressed the popular will.

✳   ✳

In 1921 the membership of the Communist Party of China was about sixty. From the high of three hundred thousand attained in 1934, it was down to forty thousand in 1937, after several purges and persistent attacks by the Kuomintang. Between the end of the Anti-Japanese War in 1945 and its conquest of power in 1949, the Party expanded from 1.2 million members to 4.5 million. In 1963, there were nearly 18 million members of the Communist Party in China. That figure represented an increase of much more than 16.8 million within a fifteen-year period, for wastage by death and purges had been considerable.

The enormous Party was a powerful instrument in the hands of the hierarchy, but it was not a handy instrument. It was an overwhelming task to try to control the actions and thoughts of every member of this vast organization, which was no longer made up of men of common background dedicated to a simple purpose as it had been in the beginning. To perform the task, the hierarchy created a welter of interlocking organs, committees, and commissions that outdid the gaudy Confucian structure of boards, pavilions, and colleges. The heart of the Communist Party was the Central Committee. When the rolls were full, it had about a hundred full members and one hundred alternate members, all elected by the National Party Congress; they met in plenary sessions, special sessions, expanded sessions, and emergency sessions. The hierarchy proceeded downward from six multiprovincial Regional Bureaus through provincial, border-area, and special municipality bureaus, to county or city committees, and ended in branches in communes or factories. At the bottom was the cell, made up of about twelve men and women.

To govern this sprawling organism the Central Committee selected one Chairman, five Vice-Chairmen,[4] and one General Secretary. The policy-making body was the Political Bureau, made up of nineteen full members and five alternate members. The Politburo's Standing Committee of seven men was the group that really ruled Communist China. A Secretariat of ten full

[4] In 1966 a decision of doubtful legality by an intimidated Central Committee reduced the number of Vice-Chairmen to one: Lin Piao, Mao's chosen successor.

members and three alternates administered the day-to-day business of the Party, executing the decisions of the Political Bureau. The Control Commission, with twenty members in addition to a secretary and five deputy-secretaries, sought to enforce ideological recitude and to insure that every Party member behaved in a manner befitting a "vanguard of the revolution." The Control Commission was, however, powerless to deal with major ideological controversies, like the massive resistance that began Mao Tsetung's eclipse after the excesses of 1958 and rose again even stronger after the Central Committee's sweeping confession of failure in 1961.

The intricate structure of the Party, complemented by a People's Government equally complex, obscured only slightly the fact that China was once more ruled by men rather than by laws. Unwilling to yield a jot of its power to settled institutions that functioned according to fixed rules, the Communist Party maintained a simulacrum of a functioning political system. But in practice only personal authority could control personal excesses. The quality of the individual cadres therefore assumed critical importance, much beyond the significance of individuals in systems in which established institutions not only limit personal power but actually fulfill specific functions over extended periods. Despite conflicts between different strata of the Party and within the supreme leadership itself, the CPC still possessed several million reasonably honest and reasonably able cadres. Most of the men who have challenged the absolute Party did not seek to overthrow Communism, but rather implored the Party Center to permit reforms, which, they argued, would equally benefit the masses and the Party itself. Unremitting excesses alienated these remaining idealists from 1961 to 1965. Those men would—under great provocation—rise *for* the Party, but they would not rise *against* the Party, which was their life. It remained for Mao Tse-tung, Lin Piao, and their few followers to rise against the Communist Party of China.

Only one major institution in Communist China possessed vitality that was not drawn directly from the Communist Party. The People's Liberation Army of about three million men was at once the strongest buttress and the greatest potential threat to the regime. Until 1949 it was almost impossible to distinguish the Army from the Party or the generals from the politicians. Assaulting the citadels of power with captured rifles and homemade grenades, the Chinese Communists made little distinction between the men who conceived policy and the men who carried it out on the battlefield. Little distinction was necessary, for the same men frequently played both roles. After the establishment of the People's Republic as a vast modern state, distinctions were essential.

Becoming self-conscious of their power and distinctiveness, the military might otherwise have swallowed the Party—and perhaps the state as well.

Mao Tse-tung's first response to the challenge of organizing a new China was nonetheless to entrust the task to his generals, as he had entrusted them with the conquest of power. Six Military and Administrative Areas, all but semiautonomous Manchuria ruled by generals, enforced the first reforms upon the Chinese people. But those Areas were weakened in 1952 and abolished in 1954, so that the Party's direction might replace the Army's. Nonetheless, the regular armed forces remained the regime's chief instrument of coercion, though militia and police units directly under the Party were given greater "responsibility for internal security" as the years passed. But the Army was no longer an integral part of the Party. Only one People's Marshal, Lin Piao, was still counted among the half-dozen men who controlled China before the total disruption of the Cultural Revolution. Even then Lin was considered a "political general," the term, unusual in Communist China, meaning that his chief impetus was loyalty to Mao Tse-tung rather than to his troops or to the profession of arms. When the final climacteric began, Lin's behavior revealed that great personal ambition and a startling degree of ideological fanaticism also guided his actions.

Set apart from the Party, the Army remained a highly privileged group which was the ultimate recourse of China's Communist masters. The Politburo depended upon the soldiers to control the masses in any major test and to give substance to its external threats. The original Cromwellian structure of government was altered chiefly because Mao did not wish the People's Republic to share the fate of the English Republic. The generals, the only group possessing both power and competence in an area distinct from politics, had already proved exceedingly difficult to manage.

The first separation of the Army from the Party occurred at the height of the Army's success in the Korean War. Disturbed by his generals' growing independence, Chairman Mao restored their sense of proportion by curbing their political power. He reorganized the structure of government to abolish the five great Military and Administrative Areas—four ruled by generals—into which all China had been divided. The second degradation, disguised as glorification, came in 1955, when the military were inclined to feel that the goals of the revolution had been attained. The Politburo gave the generals the conventional military trappings for which they longed and, by the same stroke, reminded them that they were the servants of the Party and the state. Mao transformed his revolutionary generals into People's Marshals, hanging them with gold braid, medals, and stars—and creating ten in all to forestall the *folie de grandeur* a smaller group might have felt.

After their translation, most of the gold-braided guerrillas were utilized for ceremonial purposes, while younger generals took over their commands. One of the old guard appeared as the official Chinese representative at the glittering reception given by Prime Minister Mohammed Ali to celebrate Pakistan's becoming a republic early in 1956. Stocky Marshal Ho Lung, his stubby pipe clenched between his teeth, held court in a corner of the garden under a string of colored lights. He was surrounded by an entourage of bright young captains and majors. The semiliterate old peasant was impassive in his gaudy new uniform: red-striped trousers, high-necked tunic littered with gold braid, a cluster of orders as big as silver dollars and twice as weighty, and, on his shoulders, gold-encrusted epaulettes bearing the single red star of a People's Marshal. Ho Lung was outstandingly dignified, and he was amiably prepared to chat even with an American who spoke his language. But his function was, quite apparently, wholly ceremonial; his usefulness for diplomacy was limited by the fact that he spoke no language other than Chinese and was making his first trip abroad. Only Chen Yi and Defense Minister Lin Piao among the marshals truly exercised important political power before the Cultural Revolution began in 1966, while the former *primus inter pares*, Peng Teh-huai, was degraded in 1959. In 1964 Lin Piao, as Defense Minister, abolished all formal ranks in an effort to solidify his personal control of the People's Liberation Army.

After 1956 the ranks of the People's Liberation Army were as dissatisfied as their generals. Some of the sources of discontent are also common in bourgeois armies, though they were somewhat surprising in a Communist army. Some were peculiar to China. The Army was angry at political discrimination in promotions, particularly in the officer ranks, and at the caste line drawn between officers and men. The peasant soldiers were also shocked at the sacrifices demanded of their families in China's myraid farm villages. The Party never satisfactorily explained to the military elite why their families were reduced to toiling peasants, when they had previously enjoyed great privileges as a reward for their men's military service. Officers, in particular, were infuriated when their wives were sent to far-off villages to labor on the land.

Personal discontent intensified the friction generated by the Army's conflicting missions. The Army was, on the one hand, a defensive force and a vehicle to carry the revolution abroad or to border areas like Tibet. Internally, on the other hand, it functioned as the chief repressive arm of the state and as a shock labor force. Attempting to fill both roles, the People's Liberation Army could perform neither efficiently.

The Party's first attempt to reconcile the conflict by creating a professional military caste after the Russian model merely created new sources of discontent. Instead of rendering grateful service in return for status, the generals began to act like generals. Intent upon its transformation into a force capable of fighting technological wars, the Army violated political discipline. As early as 1957 the Party complained that the generals "insisted upon solely military considerations and neglected political work, growing slack in their primary responsibility to the people." When Mao Tse-tung bestowed epaulettes on the professional officers, he also gave them sanction for considering themselves a breed apart. If they were to dress like Russians, the old guerrilla fighters reasoned, then they would act like Russians, placing professional concerns first. Generalissimo Chu Teh himself found it necessary to remind his subordinates in 1958 that it was not the tricky new Russian techniques that had brought them to victory in the revolution, but the strategy, tactics, and training developed by Mao Tse-tung, who had brought mankind's "military doctrines to their highest development."

The Party, therefore, determined to humble the arrogant generals. In 1958 more than a hundred were "sent down" to serve as privates for several months. In 1959 Defense Minister Marshal Peng Teh-huai and his hand-picked chief-of-staff were replaced by Marshal Lin Piao, a Vice-Chairman of the Party, and Lo Jui-ching,[5] who was a professional security policeman, not a soldier. Veterans, who had grown apart from the Party and the peasants, were discharged to make way for unblemished recruits. These measures did not, of course, contribute to the creation of a modern army; they wrecked morale without noticeably improving political reliability. The Maoists had not mastered the conflict created by its demand on the one hand that its soldiers be highly skilled and on the other that they render blind obedience to Party directives which violate all their professional standards.

Coincident with the creation of People's Communes in 1958, the Party proclaimed the Everyone-a-Soldier Movement to mobilize a People's Militia of hundreds of millions of men and women. This citizen army was to fulfill two chief functions: under the direct control of local Party organs, it served as a coercive force ouside the regular military establishment; and it provided defense in depth against nuclear attack.

Nonetheless, the People's Liberation Army of 2.8 million men is a formidable force. In conventional arms and military skill the Liberation Army is dominant in Asia. Only in contrast to the ultimate enemy, the United States, does it appear weak.

The People's Air Force musters about a hundred thousand men and four thousand to forty-five hundred airplanes, of which twenty-five hundred to three thousand are Russian-designed jet fighters and bombers. China can make a limited number of Mig-17 and Mig-19 airframes, and a factory manufacturing the ad-

[5] Lo Jui-ching was himself degraded in 1966 for "professionalism."

vanced Mig-21 began operating in 1964. Handicapped by inefficient ground radar, Communist fighter pilots distinguished themselves neither in dogfights against Nationalist Sabrejets nor in preventing reconnaissance and airdrops by cumbersome Nationalist C-46s. But the radar gap was finally closed, and the Migs now mount a Russian version of the Sidewinder air-to-air, heat-seeking missile. Migs have sallied successfully against American fighter bombers entering Chinese airspace during missions over North Vietnam. They are backed by sophisticated ground-to-air missiles.

Before the Cultural Revolution an elite was undergoing modernization and training for nuclear warfare. The regular People's Liberation Army numbers about 2.6 million ground and support troops of varying quality, the best units excelling in sheer physical endurance and the use of small arms, mortars, and artillery. Most are trained as guerrillas, but even the best units are severely handicapped as conventional forces by lack of standardized equipment, by bad logistics and communications, and by a shortage of staff officers who can control large formations. In the last days of the Korean War, Chinese attacks, staged by three army corps of thirty thousand men each, broke down after three days, when the troops outran their supplies. Staff work has undoubtedly improved in the last decade and a half, but during the 1958 bombardment of Quemoy, Communist guns were handicapped by the need to provide separate ammunition for a variety of artillery pieces. Supply problems, as well as political reasons, were a major factor in halting the Chinese attack on India in the autumn of 1962. Nor is the internal Chinese transportation network adequate to support large formations engaged in continuing combat on the country's borders. Although obsolescent Russian tanks and guns equip the new formations, the Chinese themselves complain that quantities are inadequate—and the flow decreased radically after 1960, virtually halting after the public quarrels of mid-1963.

The People's Navy is still a negligible force, symbolized by its flagship, the obsolete light cruiser that was once the U.S.S. *Canberra,* given to Chiang Kai-shek in the mid-1940s. Between thirty and forty submarines and about a hundred motor torpedo boats are the Navy's chief offensive weapons. They are backed by a handful of destroyers and frigates, as well as smaller units numbering about six hundred and fifty.

Calculations of conventional strength have been rendered somewhat academic in the eyes of men charged with the defense of American interests in Asia—and the American nation itself—by China's rapid development of nuclear weapons. Concentrating their technological resources upon atomic and rocketry development and spending lavishly of their economic resources, the Chinese moved from the explosion of their first nuclear device in 1964 to their first hydrogen bomb in mid-1967. The time elapsed was less than three years, a remarkable record. Estimates of China's capability to deliver her nuclear weapons vary, but even the most conservative agree that the Chinese will possess intermediate range ballistic missiles by 1970—and true intercontinental ballistic missiles two to three years thereafter. The fantastic pace of the six Chinese nuclear tests makes any other assumption unreasonable.

No Chinese leader—Maoist or pragmatist—was opposed to the development of atomic weapons as rapidly as possible. For the Maoists those weapons represented a formidable offensive weapon—although a weapon whose psychological effect would perhaps preclude its use. The pragmatists, quite logically, viewed the weapons as a guarantee of China's security.

Fortunately for the United States and her allies, the overwhelming weight of American nuclear superiority has tended to reduce the psychological effect of China's developing nuclear arsenal. Although the U.S. Seventh Fleet was in 1968 a somewhat less formidable weapon than it had been in 1963 because of China's nuclear capabilities, American intervention on the ground in Southeast Asia had radically reduced the danger of a nuclear confrontation between the United States and China. In the first place, that intervention had given heart to native governments and checked the decay—moral, political, and economic—that invited the Maoists to press their "people's wars." Those campaigns of subversion and guerrilla warfare, of course, brought the nuclear confrontation closer by enlarging China's influence in the troubled area. In the second place, the demonstration that Maoist tactics are not "inevitably victorious" had been a significant factor in bringing about the collapse of the entire Maoist mystique. It was, of course, the obsessed Maoists in their dedication to "liberating" the entire world who created the danger of nuclear confrontation by their adventurous forward policy.

Nonetheless, all future American policy must be based upon a respectful assessment of China's nuclear power. The decision to proceed with a "thin" anti-ballistic weapons system in mid-1967 was but the first acknowledgment of the new reality.

The chief involvement of the People's Liberation Army in 1968 was political rather than military. The greatest array of guerrillas in mass formation the world had ever seen and its dedicated petty bourgeois generals were Mao's own pride and the darling of the Chinese people when the Communists took China in 1949. For the first time in her history, soldiers were welcomed with joy by the civilian populace of the cities and the countryside. A new world was in birth, and the People's Liberation Army was the adored midwife. The Maoist regime "grew out of the barrel of the gun!"

In 1968 the PLA played an utterly different role amid anarchy that made the chaos of the Kuomintang's last days appear an orderly retreat. "Commanders and warriors," to use the Communists' own terminology, were bewildered by the conflicting demands made upon them. The central command of the largest and most effective Chinese army of modern times was split into two major factions—and many smaller factions, though no one outside headquarters knew the precise divisions. The rough khaki uniforms and the red stars on shapeless caps were the same as they had been in 1949. But the civilian populace looked upon the Liberation Army half in antipathy and half in utter puzzlement. The military's chief assignment was no longer either "liberation" of the Chinese people or their defense against external enemies, but the control of civil disorder, the suppression of political riots, and the maintenance of industrial and agricultural production.

The Army occupied vital installations from warehouses to banks, from railroad depots to radio stations, from schools to shipyards. If the Army had not held them, they would have been the focus—and the prizes—of strife between a welter of conflicting factions.

The deceptively straightforward assignment given to the PLA by politicians who exercised only titular authority tried the Army's ability—and its willingness—to carry out the mission. Under commanders who were either loyal to the Lin Piao–Mao Tse-tung faction or were impelled by personal ambition, some units supported the Maoist campaign to "take power" from the regular structures of the Communist Party and the People's Government. Those units were, however, a minority. Another minority supported the anti-Maoist officials of their particular provinces. The majority of the PLA tried simply to maintain the normal pulse of China. Like policemen in the midst of a gang-fight, the soldiers hardly attempted to distinguish between "good elements and bad elements." Considering the preservation of order their mission, they sought above all to suppress strife rather than fighting for the victory of one side or the other. Like any peacekeeping force, the PLA instinctively favored that side which gave them the least trouble—that is, the moderates.

The Liberation Army at once epitomized and minimized—insofar as it could—the total confusion that was the state of China in 1968. Bewildered by the lack of either clear directives or clear objectives, it was not notably successful in suppressing internal strife.

Despite the threatening presence of armed soldiers in every major factory and People's Commune, the economy was spinning toward chaos because of mismanagement, absenteeism, and sabotage. Yet matters would have been much worse if the Army had not intervened. Whatever stability was preserved was maintained by the troops in baggy uniforms. The Army was omnipresent, if not omnipotent.

In Sian, the capital of Shansi Province, in mid-February 1967, opposing factions made up of workers and students fought for possession of the loudspeaker installations dominating the city's main square. Since both claimed to be "true revolutionary rebels" (Chinese cant for loyal Maoists), the troops merely stood by. When the mob clashes swelled into a battle to occupy the offices of the provincial newspaper, the Army stepped in to prevent either side's winning. Neither faction could claim a victory, but the more militant was, without question, frustrated by the PLA's intervention.

The same pattern had already displayed itself in Shanghai, China's greatest city, when extremists laid siege to *The Liberation Daily,* the organ of the Municipal Committee of the Communist Party. As attackers hammered on the doors with makeshift battering rams, soldiers preached restraint to them through loudspeakers. When the attackers refused to give way, the troops themselves occupied the building. Again the ultra-militants were checkmated.

Hooliganism, theft, and violent clashes between rival political factions were epidemic in China. Nonetheless, the Liberation Army did not generally attempt to suppress disorder by the direct application of armed force. Officers preferred to calm tempers by moral authority and by the weight of the soldiers' presence. Although intimidation was implicit when uniformed soldiers were ostentatiously present in classrooms, workshops, and fields, the military's chief weapon was conciliation. Patient officers not only attended mass political meetings, they sat down with groups of a half-dozen students, workers, and farmers to offer instruction in the canonical Thought of Mao Tse-tung and to urge moderation. Army dramatic troupes toured the countryside, to plant the red banner of the Thought of Mao Tse-tung. The spate of directives that transformed the Army into the chief agency of authority throughout China stressed that soldiers must "learn from the people and behave humbly toward the masses"—negative but convincing evidence that they had not always done so. The masses were exhorted time and time again, to look upon the troops as their "staunch defenders and their dearest friends." The necessity for such constant exhortation was a convincing demonstration that the people held quite another view of the troops they had once idolized.

The Army's formal assignment in those troubled times was to serve as a "great school of the Thought of Mao Tse-tung," in other words, an instrument of mass indoctrination. Nonetheless, Vice-Chairman of the Communist Party and Defense Minister Lin Piao, Mao Tse-tung's "deputy great commander" and heir presumptive, indicated both the scope of the Army's involvement in the turmoil and his own appraisal of its gravity when he told senior commanders: "Many men and women have committed suicide, and many others have been murdered. Production has fallen . . . but our losses are not as great as they were during the War against the Japanese or the Civil War against the Kuomintang!" In the same speech, delivered at the beginning of April, Lin instructed all units: "You must take no action without clearing it with higher authority. But you *must* pay *no* attention to the Provincial Committees of the Party. They are all rotten!"

The PLA was not strengthened in its endeavors to keep the peace by the fact that a major source of the controversy that has splintered the Chinese nation was military doctrine—and the future of the Army. Two fundamental questions were at issue: Was the Liberation Army, descended from the grand old guerrilla forces of Mao Tse-tung, to become a modern, technological force, or was it to depend primarily upon what Lin Piao called "our spiritual atomic bomb, the great numbers of the courageous Chinese people"? Was Peking justified in pursuing a dangerous policy of confrontation with the United States—and the Soviet Union—in order to "liberate the oppressed masses of the world" through guerrilla wars and subversion when the PLA was obviously incapable of turning back an attack by either great power?

The anti-Maoists argued that an adventurous foreign policy could not be justified until the Liberation Army was fully equipped with modern arms—and skilled in their use. The Maoists contended that the Thought of Mao Tse-tung, "who is the greatest military thinker of modern times," not only made the guerrilla strategy invincible, but guaranteed the victory of a "forward" foreign policy. They further insisted that "politics must command," which meant promotion of officers and men for ideological fervor rather than professional competence; the slogan also meant employing the troops in a variety of non-military activities, ranging from farming to building dams. Lo Jui-ching, Chief of Staff of the PLA from 1959 to 1966, espoused the first position. He was purged by the Maoists. Lin Piao, Minister of Defense since 1959, was a whole-hearted public advocate of the second position. Their clash, preceding the formal beginning of the cultural Revolution, was the last of the incidents the Maoists characterized as "three great mutinies" within the officer corps of the PLA. All three ended with sweeping purges of the "professionals."

The continuing difficulties in controlling both the Communist Party and the People's Liberation Army from 1949 onward were manifestations of fundamental questions confronting the regime: Could men effectively rule a vast and complex nation like China if they insisted upon exerting absolute control from the center over the organism's every movement—much less frogmarch it into the twentieth century? With tension increasing, was it possible to avoid a breakdown before the regime's objectives were attained? Could any people endure the unending strain of absolute obedience and absolute conformity while toiling to fulfill their masters' illimitable ambitions?

The Maoists answered *Yes* to all three questions. The pragmatists answered *No*. Finally, the Maoists were forced to exert their authority by denying all formal structures of authority. The pragmatists wished chiefly to reduce the scope of authority by making existing institutions of authority at once less intrusive and less officious.

12

Government with Mirrors

The Organization and Working of
The People's Government Before It
Was Shattered by the Great Proletarian
Cultural Revolution

When Count Potëmkin, Catherine the Great's lover and prime minister, built the façades of thriving villages along the Volga River, he deceived his sovereign by creating the appearance of prosperity in the ravaged land.

Elaborate façades called the People's Government and the People's Law Courts existed in China, in part because the hierarchy knew that nations always possessed governments and in part to display the hierarchy's good intentions. But the government did not rule, and the courts did not judge. Despite a seemingly unending proliferation of administrative organs and decrees, the government's component branches neither took decisions nor executed policies, as do bodies called by the same names in the West—or even in the Soviet Union. After years of debate, the courts had rejected both the Anglo-Saxon principle that the accused is innocent until proven guilty, and the principle of Roman Law that the accused is presumed guilty until proven innocent. In China the accused was always guilty. The function of the courts was to prove the charges laid by the Party. "Politics was in command," in Mao's motto, and the courts were held to be merely another instrument of the "dictatorship of the proletariat." Abstract justice was neither executed—nor even pursued.

Mao Tse-tung, however, was his own Potëmkin. He deceived himself as to his government's true nature by contemplating it

255

through the distorting prisms of certain ideological assumptions. The People's Republic of China, in the authorized definition, was "a democratic dictatorship by the entire people, with the proletariat in the vanguard, all under the guidance of the Communist Party of China." It was not formally government by the Communist Party since representatives of other parties sat in the National People's Congress, the instrument through which the people exercised their presumed sovereignty.

Although "dictatorship" was the authorized translation into English, the word used for "dictatorship by the masses" was different in Chinese from the term describing the "dictatorship" of Chiang Kai-shek or Adolf Hitler. The first, *chuan-cheng*, means "special rule," while the second, *tu-tsai*, means "one man's oppressive rule." By calling their government a dictatorship the Communists were far from acknowledging that the people had no voice in public affairs. The Marxist thesis holds that governments—before the blessed state of Communism, when they disappear—are the instruments by which the dominant economic class exercises control, *i.e.*, dictatorship, over other classes. Dictatorship of the people accordingly meant that the masses, having displaced the bourgeoisie, now operated the machinery of the government for their own benefit.

By its own lights the Communist Party governed neither arbitrarily nor exclusively. By Western lights the Party's "guidance" was indistinguishable from absolute control. Most startling perhaps was the aristocratic prohibition on popular election of "representative" bodies. Instead of electing the twelve hundred and twenty-six delegates to the National People's Congress by direct vote, the people voted for local councils. Those councils, in turn, chose Provincial People's Councils, which elected delegates to the National Congress. The Chinese selected their local councils from a single slate of candidates, usually by a public show of hands in which only "citizens" might participate. In addition to the feeble-minded, several additional millions were disfranchised. They were classified as "nationals" rather than "citizens," because they were landlords, counter-revolutionaries, high officials of the Kuomintang, or simply "enemies of the people." Since the proletariat was the vanguard, a hundred thousand city dwellers were entitled to a representative in the Congress, while each deputy from the rural areas represented eight hundred thousand persons. A number of seats were also reserved for special groups like ethnic minorities and the armed forces. The Congress generally was supposed to meet annually, although its sessions rarely occurred at the precise interval fixed by law. Those sessions generally lasted no more than two weeks. The Congress heard speeches and approved, without amendment, the policies and appointments placed before it. The 1954 National People's Congress was a particularly efficient body, for it sanctioned two hundred and eighty-seven appointments in just twenty minutes.

Two anomalous, quasi-governmental bodies existed on the same plane as the Congress. The Chinese People's Political Consultative Council, composed of "representatives of all classes," did not change in composition from the time it was chosen by the victorious Communists in 1949 to sanction their conquest by arms. The Consultative Council met at irregular intervals—in practice, whenever the Communists desired a more sweeping expression of approval than the National People's Congress could provide. But it had no power whatever, not even the right to approve decisions. The second body, the Supreme State Conference, was a most curious organization, probably unique in lacking the slightest pretense of popular representation in an era when even the most arbitrary dictator claims that he rules "democratically." The Conference, selected and convened by the Chairman of the People's Republic as he chose, officially "advised" the Chairman on critical issues. In practice, it bolstered the Chairman's personal power, since he could invoke its authority to impose his will in the unlikely event of his meeting opposition from other branches of the government.

The Chairman of the People's Republic of China possessed unique formal powers, which were crowned by his *ex officio* chairmanship of the National Defense Council, the body that controls the armed forces. When one man, Mao Tse-tung, combined in himself the chairmanship of the People's Government and the chairmanship of the Communist Party, with all the powers appertaining to that latter state, his position was beyond challenge except by a determined—and necessarily reckless—alliance of the most powerful men in the Party. When Liu Shao-chi held the chair of the People's Government, his power was effectively limited by the overwhelming prestige of Mao Tse-tung and by the overriding power of the CPC's parallel structure of organization. The Party's Military Affairs Commission, rather than the National Defense Council, for example, really controlled the military arm.

The Communist Party remained supreme in practice, though the relationship between the Party and the People's Government was not precisely defined. Tung Pi-wu, then a Vice-Premier and later Chief Justice of the Supreme People's Court, wrote in 1953: "The Central Committee of our Party has never given direct orders to the Central People's Government. However, all the laws and directives promulgated by the Central People's Government are instigated by our Party. Most of the documents are drafted by the Party. There is no such thing as a resolution which is not prepared and considered by the Party."

Tung, who was one of the architects of the governmental structure, added: "The Party should issue proper directives to the administrative mechanism on the nature of the task to be carried out and the proper course to follow in their implementation; and through the administrative machinery and its subsidiary departments, the policy of the Party should be enforced, while the operation of the machinery should be supervised [by the Party]." [1] Although this relationship was constantly disrupted, the Party maintained provincial and local bureaus parallel but superior to the state's machinery. The Party Secretary, rather than the administrative chief of a locality, delivered major pronouncements and enforced them. In many cases, of course, one man combined Party and government offices in himself. Even then, his Party manifestation was dominant.

The State Affairs Council [Cabinet] under Premier Chou En-lai carried out the Party's decisions as legitimized by the National People's Congress. Chou's government, with its labyrinth of six general offices, thirty-two ministries, eight bureaus, six commissions, and seven still smaller units, constituted a bureaucracy so vast and so intricate that any two other bureaucracies could fit into it comfortably—with a profusion of employees and agencies left over. The Party commanded through a system of overlapping

[1] *Peking People's Daily*, January 31, 1953.

directorates, since all the major positions in the government, from the premiership down, were occupied by men high in the Party. Nonetheless, service in the state bureaucracy was a thankless assignment, for government administrators at the operating level were constantly required to execute decisions of which they disapproved, decisions often made by men who were far removed from the practical problems of administration. It was also unusual for the government to be functioning "normally," since there were few moments when a special "campaign" had not diverted so much of its energy that the People's Government was more than a formal framework for chaos. The revolt of the practical administrators against the fanciful making of policy was a decisive factor in precipitating the Cultural Revolution.

The supreme body in the government was the Standing Committee of the National People's Congress, through which in theory the people expressed their will during the fifty weeks of each year when the parent body was not sitting. Under the chairmanship of that amiable political nonentity the aged Generalissimo Chu Teh, thirteen Vice-Chairmen and sixty-five members made up the Standing Committee. Since the Communists deliberately restricted the flow of information, any appraisal of the Standing Committee's role must be derived from the functionaries who spoke out during the brief—and much regretted—period of free speech in 1957. The testimony of those men, who were seeking reform, was copiously reported by the Communist press at the time. It still constitutes an authoritative corpus of information on political life in Mao's China before the protracted crisis which began in 1958.

The judicial representative of the non-Communist parties on the Standing Committee commented then: "I always take part in meetings of the Standing Committee. But attendance is low, barely the legal quorum, and the most frequently absent are the [Communist] Party members.[2] The fact that the Party members do not attend this body, the highest authority in the state, gives us to understand that they have no high esteem for it, that all deci-

[2] Five of the thirteen Vice-Chairmen and thirty-four of the sixty-five ordinary members were Communists.

sions have already been taken in advance by the Party. The ascendancy of the Standing Committee seems to be a mere formality." [3]

The most surprising aspect of the People's Government was the surprise the Communists expressed at voters' lack of enthusiasm. Even cadres often failed to vote for representative bodies which possessed as much independence of action as the painted puppets of donkey hide that act out traditional Chinese shadowplays. The fact that every adult Chinese knows the plot and the dialogue of all the shadow-plays has insured their popularity, but the same psychology has not appeared to operate on behalf of the People's Congresses. One electoral official, having forgotten to distribute ballots to the foundry section of a tractor factory, pursued the workers to the hall where they were holding a banquet to celebrate receiving the plant's efficiency award. "Would you mind not bothering us tonight?" courteously asked the workers' spokesman, when he was presented with an armful of ballots. "Why don't you just mark them in the proper way and send them in for us?"

It would, however, be unfair to charge the Chinese Communist leaders with selfish cynicism because they created a "representative government" which neither expressed the popular will nor indeed possessed any power of independent decision. The temptation to condemnation is great—on the basis of the political experience and the political philosophies of the West. But the Communists were, by their own reasoning, anything but cynical. They sincerely believed that their curious form of government represented a skillful compliance with "historical inevitability" during the period when the masses required tutelage and constant protection from both their implacable enemies and their own mistakes.

The Chinese People's Government, like the Communist Party of China, operated on the principle of "democratic centralism" originally laid down by Lenin and later expanded by Mao Tsetung and Liu Shao-chi. Centralism, the dominant element of the compound, meant that no decision promulgated by the Party

[3] *Kwang Ming Jih-pao* [*Enlightenment Daily* (Peking)], May 17, 1957.

Center might be questioned. The government was considered democratic because it studied the people's needs and desires through organs that reached to the lowest level, as well as through elected Congresses. The leaders were sincerely anxious to know how the people felt. No government in history so constantly stressed the necessity for its functionaries to go among the people in order to acquire "proletarian consciousness." Conflicts, as Mao Tse-tung himself has noted, arose when the center lost touch with the people's wishes or—as Mao markedly failed to note—when the ambitions of the hierarchy outran the people's endurance and their readiness to sacrifice present benefits for future glory. Mao's *Thesis on Contradiction*, which represented an original contribution to Marxism-Leninism, was, significantly, not published until 1957, when the original benefits conferred upon the people had been exhausted and the emphasis had shifted to sacrifice rather than ratification. It was those contradictions between the masses and their government, between Mao himself and the CPC's working leadership—that finally brought down the structure. Mao had called them "non-antagonistic contradictions." They proved mortal.

Although their performance often raised doubts of their knowledge, even the Maoists were aware that they could not rule by coercion alone. The periodic purges characteristic of the regime sought to make examples by weeding out evildoers. Their purpose was as much persuasion as it was punishment. To save the ideological souls of their functionaries, the Chinese Communists would torture men's bodies and minds with as much reluctant relish as ever a Spanish inquisitor showed. Though they placed their faith in historical determinism, the essentially simple Maoist hierarchy saw no contradiction in forcing the popular will—and reality itself—to conform to the vision in their own minds. Since they could not accept the clear evidence that neither the masses nor the bureaucracy could be compelled beyond a certain point, the Maoists' failure was necessarily a total failure, though long delayed by their obduracy. They had certainly had much time to adjust their vision to reality—as their own doctrine demanded. But constantly mounting evidence of irreconcilable opposition only confirmed them in their fanaticism.

The *Sufan*[4] Movement, which did not seek major alterations in Chinese society, but primarily sought to purify the Communist Party and the People's Government, was characteristic of many purges in the way it bypassed both the government and the courts. Lasting from the beginning of 1955 to the middle of 1957, the *Sufan* involved eighteen million persons, and, according to the Party's ideological journal *Study,* it uncovered a hundred thousand "counter-revolutionaries and other evil elements in our revolutionary ranks." Among the functionaries who were out of step with the "mass line of the people" were five thousand members of the Communist Party and three thousand members of the Youth League. Two hundred and twenty counter-revolutionaries were discovered in government offices in Peking itself. In addition, sixty five thousand "ordinary counter-revolutionaries, reactionary elements, and criminal offenders" were unmasked, as were nine thousand counter-revolutionary suspects and three thousand counter-revolutionary cells. Half the accused confessed immediately.

The Party "penetratingly" investigated the political history of 1.8 million persons, among whom a hundred and thirty thousand had "severe problems, but threw off their burdens and adjusted themselves, expressing their immense gratitude to the Party." Many said: "This experience was like being washed clean in a public bath." The Party measured the intensity of the struggle in astronomical statistics: seven hundred and fifty thousand "core cadres" were assisted by a million full-time activists and nearly four million part-time investigators. They reaped a harvest of two million documents denouncing their chosen suspects. Offenders whose guilt was proven totaled just that 5 percent of the nation's functionaries the Party had predicted the movement would reveal when it began.

The Party's Central Committee assumed direct responsibility for the *Sufan* Movement, ignoring both the government and the courts in giving instructions to the police. Every Party unit established a committee of five members to "guide the movement by deciding whom to arrest and for what." The effort was so concentrated that the Provincial Party First Secretaries, the twenty-

[4] Literally, "liquidating the opposition."

eight men who carried the day-to-day responsibility for running People's China, personally telephoned instructions to each of these thousands of minuscule groups at least once a fortnight. Ranging from discharge and fines to banishment and forced labor, punishments were all decided by Party organs.

The Party delighted in the intensity of the opposition, which proved the necessity for moving against "class enemies"; anyone who argued against the Party's decisions demonstrated automatically that he belonged in that category. "The *Sufan* Movement," reported *Study*, "was carried out under the guidance of the Party Central Committee and Chairman Mao. In 1956 he said: 'The opponents must be purged and errors corrected.' The rightists attacked the *Sufan*. Indeed, they attacked the dictatorship of the proletariat. They attacked Socialism. They are the same as the counter-revolutionaries. The rightists attacked the *Sufan* violently. Does this not prove the truth [of the thesis] that there is indeed a class struggle?" The doctrine was self-proving: the more violent the Party's actions, the greater the protests against them; the greater the protests, the more need for violent action to destroy the enemies who revealed themselves by protesting.

The *Sufan* Movement did, however, provoke a minor crisis of conscience in a regime which had created not only a Supreme People's Procurator's Office to perform the functions of the Imperial Censorate, but also a Supreme People's Court at the apex of an "independent judiciary." Even Party members argued that "the *Sufan* performed by the masses, *i.e.*, compulsory denunciation, was illegal." Some high-ranking members recalled "that the Eighth Party Congress [in September 1956] [5] had said that the stormy revolutionary period was past and now democratic legalism was to be introduced: Delinquents ought to be dealt with by the police, the prosecutors, and the courts." But the official review concluded: "The rightists said that this Party guidance of the *Sufan* was unconstitutional. This is ridiculous. The Communist Party is steward and guide of all works in our country. The work of the five-man committees was, therefore, constitutional."

Many lower cadres felt sincere dismay at the perversion of legal processes, as did a number of men in high positions whose

[5] The last to be held.

names have been revealed in the course of new purges. Some Communists did not wish to deface their beautiful new legal structure, any more than they sought to Sinicize the fifty million members of minority races. Railing against the undoubted venality of the Kuomintang courts, the Communists had dispensed an offhand justice during the guerrilla days, occasionally extending that justice even to cooperative landlords. But the same ambitions which forced the Communists to abandon self-realization for minorities also compelled them to "abolish old legal concepts," as they put it. Impartial justice was not merely a luxury beyond the means of the People's Republic, but actually an obstacle to its purposes. Although Mao Tse-tung has never wished that the Chinese people had but one back so that he could scourge it with a single lash, he had reason to be infuriated at the ingratitude of the masses. As he saw it, the sloth and conservatism of his own people forced him to sacrifice all of his scruples—and most of his ideals—to expediency. He could not, he found, serve both economic progress and impartial justice—nor even preserve the aboriginal tribes' folk songs and marriage customs.

Although the People's Republic was finally given a Constitution in 1954, five years after its creation, the People's Courts were never guided by a systematized criminal code—in a nation which had always felt the necessity to codify its laws. Instead, the administration of justice—civil as well as criminal—was guided by a host of administrative regulations which were frequently mutually contradictory; by a determination not to be ruled by the "Six Law Codes" promulgated by the Kuomintang; and by the conviction that the judiciary was merely another instrument of the state's power. All crimes from wife-beating to theft were, therefore, political crimes, which undermined the regime and deserved the severest punishment.

Speaking frankly of the Constitution itself during the brief Hundred Flowers thaw of 1957, a prominent legal theorist said it "has a name but no reality." Noting that all the guarantees of personal liberty, so clearly stated in the Constitution, had been violated time and time again, the lawyer added: "Everybody considers the Constitution a useless piece of paper, and from Committee Chairman Liu [Shao-chi] to the ordinary citizen nobody takes any heed of the Constitution." [6]

Confronted by the age-old conflict between the rule of men and the rule of law, the Communists unhesitatingly made the age-old Chinese choice: the law became so flexible that it lost all shape. It is perhaps worth stressing: a consequent collapse of honesty and competence within the legal system (by the Communists' own standards and according to their own statements) came soon after the birth of the new dynasty. Modern problems were infinitely more complex than those the Empire had faced, and the Communist regime compounded its problems by seeking to control every aspect of life, as the Empire had not. The Imperial dynasties had drawn upon a self-renewing body of trained men who were uniformly educated in the Confucian classics and the Confucian ethos. But the Communists could not use those few Chinese who were trained in modern legal and administrative techniques; their ideological (read: ethical) impurity made them unemployable. After the initial reform of the legal profession in 1952, according to the Minister of Justice only 20 percent of the country's trained lawyers remained in professional work, while 7 percent were purged and 70 percent were employed outside the legal field.[7] To fill their places, the Minister added, "a great number of the cadres who had passed through the revolution were entrusted with court work. Thus the judiciary became pure . . . [though] the rightist elements say that these judges of worker and farmer origin are legal ignoramuses." [8]

Lawyers became not merely officers of the court, but instruments of the people's revolution. They were told flatly that it was no longer their duty to defend the accused. Instead, they were directed to report all evidence of crime, even if their knowledge had been gained through what was formerly considered privileged communication. Judges also came under the strict discipline of the legal cadres of the Party, which declared: "Independence of the courts is a devilish deception . . . the courts must imple-

[6] Ku Chih-chung, *Peking People's Daily*, June 26, 1957.
[7] The remaining 3 percent simply disappeared.
[8] *Kwang Ming Daily*, May 28, 1957.

ment the people's dictatorship!"[9] Like all else in Communist China, the legal apparatus became an instrument for suppressing the regime's enemies. Like all else in Communist China, the law became a means to an end never fully defined, rather than an ideal in itself.

"The law of our country is a changing law, adapted to perpetual revolution . . . ," declared the authoritative journal *Research into Politics and Law* in April 1959. "A fixed law would tie the hands and feet of the Party workers, and of the masses, and would handicap both the fight against the enemy and the development of production. . . . Since the policy of the Party is the soul of the legal system, legal work is merely the implementation and execution of Party policy. . . ."

Once again, the scope of their problems and the immensity of their ambitions had forced the Communists to abandon their ideals. They might argue that they had tried to nurture an independent judiciary and to keep the law above politics; they might add that their failure proved the error of deviating from the principle that all aspects of life must be subordinate to politics.

"Reform" of the legal system was ostensibly provoked by incidents like the misbehavior of the "rapist judges of Wuhan" who insisted upon female litigants' granting them favors before they would render judgment. In these, as in many other cases of abuses, the miscreants were "retained legal personnel of the Kuomintang government."

The campaign against the rapist judges was typical: litigants were "encouraged to judge and denounce the judges who had sat on their cases, while round-table meetings, mass meetings, and the newspapers revealed the sins of the courts." The regime bitterly attacked judges who "hold to the outworn concept that the courts must be above politics . . . or indulge in hypertechnical adherence to the letter of the law." Denouncing impartial justice as "a hangover from the reactionary past," the state instructed judges that they must always weigh the class origin of litigants in their decisions. The judges of Canton were singled out for particular opprobrium for "making no distinction between the enemy

[9] *Research into Politics and Law* (Peking, February 1959).

and ourselves; giving shelter to counter-revolutionaries; and showing no sympathy for the laboring people."

"The judicial viewpoint, judicial procedures, judges, trials, examinations, and judgments all have a class nature," a major Party theorist, Teng Tze-hui, admonished. "Judicial independence, as stressed by retained judicial personnel, is the theory of the reactionary class. Theories that laws do not tamper with politics are lies used by reactionary agents. Trials must be conducted according to people's justice and must follow the line of the masses." Once again, the Party had created a moral, intellectual, and administrative vacuum which only the Party could fill.

The vacuum of talent was filled by men like Judge Liu of a village People's Court in Hopei Province. His own account[10] displays him as a dedicated man of much integrity and demonstrates, in passing, how People's China trained its judges. During the great judicial purge of 1953 Party member Liu was told that he was to become a judge. He records his astonishment and dismay, since "I thought that not everybody could do judicial work." The County Party Secretary told him: "You will, indeed, sometimes find it difficult. But remember one maxim—learn and ask for advice when in doubt." Although he did not know how to deliver a verdict, Liu began presiding at trials immediately. He mastered his difficulties by prudently asking his Party superiors to advise him.

"I was upset," he records, "when asked to deal with my first murder case. How to deal with murder cases? I asked the [Party] comrades and they told me that first you read the documents, then you draw up a list of questions. At the trial, you find out contradictions in the confessions of the accused—and so on. Thus I concluded two murder cases." Although he was innocent of any knowledge of legal procedure and was untainted by acquaintance with bourgeois jurisprudential procedure, Liu was now fully trained. He was actually qualified by his lack of legal knowledge. Sitting on a mortgage dispute, his course was simple. "Because I had no experience in such cases and, in particular, did not know the policy of the Party in this regard," he writes, "I went to the

10 *Ibid.*

District Party Committee, which gave me a small pamphlet to read. When I had studied the pamphlet, I could deal with the case with ease."

Judge Liu found that the Party was always ready to help him. In April 1957, when a mob looted a granary, Liu arrived at the afflicted village and "first went to the village Party Committee to ask for instructions. . . ." When he fell ill in the middle of a case, the County Party Secretary was kind enough to take the bench. Judge Liu also learned "to distinguish between friends and enemies." When the leader of a labor brigade was beaten up, Judge Liu ordered the severest punishment because the accused was the son of a rich peasant and the injured man was also an officer of the People's Police. When peasants, incited by a former landlord, protested against deep plowing, Judge Liu dispensed summary justice during their lunch break.

"In all these years, in all cases of any moment," he recalls proudly, "when it was a question of arrest or when the case concerned village officials, I have asked for instruction from the Party Committee before and during the procedure; and, on the conclusion of the case, I have reported to the Party Committee. I have punctiliously carried out all the instructions of the Party Committee. Each time a county Party official came to my village, I reported to him and asked his advice."

Judge Liu's meticulously judicial behavior produced an outstanding record. He handled fifteen hundred and ninety-two cases, settling nine hundred and sixty-seven by conciliation and six hundred and twenty-five by formal verdicts. Only twenty-six of his judgments were appealed to higher courts, and his verdict was upheld in all cases. During the periodic examinations of court records by higher authorities, not one error of judgment was found against Judge Liu. He generously shares the secret of his success with other honest judges: "No sentence should be meted out until: (a) the facts are clear, (b) proofs are sufficient, (c) Party policy in the case is clear."

Such punctilious attention to the Party's will was not in itself sufficient to make the ordinary courts a perfect instrument of the People's Democratic Dictatorship. The Party from time to time also called into being special judicial bodies as *ad hoc* political instruments. The People's Tribunals created to accelerate land reform resembled courts-martial more than civil courts. Their earnest and untutored cadres could impose no sentence more severe than five years' imprisonment without review—the review to be carried out by higher organs of the People's Government rather than higher courts. The tribunals, one to each of the twenty-two hundred counties of China, were ordered:

(1) To remove or minimize obstacles to agrarian reform by combating despots, bandits, secret agents, and any other counterrevolutionaries who violated the Agrarian Reform Law;

(2) To help mobilize the masses, to help back up the peasants, and to encourage the masses in waging their antifeudal struggles; and

(3) To educate the peasants in participating in and taking hold of the People's Democratic Dictatorship, thus to consolidate the revolutionary order in the countryside.

The list summed up the coercive techniques of the Land Reform Movement, the third point's declaration of intent transcending by far the mere mechanical and temporary purpose of cutting up landholdings. The men who had, to their own distress, been called mere agrarian reformers invented new standards of judicial practice and undertook land reform primarily for political purposes. Their chief techniques were: example; social pressure; and, according to their own candid testimony, the judicious use of terror.

13

Government by Upheaval

*The Periodic Campaigns Which
Convulsed China Before the Final Catharsis of
the Cultural Revolution*

A stooped figure in rusty black trousers and tunic hobbled through the low-lying mist early on an August morning in 1950. Old Mrs. Fung, carrying a hemispherical basket and a tiny sickle, was on her way to the hillside to cut grass for the family fire in the age-old manner of the women of Kwangtung Province. Almost past the stunted pine, she stiffened and dropped her basket, crying out in terror: *"Oi-yah!"* Her nephew, Fung Chun-chung, hung from the tree, his hands clenched into fists and his bare feet swaying slowly two inches above the muddy ground.

When cadres[1] of the newly established People's Court cut the body down, they found that Fung had been strangled before he was hanged. His thighs were lacerated and his genitals bruised, but his bare soles were clean. In Fung's house they found his wooden clogs, his stained underclothing near a pool of blood, and a coil of rope similar to the noose. The cadres arrested Fung's

---

[1] Since the words "cadre" and "cadres" appear so often, it may be worth recalling here that the terms are the English translations officially employed by Peking for the Chinese word *kan-pu*, meaning "the doers." It is applied to all functionaries of government or Party organs. Like the U. S. Army, the Communists now use the term, which is properly a collective in Chinese as well as in English, in the singular and plural, assigning to the individual the term which originally described the group. There is no need to make the differentiation sharp in Chinese, since the language lacks a specifically plural form.

wife, Shin-nee, for the obvious crime of passion. Everyone knew that Shin-nee had a lover, who later visited her in jail and even threw gay parties for the judicial cadres. Nonetheless, Shin-nee was released after seven days and the case was dropped.[2]

But the cadres were quietly pursuing their investigation. In December 1950 eight men named Ho from the village called Chung Tsai Ling were charged with the murder. The chief culprit was Ho Chao-ting, a veteran of the Liberation Army who had been a leader in the struggle against the landlords from the beginning of the Land Reform Movement.

Refusing to confess, the eight Hos were interrogated. One was "stripped naked, gagged, and hung from the window sill, and cold water was poured over his head; he was so roughly handled that the rope broke and he fell and injured his head severely," according to the later official report. Ho Chao-ting was "not allowed to sleep and other prisoners were encouraged to beat him up. But he was the most stubborn of the lot. . . . In his pain he shouted: 'Long live the Communist Party of China! Long live Chairman Mao!' His younger brother advised him to confess and die, but he insisted that he could not, since he had killed no man."

The County Court passed sentence on March 19, 1951, ignoring both the prisoners' protests that their false confessions had been obtained under torture and their appeals for special consideration because they were "old revolutionary workers." On April 22nd Ho Chao-ting and two others were executed, and the remaining five began serving long jail terms. Persistent investigation had revealed their motive. The cadres knew that clashes during land reform had rekindled the ancient feud between the poor Hos of Chung Tsai Ling and the rich Fungs, the landlords of Panlung Village.

Impartial justice, it appeared, had triumphed in a curious denouement for People's China: the rich landlord was the innocent victim, and the poor peasants, who were also revolutionary activists, were criminals.

However, the all-seeing Party did not let the matter drop. In April 1952 a conference convened to correct mistakes in the Land

[2] The facts and conclusions regarding this case are all drawn from the official Communist report, widely published in 1952.

Reform Movement was rendered a true account of the Chung Tsai Ling incident by several senior officials of the Kwangtung People's Government and Communist Party. Landlord Fung had in truth been tortured and strangled by his wife and her lover. The conviction of the eight Hos was a shocking perversion of justice with disturbing political overtones; "landlords and evil elements" had manipulated the judicial machinery of the People's Government for their own purposes.

The complex incident, a *cause célèbre* during the consolidation of Communist rule in Kwangtung, was finally resolved by the Provincial Party Committee itself. Two judges were executed and a third was imprisoned. The five prisoners were released and ringleader Ho Chao-ting was posthumously declared a "model member" of the New Democratic Youth League. The murder itself proved less significant politically than the contrived conviction of the eight Hos. The revelation of an internal factional struggle, compounded by serious corruption and ideological errors on the part of old and new cadres alike, forced the Party to re-examine its entire administrative and judicial structure in Kwangtung Province.

Ho Chao-ting had become chairman of Chung Tsai Ling and commander of the village militia in 1949. He and a younger brother had joined six cousins to organize a "production team" to reclaim the hilly land opposite Panlung Village. But an old controversy over land boundaries had given the landlords of Panlung a pretext for inciting several hundred poor peasants to demonstrate against the reclamation project. Despite the County People's Government's efforts at mediation, the landlords had insisted upon bringing the dispute before the People's Court, where they won the decision.

Landlord Fung Chun-chung had been murdered at the time of the movement "for wiping out bandits and fighting against despots; for reducing rents and refunding deposits on [land] leases"—the first stage of real land reform in Kwangtung. Ho Chao-ting had led the struggle against the "Chung Tsai Ling's major despots, who were known as the Three Heavenly Kings." The triumvirate, feeling somewhat naïvely that they could dispose of the threat by disposing of Ho Chao-ting, had conspired with the landlords of Panlung Village to convict their common enemy.

The cabal had bribed local security cadres to arrest the Ho production team and had produced an eyewitness whose evidence was no more improbable than his name—Ho Ho. Claiming that Ho Chao-ting's "class status was impure" because he had deserted the People's Liberation Army, the ex-Kuomintang functionaries who dominated the security organs had felt no compulsion to offend the cabal by examining the matter closely. As a result of the punishment of the innocents, the Party later found: "The enthusiasm of the peasants immediately was dampened, while the landlords became arrogant. The peasants began to doubt the Party and to be divorced from the government—and the peasant movement suffered a major setback."

The final investigation revealed that the courts, "mistaking enemies for friends," had ignored conclusive evidence of the wife's guilt and, even worse, had disregarded the "class status" of those concerned. A purge of cadres of both villages, culminating in "public trials" at which the masses pronounced sentence upon the culprits, restored the proper atmosphere. The Party added: "The Agrarian Reform Campaign could now be developed on wholesome lines."

The Communists did not seek to suppress the Chung Tsai Ling Incident's revelations of incompetence and corruption within their ranks. Instead, they gloried in "the correct treatment of the Chung Tsai Ling Incident, which educated the cadres and raised the fighting spirit and competence of the peasants." The Party delighted in unpicking the tangled web in public in order to demonstrate that "evil elements still viciously seek to injure the people's interests by corrupting cadres and undermining the regime." The incident was more than a reaffirmation of the principle that the poor peasant is always right and an example "to elements whose class stand is not firm." The sordid tale of adultery, murder, and greed was, it appeared, actually spontaneous proof of the Communists' guiding principles. The Provincial Party Committee displayed the delight of men who have stumbled upon a bonanza, for the incident confirmed their "doctrine of continuing struggle."

By Western standards the Chung Tsai Ling Incident was of supreme importance only to those unfortunates who suffered execution or imprisonment. But it was of transcendent importance to the Communists because it provided an edifying example of class struggle spontaneously generated by contradictions within the old society—with no need for the Party to apply deliberate stimuli. It was doubly welcome because it came during the Land Reform Campaign, whose purpose was not merely to distribute land to the landless, but to impose the Party's absolute control by destroying its enemies. The train of events proved the thesis advanced in a series of lectures, entitled *How To Be a Good Communist*,[3] as early as July 1939 by Liu Shao-Chi, who later became Chairman (President) of the People's Republic, and, even later, epitomized the Party's revolt against Mao Tse-tung himself.

"The cause of Communism," Liu declared, "is a long, bitter, and arduous—but ultimately victorious—process of struggle. Without such struggle, there can be no Communism. Of course, this struggle is not, as some people have said, an 'accidental' social phenomenon or something engineered by certain Communists who are 'rebellious by nature.' On the contrary, it is an inevitable phenomenon in the course of the development of a class society. It is a class struggle which is unavoidable."

Since orderly administration was inimical to the spirit of a regime based upon the doctrine of continuous struggle, the will of the Communist Party of China was exerted through an unending series of cataclysmic upheavals which were called campaigns.[4] Each tidal wave—surging over the social, psychological, and economic foundations of China—arose in the crisis of the moment. Whatever was "normal" in the nation's political life—any fixed

[3] In 1967 the same work was violently attacked by the Maoists, primarily because of its authorship, but in addition, because it advocated an organizational discipline the Maoists rejected when they discovered that they could no longer control the will of the CPC.

[4] The Chinese word for a movement, *yun-tung*, which also means exercise, is in both the literal and the figurative senses, translated interchangeably by "movement" or "campaign" in Peking's English-language texts. I have followed the Communists' practice, though the more sweeping actions are truly campaigns, with all the connotations of planning and militance attached to that word.

patterns of behavior or administration that might have begun to appear—were swept away by the impact of the new campaign. The Communists did not rule China in any conventional sense, but subjected the nation to the convulsions of intermittent shock treatments. They were careless of the broken institutions and shattered minds they produced.

Hundreds of such campaigns of varying magnitude shook China from 1949 to 1965. When they were at their peak, they created absolute insecurity. No man who was the object of a campaign could relax for an instant, and every man who was under pressure sought his rest each evening like an inhabitant of a beleaguered citadel. He knew that the city walls were breached, that the enemy spared no living soul, and that the defending troops were falling fast. He was no longer a rational creature, for all his being was concentrated upon the chimera of survival. When he would say or do anything at all in order to survive, he had finally been reduced to the condition the Communists desired. Completely malleable, he and his fellows could then be molded—for a time at least—into the shape the Party felt would enable it to effect its purpose of altering the structure of society.

Since no group could bear such intense pressure without a letup and no authority could maintain the pressure indefinitely, the cadres were forced to break off from time to time. The progression of campaigns—and each individual campaign as well—therefore displayed a wavelike motion of alternating tension and relaxation which was the essential character of life in China until the final campaign called the Great Proletarian Cultural Revolution.

Three of the major campaigns exemplified the nature of the upheavals, and are, therefore, worth discussing in detail. The Land Reform Movement, directed against landlords, destroyed the traditional social structure in the countryside. The Five-Antis Campaign, which attacked the urban bourgeoisie, destroyed private enterprise. The Birth Control Campaign was abortive.

The Republican Revolution of 1911 was militarily the least glorious of innumerable revolutions which characterize the history of a nation where the transfer of power had always been accomplished by violence. Beginning by accident, that revolution over-threw an impotent dynasty, which would probably have perished at least half a century earlier had it not been sustained by external forces. Muddled militarily and politically, Sun Yat-sen's was none-theless the most daring of China's revolutions intellectually, for it supplanted the ancient ways of thought and administration. Yet the audacity of the Republicans' aspirations tended to prevent the realization of their ideals. Agreed only on the general proposition that the traditional system was decayed beyond redemption, the reformers proposed substitutes ranging from a constitutional monarchy to perfect anarchy. The multiplicity of bold concep-tions—and the paucity of practical means—completely prevented any effective approach to China's most fundamental problems.

When the Ming succeeded the Mongols or the Manchus succeeded the Ming, the great landowners, whose rapacity stimu-lated revolt, had been expelled from their estates. The new pat-tern of small holdings was, in its turn, altered by the gradual ac-cretion of land in a few hands—and the way was prepared for a new revolution. Sun Yat-sen himself was an avowed socialist; he was committed not only to reshaping the rural land-tenure sys-tem, but also to creating a new pattern of urban landholdings through the single tax. Successive governments of the Republic of China enacted voluminous laws providing for the reorganization and redistribution of agricultural landholdings. But the sweeping program was successfully resisted by vested interests, since the central government's authority was as weak as its will. The land-tenure pattern of the Manchu Dynasty, therefore, endured in the countryside until 1949. Since the Republic proved unable to alter the relationship of men to the land they tilled, no other funda-mental changes were possible.

Throughout his career as an agitator Mao Tse-tung had promised that men should own the land they tilled. He had echoed the Taiping Emperor's decree: "Every adult, male and fe-male alike, reaching the age of sixteen, is entitled to a share of land of average fertility, while those under sixteen will receive half a share." [5] Neither the Ching Dynasty's land-tenure system

[5] Quoted in *Outline History of China* (Peking: Foreign Languages Press, 1958), p. 220.

nor even the landlord families themselves had altered materially when Mao came to power a century later. Applying the techniques developed in the various Soviet Areas to the first task of every regime, Mao Tse-tung promulgated the Agrarian Reform Law of the People's Republic of China on June 30, 1950. The first article revealed purposes far beyond mere equitable distribution of land in order to improve the lot of the peasant masses. "The landlord class shall be abolished and the system of peasant [tiller] land-ownership shall be established," that article declared, "in order to set free rural productive forces; to develop agricultural production; and to pave the way for the industrialization of the new China." Although the law itself did not explicitly so state, a series of official commentaries made it quite clear that the chief purpose of land reform was to consolidate Communist rule.

Once again the full burden of Mao Tse-tung's attention fell on sun-blackened men and women in the mud of southern paddy fields and on the spare farmers who worked the arid yellow soil of the north with wooden plows drawn by stunted mules. Mao's obsession once again presaged not favors, but greater toil for the peasants.

Land reform was inevitably a bitter process in a nation which had so few fertile fields that the *mou,* amounting to less than one sixth of an acre, was its basic unit of land measurement. In 1950 no more than 700 million *mou* of arable land were available to a farming population of at least 300 million. If no special account were taken of tens of millions of *mou* of inferior land, an equal division would have provided just 2.3 *mou*—about one third of an acre—for each person. But Mao Tse-tung's chief purpose was neither to divide the land equally nor merely to permit the peasants to vent their pent resentment against man and nature upon a few "landlords and exploiters" selected by the regime. Land reform was but the first step in a process that sought to destroy traditional Chinese society and to substitute the will of the Communist Party for all the old standards of behavior.

In the beginning the measures adopted appeared moderate. All industrial and commercial enterprises, private as well as public, were granted immunity from confiscation of their land. Regardless of his "class status," no man was to be deprived of land which he tilled solely by his own labor. Although ancestral shrines, temples, monasteries, schools, and charitable institutions were not permitted to keep the broad acres that supported them, they were to receive cash grants to compensate them for that land. In one well-calculated exception, mosques were to retain much of their own land so that the Moslem minority would not be antagonized unnecessarily. The law even permitted a limited degree of absentee ownership by particular classes; the soldiers and cadres who had made the revolution were to receive special grants of land, as adherents of the victorious claimant to the Throne had always been rewarded. On the surface Mao Tse-tung appeared to be seeking a "democratic land reform" in harmony with his pronouncement that the victory of the Communist Party had brought to China neither Communism nor socialism but merely the New Democracy.

Mao had decreed that the masses must be persuaded—rather than forced—to act. He contended that an aroused peasantry would contrive its own salvation by "spontaneously demanding" land reform. Nonetheless, small teams of outside cadres came to each small village to insure that the peasants would feel as the Communists wished them to feel. The "voluntary movement" thereafter followed a predetermined pattern everywhere from Honan Province, where the Land Reform Movement began in 1949, to Kwangtung, where its inception was delayed until 1951.

"Anti-despot campaigns" erupted in every township. "Remnant armed bands of reactionaries were rounded up; rural despots were removed; and local peace was insured by the security organs of the state," [6] reported an official commentator. Those stirring words meant that the army and the police demanded the masses' assistance in mopping up pockets of armed dissidents, while poor peasants revenged themselves upon "landlord or other capitalist elements." Thereafter, rents paid to landlords were cut by a flat 25 percent, with the additional proviso that no one might pay

[6] Chen Han-seng (the former "Asiaticus" of the Institute of Pacific Relations' American journal *Pacific Affairs*) in *Land Reform Uproots Feudalism*, No. 3, May–June, 1952, p. 33, quoted in Robert Carin's *Agrarian Reform Movement in Communist China* (Hong Kong: American Consulate-General, 1960), Vol. I, p. 40.

more than 37.5 percent of his total crop in rent. At the same time, the anti-despot campaign was intensified, with the Peasant Associations, usually headed by the poorest men of the village, supplementing the cadres' leadership. Investigating commissions "guided" by outside cadres went from village to village to compare notes, and People's Tribunals dispensed summary justice to offending landlords. While these two subcampaigns raged, cadres drilled mass meetings in every village in the provisions of the Agrarian Reform Law, and the peasants themselves spoke up to relate local conditions to the statute's abstractions. The people, it appeared, were striking a blow for themselves.

With the countryside in turmoil, the Party arbitrarily divided the rural population into five classes and set those classes at each others' throats in the bloodiest and most effective mass movement China had ever known. Those classes were: landlords, rich peasants, middle peasants, poor peasants, and hired laborers. The masses had been aroused to a sense of their own power, and legions of cadres—more than a million to a province—were deployed over the nation to lead the attacks upon the last redoubts held by the vested interests that wished to thwart the regime's desires and maintain the old order. The cadres were directed not only to lead the assault, but also "to prevent the masses from indulging in spontaneous activities," [7] which might achieve the material objectives before the political and psychological peak had been attained. Public accusation meetings followed by public trials goaded the people's indignation and increased their sense of power. Chao Shu-li, a former peasant who is now one of the literary titans of New China, his status attested by his Stalin Prize, described the scene from life in his novel *The Hurricane*. The passage has been rendered into English by Peking's official translators with a fidelity that reflects the glee of the original:

> The land reform workers and the activists met to discuss in private the coming mass meeting, and decided to make the case of Old Tien's daughter the chief indictment against Han

[7] Mulin, "Greet the Unprecedented Land Reform Movement in the New Liberated Areas," *New Observer* (Peking), Vol. I, No. 12, December 16, 1950. Quoted in *ibid*.

[the landlord]: The next day, after breakfast, the different groups of the Peasant Association went out to call villagers to the mass meeting at the school. Chao stood at the entrance to the schoolhouse, shouldering a rifle, barring the way to Han's relatives and supporters. . . . The villagers straggled in in threes and fours. They formed a semicircle before the table. . . . On a pillar and a wall of the school were posted slogans: *Down with Han Peng-chi! Poor Men, Arise! Landlords Owe Us Blood Debts! Share Out Land and Houses and Claim Back Rents! Settle Accounts with the Local Despot and Landlord—Han Peng-chi.* . . .

Han stood beside the table, hanging his head. . . .

The crowd surged nearer. People shouted: "Beat him! Beat him!" A brick came flying up from somewhere and landed quite close to Han. His face turned pale, and he stood there trembling, knee knocking against knee.

"Strip him first!" shouted somebody.

"Kill him!" added somebody else.

A man came up and slapped Han across the face. Blood gushed from his nose. . . .

One accusation followed another. Towards evening, the record in Liu Sheng's notebook showed murders, including Kuo's father frozen to death, Chao's daughter starved to death, Pai's baby boy hurled to death, and Old Tien's daughter flogged to death. Then there were forty-three women who had been raped or carried off, only to be sold when Han and his son tired of them. When these figures were announced, there was no preventing the people from taking their revenge. A forest of sticks waved in the air, and came down on Han.

"Beat him to death! Beat him to death!" somebody shouted.

"Don't let him live another day!" roared another angry voice.

"Let him pay with his life!"

"Tear him to pieces or I won't be avenged!" cried Old Tien's wife in a wavering voice. . . .

Chao and Pai, carrying their rifles, pushed Han out towards the East Gate of the village. Kuo and Big Li followed behind with over a thousand people at their heels. They were shouting slogans, singing songs, blowing trumpets, beating gongs and drums. Old Mrs. Tien, who had lost the sight of both eyes, hobbled along with Mrs. Pai supporting her.

"I've been hoping and crying these three long years for a day like this," sobbed the old woman. "Thanks to Chairman Mao Tse-tung and the Communist Party, my daughter has been avenged!"

Thus ended the tale of what the writer saw.

Executions similar to Landlord Han's were carried out all over China. No one, including the Communists themselves, knew the exact number of men and women who died because they had actually oppressed their fellow farmers, because they had aroused envy by living in modest comfort, or because they had antagonized cadres or vindictive peasants. At least 2 million persons were certainly executed—perhaps 5 or 10 million. The "landlord and rich peasant classes," who were arraigned, made up 10 per cent of a farming population of 300 million by Peking's own calculation. If but 10 percent of the men and women in those categories were executed, the deaths would have totaled 3 million.

The Party was finally ready to distribute the land. Public meetings, "in which the poor peasants and hired laborers played the most active role," in theory decided upon the actual division. After burning the landlords' title deeds, the peasant proprietors received beautifully inscribed deeds to their new land. By February 1953, when land reform was completed over almost all China, 300 million peasants had shared about 106 million acres. The great convulsion had produced an average per capita share of .331 acres, and merely .116 to .166 acres in densely populated areas like the East China region.

Although individuals had acquired no great acreage, most were undoubtedly better off than they had been before land reform. All the farmers were terribly proud of their new holdings, and their inborn land hunger was temporarily appeased. At least 10 million persons had been eliminated from the most populous areas by execution or transportation to "reform through labor"; food was more equitably distributed; and the increased efficiency of administration and transportation insured that no longer would one county starve while another only fifty miles distant enjoyed plenty. The peasants were content, for the Communists had kept their promises. The Party was content, for the gentry, who were the backbone of the traditional "exploitive society," had perished.

The planned turmoil attendant upon land reform had, nonetheless, completely disrupted life in the countryside. The productive capacity of the hardworking Chinese peasant had by no means been increased by land reform. The fields could still not provide surpluses for industrialization. The Land Reform Campaign, therefore, automatically generated a series of new campaigns. In 1954 China took the road to collectivization by creating Agricultural Cooperatives and Mechanized State Farms. In 1955 Mao Tse-tung discerned "a high tide of Socialist enthusiasm in the countryside" and ordered total collectivization. The peasant proprietors, who had retained their holdings for less than three years, began to complain aloud—and many cadres joined the chorus. The Party demanded ever greater material sacrifices and ever more arduous toil. Since the land could still not provide the surplus capital he needed, Mao Tse-tung was forced to his most brilliant—and most disastrous—conception in 1958. But before the creation of the People's Communes—a convulsion so profound that it demands discussion in a separate chapter—other great movements shook China.

Despite the exodus of capitalists when the Communists took power, the majority of China's businessmen had remained to live under the New Democracy. Seeing that the new officials neither humiliated rickshaw coolies nor mulcted merchants, they somewhat irrationally concluded that the new order would provide the security for commercial and industrial development which the old order's corrupt impotence had often denied them. There was a good measure of truth in the Communists' charge that only those private entrepreneurs who were in cahoots with the Nationalists, the so-called "bureaucratic capitalists," had been able to amass fortunes. Necessity nurtured the remainder's hope that the Communists would prove better masters, since the average businessman, who possessed neither portable assets nor deposits in foreign banks, could not flee to a life of assured comfort abroad. Many businessmen—foresighted, conscience-ridden, or both—had removed their assets and themselves beyond the Communists' grasp. But some who were big capitalists by the Communists' reckoning stayed on. They comforted themselves by citing the Communists' declarations that they bore no grudge against the honest "national bourgeoisie," as distinguished from "bureaucratic capitalists allied with foreign imperialism" who would be annihilated. Businessmen's disinclination to consider their ultimate fate was encouraged by the Communists' deliberate vagueness as to when socialization would begin.

In the autumn of 1951 private entrepreneurs concluded that their hour had struck, though their alarm had but little more visible justification than their complacency of the day before. On September 21, 1951, the Director of the Bureau of Industry and Commerce for the city of Shanghai, where almost all China's private business was concentrated, spoke with warm appreciation of the bourgeoisie's political improvement and noted complacently that eighteen thousand industrial and commercial establishments had been founded since "liberation." But he chided businessmen for their continuing "tendency to reject the economic leadership of the state." Some firms, he said, had eagerly sought state contracts, only to refuse the business when profit margins proved too small. They had, in addition, raised the prices of scarce imported goods; they had refused to cooperate with state enterprises; they had falsified accounts to evade taxes; and they had not "attended earnestly to safety provisions, labor insurance, and labor-capital consultations." The official admonished the businessmen under his charge to follow the lead of the state implicitly and promised: "To oppose profiteering does not mean to deny profits altogether. . . . On the contrary, we not only do not oppose legitimate profits, but actually encourage amassing of well-earned wealth." Despite this generalized reassurance, businessmen trembled at the specific indictment.

Their fears were soon confirmed. Hard-pressed by the cost of the Korean War—about $4.5 billion a year, a third of the national budget—Peking determined to reclaim "illicit profit" from the bourgeoisie. But, the Communists promised, private enterprise

would endure for some years to come. No more than the Land
Reform Movement was the new campaign to "cleanse the bourgeoisie" designed to abolish private property. So the Communists
said. The official decree—and the voluminous commentaries
thereto—explained that the regime wished only to correct the
abuses of private enterprise and to resolve contradictions between
the people's interests and the capitalists'. The cleansing campaign,
it was promised, would enable businessmen to operate more efficiently—for their own as well as the general benefit.

The campaign against the bourgeoisie grew from the unlikely
seed of a Rectification Campaign within the Communist Party.
With the normal compulsion for categorization, the purge of the
Party was called the Movement Against the Three Evils—the
Three-Antis, for short. The Party declared that the malevolent influence of the urban bourgeoisie had not only encouraged innocent cadres in bad habits such as "bureaucratic practices" and
"wastefulness," but had actually "corrupted" the valiant men and
women who had brought the Kuomintang to its knees in the
wholesome countryside. The Three-Antis Movement began in
scattered localities early in 1951 and, by the year's end had become a nationwide movement. Thousands of cadres were purged,
and the Communists appeared content that their own ranks had
been cleansed. The campaign demonstrated obliquely but forcibly
how desperately the bourgeoisie required purification of the evil
ways inherent in the corrupt old society. Their evil was dark indeed if it had corrupted the paladins of the Party.

The anti-bourgeois campaign, the Movement Against the
Five Evils, started in January 1952. Its purpose was to cure businessmen of bribing officials, evading taxes, stealing the people's
property, failing to fulfill state contracts, and stealing the state's
economic intelligence. The campaign followed the pattern of land
reform, with salespeople, accountants, clerks, and laborers denouncing their employers. Cadres specially trained for the task
aroused the urban masses to seek vengeance so that, at the
culmination of the Five-Antis, as Premier Chou En-lai declared:
"The work of national construction will speedily enter its new
stage." With evangelical fervor, a Cabinet order of March 1952
affirmed: "The great Three-Antis and Five-Antis Movements are

educating government workers and the people of the entire nation. They will, throughout the nation, accomplish the thorough liquidation of the dirt and poison of the old social order; they will lead to the establishment of a new moral code stressing integrity and thrift under the new order, so that the people of our country will become more united and the People's Democratic Dictatorship will be further consolidated."

Throughout China faithful cadres set out on "tiger hunts to track down and destroy the vicious commercial tigers who prey on the people's wealth." The campaign was most virulent in Shanghai, which Mayor Chen Yi called "China's bourgeois center." Teams of propagandists toured the city, pasting up posters and hanging banners with slogans written large upon them. Loudspeakers bombarded proprietors with accusations and the question repeated dozens of times each hour: "Hey, boss, have you confessed yet?" Businessmen were terrorized without open violence, since the threat was no less terrifying for being implied.

The manager of one large firm was locked in his office for seventeen days and nights with interrogators who demanded that he amplify each successive confession to reveal further sins. Other businessmen were handcuffed to their desks or allowed to wear only underdrawers while they were questioned for three days and nights in the bitter winter temperatures.

Although they were assured that they were not to be "eliminated as a class like the landlords," businessmen gave up hope when new teams of Five-Antis investigators invaded Shanghai on March 21, 1952. All private enterprises were to be classified by the gravity of their sins. "Law-abiding and basically law-abiding establishments" were those which had committed only minor crimes. Next came "semi-law-abiding establishments, whose illegal profits had not exceeded two million People's dollars" (about $8900). Last were the firms destined for severe punishment, "seriously law-breaking and completely law-breaking establishments." Even before the formal campaign began, the Five-Antis Coordination Committee had grandly determined that a hundred and forty thousand of Shanghai's hundred and sixty-four thousand private firms were guilty of crimes against the state, with fifty-seven thousand guilty of serious crimes and eight thousand guilty of "complete law-breaking." The movement itself was, like land reform, divided into three tactical phases: managers and proprietors first made public confessions after discovering their sins under interrogation; employees then revealed their employers' sins under the guidance of cadres; and, finally, fines were assessed, and other punishments were imposed.

In Canton, the commercial metropolis of the south, the campaign followed the same pattern, according to the personal account[8] of a Five-Antis cadre named Woo, who later fled to Hong Kong. In mid-March 1952 Kwangtung Province's Party Secretary swooped down on the campus of Sun Yat-sen University to release students from classes so that they might participate in the Five-Antis Movement. Medical students and the bedridden were excused, but fourteen thousand young men and women swore a new oath of loyalty before descending upon the city to stalk "commercial tigers" in company with older cadres. Before he marched into the fray, young Woo spent two days learning his mission.

The Five-Antis Movement, he was told, was essential to the people's welfare because corrupt businessmen had been stealing the country's wealth; the people would now take back what was rightfully theirs. The enthusiastic young cadres were themselves bound to the cause by terror. "If you should succumb to corruption," they were told, "the Party will inevitably know about it and you will inevitably be punished." Before they began their investigations the Mayor of Canton himself exhorted the student teams to diligence.

Woo's unit was sent to Canton's downtown district to expose firms dealing in radios and electrical appliances. A preliminary survey had already selected certain shops for special attention because they were "completely law-breaking or seriously law-breaking." Though he struggled against his cynicism, Woo noted at the time that the firms presumed to have committed the gravest crimes were invariably those whose wealth or foreign connections indicated that they would yield the greatest plunder.

The first stage of the campaign was called the "back-to-back phase." Some cadres were assigned to live among the workmen

[8] In a series of interviews with the author.

and foment hatred against their employers, while others pressed proprietors for confessions. Woo, who was assigned to encourage employees to accuse their bosses, noted that the lowest employee was usually selected for attention first because he was, presumably, most susceptible to persuasion. After feeding the shop coolie delicacies interspersed with appeals to his class solidarity, the entire banquet washed down with rice wine, cadres invited him to "come to study meetings to develop class consciousness." Finally, the coolie was told the time had come for him to "prove his class loyalty and to serve the masses" by revealing his employer's crimes at a mass meeting of all the firm's people. Once the man at the bottom had vented his resentment, the cadres used his accusations against the next man in line, beginning a chain reaction.

"If the accusation was too weak," said Woo, "we'd figure that proper hatred had not yet built up—and we'd send the coolie back for more study."

Simultaneously, other cadres "attacked the strongest point in order to overthrow the entire structure." The teams picked out the owner's son or his cousin and beset him—in private and at mass meetings. Once his closest associate accused the owner of crime, the cadres knew others would follow.

After the "back-to-back phase" and the public accusations came the "face-to-face phase." Employers were summoned to meetings of their peers, where one weak capitalist and two stubborn ones were urged to confess their misdeeds. When the two stubborn men had—as anticipated—refused to confess, the cadres would recite their crimes to their faces. They threatened dire punishment for "noncooperation" and promised "leniency for sincere repentance." Thereupon, the weak capitalist automatically confessed—and was commended for his public spirit. His example would then move the stubborn pair.

At the last meetings of the second phase, owners who obstinately denied any fault were automatically placed in the category of "seriously and completely law-breaking culprits." They were told: "You still refuse to cleanse your soul by confession. You are obviously concealing the gravest crimes, which we have not yet discovered because you are as cunning as a vicious fox." While the

obstinate pondered their fate, public meetings tentatively assessed the fines and the additional "recompensatory payments to
the people" each malefactor would pay.

The final phase was once more "back-to-back." Teams of
cadres dealt separately with the laborers, the clerical staff, and the
management. The chief responsibility fell to the team which confronted the proprietors, since, as Woo later remarked, "only they
could reveal the full extent of their own crimes." This time the
Communists used terror more openly. Woo saw some men arrested and others interrogated while denied food and water for
forty-eight-hour periods. Although no one was executed in
Canton, the proprietors sat through motion pictures of executions
in Peking.

"Persuasion corps," made up of their fellows who had re-
deemed themselves by confessing, concentrated upon the stubborn capitalists, while sound trucks parked outside their doorways
berated them by night and by day. During this phase there were
hundreds of suicides in Canton. In the long run, Woo reported,
no one could resist the torrent of blandishments, promises, threats,
mental torture, and moral despair. Eventually, all capitalists who
had not killed themselves offered confessions that satisfied the
Party.

In mid-June 1952 the Party gathered the fruits of its efforts.
Workers joined new labor unions, and employers were combined
into employers' associations, which effectively prevented the
worst criminals' doing business by excluding them from membership. Representatives of the regime joined every board of directors in Canton, and final fines were imposed in amounts far
beyond the capitalists' capacity to pay. "But," Woo said, "the Communists seemed satisfied. They had actually collected a vast sum
in Canton, and it seemed they had broken forever the power of
the commercial classes in the city."

The Five-Antis Movement, its broad methods the same
throughout China, destroyed the bourgeois class and, the Communists believed, purged the cities of "bourgeois thinking." Although the passage of the intervening years has demonstrated
that its intellectual effects were nowhere as sweeping as the Party
thought, the Five-Antis did accomplish the total disruption of

commercial life for an entire year. It also gave the Communists nearly $2 billion in fines and compensatory payments.

The movement sought to break the capitalist class and to fill Peking's depleted war chest after "voluntary contributions and bond purchases" had proved insufficient for the regime's needs. But once again the grand campaign generated new campaigns. "Public-private enterprises" took the place of almost all private business in 1954, and by the end of 1955 all private business was socialized. Nonetheless, the Communists continued to contend with the "free market" in foodstuffs and with corruption among their own cadres, who seem incapable of resisting the temptation dangled by those irrepressible entrepreneurs who are moved by greed—and sometimes by humanity—to smuggling and black-marketeering. Again, each campaign generated new campaigns.

Despite the new necessities they created, the Land Reform and Five-Antis Movements brilliantly attained their immediate objectives. Despite their initial efforts to convince the people of the necessity for birth control, the Communists completely failed to limit births by contraception. They failed in part because they could not quite override the taboos of Marxist economics and traditional Chinese beliefs to convince themselves that birth control was truly desirable. Although realistic economists pointed out that new mouths literally devoured economic progress, the Communists did not commit themselves to a full-scale campaign to limit the growth of China's population. Perhaps they hung back because they knew that they could not succeed.

The Communists first began to talk about birth control in 1955. Significantly, an ex-Kuomintang official—who had defected from the Communist Party after attending the First Congress and returned to the fold after 1949—was chosen to release the first trial balloon. In contrast to their normal efficiency, the Communists dithered about birth control. They even permitted the same politician to offer his own sure prescription for contraception: tadpoles, to be taken internally after meals.

Forty-two working women in Hangchow volunteered to test the method. They worked on a logical principle: if eating three tadpoles a day would prevent conception, it should be even safer to eat two dozen. Four weeks after the experiment began, two of the group were pregnant. Eighteen others conceived within the next three months. The *People's Daily* reported, without further detail, that the remaining twenty-two women had "gone back to traditional forms of birth control" and explained gratuitously: "Tadpoles have proved ineffective."

Experimenting with conventional Western contraceptives in 1956, the authorities found that even enlightened cadres "resented interference in the relations between men and women." Drugstores and department stores displayed a wide variety of contraceptive devices, alongside graphic charts and cutaway dummies showing the proper manner of use. The familiar teams of cadres invaded the countryside to preach birth control. Their findings were summed up by a Western-trained Chinese doctor reporting on her own visits to Peking homes: "The housewives are very bashful indeed. They are extraordinarily shy by Western standards in discussing their problems or in going to chemists' shops. The husbands do not seem interested either. . . ."

In part, the frustration was inherent in the nature of the problem. Experience in India has led a number of Western doctors to the conclusion that only sterilization can effectively control births among a largely illiterate population.[9] The Chinese did sterilize a few volunteers, but they shied away from compelling all men and women to undergo surgery after they had produced a fixed number of children. Perhaps this ultimate invasion of privacy was too harsh for even the dedicated hierarchy to order. It is more likely that they judged the doctors and equipment at their disposal insufficient to carry out sterilization on an effective scale. Besides, the reaction to such a campaign might have been beyond the regime's powers of suppression.

In part, the Communists may have been indecisive because

[9] Voluntary birth control by chemical and mechanical means has gradually proved successful on Formosa. But the eminent scholar Dr. Chiang Monlin, who directed the campaign as Chairman of the Joint Commission on Rural Reconstruction, observed in conversation with the author that it was only the high level of literacy among the island's population that made the effort successful. He added that he did not believe a similar campaign could succeed among the illiterate masses of the Chinese mainland.

the problem of controlling births was not susceptible to their normal techniques of persuasion, coercion, mass organization, and violent retribution. "Can you," asked a Western demographer rhetorically, "condemn an embryo as a counter-revolutionary or a rightist deviationist? Can you shoot every woman who becomes pregnant without authorization—or condemn her to corrective labor?"

These reasons—demonstrated and surmised—would adequately explain any other regime's decision to ignore birth control. But Peking's unvarying readiness to lavish its energy on apparently insoluble problems—and its record of never being deterred by either sentiment or fear—imply another reason for the lackadaisical manner of the Birth Control Movement. The hierarchy apparently could not quite decide that it really wanted to limit the population. A few pronouncements made just before the campaign was abandoned in 1958 frankly admitted that the masses could not live better as long as their numbers continue to expand unchecked. But most arguments in favor of birth control cited the "ill-effects of excessively large families on the health of mothers and children" or contended that the population should increase at a controlled rate determined by economic needs.

The traditionalists won nonetheless. On September 21, 1958, the *Kwangsi Daily* flatly declared: "Teeming population is a good thing because people represent the most precious wealth in the world. Our country has the largest population of all nations, and this population is a most favorable factor for our socialist construction." Shortly thereafter, the Central Committee's organ, the *Peking People's Daily*, offered a clarification: "As we all know, according to the Marxist viewpoint on the population problem, unemployment and surplus population are but the products of the capitalist system of private ownership of the means of production. In the socialist society, with its communal ownership of the means of production, productivity can be developed at a speed unapproachable in the old society, so that production continually expands and the people receive extensive opportunities for employment and better living. . . . The 600 million population is, in itself, a basic force for the solution of our difficulties." The *People's*

Daily cited Mao's dictum, "People are our capital!" and happily noted that China's population would approach 800 million by 1967.*

The debate had, for the moment, ended with a conclusive—if illogical—decision that more full wombs would mean more full rice bowls. The shade of the Emperor Kang Hsi was triumphant. When the elderly economist who was President of Peking University demonstrated that unchecked population growth created a vicious spiral that prevented economic progress in a developing country like China, he was condemned by a vehement chorus. The *People's Daily* reprovingly quoted Engels' credo: "If the Communist society in the future should need to regulate the increase of population, then, like its earlier efforts for the regulation of material goods, such a society will attain its objective without the least difficulty."

Ushered out by trumpets of strident—and, somehow, hollow —self-assurance, the Birth Control Movement slowly dragged itself into the wings. It has, from time to time, been resumed without any great enthusiasm. Acute economic distress has also checked the rate of increase of the population temporarily, since malnutrition and overwork simultaneously increased the death rate and reduced reproductive capacity. Eerily reminiscent of the Ching Dynasty's troubles, nature's birth control—floods, droughts, and epidemics—tormented the nation from 1958 to 1963, according to Peking's own reports. But the Communists themselves have been unable to check the birth rate by deliberate measures. Confronted by nature's fierce defense of her brood, they could neither win their battle nor even pretend that they had won.

* Literally no one knew the population of China in 1968. The Communists occasionally used the figure of 700 million, but it was obviously the veriest estimate.

14

The Paper Heart

The Attempt to Make All Men Think As the Communists Wish

Brought up on Bret Harte's wily "heathen Chinee," Charlie Chan, and other caricatures like Dr. Fu Manchu who applied inhuman ingenuity to crime, few Americans questioned later reports that the Chinese Communists had invented diabolical techniques to distort the human personality. The conviction that the Chinese could manipulate men's beliefs at will allayed somewhat the sense of betrayal Americans felt when two dozen prisoners of war in Korea chose to live in arduous discomfort in China, rather than return to the loving embraces of their families and their country.

Irrational fear was intensified by books like Richard Condon's *The Manchurian Candidate*, which introduced Dr. Yen Lo, a direct descendant of Fu Manchu, if not the old devil himself in flimsy disguise. Yen Lo's miraculous techniques convinced a captured American patrol that it had fought an epic battle and transformed the hero of that imaginary battle into a robot of the Communists—all in four days' time. The graphic term "brainwashing" with its occult implications, dramatized the West's fears. It was occasionally used even in China.

The Communists described the process, which was essentially as straightforward as it was ruthless, with an equally pretentious, if somewhat more descriptive phrase. *Ssu-hsiang kai-tsao*, literally "thought remaking," was officially translated "thought reform." Constant reindoctrination in a controlled environment was necessary to preserve its conversions. It embodied no new techniques, either scientific or diabolical. The scientific basis was laid by the Russian physiologist I. P. Pavlov, who taught that nervous responses in animals could be predetermined by physical means. The Chinese were unique only in their single-minded application of the principle to an entire society.

Despite its intellectual shabbiness and its practical awkwardness, thought reform was a primary buttress of the Chinese hierarchy's power and its self-approbation. One of the chief abstract concepts behind the design of the jerry-built structure called "the Thought of Mao Tse-tung" was a conviction of the infinite malleability of the human being. Their perverted idealism compelled the Communists to seek to remold every Chinese—for the benefit of the masses and for his own salvation. Since every Chinese was required to become a hot-eyed zealot in the service of the Communist Party, thought reform was Peking's most cherished project.

Determination to alter the shape of men's minds underlaid every decree promulgated in every campaign. The exhaustion that accompanied each campaign also served the Communists' purposes, since it reduced men to a state of numb mindlessness, in which they were, in theory, prepared to believe whatever the Party commanded them to believe.

Thought reform was most successful with the most unlikely group. The half-dozen men who exercised supreme power proved the most receptive subjects, just as the policeman who finally wrings a confession from an innocent man believes most ardently in the guilt he has himself implanted. From the apex of the hierarchy, China and the world were seen through mental prisms which transmitted only red and gold. The hierarchy's self-conditioning endured not only because of their isolation from the reality of their own problems, but also because they, almost alone in China, could maintain the illusion that they actually controlled the external environment. Their endless self-indoctrination—supported by mutual indoctrination—was so effective that they even found in their failures fresh evidence of their omniscience. It was written that the people's revolution, facing implacable enemies, could attain success only by overcoming constant reverses in perpetual struggle.

But the hierarchy's demonstrated inability to create a nation of 700 million devout disciples revealed a fundamental political failure and a basic philosophical flaw in the dogma. Mao Tse-tung did not merely fail to mass-produce hundreds of millions of robots among the masses, he also proved unable to command the enthusiastic obedience of a few million privileged intellectuals. Since Peking claimed pre-eminence within the international Communist movement because of its ideological attainments, this fundamental failure was of the most traumatic significance. When the most docile subjects of thought reform, the men at the pinnacle of the Party, themselves cast off the illusions of Mao Tse-tung, visions under the heat of reality, the ultimate, destructive crisis of Maoism began.

Even before that catharsis the Communist Party's record in thought reform was not merely unimpressive, but was, by its own testimony, essentially negative. The nation had been ideally prepared for "rebirth," a total catharsis followed by total acceptance of wholly new doctrines like the Taiping Emperor's dream of being washed clean and having his heart replaced while eternal truth was revealed to him. But the Communists could not effect lasting conversions. Although the Party could briefly create a few examples of the "new man,"[1] the ideal of progressive Chinese thinkers since they reluctantly admitted Western material supremacy, it could not preserve those creations.

Few of the millions of cadres, whose lives depended on their outward loyalty, long retained unchanged the dogmas so laboriously implanted. Internally, the constant demands of thought reform bred a resentful tension, which generated the need for further indoctrination. Externally, the hierarchy's obvious inability to control the new man's environment undermined his beliefs. The Communists promised so much that a crude material reality like

---

[1] The term—like the underlying concept—owes its modern currency equally to Darwin and Confucius. Inspired by the theory of evolution, the great journalist Liang Chi-chao wrote that only by evolving into a "new man" could the Chinese master the problems of the new environment produced by the West's advent. The term itself comes from *The Great Learning*, one of the four sacred Confucian Canons, which declared: "The Great Learning teaches us to illuminate virtue and to create the new man.

lack of food was sufficient to destroy the new spiritual basis of men's lives.

The myth of brainwashing was further belied by observation of foreigners converted in Chinese prisons. Enduring conversions occurred only among a few foreigners whose past lives had made them eager for a new faith. It was, curiously enough, easier for the foreigner to retain his new faith than it was for the Chinese. An American, returning to America, could retain the imposed patterns of thought more easily than could a Chinese in China. The American's faith was sustained by native Communists, who assured him that the life in the United States actually conformed to the picture presented by the Chinese. Nor was the returned American confronted daily with the breakdown of Communist infallibility in China, where it mattered most. It was not difficult for a well-fed American convert, who desperately desired to maintain his new faith, to believe that great evil hid behind the façade of American prosperity. It was almost impossible for a hungry Chinese cadre to see good in the misery around him.

The Communists failed in good part to hold the converts they made because they could sustain the appeal neither to reason nor to faith; they offered neither rigorous logic nor the spontaneous pleasure formerly derived from religious and family festivals. A few borrowed trinkets, brightened with a thin gloss of absurdities, were not a fair exchange for the heavy, if old-fashioned treasures of the spirit and the mind the Chinese people possessed before they offered them up to the Communists. Men were thrown back on the simple proposition: *The individual is naught, and all his personal beliefs are as nothing; the Party is all, and all its pronouncements are correct.*

The Communists failed repeatedly because there were no limits to their ambition to dominate nature and men's minds. Since the Communist Party, despite foreigners' beliefs, could not read the hearts of men, it reassured itself by demanding outward evidence of submission. In 1958 the schoolteachers of Shanghai and other great cities marched in torchlight processions through the crowded streets, bearing enormous red hearts molded of papier-mâché. The loyalty those intellectuals swore was as fragile as the paper symbols they presented to the Communist Party.

Mao Tse-tung, who scoffed at the West as a "paper tiger," apparently saw no disturbing analogy in the paper hearts. But by 1965 he could no longer ignore the pervasive demonstrations that thought reform had failed abysmally. The Maoists therefore proclaimed the last, the most sweeping, and the most violent thought reform campaign—the Great Proletarian Cultural Revolution.

Somewhere in each human mind there may well be a divine flame that is fed by humor and aspiration. No man, it appears, can maintain absolute control over the minds of other men indefinitely, regardless of the techniques he commands. It has been demonstrated almost beyond question that no man can control the minds of other men, even briefly, unless he controls their environment absolutely. Such absolute control can be exerted only in solitary confinement, for the interaction of the personalities of cellmates has often interfered with thought reform. Outside prison walls nature, economics, psychology, and chance mock the most strenuous efforts. No regime can absolutely alter the minds of men unless it can alter reality beyond regression.

The failure of Chinese thought control is particularly consoling to the liberal mind because the experiment began under circumstances almost ideal for the inquisitors. In 1949 China ached for conversion, longing for precisely those remedies the Communists wished to impose. Chinese society was in that state of symbolic death which ideally precedes rebirth through conversion. Having attempted in vain to find self-respect and purpose by trampling its old values underfoot, the society was totally exhausted—mentally and morally. Drained physically and impoverished economically by forty years of continuous war, the entire nation was close to the state of "terminal exhaustion," which the psychiatrist William Sargant in his penetrating pioneer study of "the physiology of brain-washing and conversion" [2] has described as the ideal condition for conversion. The intellectual leaders of China were wholly depleted. They displayed common tendencies toward hysteria, despair, and lachrymose self-pity.

[2] *Battle for the Mind: A Physiology of Conversion and Brain-Washing* (New York: Doubleday, 1959).

Despite the nation's unending diversity, there has long been *one* intellectual class in China, called in Chinese the "knowledge-able elements" and including almost everyone who can read and write. The intellectual class has been quite homogeneous, particularly at the higher levels where the Western term "intellectuals" is really justified. In the past they were united by the discipline of the classics. During the five decades that preceded the Communist state their rebellions against orthodoxy were remarkably alike. They rejected not only the sterile Confucian classics by championing the New Literature Movement, but the entire political, social, and familial pattern created by the Confucian civilization. Whether they come from millionaire mill-owning families of Shanghai or the gentry of remote Kwangsi Province, the men born around 1900 displayed similar psychological patterns. Because their responses to new doctrines have largely determined the nature of their country over the centuries, the intelligentsia's experience of thought reform was vital.

The educated men of China have been consciously searching for salvation throughout the twentieth century. Their traditional beliefs having collapsed completely in the final welter of Kuomintang rule, they experimented with solutions that covered the widest range: anarchism, aestheticism, fascism, socialism, racialism, and even the cult of science. None of those doctrines provided solutions to either their personal problems or the nation's. By 1949 most young men, and many older men as well, were prepared to surrender their wills to any doctrine that convincingly promised them solace.

This receptivity to new beliefs was particularly inclined toward authoritarianism. In their confusion men longed for definite answers; they were moved by the age-old yearning for Utopia and by the Chinese predilection for categorical solutions. They needed authority to replace the stern Chinese father, whom they had forsworn during the tumultuous 1920s and 1930s by renouncing filial piety and by denouncing the entire social system which depended from that doctrine. Their personalities were weakened by a pervasive sense of guilt; they had not only betrayed their fathers, but had also failed to fulfill their responsibility to the nation. They

longed equally for revenge upon the arrogant West and for vindi-
cation of their personal worth. To this neurotic generation the
Communists promised all they desired—and more.

The regime's appeal was almost irresistible in the beginning,
when it had just united much of China amid promises of a new
era of glory. No matter how far from China the individuals might
be, the Communists exerted a profound attraction upon young
intellectuals who could not desert China.

I saw at close hand how strongly that appeal acted on two
young Chinese who were close friends of mine at Columbia University during the late 1940s and early 1950s. Both were trapped
in an emotional labyrinth of self-assumed guilt, though they were
quite different personalities. The first was the son of a rich Shanghai family, a student of political science whose intense idealism,
consciously directed toward the welfare of the Chinese people
and the glory of China, prevented his finding ease in the American environment. Although he clearly saw the Communists' errors, he deliberately avoided taking any step which would make
him content in the United States. He rejected both proffered academic appointments and marriage to the daughter of a wealthy
Chinese-American importer. The second was a student of business, the son of a lieutenant-general in the Nationalist Army on
Formosa. He married the daughter of a member of the Kuomintang's National Assembly and went to work in a bond house on
Wall Street. He and his wife were devoted to their two babies,
but were hardly touched by political passions.

Both men returned to China in 1955, unable to endure the
strain of exile any longer. Both knew that they went voluntarily
into an environment which was abhorrent to them in many ways.
Upon their return they were both enrolled in a "revolutionary university," an institution devoted to intensive thought reform of
young men and women who displayed either remarkable promise
or substantial recalcitrance. Residence abroad provided automatic
entrée. I have no way of finding out what became of my friends
afterward, though I would dearly love to know. But studies of
other young Chinese in similar circumstances do give a good idea
of how they were treated—and their likely reactions.

Dr. Robert J. Lifton has described the functioning of such

revolutionary universities with incisive detail and professional insight in *Thought Reform and the Psychology of Totalism*.[3] Lifton divides the process into three phases:

The Great Togetherness: Group Identification—The actual period lasted two weeks and gave the "students" at North China Revolutionary University the illusion of being "part of one great family," embarked together upon a great enterprise. No pressure was exerted upon the students.

The Closing In: Conflict and "Struggle"—Students bared their past sins of deed and thought—and accused each other of crimes against the people. The mutual trust, knowledge, and dedication developed during the initial period helped the participants search out each others' errors under the guidance of activists and student group leaders.

The cardinal sin, which instructors and fellow students pursued with the tenacity of inspired inquisitors, was "individualism," a word that had become charged with evil connotations during the Chinese intelligentsia's revulsion from Western liberal ideals in the 1920s. Individualism already meant that one scrambled for wealth and power rather than seeking personal fulfillment. The Communists made individualism read "placing one's own interests above those of the people" or, more concretely and simply, refusing to surrender one's will to the Party. From the roots of such individualism sprang a profusion of vices: subjectivism—attempting to make one's own judgments independently of the scientific truths of Marxism; objectivism—pretending to be a spectator, who was not intimately involved in the struggles of the New China; sentimentalism—retaining old emotional loyalties to friends, family, or colleagues; and such hackneyed sins as deviationism, opportunism, dogmatism, and sectarianism.

Night and day, students wrestled with themselves—and with each other—for their souls. The Communists concentrated on the individual's vulnerable points, which they had meticulously catalogued before the struggle began. The burden of concealing "hostile thoughts" became almost unbearable to one of Lifton's subjects, who later remarked: "I had to restrain myself constantly, to be patient, to avoid offending the cadres or the activists. I always

[3] New York: Norton, 1961.

had to conceal what was on my mind. . . . I could never feel easy." [4]

Pointed examples were offered. A former official confessed to a long record of misdeeds: working for the Nationalists; spying for the Japanese; resisting the Communists; stealing money from his company; and violating his neighbor's daughter. He then expressed his complete relief at "washing away all of my sins" and thanked the government for "helping me to become a new man." [5] An unsuccessful student would first undergo "public accusation." The sins he had refused to confess were then recited at length and he was led away to reform through labor in the wild frontier regions—or, perhaps, to execution. The students never knew the fate of the "failures," but they were encouraged to think the worst.

Submission and the New Harmony—Tension reached its peak when each student composed a complete confession of his past sins and then described his redemption and the attainment of a new state of mind. Inspired rumors told students that "backward elements" would go through the entire process again, while incurables would be sent to labor reform camps. After ten days spent in composition the confessions were submitted to the entire group. Each student was forced to assume personal responsibility for every confession, either approving or rejecting it. The instinct for survival was invoked. The cadres declared that failure to recognize error in another's confession could only indicate that the critic's own mind was still clouded. Activists stressed: "The most important part of the reform of an intellectual is the denunciation of his father—since the intellectual almost invariably comes from a wealthy family which must have been anti-Communist, and if he does not denounce his father he cannot be a faithful citizen of the new reigme." [6] Students found it wise to attack not only their fathers, but any person who had attained prominence independently of the Communists.

The atmosphere was as tense as the minutes before a beach-head landing until the authorities accepted the final versions of

[4] *Ibid.*, p. 261.
[5] *Ibid.*, p. 264. A curious echo of the visions of the Taiping Emperor.
[6] *Ibid.*, pp. 267–268.

confessions and affirmations. The equally intense reaction of relief upon passing the course tended to fix the conversion. Lifton's subject, who later defected, commented on his own confession: "If you put this final thought summary before me now, I could write a new summary contradictory to it in each sentence. If it isn't fear, what else could push one to do something so completely against his own will?"

Yet, he noted, it was not deliberate intent to deceive that inspired his false confession, but honest confusion of motives, ideas, and purposes. "Using the pattern of words [prescribed by the Communists] for so long, you are so accustomed to them that you feel chained. If you make a mistake, you make a mistake within the pattern. Although you don't admit that you have adopted this kind of ideology, you are actually using it subconsciously, almost automatically. . . . At that time, I believed in certain aspects of their principal theories. But such was the state of confusion in my own mind that I couldn't tell or make out what were the things that I did believe in." [7]

The strong-minded retained doubts that they could never quite resolve, since few could escape to Hong Kong as Lifton's informant did. For the weak-minded—and most had neither the education, the capacity for independent thought, nor the character to withstand the tremendous pressure—any doubts still remaining were swept away by a flood of relief at surviving the ordeal. Those doubts would reappear later, when external reality failed to conform to the image implanted by the Communists. But the remolded could hardly think in terms other than those prescribed by the Communists, since they lacked the linguistic tools, any more than Theseus could have escaped the labyrinth if he could neither have seen nor felt Ariadne's thread. Peking not only coins dozens of new terms, it also changes the shape of the traditional ideographs to destroy their old emotional connotations.

Certain generals of the Army of the Republic of Korea who had fought against the Japanese with the Chinese Communists consistently referred to their chief ally as *Mei-ti*, the Chinese for "American imperialists." Similarly, anti-Communist refugees refer to the Communist conquest as "the liberation," or speak of the

[7] *Ibid.*, p. 270.

"Halls of Happiness," where aged men and women were forced to perform manual labor on starvation wages. However, linguistic tyranny over thought is effective only until constant use finally rubs the meaning from the words—or imbues them with irony.

Accounts from other sources support Dr. Lifton's conclusion that systematic thought reformation invariably operates in a fixed progression: group identification; "struggle" to break down old beliefs; catharsis through confession; and "rebirth." The detailed accounts available to the Western world are, of course, related by the regime's failures, the men who finally escaped Communist control. But the constant succession of nationwide reindoctrination campaigns demonstrated that the men who escaped were not much different, except perhaps in the degree of their revulsion, from many of those who remained. Since most took the decision to defect while still in China, it appears that those who succeeded were merely somewhat stronger—or luckier—than those who have not fled.

The process of destroying old beliefs was the most painful phase for the subjects and the most important for the inquisitors. Since self-esteem and a sense of security are major elements of a stable personality, the Communists first broke down those barriers to indoctrination. The destruction was hasty but temporarily effective, in the case of one captured Nationalist Army officer.[8] Assigned to a "Military and Political College" in Szechwan Province, Captain Wang was allowed the usual two-week period of relaxation. Thereupon, introductory lectures impressed upon students the errors and the evils of the regime they had served.

"The main themes of the classes," Wang later recalled, "were that the old way was false, while the new way brings theory and practice together; that action always follows discussion and that labor is the foundation of the world. Heavy work always went along with the instruction in theory, even when the work was not closely related to the subject we were studying."

The arduous manual labor was designed to produce physical

[8] *Wang Tsun-ming—Anti-Communist; An autobiographical account of Chinese Communist Thought Reform* (Washington, D.C.: The Psychological Warfare Division, U.S. Department of Defense, November 1954).

exhaustion, which would make the students less resistant to new ideas. There is, incidentally, a direct parallel in the rigorous basic training given recruits by the American Army—and, particularly, by the Marine Corps—with its deliberate effort to break down civilian personality traits through hard labor and a multitude of petty tasks. It is clear that here, as elsewhere, the Chinese Communists have developed no striking new techniques, though the American basic training seeks only certain specific changes, which are desirable in a soldier and does not normally involve his entire personality. In both cases, however, the authorities also seek from the beginning to lead the subject toward new beliefs (or to "build morale") by stressing identification with the group in which he finds himself and by setting a definite time limit to the training. In both cases physical exhaustion makes men more susceptible to new beliefs, as both Sargant and Lifton have demonstrated.

Captain Wang later recalled that the prisoners of war undergoing thought reform were, like civilians, encouraged "to air their grievances" by criticizing others as well as themselves. From the beginning the Military and Political College took on the atmosphere of a compulsory course in creative writing conducted by a mad instructor. The students were continually writing and rewriting, revising and re-revising their autobiographies and confessions. They were also caught up in a rigid routine. "In this first school after the first few weeks, there were generally six class days and one 'free day'" Wang said. "But, on the free day, the students were never allowed to rest, since almost every minute had some planned activity, usually heavy labor." A typical "working day" began at 5 A.M. with reveille; then small groups made "joint resolutions" to occupy themselves usefully. Throughout the day "big classes"—two-hour lectures in which the students were required to take voluminous notes—alternated with "small classes,"in which they read their notes and "discussed the topic." In the evening "small cell discussions" undertook self-criticism under an activist leader, while other students criticized each other's daily behavior in "small classes." Relaxation came at communal singsongs, at which all the songs were ideological.

Pressure was also applied directly to each individual's vulnerable points. Wang was told that he would be sent back to his native province to stand trial as a landlord. Seeking to escape that fate, he composed a new seven-page confession and wrote a long letter urging his former squad leaders to serve the Communists faithfully. A few officers were actually removed for immediate punishment, while those like Wang who bought escape began to collapse under the burden of guilt at having betrayed all they had previously fought for. They were eager to justify themselves by adopting the new faith and affirming that everything they had previously believed was not merely vain but actually evil. "It all depended on the individual case," Wang added. "Those who were best supported by the men at the school were allowed to remain as an example that could be used with their troops. Those who were very corrupt would be used for a better purpose back home."

Wang well knew that his beliefs were collapsing and that he was playing the traitor. When he discussed his role in his subordinates' thought reform years later, he stammered in agitation and, as much in justification as in explanation, declared:

"The Communists are diabolically clever. They destroy all personal relationships and feelings. . . . They had mobilized the men against me as a target too . . . the entire company was forced to unanimously condemn me as a person . . . they worked individually on those who would not do this; and intimidated and forced them to agree to criticize me. I knew that all the men felt guilty in violating the old moral code between officers and men, and I knew they would not hold me strictly responsible for the letter I had written, because they too had realized that I had been forced to do what I did. Nevertheless it broke up something between us.

"Furthermore, I felt badly hurt in my feelings because of the unfair charges they had directed against me. I knew that the confession that I had to make was not true. I knew that I was not corrupt, but I also knew that the Communists wanted 'to kill without having the victim's blood on one's own hands.' This meant that they wanted physical and mental liquidation of one's self by one's self, so that no one could say that they had done it. . . ."

Wang apparently had a remarkable awareness of the process

he was undergoing. Nonetheless, he "felt great fear for the first time" in his life when he realized that the danger he faced was absolute. In the midst of confessions which he justified to himself as necessary to survive the peril, he still felt guilt at protecting himself by suppressing some details of his past sins. The process was beginning to work; Wang confessed to other misdeeds he had never committed. He declared that the only family he now loved was "the great family of the Chinese people" under the paternal Mao Tse-tung. And he participated with little restraint in a public trial condemning two of his close friends to death.

But the first course of four months did not perfect Captain Wang's indoctrination. He was remitted for "reform through labor" for an additional six months. During the second period his wife was also subjected to indoctrination, and both developed a morbid craving for praise from their Communist schoolmasters. Wang later became a corporal in the People's Liberation Army and was sent with the Chinese People's Volunteers to Korea. The antibodies that began to form during his forced conversion proved powerful. Wang chose to go to Formosa after a period of reflection—and undeniable counter-pressure—as a prisoner of war in Korea.

Each year from 1955 to 1964 the Communists ordered a new nationwide Rectification Campaign to correct "wrong thinking." Before 1955 these generalized thought reform campaigns, which were designed to sustain the new beliefs of millions, were often directed at historical figures or at living men who personified "erroneous attitudes." In the very early days the regime had had high praise for Wu Hsun, an educator of the Ching period who started life as a pauper and amassed enough money by begging to found a school for the poor. Later a film on Wu Hsun was condemned for "promoting the slavish attitude of the bourgeoisie." Instead of merely founding a school to educate the masses, the Communists declared, Wu Hsun should have started a revolution to destroy the bourgeois system. Another historical figure selected for vilification was the journalist Liang Chi-chao, whose son denounced his father's infatuation with Western liberalism. The Communists were deliberately demolishing the prestige and the doctrines of the great men of the period of transition from Imperialism to Communism, so that no intellectual might find emotional shelter behind barricades upheld by their theories and their examples.

Hu Shih was a natural target, for he had been a champion of the Literary Revolution and a major prophet of liberalism. He had also served the Nationalist regime. Moreover, his son was available in China to lead the attack on the man who represented the Chinese intellectual for the world and embodied progressive, non-Marxist thought for China. Young Hu, in 1950 a student at the North China Revolutionary University whose curriculum has already been described, delivered a lengthy public confession, which centered on a denunciation of his father.

"He [Hu Shih] went to the United States in 1910," the young man wrote. "He gradually acquired the viewpoint of the bourgeoisie . . . after 1919, he wandered further into wrong paths. . . . He introduced pragmatism to counteract materialism. . . . He gave first importance to education, secondary importance to politics and economics. . . . He cherished vain hopes of 'reformism,' hoping that the reactionary government might adopt his reform ideas. . . . At the same time, he became more intimately associated with the cultural exploitation of imperialism, he was an important pillar of such groups as the Trustees for the Rockefeller and Boxer Indemnity Funds. . . .

"Today, having received the education of the Communist Party, I am no longer awed by that historical 'Big Mountain'. . . . From the standpoint of class analysis, I clearly see him as a faithful minister of the reactionary class and an enemy of the people. . . ." [9]

Hu Shih, who was to be a favorite target for the next five years, remarked, from his exile in New York, that the Communists, having already denied freedom of speech, had subsequently abolished "freedom of silence." He was not quite right. He himself was granted complete freedom of silence; his reply was not published in China.

Historian Liang Shu-ming was the next target of a full-dress Rectification Campaign with its barrages of newspaper editorials, its mass meetings of ten thousands, its "small cell" discussions, and

[9] *Kwang Ming Daily,* December 19, 1954.

its continuous criticism and self-criticism in a thousand cities throughout China. Liang had retired from active life in 1941 in protest against Kuomintang excesses and had returned to politics after the "liberation" when he offered his services to the Communists. But his personal confession, published in 1951, was unsatisfactory, and the protracted anti-Liang campaign began.

Liang Shu-ming said that he had learned much since "liberation," particularly the need for continuous struggle and the leadership of the Communist Party. Further, he added: "I have nodded my head on certain questions, but there are other questions on which I cannot nod my head, and thus I have not abandoned my original views." [10]

Unfortunately for Liang himself, but most opportunely for Communists seeking issues, the questions to which he could not give his affirmation were crucial. He persisted in his contention that Chinese society had passed the stage of feudalism with the beginning of the Chin and Han Dynasties about 220 B.C., in direct opposition to Mao's contention that feudalism had flourished until 1949—and was still a major hidden enemy which good revolutionaries must fight. Liang further made the obvious point that the Marxist method of analysis, based upon Western European models, was perhaps not wholly accurate in describing the condition—or predicting the future—of a Chinese society which possessed many unique characteristics. He daringly insisted that China was not a class society in the Marxist sense and argued, therefore, that the concept of "class struggle" was meaningless in China.

Liang Shu-ming had pinked the Communists on their most sensitive points. Their response was correspondingly violent. The exact charges laid against Liang need not be repeated, since they are largely repetitions of the old familiar phrases. It was, significant however, that the campaigns against Hu Shih and Liang Shu-ming were not allowed to subside after their first convulsions, but were renewed time after time. Despite the tremendous pressure they brought to bear, the Communists were apparently unable to eradicate the ideas of two scholars. Scores of similar campaigns

[10] Quoted in Theodore H. L. Chen, *Thought Reform of the Chinese Intellectuals* (Hong Kong, 1960), p. 48.

were mounted against prominent intellectuals. Ideas apparently die harder than the Communists—or the West—had thought.

For the varied ideas of modern thinkers, which competed with the Confucian classics but had not displaced them completely, the Communists sought to substitute their new classics. Mao Tse-tung's pronouncements on subjects as diverse as guerrilla warfare, education, literature, and psychology were studied, memorized, and regurgitated by tens of millions. Authorized commentaries came from the pens of Liu Shao-chi and a host of others. The Chinese works were supported by the collected writings of Stalin, Lenin, Engels, and Marx. Rote knowledge of the Marxist classics became the first requirement for advancement. Like aspiring Confucian scholars, the disciples of Communism were to expend so much effort on memorizing the classical texts that they had neither time nor energy for other pursuits. A deluge of canonical words was to sweep away all vestiges of independent thought.

Only one significant new element appeared in the traditional pattern. Presuming greatly upon the conclusions of Pavlov, the Chinese declared that all emotions were mere conditioned reflexes produced by the individual's class status and his external environment. The only vivid emotions for the new man were to be "love of the people, the Party, and Chairman Mao Tse-tung." China established a Pavlov Research Committee under the once-prestigious Academia Sinica, and in 1956 the leading professor of psychology at Peking University wrote: "In 1950, I began to understand that the basis of psychology is the doctrines of Pavlov, and it must be so because the doctrines of Pavlov fit into the dialectical materialism. After the liberation, all those who worked in psychology learned Marxism-Leninism, and a new psychology began." [11]

Pavlov, as interpreted by the Party, remained the basis of psychological and psychiatric doctrine in China. Two generally accepted Western concepts were excoriated. The first was the assertion that certain elemental emotions are common to all mankind. An erring Chinese psychologist contended that it was obvi-

[11] *Peking People's Daily,* February 7, 1956.

ous "that there are common affections [emotions] of all human
beings which the traditional Chinese saying calls 'joy, anger, sad-
ness, and happiness.' Meet a tiger in the mountains, and the bourgeois and the proletariat will be equally frightened." [12] Not so,
said the hierarchy. The Party member will never be frightened by
a tiger, for he has learned to prevail over all perils. The second
Western concept rejected by the Chinese was the belief that
young children do not generally display strong emotions regarding abstract social questions. A child psychologist was abused because "she taught that Chinese children have no emotions of hatred, when, in fact, our children love the Party and Chairman
Mao and hate imperialism and the counter-revolutionaries." [13]

A striking new psychiatric concept appeared in the assertion
that a faithful Party member, who had been reborn through
thought reform, could not possibly suffer a mental breakdown.
Insanity therefore proved guilt. Just as a suspected witch undergoing the ordeal by water could drown only if she were indeed a
familiar of the devil, manifestation of mental illness under the
constant strain of normal life in Communist China were taken as
prima facie proof of guilt. The loyal convert was held to be im-
mune to psychiatric disturbances because he had sincerely surrendered his heart to the Party. A psychiatric textbook prepared
by Peking University stated that acute or chronic excitement
might "affect the skin, derange internal secretions, and create
pathological [physical] deformities." A Party commentator refuted the ludicrous notion that hives, ulcers, or hypertension
might be caused by stress. "We cannot," he wrote, "help asking:
The Leap Forward of our economy and the daily efforts required
for that, should these be counted among the excitements which
upset mental balance? The nerves of heroic Communists are not
shaken at such things." [14] This approach was especially interesting
in a country where the number of psychiatric ailments had more
than doubled in a decade, according to the reports of a number of
Chinese doctors in private conversations.

Although the Party was concerned with the high incidence of

[12] *China News Analysis,* No. 260, p. 4.
[13] *Kwang Ming Daily,* September 14, 1958.
[14] *Ibid.*

mental illness, the final word came from a loyal professor: "A strong revolutionary," he declared, "can stand torture at the hands of the enemy. A woman during the revolution went so far as to cover the mouth of her child lest it should make a sound and betray the presence of soldiers; the child died, suffocated. And so heroes act; they do not respond to intense stimuli by nervous disturbances. On the other hand, during the *Sufan* [the sweeping purge of 1955–56] there were many hidden counter-revolutionaries who became insane under the pressure of the fear that they would be detected." [15]

Thus, superman confronts the witch to prove madness a crime. And thus to the ultimate conclusion, published in a Hupei provincial paper,[16] that no task is impossible and the laws of nature can be annulled if the Party but strengthens its ideological persuasion—and "issues the proper instructions."

Until mid-1957 there had been some room for academic discussion. Men still exchanged ideas on psychiatry, economics, genetics, and sociology, remembering always to consider reality in the light of Mao Tse-tung's teachings. The quasi-intellectuals, young people and men of affairs, compressed their minds into the mastermold of Communist thought; they were happy as long as they believed their submission served the ultimate purpose of making China strong, respected, and prosperous. They dismissed doubts with the rationalization—not unknown in the bourgeois world—that abstractions were none of their concern. If thought reform had not yet attained its ideal of a nation of zealous robots, it certainly appeared to have attained its practical objective— a quiescent nation, laboring without protest to achieve the Communists' purposes.

But the quiet ones revolted when stringent limitations on original thought began to produce deleterious practical results. Among the first to manifest the new heresy were some of the Communists' most fervent disciples. The ardent and dedicated dispositions which had originally carried them into the Commu-

[15] *Ibid.*, October 7, 1958.
[16] And reprinted with approbation by the *Peking People's Daily*, February 16, 1958.

nist camp reacted against the Communists' excesses—and, even more than their excesses, against their stupidities.

Something was seriously wrong when a twenty-one-year-old girl, who had joined the People's Liberation Army at thirteen, rose on the campus of Peking University to declare that the socialist system was "in a complete mess" and to urge her fellow students to "raise the torch of the May Fourth Movement." Worse yet, this student, who had been a stalwart in the campaign for orthodoxy in literature, complained of the "suppressive influences" at work in China and declared that the Communist system must be "rent asunder." With Lutheran simplicity, she added, "After I finish talking, I am ready for jail." [17]

This outburst, like the public complaints of additional thousands the Communist press called "black sheep," was invited by Mao Tse-tung himself. He was confident in late 1956 that the thought reform campaigns of the preceding seven years had produced a nation so docile that he might stimulate lagging enthusiasm by permitting a measure of free speech. He justified the measure by applying the principle that "contradictions" between the people and the government could occur even under socialism. He carefully distinguished "antagonistic contradictions," which arose between the regime and irreconcilable rightists, from "non-antagonistic contradictions," which arose between the regime and the faithful. With naïve complacency, which he later tried to camouflage by the consciously Machiavellian avowal that he had wished "to allow our enemies to expose themselves," Mao Tse-tung encouraged the intellectuals to speak aloud of their dissatisfaction so that the regime might know better how to resolve "non-antagonistic contradictions." "Let a hundred flowers blossom!" he proclaimed. "Let all schools of thought contend!"

The intelligentsia's accumulated resentment poured out in floods of protest in May and June 1957. In addition to students, other groups spoke up. Professors, writers, technicians, and even non-Party cabinet ministers revealed searing grievances. They attacked every aspect of Communist rule, from unrealistic economic policies through mistreating the masses to unthinking adulation of Russia. But the most frequent complaints deplored the intellectual

[17] *Chung-kuo Ching-nien Jih-pao (Chin Youth Daily)*, July 12, 1957.

stultification that followed thought reform. The flood tide cast up from the depths millions of "antagonistic contradictions" that stank in the sunlight. Aside from the courageous and foolish thousands who actually demanded that the Communists abdicate power, most critics complained of the Party's arrogant bumbling.

One diatribe, which rings with honest purpose despite its bitterness, caught the people's spirit. "The Party has arrived at a point where it confronts a profoundly dangerous crisis . . . ," declared a young student at the hyperorthodox Chinese People's University. "When pork is unavailable and the price of vegetables has increased 600 percent in a year, it is difficult to convince the people that living standards have improved. The people have begun to lose confidence in the Central Committee, and they say that, in certain respects, the situation is worse than it was in the days of the Kuomintang. . . .

"To say that the Party has divorced itself from the masses is not so true as to say that the masses have divorced themselves from the Party. The Party will collapse soon. . . . It is, of course, possible to emplace machine guns to deal with trouble, but what should be feared is that the machine guns will be turned against those who first fire them." [18]

The Communist Party ignored the warning. Mao decreed that the Hundred Flowers Movement would continue, its new purpose "to distinguish fragrant flowers from poisonous weeds, which must be rooted out mercilessly." Violent repression was essential to the regime's survival in its existing form—and a new Anti-Rightist Campaign began. The Hundred Flowers Movement had already revealed the failure of thought reform. The new Rectification Campaign destroyed mutual confidence between the regime and the intellectuals. Mao ordered the most strenuous repression and the most arduous forced labor any country has known. If the intelligentsia would not cooperate, the intelligentsia would be destroyed as a class and, if necessary, individual by individual. Nearly ten million technicians, students, and professional men and women were "sent down" to farms or to mass-labor projects "to acquire proletarian consciousness from the masses"—and to learn humility. If the intelligentsia would not surrender its heart

[18] *China Youth Monthly,* June 1957.

in sincere contrition, China would do without the corrupt bourgeois intelligentsia. The new man would not be an intellectual washed clean of his vile individualism, but an honest proletarian who had learned the new technology, which was untainted by "the superstition attendant upon Western science."

It apparently did not occur to Mao Tse-tung that his revised version of the new man might be led astray from submission by his newly acquired skills. Nor apparently, did it occur to Mao that proletarians, too, might lose their faith because there was no pork.

Part Six

THE SHAPE OF PARADISE
What the Communists Wrought

Proclaiming in 1958 that all Chinese must become both Red and Expert, the Communists recognized their fundamental problem with human beings.

The Party was expressing a pragmatic conclusion. It could not rule as it wished if men were merely experts—in poultry raising, bridge building, flood control, accounting, or nuclear science —unless those men were wholly subservient as well. To be Red is to accept the Diktat of the Politburo without a single question— spoken or tacit, conscious or unconscious—no matter how those Diktat mock objective reality. China's established experts, "tainted by bourgeois thinking," had refused such submission.

Having found the experts intractable, the Party decreed that being Red was all that really mattered, since true believers could easily acquire expertise which was not adulterated by bourgeois doubts. Millions of technicians were exiled to the countryside, *while unskilled workers took over their tasks. Western-trained scientists were excoriated for "slavish adherence to Western scientific superstitions," and a semiliterate peasant boy who invented a new way to kill termites was made a full professor of entomology at Sun Yat-sen University in Canton. Students were admitted to advanced scientific study solely by political qualifications. When technical standards plummeted, the Communists were forced to bring millions back from the countryside to administer the nation and operate its machines. But the intelligentsia's obduracy soon forced new thought reform campaigns.*

The conflict between the Red and the Expert persisted, the advantage shifting first to one side and then to the other. Tension endured because the Expert would not acknowledge the Party's omniscience, while the Party hack made a bad technician.

Stemming from a nearly classless, nontechnological society, the Maoists have discovered that they could not attain their goals without the services of a distinct group of technicians. Yet the new class demanded special privileges and developed an esprit *that was spontaneously anti-Party and anti-egalitarian. The inherent contradiction manifested itself in every aspect of life, from literature to latrine construction—and wracked the People's Liberation Army. It was, for example, essential to purge the military of their professional* esprit *so that they would be wholly responsive to the Party's will. But short-service peasants could not tend missiles or operate radar, and only professional officers could command a modern army. The new class, inherently anti-dogmatic, appeared again.*

The same basic conflict scarified relations between the expert Soviet Union and Red China. The interests of a maturing society and an adolescent society inevitably clashed. The new class of specialists—managers and technicians—was already becoming dominant socially, if not politically, in Russia. Simultaneously affirming Marx by pursuing its own class interest and refuting Marx by its existence, it tended to identify with similar classes elsewhere, rather than with the fanatic and importunate Maoist leadership.

15

The First Climacteric: the Great Leap Forward and the Great People's Communes

Mankind's transfiguration occurred in the late summer of 1958. Utopia was enacted by decree, and the Chinese race was exalted. The Golden Age was re-created, and the People's Republic attained a peak of power and confidence on which, the Maoists congratulated themselves, no nation had stood before.

The self-deceiving Maoists contemplated a world wholly in accord with their desires. Other powers trembled as the People's Liberation Army toyed with the offshore islands of Quemoy and Matsu. Even the Soviet Union stared in awe as China, carelessly confident, dared the Armageddon of American nuclear retaliation by her protracted campaign to reclaim those groups of coastal islets from the rump Nationalist regime on Formosa.

Just nine years after coming to power in China, Mao Tse-tung commanded an internal metamorphosis to astonish all the world—and surpass even the Soviet Union—by leading the Chinese people into a radically new phase of man's history upon earth. Greed and strife, lust and envy—indeed, all ignoble emotions and actions—were abolished in the same moment through destruction of the last vestiges of the society which had bred them. Since "man, at his birth, is by nature good," as Marx and Confucius agreed, the new social environment, eliminating both psychological and economic conflict, would inevitably produce the new man, that ideal of centuries of seeking.

317

Nature herself—always troublesome and often malignant—would abate her harshness, gracefully yielding her favors to the industrious wooing of hundreds of millions of Chinese under the inspired guidance of the Communist Party. The mighty rivers would become servants as docile as placid water buffaloes heaving against their traces in obedience to switches in small boys' hands. That transformation would be wrought by China's "most abundant natural resource, her innumerable people," for even the earth would surrender its iron to tens of millions of questing hands—the ore to be transformed into steel by massed human labor.

All "objective phenomena" and all doctrine coalesced in a massive synthesis, which was highly gratifying intellectually and emotionally to the hyperlogical Chinese mind. Every aspect of man's life upon earth was dovetailed into the final, perfect system, whose logical symmetry provided the ultimate aesthetic and philosophical satisfaction Chinese thinkers had always sought. The corrupted nature of man was to be washed clean of the encrusted filth of millennia. *All* contradictions were to disappear in a new system of administration which avoided both the inefficiency of democracy and the excesses of authoritarianism. The arduous process of industrialization would be purified of its inherent social evils by *direct* application of human labor and Chinese ingenuity. Even time would be vanquished, since man's energy and enthusiasm, freed from all previous restraints, would "accomplish twenty years' work in a single day."

Believing still that the spirit of man was clay in their potters' hands, the Maoist hierarchy in Peking decreed a new social organism in mid-1958. The Great People's Commune was to supersede conventional government, for it would comprehend the chief aspects of man's life: agriculture, industry, arms, commerce, and culture. The Commune would supplant not only the family, but even the individual human being. He would be idyllically happy, but he would no more be an independent organism than the individual part of a colonial animal—the polyp of coral or the segment of a tapeworm. Exulted the fortnightly ideological Bible of the regime *Red Flag*: "People's Communes are a brilliant new conception which will create an entirely new kind of human being in an entirely new kind of society."

The rural People's Communes were created with frantic speed and based largely upon the intuition of the zealot Mao Tse-tung. In three wild months, from the beginning of August to the end of October 1958, the regime sought to create a new society. When the metamorphosis was complete, 500 million peasants were to have entered an epoch of common ownership—except for their clothing, the notebooks in which they scrawled political maxims, and, for some, their toothbrushes. Organized along military lines "to live collective lives dedicated to production," they were to possess neither garden plots, nor domestic animals, houses nor cooking pots, nor even their own hearth fires. Drawing their clothing from central supply depots, eating in public mess halls, and bathing in gigantic public bathhouses, they were to become perfect "producing units." After the unavoidably individualistic acts of conception, parturition, and lactation, parents were to be allowed neither responsibility nor control over their children, who would be cared for by the state. Parents and children alike were to cast off the "narrow, selfish bonds of filial love," so that all their love might flow to the Motherland, the Communist Party, and Chairman Mao Tse-tung, whose "love for all the Chinese people is far deeper than any parent's love for his children."

No Chinese was to sit in sinful idleness for an instant. Grandmothers were to weave baskets and tie brooms in Halls of Happiness aset aside for the aged, while mothers and daughters worked in the fields or in small workshops. Perhaps one woman in five was to be occupied with domestic tasks, caring for children, mending clothing, keeping house, and preparing food on behalf of all her sisters. With the disappearance of distracting family ties, distinctions between the sexes were to vanish in the crucible of perfect equality.

Women would differ from men only in the divergent roles in procreation imposed by biological necessity. Already dressed alike in drab, shapeless garments like baggy snowsuits, their secondary sexual characteristics never pronounced, Chinese men and women alike were to be heroes of the revolution. Men were not to assert their masculinity by assuming responsibility for women and children—or exerting authority over them. Women were to give up the feminine prerogatives of adorning themselves, caring for children, and exercising their tactful domination over men.

A perfect egalitarian society—perfectly featureless and perfectly responsive to authority—was to emerge when the Great People's Communes had destroyed distinctions between manual and intellectual labor, between agriculture and industry, between city and countryside. Under the sway of Maoist priest-kings, who instinctively hated any differentiation, the unitary Golden Age would reappear.

The Communes were a brilliant answer to the perplexities and compulsions that vexed the Communist Party. They asserted China's ultimate supremacy in the world by introducing a wholly new concept which, the Party promised, would bring China, first among the nations, to the ultimate stage of true Communism, when all repression would vanish as Karl Marx had predicted. "Men of seventy—and even eighty—will live to see Communism," the regime pledged. At the same time, the Communes were designed to solve the problem of insufficiency of resources which had plagued Mao Tse-tung's efforts to make China a major industrial and military power. Reducing consumption by stringent controls, they would also increase production by regimenting labor. Creating autonomous military units, they would provide an impregnable defense-in-depth against any attack, even one employing atomic weapons. As self-sufficient economic units, they would relieve the pressure on China's transportation system and allow heavy industry to concentrate upon capital construction. They would also stimulate men to new, creative intellectual efforts by providing an immediate object for pride and loyalty.

Seeking to simplify the repressive bureaucracy, the government surrendered much of its power to the Communes. They would not only take the place of local government, they would also supplant the complex machinery which contrived the exchange of goods. Each Commune would first produce the bulk of its own needs and would then trade its surplus for whatever else it needed in direct barter with other Communes. General supervision outside the Communes would come from the all-wise Party through its local branches.

Mao Tse-tung believed he had finally discovered the true Philosopher's Stone which would resolve *all* human difficulties. He asserted that all mankind would eventually be glorified by following China's example. His perfect vision of the People's Communes becoming the human race—and rendering the human individual obsolete—was thwarted only by the Chinese masses' manifestational human incapacity to attain perfect faith or to offer perfect obedience.

The millennium was not quite unveiled in a single day to Sansung Village in southwest Hunan Province. In mid-August 1958 cadres hinted to small groups of activists that a "new, bright life" would soon be revealed to the people by the Communist Party. A few days later town criers paraded through Sansung's dusty lanes, proclaiming that the people would shortly begin to receive all the benefits for which they had so long fought and suffered. Every night for an entire month lanterns glared over mass meetings enlivened by singing and folk dances; thus the pattern of future bliss was gradually unrolled. Students and members of the Young Communist League gathered in special sessions to study their new tasks, while the Women's Association, the Farmers' Association, and the Producers' Cooperative discussed their new functions.

In brief, all the familiar techniques of previous campaigns were used to persuade the villagers, though there were this time no exhortations to "struggle against enemies" and no call for suggestions from the people. Late in September the men and women of Sansung drafted a "voluntary petition" requesting the People's Government to combine their village and a number of neighboring communities into the Great Peace and Prosperity People's Commune. Fortunately, the cadres had not been caught unaware. Martial music blared through loudspeakers, banners waved, and posters fluttered in the wind when the massed villagers presented the petition imploring the authorities to grant the benefits for which they yearned.

The transformation occurred a few days later, more than a month before November 1st, when communalization was to be completed throughout China. According to eighteen-year-old Lee Teh-ming, an intense schoolboy who fled to Hong Kong in December 1958, the villagers did not at first grasp the full scope of the social revolution.[1]

"No one really understood what a Great People's Commune meant," he later observed. "But it certainly seemed good to us in the beginning. Unlike other campaigns, no 'foreign cadres' were imported to tell us what to do. As far as we could see, the government was going to leave us alone in the future—the county government and the People's Commune were to become the same thing, and we were to govern ourselves. It sounded wonderful! We were promised that we could grow more food by uniting our efforts more closely and that everyone would have more to eat. Everyone was guaranteed better clothing, a generous minimum ration—and even baths and haircuts—all free. We learned that the Commune would itself produce many of the goods we needed —hoes and shovels, baskets and plows, cloth and thermos bottles, even iron and steel. Because we would become an 'industrial complex' ourselves, we would not need to spend our money outside— or to exchange our crops with outside producers. Schooling was to be vastly enlarged, and we would even be our own soldiers to defend the country and carry out the will of the people of the Commune themselves."

The youth paused, smiling wryly at his memories of enthusiasm. "There were a few changes people didn't really understand," he continued. "Mainly, I think, we didn't want to understand, because they seemed so incredible. We were all agreed to eating in a public mess hall to get our free meals, but we couldn't believe we would not be able to cook our own meals when we wanted to—or that all celebrations, festivals, and even private parties were to be prohibited. People were glad that they were to have new houses and that old men and women and young children would be specially cared for. It seemed incredible, however, that families would be split up: husbands and wives separated from

[1] In a series of interviews with the author. His name and the name of his village have been altered to protect his family.

their children and each other. That sort of thing was obviously a misunderstanding, for it simply didn't fit with the words the cadres kept quoting from the *People's Daily* and other Party organs: 'The Greek mythology of ancient times was only a tale, a dream, an impossible ideal. But today in the Mao Tse-tung Era, heaven is here on earth!' Or they would shout the slogan: 'One for all and all for one!' and tell us: 'The new era of universal, almighty man has arrived!' "

The regime's failure to fulfill its extravagant promises soon dampened the real—if somewhat sheeplike—enthusiasm that had greeted the Commune's advent. Somehow, the people of Sansung had convinced themselves that the Great Peace and Prosperity Commune would mean more food, less work, and less regimentation. When the reverse proved true, the farmers' enthusiasm turned into hostility toward the regime and all its works. There was less food, and that little was badly prepared; compulsory labor was intensified, and the people lost even the simplest freedom of choice in their daily lives. Lee Teh-ming, who had grown up in Sansung as the son of a village schoolmaster, first understood what the Commune would mean to him when he was enlisted in a "shock labor battalion"—alongside every able-bodied villager between sixteen and forty—to gather the autumn harvest. Older adults and children in theory worked a "normal schedule." But in the first flush of communalization all schools were closed for a month "so that pupils may devote their full time to productive labor." When classes were resumed, they met only two or three hours a day—and most pupils were too exhausted to concentrate on their books. "The cadres," Lee said, "didn't seem to care at all about ordinary studies, as long as we made passing marks in politics."

In the labor battalion the workday began at five-thirty in the morning, when Lee was awakened and mustered to the fields "without munching a grain of rice or sipping a mouthful of hot water." A breakfast break at ten provided a small bowl of rice gruel. After half an hour's rest, the battalion marched back to the fields to work until six in the evening.

"All the time we were in the fields, our group leaders would threaten us," the schoolboy went on. "They would swear that we

were lazy—probably reactionary elements—and warn: 'There'll
be no food at all tonight, unless you all work harder!' I saw two
twelve-year-old boys working side-by-side in the fields, so exhausted they were dazed. One stumbled and fell into the furrow,
and the other mechanically lifted his hoe and hit his friend on the
head. Another time, three men were heaving at a boulder so big it
slipped away and crushed one man's leg. The group leader swore
at them for malingering."

From the beginning the peasants complained most bitterly of
their straitened rations.

"In the Peace and Prosperity Commune," said young Lee, "an
adult got twelve ounces of rice a day, and a child nine ounces.
Each adult also got a pound of sweet potatoes, and every family
was given four ounces of boiled vegetables twice a day. They
promised us each four ounces of pork a month, but we never saw
meat or eggs—or even bean curd. There was no black market, and
the government stores had closed down. We simply couldn't buy
food. We couldn't save rice from our crops because everything
went to the Commune. Even the chickens and pigs we used to
keep and slaughter when they were fat were put into the Commune's pens. The cadres didn't try to take our household furniture, as we heard they did elsewhere, because the separate dormitories for men and women were not ready yet. But all our pots
and pans were confiscated for the iron and steel drive to help the
Motherland resist American aggression in the Taiwan [Formosa]
area. So we couldn't cook, even if we managed to steal a handful
of our own rice or hide an egg."

Although Chairman Mao had proclaimed that the family
would "cease to be the basic unit of social and economic life," the
cadres still insisted that the entire family bear responsibility for
each member's misdeeds.

"If you didn't work, you didn't eat," Lee Teh-ming recalled
his eyes wide with anger. "If one member of the family failed to
answer roll call, no one in the family would eat that day. You
could report sick, but there were no doctors in the Commune—
and the group leader alone decided whether you were well
enough to work. . . . He almost always said you were not sick."

The Great Peace and Prosperity People's Commune is an example, not a typical Commune. No completely representative Commune ever existed, since local cadres were given the widest scope as to the pace and the manner of creating segregated dormitories for males and females, Halls of Happiness for the aged, and crèches and kindergartens for preschool children. But it was intended that all those appurtenances would eventually arise to shape every locality into the semblance of the ideal People's Commune that existed in the mind of Mao Tse-tung.

Aside from certain areas inhabited by hunting or pastoral minority groups, all China's rural area underwent communalization despite its wide divergences in speed and intensity. Two features were almost universal from the beginning: public mess halls and regimented labor. Mess halls—or at least communal kitchens —were essential to control consumption and as Lee Teh-ming put it, "Everyone, without exception, had to work as hard as he could —and then a little harder." In the Peace and Prosperity Commune, unskilled males over sixteen worked the fields in the shock production battalion. Young women tilled the land beside the men or assisted the skilled men in the Commune's two new iron and steel foundries. Older women worked in the mess halls or ran the nurseries, each caring for three or four children. Politically reliable men and women between sixteen and thirty-five joined the People's Militia, which trained with ancient weapons and dummy rifles to defend the Motherland against American invasion. Drilled by veterans of the People's Liberation Army, the militia was under the direct command of the Commune's Party Secretary rather than the regular armed forces.

"After work and drill," said Lee, "came special 'light' tasks, depending upon the season. We planted rice, spread fertilizer, or dug ditches—until the light failed. If we were on a special project, like building a dam or a big irrigation system, we slept where night found us. Women were supposed to bring our food from the mess hall, but often they did not arrive. We were given no holidays, and our only times of rest came when heavy rains made it impossible to work in the fields. Then we attended special study sessions.

"There were regular study sessions every night after work—in addition to the special classes—and confession meetings at least once a week, where we had to 'speak clear' our problems, so that the entire group could help us 'cast off our burdens.' Each of us had to accuse the others of bad deeds and evil thoughts—in order to assist them in solving their problems. But most of the people were so tired they just fell asleep. Even when the cadres blew the whistles that regulated our every movement, they didn't wake up."

The rapidity of the transformation generated resistance almost as rapidly. Some of the staunchest supporters of the regime lost their enthusiasm and were denounced as opportunists.

"A man named Yuan," said Lee, "had been a strong supporter of the Communists from the very beginning. He was a poor peasant who got a big plot of land because he participated so vigorously in the Anti-Despot Campaign against landlords. Then he became head of the Farmers' Association, and he was a leader in the Cooperativization Movement in 1955. But he was fairly prosperous by the time the Commune came along, and he didn't like the change at all. He tried to resign from the Farmers' Association and even told us: 'The work's all ours, but the food, none of it belongs to us!' The cadres put pressure on Yuan, and he reformed.

"Somewhat different was the case of a group of ten men headed by a farmer called Kwan. They spoke up in public to urge the people to sabotage the Commune by idling on the job. They were so strong that some of the cadres began telling us behind their hands to take it easy. One let it slip that no matter how hard we worked we still couldn't meet the grain quotas, so he'd have to lie anyhow. But a team of cadres came in from outside to hold mass meetings, and we were forced to denounce Kwan's group as counter-revolutionary. They offered lenient treatment to those who would confess. Most of the men did confess, and they discovered that lenient treatment meant a reform-through-labor camp. But that was better than what happened to the leader. Kwan was tried by a People's Court and executed. After that there was no more trouble or sabotage."

The Peace and Prosperity Commune was quiet for a time, but universal discontent with the Communes detonated sympathetically across a nation in which all formal channels of information were state-controlled and no man could travel more than ten miles without the proper documents. Since everyone in China had roots in a village that was communalized, pampered urban cadres and the proletariat reacted almost as violently as the peasants themselves. Everyone soon knew that Communes were producing toil and deprivation rather than a land overflowing with rice and yellow wine. Not only intellectuals but shrewd old peasants as well reappraised all the regime's promises and threats.

The Communists had finally exhausted the people's credulity by this ultimate contrast between their promises and the reality they created. The vision of a bright new life in People's Communes was the last Maoist tale the masses would ever swallow. The Chinese even began to laugh behind their hands at the regime's threats. That laughter, breeding contempt, was finally to break the regime's iron discipline. It forced local cadres to accommodate their local policies to what was possible despite the wholly unrealistic and totally visionary orders emanating from Peking. Finally the local cadres prevailed upon all but the Maoist hard-core to come to terms with reality.

"When the Communists first came to our town," explained a young woman[2] from western Kwangtung Province in 1962, "they pleased many people, angered a few—and frightened everyone. We thought they were terribly fierce . . . and there was nothing we could do against them. But, now, after the ten years' shouting, they still have not 'liberated' Taiwan [Formosa]—or even Quemoy and Matsu. Nor have they increased crops or given us a better life. After all the fuss of 1958 people now just laugh into their sleeves when the cadres talk of increased production—or even mention Taiwan. And they laugh in their hearts when the cadres promise to 'liberate' Quemoy and Matsu. How can the Communists accomplish half of what they promise—all those impossible promises—when they are completely stopped by the rotten Kuomintang and the American 'paper tiger'?"

The Communists discovered a new outbreak of individualism. Youths once hailed as the "natural champions" of revolutionary change, were "crushing the sprouts of Communism,"complained *China Youth,* the official organ of the Young Communist

[2] In conversation with the author.

League. Rather than greeting the transitional era with joyous dedication, "many young people are stealthily and painstakingly promoting their individual interests," the magazine added. Fearful that the state would confiscate personal property, many young men and women sold or destroyed furniture and implements—and "hastily withdrew their bank deposits to buy wrist watches or other consumer goods, squandering all the remainder on feasting and drinking."

"We are in danger of being bogged down into a mire of anti-Communism," warned *China Youth*, "because of the mounting conflict between individualism and Communism. . . . Many people became frantic as frightened chickens upon hearing of the immediate advent of Communism, or listening to the current crop of rumors that women will be Communized within a few years; that father and son will be unable to identify each other; that food and clothing will be uniform for all. . . ."

Stolid peasants also "precipitated a series of political and ideological struggles" early in 1959, according to the theoretical journal *Red Flag*. Even the Sputnik Commune in Honan Province, the very first People's Commune, produced its dissidents. A member of Sputnik's Model Production Team denounced the Commune's creation, contending, "We could produce just as well in the old cooperative." Like so many peasants, "he slaughtered his hogs, rather than make them over to the Commune, and encouraged his friends to kill fish, to steal grain—and even to chop down fruit trees for firewood." Discontent in the Sputnik Commune was fostered by cadres, *Red Flag* said. "Even Party-member cadres opposed the elimination of private ownership . . . probably because their individualism led them to serve their own interests, rather than the interests of the broad mass of the people."

Selfish cadres, charged the Maoist publicists, let crops rot in the fields, rather than harvest them for the state's account. They had so little confidence in the People's Dollar that they hoarded vast quantities of goods, including raw materials that should have been processed and machinery that should have been employed in production. Many cadres feared that their own Communes, having sold their goods for worthless banknotes, would starve, while more canny Communes survived. Rather than stimulating selfless cooperation, communalization set the Communes against each other—and against the state.

The Communist Party was justifiably alarmed by the cadres' disobedience, while both the Party and the erring cadres had even greater justification for alarm in the state of the nation. Six months after the creation of the People's Communes, the entire distribution system of Communist China began to break down. Few Communes were actually self-sufficient, but no efficient mechanism had been provided to facilitate exchange of goods among the "new social organisms." Sabotage, wild competition, and the lavish misuse of China's inadequate transportation network aggravated the problem of distribution. Instead of simplifying China's economic life, the Communes generated complexity verging upon chaos. China's thriving export trade fell from the peak attained in the first ten months of 1958 to almost nothing by the middle of 1959.

The abstract logic displayed by the concept of the People's Commune compels the outsider's respect, despite the organizations' practical and moral flaws. The Communists themselves saw only a perfect unity, which would finally create a perfect, harmonious Utopia in the material world. Although it still believed that the Commune was the supreme creation of the human mind, the regime was forced to recognize difficulties in execution a few months after the millennium was proclaimed.

When massive resistance to the Communes indicated as early as mid-November 1958 that the Chinese people were not as thoroughly disciplined as the Party had believed, the Maoist-dominated Central Committee's first reaction was to intensify repression. The Party had soared so high upon the thermal currents of self-congratulation that it could not believe that the criticism came from loyal Communists. Instead, Peking gleefully concluded that millions of hidden rightists were revealing themselves. By a gift of fate the People's Communes were not only to transform society, but were also to produce the final catharsis of mankind's highest political expression, the Communist Party of China.

A great purge swept China's thirteen chief provinces. The Central Committee cut from the herd nearly a million activists, and technicians who questioned the regime's fantastic goals and ruthless methods. Forty thousand cadres were relieved of Party and government positions in Shantung Province alone—Shantung, whose conquest by Lin Piao's Manchurian armies, aided by local guerrillas in their tens of thousands, had provided the final impetus toward the conquest of all China. The Governor of Shantung was removed from office, as were the Vice-Governor and the directors of the bureaus of planning, trade, and finance. Elsewhere, governors and Party First Secretaries were relieved one by one—and working cadres in their hundreds of thousands.

By the end of November it appeared that doubters had been swept from the Party. Those who remained were qualified by their absolute obedience to the commands of Mao Tse-tung, that obedience presumably based upon unwavering belief in his infallibility. Dozens of loyal officials rose from minor positions to major responsibilities, for the leaders believed that they required only a perfectly responsive instrument in order to perform deeds men called impossible.

The Maoist hierarchy's conviction that it could command not only the souls of men, but the winds of nature as well, was revealed in a play called *Everywhere the Red Flag Flutters*, which official critics hailed as a masterpiece of the new people's literature. A Labor Hero, injured by his new blast-furnace, is brought to an "old-fashioned," *i.e.*, Western-style, hospital, with second- and third-degree burns covering 90 percent of his skin surface. Backed by every medical precedent, the doctors decide that they can only make him comfortable till he dies, though he cries out: "We are surpassing England . . . surpassing America . . . I must not die . . . I cannot die. I must go back to tend my furnace!"

The Party decrees that the Labor Hero must live. The patient is entrusted to younger doctors, whom the Party has taught to cast aside "superstitious faith in scientific research" and never to surrender to the—apparently—inevitable. By daring experiment and devoted care the young Communist doctors save the Labor Hero, who returns to his furnace to battle for the Motherland's reconstruction. The new medical techniques, their nature unspecified, are so efficient that the Labor Hero undergoes none of the infections, the relapses, or the unsuccessful skin grafts characteristic in the West of the recovery of many patients less severely burned. He is back in the "front lines" of production within a few months.

"This play proves our contention," observed the regime's favored critics. "What foreign science cannot do, the Communist Party in the New China can accomplish." A campaign based on *Everywhere the Red Flag Flutters* exhorted the new men to "discard their unthinking deference to Western precepts." They were to realize that "nothing is impossible to man," if he drew upon his inherent ingenuity and the "native Chinese methods" devised through the centuries. Then the production quotas set by the regime would be attained with ease—and even "overfulfilled" manyfold.

Shock underlined the lesson. Children were assigned quotas of human bones to deliver to the Communes' fertilizer factories so that they might simultaneously contribute to agricultural production and purge themselves of superstitious reverence for the dead by pillaging their graves. That mission was but part of the organized madness of the Flying Great Leap Forward, proclaimed with the establishment of the People's Communes in 1958 to supersede the mere Great Leap Forward of 1957. More than 100 million men and women served minuscule "native blast-furnaces," whose output would increase China's steel production threefold in a single year. Another 100 million heaped up primitive earthworks to supplement great modern dams in harnessing the nation's rivers to man's service. Farmers were ordered to "plow deep" to depths of six to ten feet, using explosives when necessary, so that they might tap the resources of the subsoil and grow three plants in a furrow where only one plant grew before. Railroad engines—and their crews—worked three and four times their normal hours without proper maintenance or rest. Geologists completed surveys in a week that would have taken years of finicky effort under the old dispensation.

Convinced that giving the proper name to a phenomenon conjured it into reality, the hierarchy actually believed that the Flying Great Leap Forward and the Great People's Communes had tapped 100 million new springs of enthusiasm and skill throughout the entire country. A hundred impossible feats would be carried out simultaneously. It did not matter that the "native blast-furnaces" consumed badly needed utensils, tools, and agricultural implements to produce "steel" that looked like petrified, gray Swiss cheese; or that the "native steel," adulterated by the bricks lining the furnaces, was of less value than the crude pig iron previously produced in the countryside. It did not matter that earthen dams burst under the pent waters, creating the conditions for what the Communists themselves called "the worst floods in a century" in 1959. It did not matter that exhausted shock brigades neglected their ordinary tasks and performed their special assignments without energy; nor did it matter that pigs and livestock did not "leap forward," but actually decreased in numbers under Communal care. The Party had decreed the new spirit—and it would prevail. "Man is a productive animal; he must produce!" replied the faithful, when visiting foreigners observed that some aspects of the Great Leap were wasteful.

The spirit which at once defied tradition and drew inspiration from the past was expressed in a stanza composed by a Shanghai cotton mill worker, who became a hero of the Literary Leap Forward:

> The poet Li Po wrote many an immortal line,
> Tossing off poems as he toasted the seductive moon.
> The steelworkers have no need for wine,
> When they hammer out ten thousand poems.

As much as the massive dams, the barrackslike insane asylums on the edges of major cities were monuments to the regime's energy, for each major campaign produced a new wave of mental illness. Nonetheless, indoctrination and thought reform made the greatest leap of all. The strenuous affirmations of a horde of professional and part-time propagandists were apparently insufficient, though one area of just three counties in north China was stirred by 2 million Agitprop activists. All Chinese would become propagandists. Employing a metaphor of the continuing Hundred Flowers Movement, the Party commanded "blooming and contending." New ideas would in theory bloom spontaneously—to be tested in public debate. Repression insured that only "correct ideas" would survive the war of the flowers.

Magnificent absurdities blossomed indeed, forced by the hierarchy's basic premise: "Thus we believe, and we are omniscient; therefore our beliefs are true." Discussing the consequences of nine years of Communist rule in China, *Red Flag* ponderously observed: "The West . . . has become decadent. Now the East Wind is advanced and the West Wind is backward. . . . The East Wind is prevailing over the West Wind!" That analysis of the comparative technological positions of the parties to the Cold War owed its inspiration to a collection of Mao Tse-tung's writings on international politics entitled *All the Reactionaries Are Paper Tigers*, published in late 1958. (Mao also taught: "To start a war, the U.S. reactionaries must first launch an attack on the American people. They are already attacking the American people, oppressing American workers and democratic elements, and actively preparing to institute Facism in the United States.")

Couéism attained new heights. The *People's Daily* asserted on behalf of its publishers, the Central Committee: "There are no obstacles in nature which man cannot conquer . . ." and cited the benefits conferred upon impoverished Kweichow Province by the People's Communes and the process of "blooming and contending." The people of Kweichow used to say: "We never see three clear days without rain, and nowhere can we find more than one square foot of level ground to plant our crops!" Now the people of Kweichow, transformed by re-education, gleefully remark: "We are fortunate in having balmy weather, with all four seasons just like spring elsewhere. Besides, our province is full of mountains and, therefore, full of wealth!" After an inspection tour of revitalized Kweichow, the Communist Party's Secretary-General, Teng Hsiao-ping, declared that People's Communes were proving immensely beneficial to the masses, each of whom might confidently expect—after five years had passed—to consume 1.3 pounds of pork a month.

The comprehensiveness of the new concept also displayed itself in the Everyone a Soldier Movement, which sought to make the discontented into their own overseers. By mid-November 1958 one of every three Chinese—men between sixteen and thirty and women between eighteen and twenty-two, 200 million persons in all—were enrolled in the People's Militia. Only a few political stalwarts were issued weapons, though peasant girls in flowered jackets drilled with long Japanese Nambu rifles for the photographers and, Peking's publicists insisted, "did not bother about oil stains." The movement's first purpose was not to train soldiers, but to organize one third of the nation into "the shock troops of production under military discipline." The elite militia served as a constant threat to potential slackers, who were merely under "collective discipline."

The Maoists came to depend ever more upon the People's Militia for strategic defense and internal security. Core units were organized as paratroops, guerrillas, and assault troops, training with mortars, machine guns, and small arms "to form a strong special service corps." Officers of the People's Liberation Army trained the People's Militia. They were withdrawn from regular units in which the weeds of military "professionalism" flourished, choking the healthy blossoms of the principle that "politics are king." The officers would teach the peasants military skills, and would "learn proletarian consciousness" from the honest peasants.

A Party tormented by fear, suspicion, and great ambitions sought to create a new armed force under its direct control and to shear the regular armed forces of their prestige and political power. Too many regular officers, infected with "Zhukovism" by Russian advisers, had begun to believe that they were a class of experts who were set apart from the seamless new society. They presumed to argue that Mao Tse-tung's military doctrines, drawn from his guerrilla experiences, were outmoded in an atomic age, which required heavily armed and highly mobile units made up of skilled technicians. They actually obstructed the Army's "employment in productive labor," arguing that such tasks hampered technical training. They even protested against the regime's ruthless exploitation of the masses.

The Army and the Party, which had been a single organism for decades, were being divided by the strain of administering and defending the vast nation. The Party was determined to recreate a perfect unity, free of vexing distinctions.

The People's Militia would provide a defense in great depth, if nuclear war, which the Communists affected to scorn, should follow their reckless international maneuvers. Defense Minister Field Marshal Lin Piao, the only active general who was also a Vice-Chairman of the Communist Party, warned the "imperialists" that they would be "engulfed in a sea of flame" by swarms of People's Militia if they dared to attack China. "As war becomes more cruel," he said, "more emphasis must be given to the role of men. Human beings are the 'spiritual atomic bomb,' which is *our* monopoly." Theoretically, the People's Communes, with their integral militia units, were the perfect strategic defense against the nuclear maelstrom. China would be impregnable, divided into watertight compartments, each completely self-sufficient industrially, agriculturally, and militarily.

The reality of enfeebled adults and exhausted children—and, above all, wasted resources—finally silenced the choruses of self-deception. In the stillness new voices argued that the vision of the ideal must, for the moment, defer to "objective conditions." But other voices insisted that the Party had erred, not by going too fast, but by leaping too slowly. Previous intra-Party crises had been resolved in secrecy, but this time the battle lines were drawn before an inquisitive world. Though the Party tried to conceal the emergency meetings of "leading cadres," it was not granted an extended period during which it might resolve its conflict in secrecy because the outside world learned too soon of the true nature of the debate.

The denouement came in mid-December 1958. For a week telephone lines and radio circuits linking Party bureaus, county offices, and local cells across the vast breadth of China crackled with confidential messages. Stunned cadres mechanically replaced receivers and haltingly told their subordinates the news. Then all the cadres went forth to "give the masses explanations immediately." When Nationalist monitors on Formosa broke the news to the world, the Foreign Ministry in Peking hastily summoned diplomats for the first official announcement: Mao Tsetung was resigning as Chairman (President) of the Chinese People's Republic. It was also revealed elsewhere that there had been "great debates" on the Communes within the Central Committee and in two extraordinary assemblies of provincial officials, but the resignation and the controversy were not explicitly connected by the announcements.

"At first it was as incredible as an announcement that the sun would henceforth rise in the west and set in the east," said a leftist editor in Hong Kong, expressing the shock which swept China when it learned that the incarnate symbol of Communism was retiring. The Communists had hoped to precede the revelation with reassurances, though the decision's abruptness forced them to rely on emergency "telephone conferences" to let the "leading cadres" know. When Taipei's premature exposure forced Peking to make the announcement before the explanations were complete, the official interpretation remained unchanged. Mao Tse-tung, having seen his great plans culminate in the People's Communes, could finally give up the ceremonial duties of the chairmanship of the state. He would thenceforth devote himself to perfecting his theoretical doctrines, but would remain Chairman of the Communist Party.

Flaws other than timing became obvious in the authorized version of Zeus's retiring to Olympus to brood on his perfected accomplishments. Mao Tse-tung withdrew abruptly, when he might have waited just four months for the next regular session of the National People's Congress. He thus demonstrated clearly that not achievements but failure had provoked his resignation. Although he won a formal victory in the protracted ideological struggle that followed his forced resignation and packed the Central Committee, he had not encountered such determined opposition since the Tsunyi Conference assented to his elevation in 1935. Liu Shao-chi became Chairman of the Republic in Mao's place. The decision at first appeared a victory for the Maoists, since Liu was Mao Tse-tung's designated successor. Subsequently Liu began to ally himself with the pragmatic opposition to Maoist excesses.

The Central Committee session that accepted Mao's resignation also postponed urban communalization and decreased the pace of rural communalization. It further admitted great failures in meeting production targets, those touchstones of a Communist regime's attainments. Despite the deliberate confusion of Chinese statistics, the official figures on steel production revealed the true state of the economy. After the remarkable feat of producing 5.5 million tons in 1957, the Communists determined to double production in 1958, and redouble it to 22 million tons in 1959. The Central Committee, meeting in December 1958, reduced the 1959 target to 18 million tons—a figure, incidentally, whose achievement was not to be claimed until 1960. It later admitted that the 11 million tons produced in 1958 included 3 million tons of "native steel, which was not suitable for industrial use." Accepting the Communists' own figures—and their own assertion that steel production is the proper measure of their accomplishments—one may fairly conclude that an increase of 2.5 million tons in 1958 was most impressive. But that increase did not approach the fantastic demands of the year of the Flying Great Leap Forward. Concentration upon agriculture rather than industry was subsequently decreed, and effected a nearly complete cessation of new investment as well as major retrenching in established plants. Steel production for 1963 was about 9 million tons, a most respectable figure for a country that operated under so many handicaps, but it was a far cry from the impassioned promise to "overtake England in fifteen years."

The Central Committee's "Resolution on the Problem of the Communes"—fourteen single-spaced foolscap pages without a single mention of Mao Tse-tung—ordered China to retrench in 1959. Rural communalization was halted for "tidying up after the re-examination," and the rate of capital investment in industry was reduced. The Central Committee revealed a major schism within the Party through the resolution's declaration that the Party's "urgent tasks . . . include achieving uniformity of views on the People's Communes among all the people and all Party members." It reprimanded "those people in our own ranks who are over-eager," stressing repeatedly: "There is still a long distance to go before we reach our goals." The promises of imminent transition to Communism, made only five months earlier, were repudiated. It was an anti-Maoist resolution.

Although the Party had concentrated upon the creation of rural Communes during the period from August to December 1958, a few urban Communes had appeared in Peking and Shanghai. However, the Central Committee ordered that no more urban

Communes were to come into existence until "skeptics are convinced . . . [since] bourgeois ideology is still fairly prevalent in cities, and they [the cities] still have misgivings about the system of People's Communes." The Central Committee assured rural communards that men and women would not be segregated during "tidying up" and directed cadres to "construct new residential areas, with provision for families—children, husbands, wives, and the aged—all living together." The Party flatly denied any desire to destroy the family. Blandly disregarding its sweeping earlier statement that the Communes would "create a new kind of society," the "Resolution on the Communes" said the Communists sought only to destroy "patriarchal feudalism"—a phenomenon most Chinese believed in their innocence the Land Reform Movement had extirpated.

The "tidying up" (read: "retrenchment") was extended beyond the Communes to Party and government organs. The failure of the Great Leap Forward had revealed fundamental faults in the People's Republic. Leading cadres were peremptorily ordered "to refrain from exaggerating their accomplishments and *to learn the difference between reality and appearances.*" [Italics supplied.] Mao "retired" in December 1958, and at the beginning of 1959, 10 million erring intellectuals began returning from the countryside, no longer destined "to become the first generation of educated peasants." A new wave of liberalism was rising, but it would soon break on the rocks of fanaticism.

The Party Center reasserted intimate control over economic life, then relaxed somewhat; major responsibilities for production and distribution were shifted from the unwieldy Commune to smaller "production brigades"; peasants were, for the third time, given deeds to garden plots and permitted to consume—and even sell—a fraction of their own produce; segregated dormitories were built, abandoned, and reoccupied; children were forced to live in crèches, then furloughed to their parents. Only flux was constant, but the general tendency was toward political relaxation and economic liberalization which would produce a more contented China during the next five years. The moderates—"realists" or "pragmatists" are also applicable terms—were in practical control.

In a travesty of Hegelian doctrine, the Maoist regime was

always the battleground of opposing tendencies, from whose resolution emerged not synthesis but new struggle. Impelled to seek solutions ever more extreme, the Party periodically recoiled from the excesses imposed by the Maoists. The mainstream of Chinese history continued to flow within the channel of the People's Commune, alternately rising toward liberalism and ebbing toward regimentation. When the current rose so high and the alterations grew so rapid that the mainstream leapt its banks, China experienced the devastation of the Great Proletarian Cultural Revolution from 1967 to 1968.

But before that final climacteric the Maoists won a victory at a plenary meeting of the Central Committee in September 1959. The anti-Maoist hard-core was purged and the chief exponent was disgraced. It was Defense Minister Field Marshal Peng Teh-huai, who was replaced by Mao Tse-tung's preferred successor, Field Marshal Lin Piao.

After the initial "tidying up," the hierarchy arrived at its own explanation for the fact that the Maoist Communes had been less than a complete success. The Party concluded that the minds of the people had not yet been fully prepared for the new manner of life. The persistence of bourgeois thought, evidenced by the peasantry's clinging to the old ways, demonstrated that cadres had shirked the essential task of seeking out and destroying the hidden enemies of the regime. The self-purification of a new Rectification Campaign was obviously essential, but still more rigorous measures were needed. The Central Committee concluded that the best way to shore up the ramshackle structure of twenty-five thousand rural People's Communes was to expand the Commune system. The urban People's Communes, whose creation had been halted in 1958 because the people were "not ready" for them, were to become the spearhead of further attacks on the entrenched bourgeoisie. However, the hierarchy moved more discreetly, apparently reckoning that the blaring publicity attendant upon the creation of rural Communes had exacerbated opposition. This time the urban People's Communes would first be made a reality—and only then, would they be announced to the Chinese people and the world.

Late in 1959 terms of young zealots equipped with surveyors' transits and measuring tapes appeared in every district of the metropolis of Canton. They invaded factories, workshops, markets, public buildings, and private dwellings, meticulously measuring cubic areas and cataloging the number of persons using each structure. They answered persistent inquiries with silent shrugs or said merely: "The authorities have ordered it!"

There was also bewilderment in Chungking, the mist-hung city clinging to the cliffs above the Yangtze River. In that industrial and commercial plexus of southwest China the authorities were behaving most peculiarly. They displayed an intrusive curiosity beside which their previous prying seemed mannerly. Cadres of the Street Committees convened special meetings to ask citizens their specific needs in housing, manufactured goods, and food. State-owned Factory Stores and the Municipal Friendship Store joined in compiling an *Economic Directory of Individuals and Households,* which enumerated each district's families by race, place of origin, age, and state of health. A special section listed expectant and nursing mothers.

There was one useful clue to the Chungking riddle. Cadres constantly referred to the "guiding experience of Upper New Street," a district in the new industrial quarter on the opposite bank of the Yangtze River. The local authorities had for a year been reorganizing that district for the announced purpose of "collectivizing the masses' life." They had by the fall of 1959 created a distinct new municipal pattern. At the apex of a pyramid of new "guiding organs" was the all-powerful Committee to Organize the People's Economic Life. From its offices in the premises of another new organization called the District Store, the Committee had wrought radical changes in the lives of the thirty-two thousand inhabitants of the Upper New Street District. It had found work for seventy-two hundred and twenty-one previously unemployed adults, 85 percent of them women. Of that number forty-three hundred and seventy-eight worked in state-operated factories and the remainder in a multitude of small "street service and production units" or in nine "street production workshops." Women could "engage fully in productive activities" because 80 percent of the children under school age had been entrusted to twenty-eight crèches; because most of the aged and infirm had been shunted into the Honor Age Hall; and because the "street service units" had opened twenty public mess halls to feed more than 90 percent of the district's people.

Their new manner of life offered the people of Upper New Street not only fulfilment through labor, but also "equitable distribution of the necessities of life." The District Store "analyzed each family's needs and guaranteed to fill those needs," providing no more than was judged appropriate, regardless of the family's financial resources. Any wages earned by the family in excess of the sums charged for "necessities provided" went into the Savings Stalls that were established at every major intersection and in every semipublic building. Savings were registered to the individual's credit, but he had no more control over his rate of saving than he did over the goods and services he received—and there was no indication as to when or how he might draw on his funds. Although his salary was still determined by an individual's labor, he might spend no more than the state felt he needed.

It was soon clear that all of Chungking was to be reorganized after the model of Upper New Street. That process was completed by the early spring of 1960. Other cities began to follow suit. But the official, public declaration that China was establishing urban People's Communes came hesitantly, its manner obviously restrained by the lesson learned in the confusion created by the rural Communes' establishment "with great speed and fanfare." In March 1960 the *People's Daily* revealed to all China that "the economic life of the people of Chungking has now been completely organized in order to provide a better life, to rationalize distribution, and to conserve resources." The term "urban Communes" was still taboo. For a time the key phrase was "new Socialist cities," though the first Party Secretary of Chungking did acknowledge: "The example of the rural People's Communes has been paramount." When the National People's Congress met in May 1960, the Communists finally announced that all the cities of China were undergoing transformation into urban People's Communes.

The final stage in the ideal transformation of Chinese society had begun. The Party was determined to conquer the cities, the citadels of bourgeois resistance. With that conquest the traditional

patterns of life would finally be destroyed. The industrial proletariat, long the coddled darlings of the regime, were to be exploited
as ruthlessly as their rural cousins. Creation of the urban Communes was a thorough, deliberate process which had obviously
been planned with great care. The regime ordered thousands of
workers to move from their old homes to dwellings near their
places of employment in order to create "organized people's districts," each characterized by a central factory surrounded by its
labor force. For the moment distinct industrial, commercial, and
cultural districts would continue to exist in each city, but eventually the distinction between town and countryside would vanish
in the creation of new garden cities.

"It will not be long before our cities become *city areas,*" rhap-
sodized the *Hunan Daily.* "In each, several big factories will form
the backbone; workers, peasants, students, and soldiers will become one; and complete facilities will exist for cultural, educational, and welfare work. By that time these cities will be like orchards, with green fields and forests separating one industrial area
from another and numerous small cities lying hidden in the green
sea like small islands. Each single *city area,* set apart, will have
clear creeks, calm lakes, rows of buildings separated by fruit trees
and flowers, broad streets, and winding paths. Busy markets are
set in the depths of orchards, and orchards surround busy markets. These are the new Socialist and Communist cities we are
building."

While the Maoists planned the new paradise, they happily
measured their wisdom by production statistics. More than 20 million women were "liberated for productive labor" by the urban
People's Communes. "Household service teams" mended and
washed clothing, tidied flats, prepared food, raised children, and
cared for the sick. They even ran mobile stores, so that workers on
the production line could buy whatever necessities they had not
already received from the District Store. Peking boasted that the
new "household and street workshops" alone produced $500 mil-
lion worth of goods in the first three months of 1960.

Less than a year after the measured creation of urban People's Communes the new movement came to a "temporary halt,"

as had communalization in the countryside before it. The Communists had again miscalculated the restraining factors. Maladministration and bad weather—in a nation where most wealth still comes from the fields—meant that there was insufficient food and raw materials to meet the increasing demands of men and machines. Reduced to four ounces of rice and a shred of greens a day in the rural Communes, men looked back longingly to the "bad days" of 1958 when they had received twelve ounces of rice, a pound of sweet potatoes, and four ounces of vegetables. The people's conservatism hardened under pressure, and men who had nothing more to lose except miserable existence simply refused to work. Each sweeping new reorganization designed to simplify administration produced a dozen new layers of bureaucracy, and inefficiency increased geometrically with the expansion. China was, as even the official press declared, "in a muddle."

In 1961 a frantic hierarchy went to the presumed roots of its difficulties, initiating a Party Remolding Movement more extensive than any of the innumerable Rectification Campaigns that had marked its previous eleven years in power. It was followed by a nationwide Rectification Campaign in 1963. In 1964 and 1965 there followed the Socialist Education Campaign. The intractability of material nature and human nature was assaulted time and time again in the minds of the Chinese people. The ideal of the People's Communes was not repudiated. Everywhere in China, the masses still shouted the Three Great Cheers: "Hail the Victory of the General Line of the Party in building Socialism! Hail the Great Leap Forward! Hail the Great People's Communes!"

Laying the foundations of Utopia was not achievement enough for Mao Tse-tung. He could not rest until he saw the shining towers of the future rising against the skies of the present. From those towers would hang gaudy banners, proclaiming—in his own brusque phrase, as self-consciously naïve as an American cigarette advertisement—the motto: *People's Communes Are Good!*

16

The Kaleidoscope Stops

The Shape of China After the First
Climacteric: Economy, Education, Art,
and Religion

There are moments when history halts, though time goes on. No more than an individual's is a nation's energy without limits. Sometimes an entire people will slump into inaction—no matter how harried by nature, politicians, and enemies. Such a protracted fit of apathy seized the People's Republic of China in 1959 and persisted until mid-1965, hardly disturbed by the abortive urban People's Communes, the vitriolic Sino-Soviet quarrel, or the developing confrontation in Vietnam.

The pause was overdue. No nation in this frantic age had moved as rapidly as had China since 1949. The pause was all the more dramatic in contrast to the frenzy that had preceded it. Even more than the stubborn, massive non-compliance of the masses, expressed in the passive resistance of hundreds of millions, the apathy of the cadres of the Communist Party and the People's Government created the new atmosphere. From the heights of the Political Bureau to the plains where the lowest-level officials labored, a substantial portion of the Party's membership was in revolt against the boundless romanticism of the Maoists and the unremitting harshness of their unworkable policies. The majority of those men ignored unenforceable or elusively Utopian instructions from Peking and sought in their own way to work for the general welfare in unspectacular ways.

The years until 1955 had been the good years, in which Communist energy and determination yielded a bounty of industrial expansion and greater well-being for the masses—except for those unfortunate millions who were punished as enemies of the regime. Under the first effective central government in more than a century, an enthusiastic population worked hard, and their efforts were supported by a fair measure of aid from Russia. Their industry was well rewarded, since China was enjoying stability and freedom from war for the first time since Chien Lung's reign ended in 1796. Besides, the Nationalists had left behind a multitude of half-built facilities, ranging from railroads through dams to factories. Those the Communists completed most efficiently.

But the easy gains soon ran out. Neither land reform nor the destruction of the urban bourgeoisie provided the Communists with a tithe of the surplus capital they required for their ambitious program of industrialization, while Russian aid was obviously inadequate. Since surplus capital could come only from the fields, Mao Tse-tung espied a "high tide of Socialist enthusiasm in the countryside" in the summer of 1955. Peking ordered immediate collectivization of landholdings, leaving the farmers just enough to assure their continuing cooperation. Although China was beginning to experience shortages of consumer goods and food, the atmosphere was still favorable to the Communists. But the pressure bore down on the masses ever more intensely in 1956 and 1957. Campaigns of ever increasing harshness disrupted normal economic and social life. Consumption was cut and cut again, while hours of work seemed to increase in inverse proportion. In 1957 Mao Tse-tung was shaken both by the revelations of widespread discontent produced by the Hundred Flowers Movement and his obvious incapacity to attain his economic goals. He ordered the Great Leap Forward and in 1958 the People's Communes. After these seismic convulsions the nation simply went limp in 1959.

In 1964 and 1965 China was like a giant kaleidoscope that had been violently shaken and then laid down. The pattern was frozen for the moment. All was still—the broken shards of glass, the bright pebbles, and the battered rhinestones that represented men's lives and their rulers' great designs. Before the final great upheaval of the Great Proletarian Cultural Revolution, the pattern was clear.

In Peking in 1960 a European foreign correspondent was unable to persuade the Chinese Customs to release an atlas of the world sent from abroad. After several vain inquiries through the Foreign Office, he was finally given an explanation.

"Your atlas," said a senior official, "has a map of the Far East. On the map of the Far East, our island of Taiwan is called Formosa. That imperialist name implies that the island is not a province of China. We cannot, therefore, permit you to import this atlas."

The correspondent offered to paste the name Taiwan over the offending word Formosa.[1] Weeks of consultation followed, but the answer remained: "No, we are terribly sorry, but you cannot import this imperialist atlas."

After months of negotiation, a compromise was finally arranged.

"If you will write us a formal letter, stating that you acknowledge the error in terminology and deplore it; and that you realize that Taiwan is Taiwan and not Formosa; and further affirm that the island is a province of the People's Republic of China. . . . If you do this, we will release the atlas to you," said the Foreign Office.

In mid-1961 in Canton a British businessman looked down from the fourth floor of the Love the Masses Hotel. He saw a tableau reminiscent of the Great Depression in the United States. Groups of listless men stood on every streetcorner smoking dried papaya leaves wrapped in brown paper. They scuffed the dust with tattered cloth shoes as they chatted. A few workers half-heartedly trundled lightly laden handcarts down the street, pausing every few minutes to spit or wipe their faces. One cart took three-quarters of an hour to traverse the fifty-yard span of the

[1] Formosa, meaning "beautiful," is the name early Portuguese explorers gave the island. Taiwan, the pronunciation almost identical in Chinese and Japanese, means "Table Bay."

visitor's vision. Along the waterfront makeshift stalls sold vegetables and slivers of slimy meat to anyone who could pay two People's Dollars[2] for a wilted cabbage the size of a small bunch of celery. At the railroad station, travelers arriving from Hong Kong with food and clothing were assaulted by thieves who snatched away their parcels. The omnipresent People's Police watched, but took no action against either the loafers or the thieves.

A breakdown of authority demoralized not only the masses, but the cadres too. A middle-rank cadre fled to Hong Kong when his own crimes were discovered to be more serious than the petty graft on which most of his fellows lived. He had conspired with the principal of a middle school to counterfeit ration tickets by using the school's official rubber stamps to authenticate forgeries prepared in the school's printing shop.

"China has become the country of the ration ticket," a letter from a teacher in Shanghai reported. "We can buy nothing without those flimsy slips, which are themselves only about one inch square because of the universal paper shortage." The ration set a limit on the food an individual could purchase outside the "free" markets; it did not guarantee him a minimum amount. In central China road accidents increased manyfold because truck drivers suffered from night blindness caused by malnutrition. Beriberi, dropsy, and rickets were widespread. A doctor of herbal medicine who fled a rural People's Commune in Kwangtung Province reported:

"About two hundred came to our 'hygiene station' each day, but some of these were patients from neighboring towns. Dropsy was the most common disease—caused chiefly by vitamin deficiencies, because the people in the countryside just didn't get enough to eat. Nine out of ten of the cases treated at my station were dropsical cases, and there wasn't much we could do except to try and prolong their lives by feeding them on a kind of brew of red dates and rice bran.

"The most common disease in towns was inflammation of the liver—one of the symptoms was the patient's complexion turning yellowish.[3] Bone diseases and tuberculosis were also increasing.

[2] U.S. $.90 at the official rate, but more than $10 in terms of income.
[3] Apparently hepatitis, perhaps infectious, made virulent by avitaminosis.

chiefly because of malnutrition. Lack of cooking oil and proteins was responsible for a number of ailments like abdominal infections and stomach disorders. We had cases of farmers fainting in the fields every day, and sometimes they just dropped dead without any warning."

From 1960 to the end of 1963 the Communists spent more than $900 million to buy more than 15 million tons of grains and flour. They bid up shipping rates in order to obtain rapid deliveries from their chief suppliers, Australia and Canada.

A Frenchman, leaving after three years' residence in Peking, observed, "The feeling in the city today is like that in Paris in 1944. If you see a queue, you join it first and ask what it's for later."

With deficiency diseases epidemic, reducing the birth rate radically and rendering hundreds of millions of Chinese incapable of sustained labor, one great riddle obsessed students of China: What had happened to the food crops which, before the Communist conquest, were just adequate to feed the entire population though inadequate transportation facilities sometimes produced famine in one province while neighboring areas enjoyed abundance?

The Communists had a pat answer. Floods and droughts of unprecedented severity, they said, had radically reduced China's food production since 1958. But a young overseas Chinese named Herbert Lam, who arrived in Hong Kong early in 1962 after spending five years in Yunnan Province in the far southwest, had another answer.

"There was no drought in Yunnan in 1960," he said, "and only a mild drought in 1961. Since natural forces had no significant effects, Yunnan's agricultural production in those years was as high as ever. But we were all on severely straitened rations. The Communists told us that our production had to be shipped elsewhere. They gave four reasons: (1) Yunnan's grain was being shipped to provinces that had suffered badly, as Szechwan had from drought and Fukien from floods; (2) China was sending grain to help other countries, like Cuba; (3) it was necessary to build up stockpiles for the army against a possible war; and (4)

Russia was pressing China for payments on outstanding debts, demanding rice and other foodstuffs."

The Communists offered slightly different explanations at home and abroad, but testimony from elsewhere in China demonstrated that the basic reason for shortages was one they preferred not to cite. Chou Li-fan, an American-educated psychologist who lived in Manchuria from 1957 to 1962, presented a more searching explanation.

"The Communists said that natural catastrophes began in 1958, but Manchuria had spectacularly good crops that year," he said. "Sadly, most of the grain never got to the warehouses, and much that did rotted because of bad storage. During the vital harvest months, almost every peasant—and clerks, doctors, teachers, and engineers as well—was engaged in tending small backyard furnaces that produced a grade of steel useful only for sinkers on fishing lines. While the peasants were wasting their time, the crops rotted."

Studies of the weather in neighboring countries substantiated the evidence that nature had *not* taken a catastrophic toll of China's agricultural production. The real causes were maladministration and waste on a fantastic scale. More than 100 million persons were employed in making backyard steel, and another 100 million in making jerry-built irrigation works. This lavish use of manpower not only produced a major labor shortage in populous China, it also resulted in an average grain crop somewhat less than 170 million tons annually from 1958 onwards. Only from 1962 to 1965 did the figure begin to inch upward again toward the minimal requirement of 180 million tons. That increase, produced chiefly by lack of official interference with the farmers, was, unfortunately, largely negated by renewed acceleration of the rate of population increase.

The economic effects of lower food production were cumulative. Weakened farmers produced less food, while industry, deprived of raw material for machines and workers alike, produced less goods. At the beginning of 1961 the Communists announced a virtual cessation of industrial construction in order to concentrate upon agriculture. Although all available resources were directed to the land and large quantities of grain were imported, the regime still could not provide enough to eat. The more spectacular excesses of 1958–59 disappeared, but economic administration remained in a state of near chaos, and the morale of the farmer was broken.

The compulsion to dominate, which led the Chinese Communists to defy first the West and later the Soviet Union, produced curious results domestically. Realizing that they could obtain little assistance from abroad, the Chinese determined to create a major industrial and military power by their "own unaided effort." Approaching the task of industrialization with desperate fervor, the Communists themselves contrived their greatest failures.

Wang Po-hwai, an engineer from Wuhan, China's Detroit, told a story that epitomized the Chinese approach to industrialization in the critical years 1958 to 1960.

"We had two tremendous Russian cranes at my foundry," he said. "Everyone was very proud because they could lift such heavy loads and because they speeded up our work so much. But one day two of the younger engineers came forth with a brand-new suggestion. They told the Party Secretary that their calculations showed the cranes could lift 30 percent more than the weight specified. Both the Russian experts and I said this was impossible, and we warned that such loads would break the cranes. The Secretary denounced me as a 'negativist 'and went ahead. First one crane collapsed and soon the second. Then came the craziest thing of all—the two younger engineers were commended for their inventive spirit, but warned mildly to be more accurate in the future. I was subjected to public criticism for my 'negative attitude and lack of faith in China's potential.' "

That incident occurred in 1958, at the most frantic moment of China's attempt to industrialize overnight. But basic Maoist attitudes changed little thereafter, despite repeated demonstrations that genuine progress usually proceeds step by step, rather than in great bounds.

"Life in China today is a series of endless upheavals," explained psychologist Chou Li-fan from Manchuria in 1962. "The Communists call them *yun-tung* [campaigns], and we are never without one. Active campaigns, like planting trees or building dams, are succeeded by passive campaigns, like the Movement Against Waste. Sometimes, two successive *yun-tung* are direct opposites. At my university, for instance, there was a movement called Emphasize the Modern, Neglect the Old. A few weeks later the Party Secretary announced another *yun-tung* called Study the Old for Practical Use. Some of the students came to me in tears, for they had already burned their lecture notes and texts on all history before 1800.

"The constant campaigns produce a strange psychology on the part of students and teachers alike. The Three Coordination Campaign was supposed to remedy our acute shortage of textbooks by a concerted effort on the part of writers, teachers, and students. Each academic department was ordered to submit a list of the textbooks it would produce by a deadline three months off. My own department said it would write a hundred and twenty to a hundred and fifty books, but the Party Secretary said the figure was not high enough and demanded that we produce three hundred. The chairman of the department readily agreed.

"When I said I was sure we'd never be able to write that many, he answered: 'It doesn't matter whether we do or not. There'll be another campaign long before three months are up, and they'll forget about this one. All we have to do is to produce the list—not the books.'"

That attitude, multiplied many millionfold throughout the nation, thwarted the fanatical Maoists.

Herbert Lam from Kunming noted that campaigns were a constant feature of life everywhere in China, each climaxed by the disappearances to "corrective labor" of a few culprits who seemed to be selected almost by whim as an example to the remainder.

"I think the Communists are so unsure of the temper of the people," he said, "that they deliberately relax restrictions on speech and even employ *agents provocateur* to get others to speak out. Their purpose, of course, is to determine how much control they must exercise—and where. But the campaigns are self-defeating. Life in China is like the dance marathons my father told me about when I was a little boy in Jamaica. When the new campaign starts, everyone automatically throws himself into its rhythms in order to protect himself. But the individual campaigns have no more meaning—or effect—than the switch from a foxtrot to a waltz to the Charleston in the marathon. And everyone ends up totally exhausted."

The campaigns of 1961 to 1965 were, however, in a minor key. The Maoist hierarchy retained its characteristic style of operation, but the fires were banked by exhaustion and passive resistance. Nearly 50 million Chinese "returned to the front line of agricultural production" early in 1961, for the fields were not yielding enough to feed China—much less finance industrialization. New construction was halted, and established factories worked half-days.

The most pathetic campaign of all was expanded—the Technical Innovations Movement. A major element was the construction of "local railroads" running on rails made of wood covered with thin sheets of the brittle steel produced in "native furnaces." Small steam engines and converted trucks pulled narrow-gauge carts, and the propagandists rejoiced because "one truck can now move ten times as much as it formerly did." But the local railroads were an unstable prop for a populous nation's attempt to build modern industry; constantly breaking down, they required so much maintenance that they defeated their own purpose of saving labor power. Another improvement was mounting sails on bullock carts. These "sailcarts" did have one negative virtue absent in most of the other primitive machines, which showed a distressing tendency to break down and injure their servants. The sailcarts injured few; they did not move fast enough.

In mid-1962 the People's Dollar was almost valueless. "High-class and special restaurants" in Shanghai offered meals that cost the individual as much as a hundred dollars.[4] The black market made farmers rich in money they could not use, and coolies said they preferred food to money as tips. Hotel servants lined up to beg departing guests for scraps of food or clothing, though tipping was officially forbidden as demeaning—and tips had actually been refused until 1959. With control breaking down, people no longer feared, as one Chinese woman had said despairingly in

[4] U.S. $40 at the official rate, or, more realistically, in terms of income, U.S. $200-$400.

1957, that "No matter where you go, your dossier will go with you."

In 1961 a resolution of the Central Committee quietly furled the banners of the Great Leap Forward. The Communists ordered that "the nature of basic construction must be readjusted and its speed reduced. . . . More attention must be paid to bettering the state of consumer supplies." The Communist Party complained, somewhat petulantly, that 10 percent of the population was actively opposed to the regime, raising the intriguing question of how many Chinese *actively* supported the Communists.

The logical—if somewhat absurd—culmination of the alternating waves of tension and relaxation, pressure and permissiveness that swept China after 1957 was hardly the old Taoist state of *wu wei*, inaction. The stage in which China found herself was nonetheless a fascinating example of the ends to which strict application of the Hegelian dialectic can lead. The thesis of repression and the antithesis of relaxation came together in a new and unique—if somewhat schizoprenic—synthesis. Both elements operated at the same time—with official sanction. Nonetheless, the Communists had learned much from their previous failures, for the degree of the pressure and the permissiveness was never as intense as it had previously been. The administrators quite simply ignored the planners' visionary zeal.

In September 1962 a plenary session of the Central Committee most explicitly decreed a new wave of tension. "Class struggle" was to be intensified in the cities; the state was to assume greater control of economic life; petty bourgeois tendencies, rekindled among the peasantry by granting them control of private plots, were to be quashed; the intellectuals were to be brought into line; and industrialization was once more to be pressed. In short, the Maoists were determined to resume a straight course toward their obsessive goals. The slight economic betterment which followed upon the general relaxation that began in 1960 had restored the Maoists' self-confidence. At the same time, the manifest danger of the country's lapsing into a contented state of bourgeois material well-being impelled the extremists to order ever more evident campaigns of ideological "rebuilding." But the pragmatic cadres resisted the fanatics' directives: no major new convulsions occurred, but merely a tightening up all along the line. The orders that were intended to get China moving again had only sporadic effects. Tension increased, but the degree was remarkably lower than that which characterized previous periods of pressure.

China specialists expected a new wave of tension as soon as the *laissez-faire* policy which began in 1960 resulted in a slight improvement in living conditions. The reality initially proved more complex. In November 1962, for example, the Party itself concluded that the *sine qua non* of mechanized agriculture could not be achieved until the passage of twenty to twenty-five years. Having already proclaimed that agriculture must remain the basis of the Chinese economy for the foreseeable future, the hierarchy was, in effect, admitting that industrialization on any major scale could not be realized before at least two decades had elapsed. Meanwhile, the Chinese people were eating better than they had during the Great Leap, though still not so well as they had before 1958. A more reasonable attitude characterized the Party's approach to everything, from distribution of goods and irrigation of farms to production of clothing and scientific research. Unfortunately, the reasonableness manifested itself only in the immediately practical and material fields. With regard to the arts, Marxist doctrine, and foreign policy the Chinese were just as dogmatic as ever. Having been forced to make major concessions in practical policies, the Maoists lashed out in the abstract areas.

However, the historical hiatus touched every aspect of life. Education was particularly affected.

The heart of the Confucian system had been the schools, which transmitted classical learning. Abolition of the Civil Service Examinations in 1905 destroyed the reason for the old schools' existence, and five years later the Empire perished. No effective substitute for either the Confucian classics or the strict Confucian education was discovered during the chaotic years from 1905 to 1949. The Communist hierarchy came to power determined to replace the old Confucian strictures with a mechanism which would instill the new orthodoxy. The sanctified Thought of Mao Tse-tung played the same role in the Communist state that the sacrosanct classics did in the Confucian Empire. The *only* course allotted a sufficient number of hours in all Chinese schools at all levels was political study. Only in politics were all students required to take rigorous examinations.

From the Empire's disintegration in 1911 until the establishment of the People's Republic in 1949, all major political movements, including the Communists', originated in the "new schools and universities," which were built after European and American models. Although they were much modified after 1949, these schools and universities still existed in 1958, when Mao Tse-tung decided to destroy the academic system that had given birth to the Communist movement. He took that decision because the schools, as they were then constituted, could not produce the hordes of technicians he required and because potentially effective opposition to the regime was concentrated in the academic world. Having failed to break the bourgeois intelligentsia, he determined to raze their citadels.

Even before he declared total war on the old intellectuals and the old educational system which had produced them, Mao had known quite clearly what he desired of education. The basic thinking of the Party he then controlled absolutely was shown in a light all the more revealing for being oblique in a thesis that was technically excellent—and occasionally brilliant. Published in 1956 in English as a manual for college students training to be English translators, *Translation: Its Principles and Technique* opened with this passage: "What is the object of studying foreign languages? The answer to this question is now different from that ten or twenty years ago. A foreign language is now to be studied not to serve the foreign imperialists, but to serve our own people, not for the sake of foreigners, but for the benefit of ourselves."

The author's preface illuminated the basic philosophy of China's new culture more sharply than volumes of analysis.

"One of the main points in our philosophy," he wrote, "will be, I suppose, how to make translation a science. Translation, as I told you, is an art. True, it is an art. But as an art, it will be considered as the work of gifted people only. Painting, singing, dancing, and other arts are not supposed to be mastered by everybody. High attainments and successful achievements seem to come only through the unusual gifts of some prominent figures. This is, however, the old point of view, which checks the progress of society. We are now taught to hold a new point of view, a view different from the traditional theory. We are taught that in order to make it popular, any and every art must be turned into a science. There is, in fact, no pure art as people supposed. Translation as an art is the work of only a few; translation as a science will be within easy reach of many."

The professor of English did not restate the conclusion of Lu Ting-yi, then Chairman of the Propaganda and Cultural Bureau of the Central Committee of the Communist Party of China.[5] He asserted flatly that the object of education was "to produce constructive workers of Socialist consciousness, each of whom can undertake any task and practice any profession whatsoever." But the professor did contend that translation was best conducted as "a collective project." In an *obiter dictum* he revealed the basic purposes of education in China:

"Psychology tells us that where there is a stimulus, there is a response. . . . When somebody passes criticism on your work, you may get angry at his improper speech, or you may doubt his judgment, or you may be glad to accept his advice. Among the different responses, only one is considered to be appropriate. *Education is to lead us to respond correctly and properly. All learning is nothing but leading us to hit upon appropriate responses to stimuli.*" (Italics supplied.)

A footnote defined the psychological basis of education in Communist China: "Pavlov's experiments show that one of the most important and most characteristic properties of the conditioned reflex is its temporary nature. If the fundamental condition is in any way not fulfilled, then even old and strong conditioned reflexes will gradually weaken and disappear. So the [constant] association of the extraneous stimulus with an unconditioned reflex is necessary not only for the formulation of conditioned reflexes but also for their preservation."

Always temperamentally inclined toward preferring "instant"

[5] Lu, whose public utterances appeared totally Maoist, was deposed in 1966. He was charged with being a leader of the anti-Maoist pragmatic faction.

indoctrination to the laborious process the West calls education, Mao finally decided that only the application of Pavlovian principles could attain his purposes. He was compelled to that decision by the treachery and the total disaffection the intellectuals and the academic community displayed during the Hundred Flowers Movement. Unwisely accepting Mao's invitation to frank criticism, the intellectuals earned the enmity of the regime—and the gratitude of the outside world—by describing the true state of education in Communist China. During the "flowering" months of May and June 1957 a series of forums sponsored by the *Kwangming Daily*, a Peking paper "representing the minority parties," revealed the depth of academic discontent. A forum at the Academy of Science complained that bureaucracy was hamstringing scientific research because "the leadership of the Communist Party merely wastes time and money, without leading." In Manchuria another forum declared there could be no "blossoming of fragrant flowers" until the Party relaxed its rigid controls. The refrain of all complaints was the domineering dogmatism of these Communist Party members who were concerned with education. Professional educators displayed righteous fury at being "reduced to lackeys" within their own schools.

At Wuhan University the faculty complained that Communist Party members, believing themselves to be made of special stuff, dictated all academic decisions down to the appointment of junior staff members and the selection of students for study in the Soviet Union. They insisted on their own politically qualified candidates, regardless of their scholastic attainments. The Party group, "considering themselves specially appointed to reform all non-Party intellectuals," regularly called faculty members from their classrooms to demand "complete self-examinations" before permitting them to return to their teaching. At Tsinghua University, one of China's oldest and most distinguished, the Dean of Studies had no practical authority, but merely followed the orders of his "secretary," who was a Party appointee. Party members did not bother to talk to outsiders, because they were "too busy," while ordinary faculty members were never permitted to converse with foreign visitors in foreign languages. One senior professor complained that the quality of instruction had deteriorated with the change in the student-teacher relationship. Authority was dead, and students "waged struggles" against their teachers, even to "digging out intimate details of their private lives in order to expose their faults to the world."

A professor of the Central China Normal College reported that the Communist vice-president of that institution had admonished non-Communist teachers: "Do not think you are indispensable. In three years we shall have a new crop of experts and we shall not need you any more." Teachers also attacked excessive reliance upon Soviet methods and the regime's disregard of modern Chinese experience in education.

The *People's Daily* discovered a "wave of unhealthy phenomena among students . . . slacking, engaging in promiscuous sexual activity, dancing, frequenting cafés, and brawling." But the dedicated and puritanical Chinese students, unlike their Russian counterparts, vented their discontent in political action, rather than mere hooliganism. At Sun Yat-sen University all classes were suspended for a week after students demanded "a fundamental change in the nature of the nation's political life." Szechwan University students appealed to their fellows everywhere: "Sound the clarion call for attack . . . call for the sword and the spear."

The worst shock was the near revolt of the chosen elite at Peking University. Undergraduates formed a Hundred Flowers Club, inspired by a girl who declared in a dramatic public speech: "There is no real democracy in China. Exactly what kind of democratic rights have you achieved [since Communist rule began]?" A senior physics student who supported her argued: "The study of philosophy is steadily deteriorating under Communist pressure. Physics and natural science are being totally ruined. China's greatest scholars and teachers are being driven to ignorance and confusion."

Wall posters attacking the regime made university buildings look like enormous billboards. Seated on the lawns, students gazed at a poster proclaiming: "The Communist press is another Great Wall of China! It keeps out knowledge and keeps us in ignorance!" Another poster, perhaps the boldest of all, asked quietly: "What is there that is more precious than individual liberty?"

The Communists had sought to win the support of the students by destroying the authority of their teachers. The "feudal superior-inferior relationship" between instructor and pupil no longer applied, either in personal relations or in intellectual endeavors. Students and teachers, the Communists declared, were "equal Socialist workers."

Somewhat surprisingly, the students' final revulsion was more violent than their elders'. At Hanyang Middle School a thousand students imprisoned the Communist principal and commandeered the school buildings for three days to demonstrate against inadequate instruction and the arbitrary assignment of jobs after graduation. Apathetic police stood by while the students hoisted great placards reading: "Mao Tse-tung must go! The Communists are leading us downhill! We welcome an early return of the Kuomintang!" Nor did the police act when the demonstrators seized the offices of the County Committee of the Communist Party.

Retribution came later. The repression that followed such outbursts briefly overcame the hierarchy's preoccupation with producing great quantities of graduates as quickly as possible. Instead of piling additional hundreds of thousands into inadequate middle schools and universities to be taught by unqualified instructors, the regime reduced the number of new entrants. New college freshmen in the fall of 1957 were a hundred and seven thousand, about 60 percent of the hundred and eighty thousand who had enrolled in 1956. There were similar reductions in middle- and primary-school enrollments. Those middle-school graduates who could not secure admission to universities were "sent to the countryside to become the first generation of educated peasants." Some saw their former teachers tilling the next furrow.

Only the next year the trend was reversed by the demand for an ever increasing number of graduates to satisfy the mystique of the Flying Great Leap Forward. The Party hierarchy again succumbed to the fascination of quantities. The obsession was not new. It had manifested itself as soon as the Communists took power, with the creation of "short-course and specialist universities" designed to pour out streams of technicians. They were built upon the principles of intense specialization, described by Howard L. Boorman of Vanderbilt University as "teaching one man to build the bottom part of a bridge, while another learns to build the top." Debasing teaching standards even as far down as the primary schools, those technical institutes left a legacy of mediocrity. "Students spend so much time in political work and manual labor from the beginning of their education, and teaching standards are so low," agreed three science teachers, "that the great majority of students entering colleges are simply not equipped to do middle-school work, much less college work."

A shortage of qualified teachers aggravated the crisis of standards. Lu Ting-yi himself admitted in late 1959: "According to next year's plan, five hundred thousand additional teachers will be needed for full-time and part-time schools [even after inadequately trained graduates are included.]" Despite a variety of such makeshifts as recruiting Party members and bureaucrats as part-time teachers, by Lu's own account the shortage of teachers remained the single greatest difficulty of China's educational system. That shortage, in good part produced by the Party's unyielding determination to strive for results beyond its means, remained the chief problem of education until the schools were closed by the Cultural Revolution.

The Communists themselves created the problem by their infatuation with numbers. In 1949 there were 117,000 students in higher institutions; 1.27 million in middle schools; and 24.39 million in primary schools. There was thereafter great quantitative progress. In 1957, the totals were: 440,000 students in colleges; 7.08 million in middle schools; and 64.20 million in primary schools. Then came the Great Leap. At the end of 1958, there were: 790,000 college students; 14 million middle-school students; and 92 million in primary schools. Many middle-school and college freshmen had never been exposed to formal education; they were "qualified by experience." All were hurled into the sausage machine to meet the quotas fixed in the Second Five-year Plan.

Despite the laxest standards, 30 percent of the new students dropped out of middle school and colleges, forcing the regime to recruit additional hundreds of thousands of unqualified students. A brief return to sanity in 1959 produced a slight decrease in the student population, but the inflation began again the following year.

An intermittent adult-education campaign, the Communists

claimed, taught tens of millions to read. The figures were immediately suspect because the fifteen hundred basic characters the illiterates studied were barely sufficient for daily use. Besides, the Communists themselves spoke of a phenomenon called "returning to nature"; new literates rapidly forgot their hastily acquired knowledge because they could find little reading matter written in the few characters they knew.

"The policy of walking on two legs" justified the regime's constant readiness to undertake two diametrically opposite—and often mutually antagonistic—approaches to the same problem. On the one leg, education sought to produce a corps of specialists, highly trained and ideologically pure. On the other leg, masses of illiterates required elementary instruction. The bureaucracy's answer to the debacle of the Great Leap in education was enunciated late in 1959: "State-run and people-run schools; professional academies and part-time schools; half-work and half-study schools!"

Under Mao's direction, the authorities applied to education the new principle: "Red before Expert." Educated Chinese had always held manual labor in contempt. Determined to destroy "class pride" by inculcating respect for honest work, the Communists decreed that all students and almost all teachers must devote at least half their time to physical labor. "We cannot waste able-bodied, full-labor power—even the students," the regime said. Early in 1960 the schools of Hupei Province adopted the Half-Work, Half-Study Program. Soon students throughout China were spending alternate weeks in "practical work" in the fields or factories. "Students under the age of sixteen should not be required to work more than eight hours a day," the directives ordered, but all attended political indoctrination courses for two hours a day, week in and week out.

Peking declared that its purpose was to create a class of "learned laborers with Socialist consciousness, to wipe out all distinctions between mental and physical labor." The Half-Work, Half-Study Program was the foundation of "the new Socialist educational system" planned in great detail at Peking Normal University. Lu Ting-yi, Cultural Director of China, on behalf of the Communist Party, issued detailed instructions: "Education and teaching must be combined with productive labor. Our main purpose in having schoolteachers and students participate in physical labor is to remold their ideology; to change the present situation in which education is divorced from productive labor and from reality; and to alter the relations between intellectuals on the one hand and peasants and workers on the other."

Under the impetus of the Socialist Education Campaign from 1960 to 1965 political indoctrination and "class remolding" formally became the primary aims of education. Stimulating agricultural and industrial production was an educational aim of almost equal importance. Developing the individual's talents was desirable only insofar as it enabled him to serve the regime. The Communists were committed to the logic of egalitarianism run mad—a philosophy that sought to deny the existence of any distinctions among individuals. A refugee named Wong who had taught in primary and secondary schools in Shanghai for five years recalled the specific instructions issued to teachers: "All students are considered to be of equal ability, and all must attain a mark of four or five points [85–100 percent]—or the teacher is punished for not knowing his business." Lu Ting-yi himself declared: "The 'capacity principle' of bourgeois pedagogy is actually an excuse for achieving only slight, slow, poor, and expensive results in education, making it hardly possible for the working people to obtain higher education."

The strain of attempting to meet the Communists' demands for ever "quicker, better learning" on a part-time basis enfeebled students' intellectual vigor, regardless of whether they were concentrating on physics or on literature. "Political considerations overrode all else," observed a Japanese scientist who was employed until late 1960 as a microbiologist in the Agricultural Research Institute of the Academia Sinica, China's premier academic institution. "I was the only man in all China in my specialty, but I had to secure permission for every single experiment from the secretary of the faculty, whose only qualification for office was his standing in the Party. All my students were at the doctoral or postdoctoral level. Some were quite good, but all were so exhausted by outside 'constructive manual labor' they could give little energy to their researches."

The new policies cut just as sharply at other levels.

"Dear Mother [wrote a ten-year-old, fourth-grade schoolboy in Canton in 1960], Life is too busy here. Every morning I get up at six and go to school with an empty stomach. I rush home at noon for a fast meal, then I must go out to kill flies. From one-thirty to five, I just sit in the classroom woolgathering. I am always so exhausted I just want to go home. Second-sister and third-brother will be going to Shumchun this weekend to help the Customs officials. We usually do several hours of 'constructive work' each day, in addition to 'joint labor' during school hours. On Sundays and holidays, we have to attend meetings or participate in other activities. During the summer holidays, all my elder cousins will be going to nearby villages to do manual labor. Perhaps I will too."

The Half-Work, Half-Study Program hit particularly hard at secondary schools, which had already been disrupted by the demands for "voluntary labor." Those schools, which supplied the great bulk of the lower and middle "intellectual cadres" as well as most university-level students, were largely negated as educational institutions. A series of verbatim questions and answers may indicate something of their state in 1962, when the worst excesses of the Half-Work, Half-Study Program had temporarily come to an end. The effects, however, lingered. The speaker is twenty-two-year-old Lee Hsin-min from Swatow.

LEE: Before I left China, I had completed the junior middle-school course in the Third Middle School of Swatow Municipality. It was a coeducational school of over eight hundred boys and five hundred girls, divided into twelve senior and thirteen junior classes.

Q: Who ran the school?

LEE: The Teaching and Guiding Office. A schoolmaster's authority depended on whether he was a member of the Party or not, because the school was run by the Party cell. All the responsible school officials were Party members, but the Chief of Teaching and Guiding was certainly the most important.

Q: Tell me about your studies.

LEE: We spent about twenty-eight hours a week in the classroom, and we also had to take part in "voluntary labor service," sports, and recreation. We had to attend political lectures for four hours each week. These lectures were usually about current international affairs. Afterwards, we were divided into small groups for discussion, led by the class cadres. Not many of us were interested in the political lectures, which were dry and uninteresting.

Q: Suppose you do well academically, but fail in the political test, what will happen to you?

LEE: Failing the political test is as serious as failing *every* other subject, and you would not go up into the next class.

Q: How much time was devoted to physical activities?

LEE: All the boys and girls had to have one hour's sport and a one hour of so-called voluntary labor service each day, outside of classroom hours. Sometimes, however, our classroom time was taken up completely by a "special labor project" that lasted for several days. We often had to help in the fields at harvest time or on different kinds of construction jobs in Swatow, and we weren't paid for any of it. Because we were always hungry, we hadn't much energy for that kind of work, and we did it most reluctantly —although we knew we would get bad marks in personal conduct if we were found idling.

Q: Did the boys and girls spend time together outside school —at the cinema, or rowing, or fishing?

LEE: No, all our time was taken up by either classroom studies or "labor service." Perhaps you won't believe it, but we had very few school romances. We had to work hard all day, and when you're always tired and hungry, you don't have much interest in that sort of thing. Life was really very dull.

Q: Do you think the general academic standard of the students is declining?

LEE: Yes, the students are not very interested in learning now. They are preoccupied with the thought of their [post-graduation] labor assignments and how much longer they will have to tighten their belts before they get a full meal. We found it difficult to keep awake in the classroom because of our hunger, and this encouraged lots of students to play truant. Lots of them couldn't pass their examinations; I was lucky enough just to pass, but that was about all.

Q: Where did you take your meals?

LEE: I ate in the school mess hall. . . . Our chief food was rice, and there was never enough of it, although the student's ration of twenty *catties* [about twenty-six pounds] a month was a little more than the peasant's. The school menus used to be varied in the old days, but since 1956, we have rarely had anything but a kind of thickened rice gruel and perhaps a small amount of vegetables. Fish was very scarce, but we could get a few ounces of very bad cooking oil each month.

Q: How did you escape?

LEE: I applied for an exit permit on the grounds that my father in Hong Kong needed my help. The business of application was very complicated as it had to be approved by three government organs: first by the Street Residents' Association, secondly by the People's Police in my district, and finally by the police substation. It took me some time to win the sympathy and help of all these people.

Q: How did you do this?

LEE: Chiefly by giving them presents. I knew that I was safe in doing this, as they would keep quiet about it for their own sakes. When my father sent me food parcels from Hong Kong, I shared them with the cadres in the Street Residents' Association and the census policeman. They were very grateful because everybody wants food more than anything. After the cadres in the first two departments had forwarded my application with favorable comments to the substation cadre, I did the same thing with him. This time my father had sent me money, too, and so I was able to give the cadre twenty People's Dollars, as well as the usual mixed grain. I gave him about two *catties* [2.6 pounds] of grain, and I can tell you that it was more important to him than tens of dollars.

Q: Does this mean that even the police cadres do not get enough to eat?

LEE: That's right.

Q: Do you think your gifts really helped your application?

LEE: My application was approved by the cadres only after I had given them presents. Without the gifts, they would probably have turned down my application, and even if they had forwarded it, they would not have added the favorable comments that made all the difference. I was lucky that my political background was all right, as they would never have dared to take the gifts if I'd been involved in any political troubles. Of course, I took the gifts very quietly to the cadres' homes. But each of them knew about the others.

The program's results were summed up by Woo Ming-way, an engineer living in Hong Kong, where his younger son, a middle school student in Peking, was permitted to visit him several times.

"My son is not as advanced as he should be," said Mr. Woo. "The present system of studying is not the same as it was when I was in school. We used to study for at least six complete days in a week, but now classes are continually interrupted and depend on the requirements of the government. . . . At harvest time, pupils are taken out into the fields to work. They are paid a small wage, which varies, but the money is paid into school funds and not to individuals. The young people like to work in the open and are proud to do so, since they are told of the importance of the work they are doing for their country."

His fifteen-year-old son told Woo: "Every class has at least two pupils who guide the others, giving help and advice when it is needed. Most of us are a little bit afraid of these monitors, because they have great power as the representatives of higher authority in the schools."

The father added: "My boy likes it in Peking, but even if he didn't he could not complain. If he did complain, he'd be sent to work in the students' gangs as punishment—and to remake his thinking. Everyone fears those gangs, because they are required to work at strenuous tasks for long hours—sometimes for months on end."

Mr. Woo went on: "When my son came to Hong Kong, he brought an English textbook with him, the latest book used to teach English in his school. It was at the time of the Taiwan [Formosa] trouble, when the Communists were very angry with the Americans. The books said that the Americans were not as rich as they claimed. They were short of houses in America and many, many people were sleeping in the streets, particularly in the larger cities. The book said the British were better than the Americans—

and generally more honest. Most pupils who have been brought up since the Communists came to power believe all this is true. They have not seen or heard anything other than what the Communists tell them."

The young teacher Wong observed: "In addition to formal classes in politics, every course had its political content, particularly Chinese literature."

A typical textbook for primary-school students, entitled *Presenting an Embroidered Banner to Chairman Mao*, told of a group of Young Pioneers, nicknamed the Red Neckerchiefs.

The boys and girls were happily reading in the library of the Worker's Club, when:

" 'Chairman Mao! Chairman Mao!' Yah-ching suddenly called out.

"The troop's members laid down their papers and books and crowded around to look. In a picture magazine, there was a photograph of Chairman Mao standing with a smile on his face and, beside him, two Young Pioneers."

The troop immediately decided that they, too, must make a presentation to Mao Tse-tung, perhaps something like the bouquet of flowers which had won the two youths an honored place beside him on the podium. They finally decided on an embroidered banner showing a dove of peace, the five-star Red flag, and the Gate of Heavenly Peace. With the assistance of adult cadres, the Young Pioneers surmounted innumerable obstacles, even becoming involved in a communal hay-mowing project, and the completed banner was finally mailed off. One day, a reply came from Peking.

"The Red Neckerchiefs," the story ended, "all crowded around, while Ma-chu, the troop's leader, carefully opened the envelope and extracted the letter. He read in a loud voice: 'Dear Comrades of the Young Pioneers: Thank you for your embroidered banner. I hope you will study hard and temper your bodies so that you become talent useful for building up the Motherland!'

"Ma-chu paused a moment, then said: 'We will certainly heed Chairman Mao's words!'

" 'We will certainly!'—That was the rousing chorus of the Young Pioneers."

＊　＊

The Maoists had by 1960 succeeded in implanting many of the factual notions they favored—some valid, some invalid—and in giving a smattering of knowledge to many who would have learned nothing under the old order. But they were themselves dissatisfied with those accomplishments.

"Walking on two legs" had resulted in another inglorious pratfall. Trying to do everything at once, the Chinese Communists had negated their own efforts. Summing up, Lu Ting-yi said in April 1960: "It will take ten to twenty years to reform China's educational system properly. . . . The signs of fewer and slower, poorer and more expensive results in primary and secondary education are really so clear there is no apologizing for them . . . the development of educational work still cannot meet the diverse demands of Socialist construction."

The inevitable reaction came in 1961, the third in the waves of alternating tension and relaxation which disrupted the Chinese educational system after 1957. Recognizing the confusion into which education had been cast by the proliferation of institutions and student bodies during the Leap and by the subsequent Half-Work, Half-Study Program, the Central Committee,[6] in January 1961, promulgated the Temporary Draft Resolution Concerning Higher Educational Institutions Directly Under the Central Government. From this resolution subsequent pronouncements and practical measures drew their inspiration until 1965. The Party pragmatists issued a call for a partial return to sanity under the slogan "teaching comes first!" One of the most important results of this decision was the partial restoration of the dignity and authority of the older generation of professional scholars and pedagogues.

Historian Chen Yuan, of the same Peking Normal School which had in the spring of 1960 drawn up the abortive plan for nationwide Half-Work, Half-Study Education, noted the new direction in an article published in the *Kwangming Daily* on May 5,

[6] It is perhaps worth stressing that all statements and facts in this section, except the personal reports of participants made in Hong Kong, which are plainly identified, are drawn either from official Party and People's Government statements or from the controlled press of Communist China.

1962, to commemorate the Normal School's sixtieth anniversary.

"At present," he wrote, "we are taking the first steps toward drawing conclusions from past years' experiences and lessons, and we are further implementing the principle 'teaching comes first' and drawing up a comprehensive scheme balancing studies, labor, and scientific research, making efforts to raise further the quality of teaching."

In practice the revulsion from the excesses of the preceding years produced a measured return to more traditional academic subjects and pedagogic methods, though many of the highly specialized and highly technical institutions created during the Leap survived. There was, for example, the Loyang Agricultural Machinery Institute and the Chiaotso Mining College, the latter dealing exclusively with highly practical aspects of coal mining. But the general tendency was to distinguish between such trade or technical schools and true institutions of higher learning. Peking University, China's premier university, for instance, in 1962–63 offered new courses in the following subjects: biophysics, genetics, foreign languages,[7] Chinese literature and history, economics and philosophy. In the latter two fields a refreshing retreat from dogmatism was apparent in the subject matter of the new courses: Keynesian theory, statistics, and the history of Chinese economic thought; Chinese Buddhism, the history of Japanese philosophy, and Chinese historiography. The last was taught by the eminent philosopher and historian Fung Yu-lan, who was shielded by his international reputation and somehow survived all the gyrations in the intellectual line. Fung bore intense official displeasure without either vanishing or completely surrendering his integrity.

Despite the partial return to dogmatism and extremism manifested in the Central Committee's sweeping resolution of September 1962, education was by and large not sucked back into the maelstrom of fanaticism. The pragmatic faction, supported by Chairman Liu Shao-chi of the People's Republic, was largely responsible for the moderation. Those practical men, their instinctively practical approach strengthened because they were charged with the execution of policies conceived by the visionary Mao Tse-

[7] The new languages were Korean, Burmese, Indonesian, and Thai.

tung, displayed a special concern with education and the intellectual classes. Although he was, on many occasions and sometimes publicly, overruled by Mao Tse-tung, even the supple Premier Chou En-lai almost invariably stood for a policy of moderation toward the technicians, managers, and intellectuals whose services were essential to effective government. Foreign Minister Chen Yi himself declared several times that political study was not as important as serious academic work. At least once he remarked publicly that he would be content if the intellectuals knew their jobs well and were dedicated to their own work—even if they were not the most zealous socialists.

From mid-1962 to 1965 China's professional educators strove, with remarkably little interference from the Communist Party, to undo the excesses of the preceding years. Of course, politics was still king, and ideological demands still encroached upon pedagogy. But within the broadened limits permitted by the pragmatists in the hierarchy, who had obviously been alarmed by the earlier debacle, educators were permitted to go about their business of teaching. Much of their work was directed toward reconstructing a shattered educational system and filling in the yawning gaps in the knowledge of students who "leaped" or labored when they should have been learning. The first task, according to the professors' own testimony, was to arouse students to the point where they were willing to reason independently instead of merely regurgitating the words of authority. Intensified by the fear inculcated by the Communists, the normal Chinese tendency toward learning by rote had become the norm—in physics, chemistry, and botany, as well as philosophy and political science. Students expected all their lessons to be predigested by the professor. To remedy the lamentable lack of real teaching during the bad years, educators adopted an odd new slogan—"little, but essential." They sought to teach the fundamentals to students who had never been given the opportunity to acquire basic knowledge in their subjects. Even the teaching of superficially nonpolitical subjects like foreign languages was substantially reorganized, and the direct method was introduced. New textbooks appeared; they treated seriously of such subjects as anatomy, archaeology, agronomy, and even the history of philosophy and Chinese history. Finally,

new standards for admission to educational institutions were enacted. Party and governmental units still recommended students
without formal qualifications for admission to universities, but
none was admitted without passing the uniform entrance examinations set by the faculties.

Life for students was, therefore, quite different from what it
had been a few years ago. Manual labor was still "volunteered" to
the state, but it did not take up most of the students' time and
energy. The Communists themselves complained of apathy
among students, for there was little enthusiasm for either academic work or service to the people. Instead, students were concerned primarily with being safe, with their job assignments after
graduation, and with their romances, though the authorities discouraged both dalliance and early marriage. The Communists
had created so much suspicion and fear that the morale of students was broken. They were concerned, almost to the exclusion
of all else, with the simple problem of survival.

The attitudes of students reflected the attitudes of the entire
intellectual class. Having been wooed, abused, exiled to "productive labor," called back, and attacked again, the vital managerial
and technical class was understandably as wary of Communist
inducements as it was distrustful of the Party's ability to lead the
nation. But that class was, more than ever before, essential to a
regime whose capacity had been weakened by its failure to train
its own Red experts—and by the withdrawal of Soviet experts.
The Communists wooed the technicians and managers with every
inducement at their command. Some of the devices were bizarre,
like the Meetings of Immortals, which brought Party cadres and
intellectuals together socially in the hope of creating new
confidence between the two groups. Intellectuals were continu-
ously reassured that their work came first and their ideological
purity second. During the Spring Festival of 1963 the Chairman
of the Republic, Liu Shao-chi, gave a gala reception for the nation's
hundred most eminent "scientists." Philosophers, linguists, and
historians were included in that most brilliant Meeting of Immortals. In Shanghai, Premier Chou En-lai presided over a similar
reception, and the *People's Daily*, speaking in uncharacteristically
humble tones, admitted that the Party was not infallible on scien-

tific matters. The editorial called for "combining the three"—the masses, the experts, and scientific problems—with each element in the equation given "equal respect."

In Chinese Communist terms the policy—and the editorial's flat admission of error during the Great Leap—were spectacular concessions to the intellectuals. That group did not, however, display any general acceptance of the new promises. It gratefully used its new freedom to go ahead with its work—academic, scientific, or managerial. But the Party's own pronouncements stated clearly that intellectuals had surrendered neither their suspicion of the Communists' promises nor their distrust of the Communists' leadership. Once again the Party was forced by necessity to moderate the pressure for ideological conformity directed against intellectuals. But it could not restore anything approaching full freedom of teaching, research, or expression without denying its own fundamental beliefs and purposes. A new Rectification Campaign, which began within the Party late in 1963, spread rapidly to the intellectuals. Nonetheless, a definite decrease in the intensity of fanaticism was clearly apparent, in the intellectual realm.

It appeared at first that the rise of the new intellectual current—or perhaps more accurately, the lessening speed of the currents of fanaticism—was stimulated primarily by the historical hiatus. It appeared that sheer exhaustion had deprived the obsessed Politburo of its vigor. But the subsequent revelations attendant upon the Great Proletarian Cultural Revolution, which began in 1966, drew the curtain from a picture of systematic resistance to the excesses of Maoism in the name of rationalism. The senior members of the Communist hierarchy who—almost furtively—directed the substantial economic and political recovery of China between 1960 and 1965 were supported by the great majority of the operating cadres. They were also sustained morally and guided practically by a stubborn core of academicians, writers, economists, and other intellectuals whose devotion to China—and the abstract truth—had not been broken by Maoist repression. It was neither coincidence nor misjudgment of the strategic situation that impelled the Maoists to open their drive to regain power by attacking the intelligentsia. The Maoists knew exactly where their enemies were entrenched—and how strong were their enemies' positions.

Oppressed by insistent demands for politically edifying works, the arts were stultified before the great pause.

Despite its early promise of vigor, the Chinese Literary Renaissance never came to maturity. Late-nineteenth-century and early-twentieth-century Western writing—particularly the Russian novelists—provided the most powerful external stimulus Chinese culture had felt since the high tide of Buddhism. But there was no responsive resurgence of the native vernacular tradition, whose vigor the literary reformers, avid for historical sanction, had, in any event, exaggerated. In the late 1920s, there had been real hope that the enthusiasm of the new writers might produce a vital new literature. In the first years of the 1930s, however, Japan invaded China, and the Communists captured the League of Left-Wing Writers. Thereafter, the best minds and the most passionate pens were driven by the conscious purpose of "service to the nation." An entire generation which might have become novelists, poets, and playwrights instead became brilliant tract-writers, exploiting their media in propaganda for Chinese nationalism—and revolutionary social change.

With few exceptions those writers who had not declared for the Communists before "liberation" hurried to Peking when the People's Republic was established. Along with "old Party-member writers" they were soon assailed for individualism, romanticism, intractability, and deviationism—all the qualities that helped to make them writers. It was one thing to exalt the spirit of revolt under a bourgeois regime and quite another to breathe a hint of discontent under the people's democratic dictatorship. In the latter half of 1957, after the revelations of the Hundred Flowers Movement, the regime condemned most of its favored writers for crimes as diverse as espionage for the Kuomintang and misinterpreting the social significance of the historical novel *The Dream of the Red Chamber*.

During 1957 just thirty-eight novels were published in Communist China. In part the paucity of production arose from the fact that there were just three acceptable themes: (1) the sorrows of the bad old days under the corrupt and evil bourgeoisie, who had ruled through the Kuomintang and served the imperialists—with the invariable ending that can only be called "up-beat" as the oppressed rise under the guidance of the Communist Party; (2) the joyous, productive life of the masses in the New China—masses inspired by their dedication to continuing struggle; and (3) political morality tales centered on the folk heroes of China's glorious past.

In 1958, the year of the Great Leap Forward, the regime decreed that professional writers would produce on schedule like industrial workers, while hundreds of thousands of worker-writers would directly express their own unsullied proletarian consciousness. The *People's Daily* heralded "a new nationwide cultural revolution" that would produce pure culture in great quantities. "A heightened popular cultural level is an essential condition for mechanization, electrification, and industrialization of the nation," declared the newspaper. "We must, therefore, have a constant flow of writing which will educate the people and stir them to greater productive efforts."

As cadres in the balconies beat gongs and set off firecrackers, a political commissar informed the All-China Union of Writers: "Everyone must submit himself to collective supervision. . . . Just as we are eager to know how many tons of steel our country will produce this year, the people want to know how much we writers will turn out. You must pledge yourselves to production quotas."

Writers, too, were to become all-round production workers.

"Those who have never tried their hands at poems should write a few," the directive continued, "because poetry depicts reality more effectively than do other media. Those who have never written song lyrics should give them a try." Although it might have seemed that bad enough was well enough let alone, the Communists wanted more songs like the ballads that headed their own Hit Parade at the time: "Surpass England Industrially in Fifteen Years" and "Mama Wants Me To Go to the Countryside To Assist in Building Up the Nation's Agricultural Production." The Party observed: "The people everywhere in the nation are eagerly awaiting new songs about the Great Leap Forward—songs which will further raise their productive enthusiasm."

Critics were advised to try creative writing and novelists criticism, amid their mutual sneers. All professional authors were urged to write opera librettos, plays—and gags for comedians. "We should include everything in our plans," said the commissar expansively, "just as a department store supplies everything the people need."

While Lao Shaw, the author of the 1947 American best-seller *Rickshaw Boy*, beamed from the chair, China's professional writers worked out their production quotas.

A seventy-nine-year-old historian, the oldest person present, observed that his fellows, like himself, "must concentrate on improving quality through quantitative production." He promised that all his future works "would be tens of thousands of characters longer than previously." Expressing the firm determination to exceed the norm he pledged, a poet promised to produce at least twenty poems, including a long epic on the Communist revolution, fifteen prose works ranging up to fifteen thousand characters in length, and many song lyrics. A lady author offered the most comprehensive program, declaring that she would cap her three-year production plan by translating five collections of the work of the Indian writer Rabindranath Tagore in the year 1961.

The new wave of literary production was intended not only to arouse productive enthusiasm, but to sweep away "yellow culture," which was exemplified by Western popular songs that "set hips twitching and feet tapping decadently." Yellow culture may have been so insidious because of what else was available. The most favored play in China at the time was a minor masterpiece called *Do Not Spit at Random!* The heroine was a sixteen-year-old girl, whose self-assigned mission was to stand on streetcorners and chant through a red megaphone: "Spitting is an evil habit which spreads germs and disease . . . affecting our people's health adversely!" The playlet's climax showed the dedicated young lady reprimanding a "random spitter" and convincing him of the error of his ways.

It was, after the passage of a few years, deplorably clear that the writers had not met their quotas, any more than the worker-

writers' tens of millions of effusions had inspired the Chinese people to prodigies of production. The worker-writers did, however,
prove more amenable to discipline than their professional colleagues. Hu Wan-chun, one of the most prolific of that group,
confided that his literary career had been guided by the advice of
a senior Party official. "From now on, your pen will be your
weapon. Take good care of it, as a soldier cares for his gun. Make
it serve Socialist construction. See that your gun is always aimed
at the enemy; take care that it never hurts your own true comrades."

Hu affirmed that he had followed his own counsel. "The level
of one's creative writing is inseparable from the level one has attained ideologically. . . . Without the Party, there could never
have been a Hu Wan-chun, the writer." Hu unselfishly revealed
the secret of his success to guide aspirant writer-workers: "Many
people have asked me what I have done to improve my writing
technique and what is the secret of my creative writing. I have
always answered: technique is important; but what is more important is a proletarian world outlook and the mastery of the ideological weapon of Marxism-Leninism."

The only guiding principle Hu failed to restate was the
Party's mandate: "Literature which is not revolutionary is counter-
revolutionary. There is no room for neutralist writing."

It was not remarkable that the turgid literature of China did
not enjoy a wide audience nor that audiences failed to acclaim old
operas sprinkled with the new "social comments." One Maoist
critic seriously complained in late 1961 that "actors and actresses
are more enthusiastic about improving their performances than in
studying politics."

Even musicians were attacked for believing they could compose best behind the closed doors of conservatories, rather than
amid the proletarian life of the fields and the factory. Chastised
for producing works entitled "Musing," "Sorrows," and "A Solitary
Lamb," the students of the Central Conservatory of Music in Peking then composed "The People's Commune Chorus," "The Anti-
American Storm Concerto," and "The Youth League Piano Concerto." But such devotion was not appreciated by their audience.
Although they drew their inspiration from life in Communes and

from the battlefields of agricultural and industrial production, the musicians found the public fickle. Peasants complained that the new cantatas "are too full of production figures and slogans, which are not only uninspiring, but dull." The total effect, the workers and peasants said, was "childish and dry."

Since the Party's artistic strictures, never substantially relaxed, were actually intensified later, there was little change from the period of the Great Leap. Although the traditional theater was allowed to function as a diversion during the years of great repression and misery from 1959 to 1961, the September 1962 Central Committee Plenum ordered that this isolated example of relaxation be expunged. The theater was once more almost purely a vehicle of propaganda, as *belles-lettres* had been since the Communist takeover. As a result, inspiration remained frozen; few works were produced and fewer were published. In 1961, for example, just twelve novels appeared; in 1962 twenty-one. Even Maoist critics attacked them for their flimsy characterization, bad writing, and "stiffness." There was little hope of any change as long as literature remained solely a revolutionary weapon and writers were forced to weigh every word for fear of incurring official disfavor—with all its disastrous consequences.

Nonetheless, the Maoists valiantly rallied their artistic shock brigades. Somehow, the Maoist hierarchy remained convinced that arduous collective efforts could produce works of art that not only served the revolution, but also entertained the masses. Only in painting did Chinese art advance under the Maoists—and painting advanced only in one direction. The clear line of traditional Chinese draftsmanship was combined with the glowing colors of the West to produce some magnificent posters. Happy aborigines and nomads danced and chanted in paintings, while charming little black-and-white figures, drawn with a highly sophisticated simplicity, went about the joyous tasks of the New China. They built houses, planted fields, raised steel mills, and dined in abundance in communal mess halls. Mao Tse-tung had finally created the ideal world, which, somehow, evaded him in three dimensions.

The opposition within the Party made more effective use of literature than did the Maoists. Series of essays ridiculed the Maoists—and even Mao himself—in barely veiled terms from 1962 through 1965. The message to the discontented was clear; ignore Mao and build China. When the Maoist counter-attack reached its peak in mid-1966, not only Lu Ting-yi, Minister of Culture and Chairman of the Party's Propaganda Department, was deposed, his two deputies were as well.

Since religion in China is generally of greater interest to Westerners than it is to Chinese, the absence of strong religious feeling has spared Peking a number of annoyances endured by Moscow. The Chinese regime has, nonetheless, concentrated some of its heaviest fire on organized religion seeking to bend it to the service of Communism rather than to destroy it outright. Although there were but nine million Christians in China in 1949, the stubborn faith of the three million Roman Catholics among them stirred Peking's reformist compulsions. Since they reflected the experience of other sects in heightened form, the tiny Catholic pebble in the kaleidoscope is worth a glance.

The first campaign in Peking's war against Christianity ended in easy victory. From 1949 to 1954 nearly six thousand foreign missionaries were expelled from China as agents of imperialism. A few were allowed to depart quietly, but many were tortured to elicit confessions of political crimes. The Communists' ultimate purpose was to displace all Christian faith, but they first sought to transform the churches into instruments of their own will. All sects were required to cut the foreign ties that bound them to the service of imperialism; Catholics, both clergy and laymen, were specifically ordered to repudiate the authority of the Vatican. It was not political expediency alone that impelled those demands, for the Communists' proselytizing fervor was inflamed by the loyalty Chinese Catholics rendered to Rome. Only when Catholics had been sincerely converted to "patriotism" could the hierarchy feel secure in its conviction that the Communist Party alone offered the ultimate creed for *all* Chinese.

Despite intensive propaganda against the Church—and particularly against the Legion of Mary—China's Catholics were the last to succumb. Not until June 1957 was the Patriotic Association of Chinese Catholics established in Peking. Under the aegis of that association, Catholics attended daily "study sessions" to review their own errors, the regime's accomplishments, and the Vatican's crimes. After three months of such sessions, one Chinese priest wrote in a letter smuggled to Hong Kong:

"The Communists pretend not to force or impose their position on us; they insist, repeat, insist again and again; always around, in and out—and back to the same statement; wearing us out, breaking us down until, unable to hold out any longer, one is finally prepared to say, 'Well, have it your way!' But they won't accept it that way. What they want is for us to concede as if we had proposed it; as if we were finally convinced of what they have said and wished to surrender ourselves to their statements as if to our own self-imposed directive. . . ."

The central issue was always allegiance to the Pope, since Peking was, for the moment, prepared to tolerate a religion it could manipulate, but not a *foreign* religion. The same priest wrote: "It is impossible to defend this point; the Vatican is 'obviously' an instrument in the hands of or under the influence of capitalism. . . ."

Despite the vehemence of their attacks, the Communists long avoided forcing Chinese Catholics to choose between Peking and Rome on a clear doctrinal issue. New Chinese bishops were "sworn in" to replace exiled foreign bishops or deposed Chinese bishops. "But the new 'bishops' merely placed the bishops' rings on their fingers," explained a Chinese priest. "They were not properly consecrated by another bishop according to the rites of the Church."

Not until mid-1958 did Chinese Catholics face the fundamental choice imposed by the consecration of two "patriotic bishops." More than a thousand priests and laymen summoned from all over China saw Bishop Li of Puchi in Hupei Province consecrate two Chinese priests as the Bishops of Hankow and Wuchang. The duly appointed bishops of those two industrial cities were in exile; one was an American, the other an Italian.

Canon law was clear. The two priests were truly bishops in the direct Apostolic Succession because they had been consecrated by a bishop according to the rites of the Church. The Vatican, having refused to sanction their elevation, considered them schismatic rather than heretical. In the absence of reliable information as to the intent with which they submitted to consecration, the new bishops were not subjected to final judgment. Rome considered that they had received only the order, not the jurisdiction.

The ceremony of consecration had been delayed because one of the bishops-designate initially refused the honor. He disappeared for two weeks—to reappear in the church just before the ceremony. The three bishops apparently submitted in the same state of mind as the priest who wrote:

"These indoctrination courses are deadly. There is no escape. Either there—in the relative open—or in prison, indoctrination will go on and on so long as we are alive. Everyone knows fully that the Catholic Church is opposed—in principle and in practice —to the ruthless rule of Communism. Everyone well realizes that, little by little, outward resistance will be weakened and whittled away, that eventually only the innermost secret adherence to the Faith will be possible."

The Communists thereafter pursued their purpose of creating the National Church, which, the Vatican has pointed out, negates the universality of the Catholic Church and therefore cannot be truly Catholic. The Catholics of China showed remarkable steadfastness, and there were even a few conversions.

But the tide of persecution flowing from the north finally engulfed the Church's stronghold in Shanghai. "They began with a big meeting in December [1957]," one of the last American Maryknoll missionaries to leave China recalled in 1960, "and establishment of the local branch of the Patriotic Catholics Association. Now hardly any Chinese priest is free in Shanghai on weekdays. I know of thirty-six imprisoned in the old cathedral grounds. Some are let out on Sundays to say Mass—but never in their own churches. The majority of priests are in jail, and many have died. They keep working on them all the time to forswear the Pope."

The priest continued: "The Communists can undoubtedly destroy the Church's formal structure, because any priest who stands up to them will not be allowed to function . . . he'll never get out of jail. They do not bother Catholic laymen as much, but they want all priests to renounce allegiance to the Pope on 'political matters,' as they say."

By 1965 thirty-one "native bishops" had been consecrated. Obviously, as an old Chinese priest said, "the only place the universal Catholic faith can live is in men's hearts."

The greatest single problem the Maoists faced finally bore them down. Even more frustrating than attempting to create a heavy industrial base with inadequate capital and technological skill, even more difficult than the Messianic effort to stage a worldwide revolution from a barren base was the task of restoring the morale of the Chinese people.

Chairman Mao Tse-tung had always displayed sheer wizardry in evoking popular enthusiasm. To this gift, above all others, he owed his eminence and the Communist Party owed its hegemony. But the turmoil and misery of the Great Leap created a crisis of popular confidence which even Mao's magic could not abate substantially. Contemplating both internal promises and external threats unfulfilled, the Chinese people looked upon their rulers with a certain contempt—and even occasional amusement. They no longer felt the awe they had known. Fear, of course, persisted, but it was immediate fear of immediate retaliation, rather than the overwhelming, generalized respect that the Communists had previously commanded. Believing in their leaders' goal—an industrialized China exercising dominant influence in world affairs—the Chinese people ceased to believe that the goal could be achieved by the Communists' methods. They were, moreover, unwilling to offer the unending sacrifices the Communists demanded.

Because of that popular attitude, as much as the Communists' own technical errors, a controlled economy ceased to function in China, and the Communist Party's influence over the masses—and even its own cadres—was greatly diluted. One major result was a widespread reversion to pre-Communist ways of thought and life in fields as set apart as social relations and marriage customs are from agriculture and the bureaucracy. Despite the violence the Communists employed in attempting to destroy the old China, it showed itself a growth hardy beyond anyone's imagining. During the pause that preceded the cataclysm, scholars once more quoted Confucius and studied the classics; old Chinese history again became a major field of study; and many common men followed the old ethics. The cadres of the Communist state were largely corrupt. Educated refugees contended that dishonesty was nearly universal, its extent beyond that known under any previous regime. "A man must steal or die," was a recurrent theme of their reports and of letters from China. With increasing relaxation the necessity for dishonesty decreased, but each intensification of pressure renewed the compulsion toward corruption.

The problem of morale among the masses and the "operating cadres" was reflected in a continuing crisis of self-confidence among "senior cadres." Even at the pinnacle normally isolated from the harsher realities. Premier Chou En-lai, charged with the execution of the plans Mao Tse-tung conceived, apparently had grave doubts as to the validity of some of the policies he had to put into effect as chief of government. The unprincipled Chou, whose only principle was self-preservation, went along. But Chief-of-State Liu Shao-chi and Secretary-General Teng Hsiao-ping of the Central Committee built the nucleus of an opposition. After the Central Committee meeting of December 1958 at which Mao resigned as chief of state, the Communist Party was purged of hundreds of thousands of waverers and the Central Committee itself packed with men whose primary qualification was their unquestioning loyalty to Mao. Nonetheless, there was growing conflict between the men who envisioned the grand designs and the men who had to carry them out.

17

The World Beyond

*China's Foreign Relations: the Sino-Soviet
Quarrel, the United States, and Asia*

In the spring of 1960, when the ideologues of China celebrated the ninetieth anniversary of Vladimir Ilyitch Lenin's birth
by attacking the doctrines espoused by the Soviet Union, Peking
University rejoiced. Students who had three years earlier rebelled
against the dogmatism of the Peking regime confided to foreigners their exhilaration because "China is finally speaking up to Russia." Their pleasure was like the thrill that stirred the hearts of
Chiang Kai-shek's followers in exile on Formosa when Mao's
forces drove the American Eighth Army to the heel of the Korean
Peninsula in 1950. Though that reaction was muted because the
victorious armies were Communist, the Nationalists, nonetheless,
rejoiced because the armies were Chinese.[1]

Some intellectuals in Communist China continued to rejoice
for some time at Mao Tse-tung's defiance of Russian obstinacy by
asserting ever more positively China's ideological supremacy—
and her rightful leadership of the Communist world. Others were,
after a time, less inspired by the sheer grandeur of China's de-
fying Russia and the entire world. The nation, which Mao himself described with lugubrious pleasure as an ideal *tabula rasa*
for his designs because it was "poor [economically] and blank

[1] Shortly after that Communist victory, a number of young Nationalist majors and colonels confided to me that they, like many of their comrades, felt
guilty because they could not restrain the instinctive racial jubilation.

383

[culturally]," was, they felt, aggravating its economic difficulties by its orthodox assertiveness. True Marxists were dismayed by the rift within international Communism. On the other hand, their heroic posture awakened the deepest emotional chords in the Maoist leadership. They felt that China, still weak, but growing ever stronger, stood at bay; they looked forward to eventual victory since their confidence was sustained by historical precedent. The People's Republic was isolated and ill-armed, just as Mao Tse-tung had been isolated and ill-armed while he forged the armies which finally carried him to victory—and brought China the first effective central government and the greatest international prestige she had known since the reign of the Emperor Chien Lung more than a century and a half earlier.

The analogy was remarkably close. From 1937 to 1945 the Chinese Communists were engaged against their formal enemy, the Japanese; but they contended most bitterly against their formal ally, the Kuomintang. In the early 1960s, China and the United States were avowed enemies; but the Soviet Union, China's "natural ally" by all the rules of Marxism-Leninism, reciprocated bitter Chinese antagonism. During the first period the Chinese Communists had been sustained by the peasantry, which they alternately cajoled and intimidated, by a corporal's guard of faithful foreign publicists, and by their own conviction of invincibility. In its second Valley Forge, Peking was counting upon the support of the vast populations of the underdeveloped nations, Communist and uncommitted. A vastly expanded apparatus of publicity promised those nations the immediate hope that Moscow's doctrines denied the depressed. Since he had already won over a few minor members of the Communist bloc and had evoked a favorable response among many Communist parties still striving for power, Mao's sense of invincibility was not diminished by his weakness. Indeed, the Maoists were perversely exhilarated to find themselves once more contending with primitive weapons against towering odds. They relied upon the strength of the "oppressed peoples" and upon the certainty that they alone understood the forces of history. Internal development having been retarded, the dedication and élan of the Communist leaders was directed to external strategy.

Ancestral memories, inflamed by personal resentment, lay behind the Soviet Union's gradual metamorphosis from ally to antagonist. The Chin Dynasty created the modern state of China about 215 B.C. and simultaneously began to build the Great Wall for defense of its inner Asian frontiers. Eighty years later the Han Dynasty sent China's first ambassador abroad to subvert an offensive alliance of the Uighur tribes of Central Asia. Since that time, every Chinese regime which could not prevent the barbarians on its northern and western borders from uniting had been destroyed by such an alliance. To the Chinese mind, inflamed by the ill treatment it felt China had suffered at the hands of the Russians, there was no moral difference between the Mongols who conquered the Sung Dynasty or the Manchus who overthrew the Sung and the ambitious Soviet Union, which controlled large areas properly Chinese. The sanguine Chinese, moreover, obviously compared the Soviet Union to the great number of barbarian combinations which had been defeated by Chinese sagacity and valor.

Yet China had never known a more powerful continental neighbor than she confronted in the critical 1960s. The Soviet Union's hold over the north and west not only threatened China proper, but also diverted China's energies. Engaged in the north, Peking could not concentrate upon developing spillover basins for excess population in the rich and sparsely populated regions to the south. Worse, Moscow deliberately interfered with Peking's advance into Southeast Asia by disputing Peking's predominant influence over the region's Communist Parties, by attempting to bind China to international agreements which would check her expansion, and by publicly taking India's side against China.

The Russians had never been exempt from the righteous hatred that animated their Chinese comrades. They would have incurred the hatred men normally feel for their benefactors if their assistance to the infant Chinese Communist movement had always been given—and received—in perfect harmony. But early friction, rekindled by Chinese dissatisfaction with Russian economic aid after "liberation," was intensified by the restrictions Moscow imposed on China after their quarrel became acute in 1958. During the latter half of that year Nikita Khrushchev rushed to Peking to restrain the Chinese from attacking "China's territory of Taiwan [Formosa]" and later stated publicly that Russia would not feel bound to support China if she provoked a conflict over Formosa. Worst of all, as the Chinese subsequently were to charge, Khrushchev reneged on a formal promise to assist them in developing their own atomic arsenal. Mao Tse-tung himself complained publicly as early as 1960 that China was "bullied and oppressed . . . by reactionary elements in various countries which do not permit us to advance and become wealthy and powerful . . . which do not permit us to accelerate our Socialist construction and rapidly prepare the conditions for Communism." The context made it quite clear who those "reactionary elements" were without directly violating the etiquette of the international conspiracy by naming names before the open break. Citing the Chinese proverb: "He who comes late to the fray, triumphs!" Mao declared that the latecomer, China, would "triumph by our own unaided efforts." He promised that a triumphant China would not hinder other nations' progress, "because that would not be acting like true Communists." Those who sought to restrain China were obviously not true Communists.

Mao Tse-tung threw back at the Russians the many grievances engendered by their inept and self-seeking interference ever since the creation of the Chinese Communist Party. Feeling that he himself was persecuted by the Comintern during the 1920s and the 1930s, Mao had no more reason to love the Russians than did the students of Peking University. A central issue in the dispute was the character of Josef Stalin, denounced by Nikita Khrushchev in 1956, but consistently defended by Mao Tse-tung for his great accomplishments and proletarian ruthlessness. In late 1963, however, when all restraints had been abandoned by the quarreling parties, the Chinese could not refrain from expressing their own dissatisfaction with Stalin in the course of a *People's Daily* editorial primarily devoted to his defense. "Long ago," wrote the newspaper, "the Chinese Communists had firsthand experience of some of his [Stalin's] mistakes. Among the erroneous left and right opportunist lines which emerged in the Chinese Communist Party at one time or another, some arose under the influence of certain mistakes of Stalin, insofar as their international sources were concerned. In the late twenties, the thirties, and the early and middle forties, the Chinese Marxist-Leninists, represented by Comrades Mao Tse-tung and Liu Shao-chi, resisted the influence of Stalin's mistakes; they gradually overcame the erroneous lines of left and right opportunism and led the Chinese revolution to victory."

Mao championed Stalin against Khrushchev's attack for emotional reasons and because he felt that his stout defense would win him adherents among orthodox, hard-line Communists everywhere. But his sense of outrage was so great and his conviction of infallibility was so sweeping that he could not refrain from demonstrating that he was Stalin's superior because he had not erred when the Georgian erred and because he had won his revolutionary victory despite the Georgian's inept interference. The Sino-Soviet dispute crystallized all the major experiences that had shaped the Chinese Communist Party and the Chinese People's Republic.

The Chinese did not nicely calculate either the external or the internal benefits of quarreling with the Soviet Union. Impelled by passion, they justified their course by a logic more mystical than rational. The materialistic Chinese Communist Party, bedeviled by material difficulties, appealed to supernatural inspiration. *"The spirit of man transcends his physical circumstances!"* declared the champions of orthodox Marxism. From that transcendental credo Mao Tse-tung drew his certainty of prevailing over the Russians—as well as his strategy for world revolution and his vision of the earthly paradise of ultimate Communism. If he had yielded, he would have been repudiating the faith that grew from thirty years of revolution: "Bitter struggle is the essence of life! Honest compromise is death!" Fundamentalist fervor animated the Maoist attacks on Nikita Khrushchev, who had betrayed the proletarian crusade for a mess of bourgeois pottage. They charged that Khrushchev was content to build up the Soviet Union's economy by exploiting other Socialist nations and by pandering to his nation's own petty-bourgeois elements, while abandoning the sacred mission of "liberating" all the world's oppressed.

The Communist Party of the People's Republic of China, new to power and wholly controlled by revolutionaries of the first generation, was obviously more ardent and more romantic than the maturing Communist Party of the Soviet Union. Although both Nikita Khrushchev and Mao Tse-tung were professing Marxist-Leninists, they were at least as far apart doctrinally as the Archbishop of Canterbury and a hellfire Georgia revivalist preacher, both formally Protestant Christians. Different approaches to paradise—terrestrial or celestial—inevitably produced creeds that were quite distinct. Mao and Khrushchev differed not only on the proper road to Utopia, but also in their conceptions of that ideal state itself.

It was blatantly apparent from any consistent reading of Chinese statements against the background of Chinese history that the Soviet Union's policies and its view of the world frustrated Peking's most ardent desires and mocked the fervent convictions of the Chinese hierarchy. China could not be pre-eminent if she submitted to Soviet doctrines, nor could she attain even her minimal national objectives, the possession of her own nuclear weapons and "liberation" of Formosa, much less her greater purpose of dominating first southern Asia and eventually the entire underdeveloped world. Replying to a Soviet position which they considered sacrilegious, the Maoists flatly asserted that they—and not the Russians—were the legitimate heirs of the orthodox Marxist-Leninist tradition. They exhorted all Communist Parties to follow their lead—and to ignore the Russians. The Chinese argued that Communist policies should be based upon two self-evident facts: first, armed revolution and even global conflict are not only inevitable, but desirable; and second, the realization of the Communist Utopia depends even more upon the spirit of man than upon his material environment.

Chinese assertiveness sprang from a multitude of irritations and fears. Understanding their Chinese brethren imperfectly, the Russians had been unable to refrain from actions that grated upon the Chinese *amour propre*. Russian pronouncements imperiled the image of themselves which was the very basis of the Maoist hierarchy's self-esteem. Khrushchev might, however, console himself that tact alone could never appease the Chinese. They demanded no less than submission. Instinctively seeking to weaken the menace on their northern borders and to pursue an independent foreign policy, the Chinese chose the only battlefield where they could meet the Russians on equal terms. They could not compete with the Soviet Union economically or militarily, but Mao Tse-tung's personal prestige actually gave him a slight advantage in ideological disputation.

Although the conflicting ideological positions of China and Russia—by no great coincidence—sprang directly from their distinct national interests, the controversy had a profound effect on the entire Communist camp. As long as there was but one center of Communism, doctrine could be adjusted to necessity by fiat, and Communist Parties abroad could be sacrificed to the changing needs of the Soviet Union. The existence of two rival centers with conflicting interests made such adjustments immediately difficult and ultimately impossible. The open polemics destroyed the myth of Marxism-Leninism as a scientific doctrine based upon revealed historical truth. The essential nature of international Communism was shattered so that all the Commissars' men could not put Marxism-Leninism-Stalinism back together again. Seeking to preserve Leninist orthodoxy, the Chinese heresy hastened its decline by exploding the mystique of the monolith. The Chinese unintentionally invoked a new era in the history of Communism, an era of polycentrism dominated by differing national interests.

Mao Tse-tung deliberately hazarded the risk of the bloc's dissolution. He would have preferred that it perish in preparation for rebirth rather than endure corrupt. He was restrained chiefly by fear that a Soviet Union which was either hostile or neutral would encourage the American enemy to attack China.

The Russians, for their part, would obviously have been pleased to be relieved of their volatile Chinese allies. But they could not know how many vassals a schismatic China might snatch from their empire.

The Soviet Union became the Chinese Communists' chief foreign concern when the war in the Pacific ended. Sino-Soviet relations had attained their greatest cordiality in 1947, when the Soviet Union presented the People's Liberation Army with the Manchurian stronghold from which it conquered all China. That service was, however, never fully appreciated, in part because

Mao Tse-tung preferred to believe that his own efforts were solely responsible for his victory and in part because the Russians' fraternal gesture came after they had stripped Manchuria of at least $2 billion worth of industrial plants. The apparent high point of Sino-Soviet cooperation came in 1950. After signing a mutual defense pact with China, the Russians provided equipment and technicians to support Chinese armies fighting their common enemy, the United States, in Korea. But the seeds of earlier enmity sprouted during that war. Resenting the heavy payments she was making to Russia for the privilege of defending their mutual interests alone, Peking hastily disengaged after Josef Stalin's death in 1953. Although the Chinese have later denied it, the new temper in the Kremlin undoubtedly made their disengagement easier.

The basis of China's new industrial construction in the early 1950s was Russian machinery and Russian engineers—bought with enormous shipments of raw materials. Although Russian assistance was the essential element in the considerable economic achievements of the Chinese before the madness of the Great Leap Forward, the Maoists clearly felt that a total of $2 to $2.5 billion in expertise and equipment from 1949 to 1962, when the well went dry, was inadequate to their needs. It is worth noting that no aspect of the tangled Sino-Soviet web was more intricate than their economic relations. The outsider was denied any clear understanding because secrecy has further concealed major details of transactions which were, in any event, obscure because they were stated in deliberately vague terms. Nonetheless, those figures that are available demonstrate the reasons for Chinese dissatisfaction.

Although China's undoubted economic progress—before the Great Leap cast all into confusion—could not have been achieved without Soviet assistance, Russia never made an outright grant of a single ruble for economic development. A few small recreational and medical facilities, presented as "gifts to the Chinese people," were probably not worth more than $10 million. It appears likely that Russia did give China several times that figure in obsolete war material, though the Chinese were also billed for much larger quantities of military equipment, the actual figures never revealed. But the lines of credit on which economic construction was based amounted to just $430 million from 1949 to 1961. That sum was considerably less than the $933 million Russia had loaned India, the $783 million to the United Arab Republic, or even the $509 million to Indonesia. Outer Mongolia, between the two powers, received more than did China from Russia. The Mongolians obtained Russian loans totaling $651 million, as well as an outright Chinese grant of $40 million and Chinese loans of more than $75 million. By 1965 the People's Republic had actually bestowed more direct grants to foreign countries than it had received.

Loans were not, however, the entire picture. Soviet sales of machinery, blueprints, and technical services to China amounted to more than $2 billion up to 1961. An additional $1 billion worth of technical assistance was originally projected through 1967. It was canceled. China was obliged to pay for these goods and services in cash, and she could have found no more funds even if the Russians had wished to continue the arrangement.

China used up her lines of credit from the Soviet Union in 1957. But she paid Russia $260 million in 1956, when she received $50 million on the basis of the final loan agreement signed in 1954; she paid another $271 million in 1957, when she received her last $10 million loan. The balance of trade between the two countries revealed a little more of the tangled skein. In 1959 total Sino-Soviet trade came to more than $2 billion, and China sent Russia well over $200 million more in goods than she received. In 1961, when the Chinese could not meet continuing obligations of about the same order, the Russians radically reduced supplies of capital equipment. Over-all trade dropped 45 percent below 1960's level, though the Chinese still sent about $190 million more to Russia than they received. The Russians offered China only a sticky sop in a loan of Cuban sugar she could neither use herself nor sell on the glutted world market. Forced to cut off almost all other imports in 1961 in order to pay for foodstuffs from abroad, the Chinese were virtually forced to halt their industrial construction. The Soviet Union was, obviously, not anxious to assist the intransigent junior partner in developing her industrial strength. Besides, China still owed Russia at least $1 billion for civilian goods in 1962—and at least another $1 billion for military equipment. In that same year trade between the pair fell 25 percent below its value in 1961, to an estimated total value of $690 million. Nonetheless, Chinese exports to Russia continued to run well ahead of imports. The Chinese nevertheless still serviced their debts; they claimed to have paid off the Russians in 1965.

Important as they were, both economic relations and formal diplomacy merely reflected the critical changes in relations between the Communist Party of the Soviet Union and the Communist Party of China. The underlying tension between the two Parties splintered the veneer of fraternal amity after Nikita Khrushchev's address to the Twentieth Congress of the Communist Party of the Soviet Union in the spring of 1956. Appalled by Khrushchev's attacks on Stalin, the Chinese were directly frightened by his intention to relax coercion within the U.S.S.R. They were equally disturbed by Khrushchev's thesis that "the era of final imperialist wars" predicted by Lenin might not necessarily occur because the basic nature of capitalism was changing, while Communist strength was everywhere increasing without armed conflict. Khrushchev finally declared himself in favor of "peaceful competition" between East and West. He contended that the Communists could seize power by nonviolent, parliamentary means, rather than armed revolution supported by the military might of established Communist states. Peking feared that Moscow was about to sell out.

The 1957 Moscow Declaration of the Communist Parties of the World attempted to allay the disagreement by cataloguing the opposing views without really reconciling them. During that same year Russia signed a secret treaty which the Chinese interpreted as a firm Russian commitment to assist China in developing her own atomic weapons by supplying her with technical assistance and a sample bomb. In September 1958 Khrushchev prevailed upon the Chinese to halt their campaign to take the Nationalist-held offshore islands; he actually declared in a one-sentence interview with Tass that Moscow would back Peking militarily *only* if she were the victim of aggression. From the Chinese point of view this deliberate interference with China's attempts to attain her rightful national aspirations was intolerable, as was Moscow's continuing failure to live up to the terms of the 1957 agreement on atomic assistance.

But the Kremlin went even farther. Khrushchev, the Maoists charged, intervened in the internal affairs of the CPC in the hope of strengthening the anti-Mao group in the Central Committee. The official English-language text of a lengthy article on the "Origin and Development of the Differences Between the Leadership of the CPSU and Ourselves," published on September 6 and 7, 1963, said: "In 1958, the leadership of the CPSU put forward unreasonable demands designed to bring China under Soviet military control. . . . [Later] Khrushchev even expressed undisguised support for anti-Party elements in the Communist Party of China." The Chinese-language text, however, differs slightly, asserting that the Russian demands sought to "control China militarily." It would, therefore, appear that Khrushchev may have offered China increased military assistance on the condition that Moscow be given a greater say in Chinese external strategy involving those weapons. The group of generals and politicians who may have advocated accepting that condition, led by the Defense Minister, People's Marshal Peng Teh-huai, had already pressed Mao Tse-tung hard by opposing his more radical agricultural policies and by insisting that the People's Liberation Army be transformed into a more professional and less political force. Their flirtation with Khrushchev sealed the fate of the group, which was purged after a brief struggle for power. An enraged Mao Tse-tung thereafter looked upon Nikita Khrushchev as a personal enemy who had tried to manipulate the balance of power within Mao's personal creation, the CPC—and had actually sought to depose Mao himself.

Early in 1959 the Twenty-first Congress of the Communist Party of the Soviet Union heard Khrushchev declare that there were "many roads to Communism"—a concession that failed to appease the fundamentalist Maoists. Rejoicing at Khrushchev's assertion that the Soviet Union was entering the stage of transition to Communism, the Congress also felt his disapproval of the Chinese People's Communes. In June, according to the later Chinese revelation, Moscow flatly told Peking that China would not receive the technical advice and the sample atomic bomb she expected from Russia. Since there is still no definitive evidence available on the relations among Moscow, Peking, and the North Vietnamese Communist government in Hanoi, it may have been coincidence that Hanoi began to increase its pressure on Laos during the following six months and on South Vietnam shortly thereafter. But it is well nigh certain that the Chinese, altering their tactics because they could not count on possession of the atomic bomb in the near future, urged Hanoi to begin the present wave of guerrilla insurgency in Southeast Asia. If they could not take Formosa by threats, they could press the "liberation" of the rich Southeast Asian territories.

Khrushchev soon offended even more directly. Immediately after his talks with President Dwight Eisenhower at Camp David had awakened China's fears of a reconciliation between Moscow and Washington that would thwart China's most profound desires, he went to Peking for the celebration of the tenth anniversary of the People's Republic in October 1959. He lectured the Chinese on the new, friendly face of their sworn enemy, the United States. He reaffirmed his thesis that the era of final imperialist wars was no longer inevitable because monopoly capital no longer dominated the United States, as it had when Lenin propounded that thesis. In public the Soviet premier warned China against "testing the stability of the capitalist world by force." In private he assailed China for the headlong pace of her economic construction and characterized the People's Communes as a "reactionary" device that could not succeed in their purpose of skipping a stage on the road to pure Communism.

On the ninetieth anniversary of Lenin's birth in April 1960 the Chinese began their public campaign to save Leninism from the "modern revisionists" of Moscow. Thereafter the quarrel was public and specific, though names were still not mentioned for a time. The Bucharest Conference in the late spring of 1960 reaffirmed the contending parties' adherence to the Moscow Declaration of 1957—in terms as equivocal as that Declaration itself. The unsatisfactory compromise was reached only after Khrushchev had attacked the Chinese, in secret committee sessions, as "madmen . . . wanting to unleash war . . . being purely nationalist on the Sino-Indian border question . . . using Trotskyite tactics." All those points are drawn from Chinese revelations in 1963.

The Russians subsequently contrived to avoid a summit conference with the West, which China had denounced, by utilizing the incident provided when an American U-2 reconnaissance plane crashed deep inside Soviet territory. Since a formal détente between Washington and Moscow would have strained the fraying bonds between Peking and Moscow intolerably, Khrushchev was in turn forced to back away from comprehensive agreements with the West while there was still hope of preserving the more important relationship with China. But the public exchange of insults between Moscow and Peking continued. When the Communist-sponsored World Federation of Trade Unions held its annual convention in Peking in June 1960, the Russians threatened to walk out because of the attitude of their Chinese hosts.

Shortly thereafter the Russians recalled their technical advisers from China and issued new collections of Lenin's works on precisely those subjects closest to the vanity of the "master theoretician" Mao Tse-tung: *The Alliance of the Working Class and the Peasantry.* Russian theoreticians marshaled heavy battalions of canonical quotations against the Chinese positions. The Chinese, in turn, accelerated their campaign to incite worldwide revolution immediately. In Hanoi in August 1960 a celebration of the joint anniversary of the Vietnamese Labor [Communist] Party and the Democratic Republic of [North] Vietnam was the occasion for a bitter exchange of insults. The Russians assailed the Chinese as "rigid dogmatists who quote Lenin to avoid thinking," and a Chinese Vice-Premier, taking his text from Lenin, warned against "modern revisionists" who exacerbate disagreements within the Communist movement "even to the point of an open split."

These doctrinal battles were fought when China's economic programs were almost halted by maladministration, unrealistic goals, bad weather—and reductions in Russian aid. The smug, prospering Russians infuriated the lean, frustrated Chinese.

The Communist Parties of eighty-one nations met in Moscow in November 1960 to resolve the conflict. Before the conference began the Chinese publicly reaffirmed their stand on all the ques-

tions at issue and wholeheartedly denounced their Russian opponents. The struggle within the sub-committees of the conference
was even more heated. Peking's delegation, headed by Liu Shao-
chi, was composed of "old revolutionaries" who had made themselves experts on the "revolutionary struggle in the underdeveloped world." The Conference was protracted for several weeks by
Chinese stubbornness, and the Chinese waited but forty-eight
hours before hailing the final Communiqué and Declaration as an
unqualified victory for their stand. It was by no means a Maoist
victory, though Khrushchev had made some verbal concessions in
return for slighter concessions from Mao.

After that conference the doctrinal quarrel temporarily became less of a public scandal. Khrushchev was for a time more
contentious toward the West, impelled equally by the irresistible
opportunities offered by American policy and by his fear that the
Chinese would seize upon any timidity on his part to discredit
him. Even the messianic Chinese were distracted by their enormous internal problems. But the Russians took a direct hand in
the crisis on China's borders in Laos; they were happy to advance
the revolution while cutting China out of an area of immediate
interest to her. In 1961 Moscow insisted upon a humiliating public
declaration of China's economic incapacity in return for slight
concessions in the terms of payment of old debts. The Russians
also reduced their assistance to China sharply. China persisted in
her efforts to suborn not only the uncommitted countries, but also
Albania and Outer Mongolia within the bloc, giving them generous economic aid she simply could not afford. And the Chinese
ideologues began sniping at Russian revisionism again.

The quarrel came to a head at the Twenty-second Congress
of the CPSU in late 1961. When Khrushchev attacked tiny Stalinist
Albania as a surrogate for enormous Maoist China, Chou En-lai
walked out of the Congress. Before he left he read Khrushchev a
lecture on the impropriety of fighting family battles in public.
Khrushchev riposted by removing the mummy of Josef Stalin
from its marble mausoleum to a simple grave and by recalling
Soviet diplomats from Albania.

Dropping all concealment, Chinese internal Party documents
began to call Khrushchev "a cowardly devil of a revisionist." The

Russian Premier replied with his most scathing attack on the Chinese in March 1962.

The quarrel entered a quiescent phase during the latter half of 1962, though both sides lobbied frantically for support among the uncommitted nations of the Communist bloc. Deputy Foreign Minister Wu Hsiu-chuan was chosen by Peking to carry the banner of the "People's Revolution" through a series of European Party Congresses, perhaps because he had proved his capacity for executing hopeless missions with élan when he appeared at the United Nations in the autumn of 1950, charged with the task of convincing that body that it should declare itself, rather than the Communists, the aggressor in Korea. Generally ignored and derided, Wu suffered open humiliation at the East German Party Congress in February 1963, when a chorus of jeers and a wave of foot-stamping drowned out his attempts to put the Chinese point of view to the assembled Communist leaders.

After this public insult Peking brooded for little more than a month before responding with a categorical defense of its position that ran to almost two hundred thousand words. For the first time the Chinese people were told in detail of the charges the Kremlin had laid against the Forbidden City. Also for the first time the Chinese publicly revealed some details of the course the quarrel had taken in secret Communist councils. They further demanded that Nikita Khrushchev expel "revisionist Yugoslavia" from the bloc, as Josef Stalin had done in 1948, before they would consider any resolution of the widening disagreement. Albania was also to be restored to her full dignity as an honored member of the group of "fraternal Socialist nations." The violent language of the Chinese pronouncements made it clear that Peking was prepared for an open break. The Chinese had already succeeded in gathering most Asian Communist Parties around them and were striving to take command of the "liberation movement" in all the underdeveloped nations. Since almost all the inhabitants of those have-not nations were colored, the Chinese strategy appeared to be directed toward splitting not only the Communist bloc, but the entire world along racial lines. The arguments used by Chinese propagandists in Asia, Africa, and Latin America were openly racist. They argued that the Russians were, after all, members of the arrogant and rapacious white race, which had for so long exploited the colored races, while they themselves, dark of skin, possessed an instinctive sympathy and an unbreakable unity of purpose with the other dark races. The differences between China and the Soviet Union daily became more acute.

In June 1963, while the two Parties were completing arrangements for a conference in Moscow to "reconcile" their differences, the Chinese issued a twenty-five-point restatement of their position. It was the most bitter attack on the "modern revisionists." Nonetheless, a Chinese delegation headed by the CPC's Secretary-General Teng Hsiao-ping arrived in Moscow on July 5. The Russians, as if to make the climate quite clear to the Chinese. delayed them in Customs for several hours, an indignity not normally visited upon even Western diplomats or tourists. Moscow had a few days earlier expelled five Chinese from the Soviet Union for distributing Russian-language copies of the twenty-five-point letter, which was banned in the Soviet Union. Attacks and counterattacks flew fast while the two delegations met. Immediately after the departure of the Chinese delegation *Pravda* published an open letter which for the first time attacked the Chinese by name. The chief charges were attempting to usurp leadership of the Communist world and advocating a disastrous nuclear war. Shortly thereafter, the Russians, the United States, and Britain signed a treaty providing for a partial moratorium on atomic testing. The Chinese, furious at both the limited détente and the implied obligation to cease attempts to develop their own atomic weapons, redoubled their attacks on the Russians.

With all formal etiquette cast aside, a spate of specific revelations followed. The Chinese charged that Russia had reneged on her secret promise to help China develop atomic weapons. The Russians in turn condemned the Chinese for baring the secrets of the Communist bloc; they flatly declared that the mutual defense pact between the two nations would not bind them to come to China's assistance if she became involved in war in pursuit of her own "special national interests," which conflicted with the purposes of international Communism. The Chinese reaffirmed their belief that Khrushchev represented merely "an interlude" in Soviet history and in their declaration of September 7 said: "The label 'anti-Soviet' cannot be stuck on us. Our criticism of your errors is precisely for the sake of defending the great CPSU and the great Soviet Union and preventing the prestige of the CPSU and the Soviet Union from being damaged by you. To put it plainly, it is you, and not we, who are really anti-Soviet and who are defaming and discrediting the CPSU and the Soviet Union. Ever since the complete negation of Stalin at the Twentieth Congress of the CPSU, you have committed innumerable foul deeds. Not all the water in the Volga can wash away the great shame you have brought upon the CPSU and upon the Soviet Union."

The Chinese had obviously given up any hope of bringing the Soviets back to righteousness as long as Khrushchev prevailed. After 1964, when Khrushchev was removed, their hopes were high —and the new Soviet leadership appeared anxious to avoid further offense to China. But both Peking and Moscow soon realized that their differences were still irreconcilable. The Soviet leadership was simply not prepared to sacrifice vital national interests to the Chinese demand for an aggressive international Communist movement under Maoist tutelage. In 1968 Moscow pressed its campaign to expel China even to provoking Roumania's partial disaffection from the bloc.

Consequences even greater than the future of the Communist bloc were at stake in the Sino-Soviet dispute. The peace of the world depended to a certain extent on the controversy over foreign policy. The essential matter of the Sino-Soviet dispute was not an abstruse ideological debate, but a desperate argument as to the tactics and strategy international Communism should employ to attain its international and domestic aims. The specific points at issue revealed how grave were the choices propounded:

(a) The Chinese insisted that the nature of imperialism was immutable. The Western World, they declared, was still dominated by rapacious monopoly capital.
Imperialism was still dangerous, said the Russians, but its nature was changing.

(*b*) Since imperialism cannot change, the Chinese argued, it must be destroyed in armed struggles instigated by the Communists.

The tides of history were running strongly in favor of Communism, said the Russians, and violence was no longer essential to Communism's ultimate triumph.

(*c*) The proper way to destroy imperialism was to isolate the capitalists through armed rebellions led by Communists in Africa, Asia, and Latin America. When the capitalist nations were isolated, rebellions within their beleaguered and impoverished strongholds would spontaneously follow.

The Russians rejoined: Violence might be necessary in certain cases, but it was not the only—or even the chief— means by which Communism would defeat capitalism. It was, on the contrary, possible to work with "national bourgeois" leaders to contrive a peaceful, parliamentary transition to Communist control. The doctrine of universal revolution was too dangerous in a world in which two great powers stood with nuclear weapons poised.

(*d*) Revolutions might possibly be so successful that big or small wars between nations could be averted, said the Chinese, but we Communists must actively prepare for international wars of all kinds, including a nuclear conflict between East and West. "Just wars" were actually desirable, since Communism had always benefited from war. Besides, nuclear bombs were only "paper tigers," devoid of either claws or fangs, despite their fierce appearance.

The Russian answer: Atomic war would be a catastrophe for the entire human race and would set back the cause of Communism. War was neither inevitable nor desirable; saying that it was, destroyed the Communist masses' incentive to work.

(*e*) Advocating peaceful coexistence and nonviolent economic competition sapped the will of the Communist bloc, spread disunity, and dissipated the perfect opportunity provided by the grave crisis of capitalism, argued the Chinese.

The Russians: It was positively desirable that Communism should conquer by peaceful means and, at any rate, pre-

dominantly pacific tactics were most effective under modern conditions.

(f) The Chinese generally argued against any détente which would isolate them among their enemies, led by the United States, and would hamper attainment of their minimal national objectives: acquiring nuclear weapons and reclaiming the lost province of Formosa. (It was obvious that they felt they required a continuing state of international tension to drive the Chinese people to further toil and that they longed for substantial external triumphs to allay the growing contempt their own people felt for an impotent and braggart regime.)

The Russians contended that a détente might well serve the cause better than tension—for the moment, though they were perfectly prepared to use limited violence when it was advantageous.

Peking asserted its position in millions of words of turgid prose. At one climactic moment in late 1960 the Central Committee chose Madame Sun Yat-sen, the "non-Party Vice-Chairman" of the People's Republic, who usually exuded sweetness, to deliver a sweeping affirmation of the harsh Chinese position.

". . . Lenin stoutly defended the teaching of Marx and Engels against the distortions of the opportunists and revisionists of *his* day," Madame Sun wrote in obvious reference to the evil elements of *this* day. "He insisted that the working class could not rely upon bourgeois-minded reformist, class-collaborationist political parties. It had to have its own political vanguard, the Communist Party, a militant revolutionary party armed with Marxist theories and permeated with the spirit of class struggle. . . . Leninism became the Marxism of the era of imperialism and the proletarian revolution."

After cataloguing the advantages the Communist movement had gained as a result of wars, Madame Sun declared: "More and more people understand that capitalism is no longer progressive and look forward hopefully to Socialism. This is an outstanding characteristic of the national democratic movement now surging throughout Asia, Africa, and Latin America. . . . The whole capitalist sector of the world is itself in the midst of a general and prolonged crisis. . . . At present, monopoly capitalism and imperialism are rotting day by day, while the situation of the people's struggle and the prospects of the progressive movement as a whole get better day by day. . . . [Nonetheless,] the nature of capitalism and imperialism is cruel and predatory—and it is impossible to change that nature."

At the same time the senior political commissar of the People's Liberation Army cited the words of his mentor, Mao Tse-tung, to bolster his points: "War, which began with private property and classes, is, at a certain stage of development, the highest form of struggle for resolving contradictions between classes, between nations, between states, and between political groups. . . . Politics is war that sheds no blood, while war is bloodshedding politics. . . . We Communists are opposed to all kinds of unrighteous wars that impede progress, but we are not opposed to righteous wars that promote progress. . . . We Communists will take an active part in such wars."

The commissar then summed up the immediate application of his master's doctrine: "All kinds of righteous wars are, instead of being a 'crime,' very good things that stop unrighteous wars, educating and mobilizing the people to topple reactionary rule and liberate themselves. Marxists hold that righteous revolutionary wars are an antitoxin, a midwife who assists the birth of a new society, and a bridge to a new world. . . . As long as classes exist, there will be armies, weapons, and wars. . . . It is childish illusion to expect permanent avoidance of war before mankind eliminates classes."

Shortly after these tortured metaphors were given to the world the CPC's theoretical organ, *Red Flag*, laid down a program for world conquest through "the united front, people's struggle, Soviet Areas, and armed revolution." The journal declared that the Chinese experience of armed guerrilla bases was the ideal model for conquest of the underdeveloped world. The fourth volume of Mao Tse-tung's collected works, appearing on the regime's eleventh anniversary in October 1960, was a handbook for revolution in nonindustrial countries. It contained Mao's writings from the end of the Second World War until his conquest of China, during the period when he was directing his own Third Revolutionary War. It was, in short, a practical manual for modern guerrillas.

Behind the torrents of self-justification and the cascades of twisted logic which marked the Maoists' position lay the solid stone of their determination to form all underdeveloped countries into a great new force in world affairs—after first installing Communist regimes by violent revolution. Recognizing that their policy might lead to nuclear war, the Communists actually welcomed that eventuality. "Only the capitalists need fear war, which will destroy them . . . ," declared *Red Flag*. "We Communists will build a glorious new civilization a thousand times higher than the capitalist system on the [nuclear] debris of the dead imperialism."

A dispatch I filed in 1960, when the new *furor Sinicus* burst on the world, may, I believe, convey both the immediate drama of the Chinese determination to impose their will on the world and the continuing scope of Chinese ambitions better than *ex post facto* accounts:

> During the past two weeks, China—struggling and short of labor—has lavished half a billion man hours on mass rallies railing against imperialism. Thousands of broadcasting hours and tons of newsprint have carried the nearly hysterial outbursts of the Chinese Communist leaders—from Mao Tse-tung downward—proving that the underdeveloped world is ripe for revolution and predicting a violent Armageddon for worldwide imperialism.
>
> The Chinese Communists are practical men—even if they are zealots. Although whipping up popular hysteria undoubtedly helps submerge growing domestic discontent, the Communists obviously expect concrete results from their vast expenditures of time, energy, and wealth. It is clear that Mao Tse-tung aims at nothing less than creation of a new, worldwide political force centered on China as a global Yenan and including all newly independent and noncommitted countries, all "progressive" political groups, and the discontented everywhere—formed around a hard Communist core.
>
> Peking hopes the Soviet Union, chastened and enlight-

ened by the U-2 incident, will join the new camp and support the Chinese strategy of glacierlike war. But Peking is prepared to press onward to the victory of socialism alone—and Peking apparently expects to go it alone.

Mao is absolutely convinced that he can isolate the West, driving "imperialism back to its lair" by creating a vast "united front to contain imperialism through peoples' struggle." The authoritative *Red Flag* said in its most recent issue: "Nothing on earth can prevent the oppressed peoples of the world from seizing national independence and democracy by [armed] struggle. This is an inevitable law of mankind's development which no amount of wishful thinking on the part of reactionaries can alter a jot."

As viewed from Peking, the world is neatly divided: ethnically, into pigmented and white; politically, between red and white. The Chinese actually believe that the oppressed masses of capitalist countries are starving in the streets and that most of the world awaits only "the spark which can start a prairie fire" to burst into flames. Knowing little of the outside world, the Chinese have taken scattered disturbances in African, Asian, and Latin American countries as proof that the final crisis of imperialistic capitalism is at hand. They are convinced that the imperialists have lost their strength and resolution, "though they are still dangerous in their death throes," according to Chou En-lai.

The Chinese, who have always maintained close liaison with the Japanese Communist Party—sheltering its leaders during the war—and have long wooed the Japanese Socialists, are encouraged by riots in that country. Unaware that discontent in Japan does not run deep, they believe they are on the verge of attaining their dearest desire: uniting the industrial potential of Japan to the manpower of China to create a new center of world Communism.

China pursues her global aim by providing funds, political organizers, propagandists, and guerrilla leaders. Arms aid is increased, as it has been in Algeria in the face of some Soviet reluctance. Peking has flatly promised all-out support of subversion and violence—everywhere and anywhere.

The Communists plan to use the united-front tactics they so successfully employed in China from 1937 onward. All the discontented will be invited to join the universal united front of the international democratic movement—and unwittingly pay the way for the victory of Communism. Mao argues: "The numbers of the imperialists are dwindling, and they will not last long." Victory is, therefore, in sight, the day when the imperialists, encircled and isolated by the "forces of peace," are forced to stand by helpless as the world turns Red.

Vice-Premier Lu Ting-yi,[2] chief of the Communist Party's Propaganda section, recently declared: "The antagonism between the oppressed nations and the imperialists is a life-and-death antagonism; between them there can be no such relations as 'live and let live or active coexistence and friendly cooperation.'"

Lu also revealed one of the chief reasons for Peking's bellicosity: the Chinese Communists, by no means secure, fear ideological penetration of China. Lu declared: "The imperialists, headed by the United States, hope that bourgeois ideology will come into vogue in Socialist countries . . . and effect a peaceful evolution of Socialist society to capitalist society." The Chinese Communists cannot permit peace, which they fear would destroy them.

Peking's conviction of its own ideological pre-eminence was not limited to asserting that the Chinese know best about the dramatic issues that received the widest external publicity: war or peace; peaceful coexistence or armed revolution in the underdeveloped nations. The Maoists went much further, actually presuming to offer world Communism their own version of holy doctrine. While criticizing Moscow for failing to employ the full coercive powers of the state internally, Peking asserted that the attainment of true Communism depended primarily upon "cultural and ideo-

[2] It is interesting—though not surprising—to see how even the highest in the hierarchy danced on Mao's leading-strings. Even in 1960 Lu Ting-yi was involved in organizing a faction opposed to the line he so loudly espoused, the Maoists subsequently charged.

logical progress" and could therefore occur without the material abundance the Russians insisted was the essential prerequisite. The question was not an abstraction. In 1958 the People's Communes deliberately sought to insure that China would attain true Communism simultaneously with—or even before—the Soviet Union, which had then been toiling toward that goal for more than forty years.

The complex debate on the evolution of socialist societies was actually more radical than the question of tactics toward the non-Communist world. Testing the faith that makes men Marxists, the disagreement involved the self-esteem of the Chinese leadership more intimately and was of longer standing than the controversy regarding external policy. On the vital issue of internal development the Chinese felt that the Russians were once more attempting to dictate the internal course of the Chinese revolution—as they had sporadically since the First Party Congress in 1921. This truly theoretical controversy was potentially so destructive that both sides long deliberately sought to mute it—without conceding their positions in any way.

Intellectually bereft because historical developments have overtaken the visions of their prophets, contemporary Marxists embark on great designs only after debating the inapposite words of men long dead. The controversy, which involved the lives of hundreds of millions, proceeded as formally as a seminar of medieval scholars citing Aristotle and Pliny to support divergent views on how the firefly glows. Briefly—and with unavoidable simplification—this was how the Chinese and the Russians differed:

Moscow held the orthodox view that "transition to Communism"—the stage of development that leads to attainment of the terrestrial paradise that is the goal of human evolution—could only occur amid the material abundance produced by massive industrialization and mechanized agriculture. The Russians recognized a number of other prerequisites. The bourgeois classes, including the petty-bourgeois peasantry, must disappear; and the people, rather than the state, must own in common not only the means of production, but all goods except personal possessions. The exact mechanisms involved were not explained, any more than Marx actually described the precise manner in which the state would "wither away." But the description of the peasantry as petty-bourgeois and the stress on the necessity for popular, rather than state, ownership were direct criticisms of the People's Communes, the device by which the Maoists planned to attain true Communism. The Russians said the peasantry could not be the basis of a proletarian state since they were essentially bourgeois. Communal ownership, they contended, was merely a cloak for state ownership. Two essential conditions of true Communism were, therefore, unfulfilled by the People's Communes.

The Chinese were driven by overwhelming compulsions, psychological and practical, to a series of opposing assertions. Arguing that "all periods of social evolution are transitional," they contended that it is impossible to determine precisely where a society has arrived on the spiral of evolution. "In any event," said Peking, "no nation can attain true Communism until every nation —however small—attains Communism." The Communist paradise, like the Moslem, was, therefore, to be attained by the sword. The conditions laid down by Marx, Engels, and Lenin for judging whether a society was actually in the stage of "transition to Communism," the Chinese asserted, rested as much upon that society's doctrinal and intellectual accomplishments as upon its material state.

Peking further contended that China had satisfied most of the theoretical preconditions of true Communism in just eleven years, surpassing the Russians in certain respects. "Common ownership by the people," the Chinese asserted, was inherent in the People's Communes, the social organization they characterized as "the best organizational structure for Socialist construction and the later transition to Communism." The Russians observed that this argument was nonsense, since the Communes, characterized by state ownership, not popular ownership, were founded upon the peasantry, who were incorrigibly bourgeois.

The Chinese replied—in the best "you're another" style of dignified political debate—that the Russians themselves had actually retrogressed by permitting the development of a privileged new bourgeoisie made up of engineers, scientists, artists, and managers. "The distinction between intellectual and manual labor must disappear," they contended—its eclipse hastened in the Chinese manner by setting intellectuals to work in the fields to teach them Socialist humility. The Chinese insisted that changes in the spirit and the mind of man, brought about by equality of labor and deliberate "thought remolding," were of greater significance than mere material abundance. "Communism," they said again, "means new men in a new society!" China's deliberate reshaping of men and society, therefore, led directly to the ultimate goal, while the Russian obsession with material goals denied it. The Chinese, mired in an agricultural society, were, of course, compelled to maintain that full industrialization was not essential to Communism, while the Russians, flexing their new economic muscles, naturally argued the opposite.

The literal-minded Maoists displayed an obsession with numbers and appearances. Unprepared students were run through inadequate courses like ewes through the sheep-dip. Adult illiterates were taught short lists of simplified characters, though there was almost nothing for them to read in such basic Chinese. Fantastic claims of industrial and agricultural productivity were advanced —apparently in good faith—and then retracted. The thorough ideological transformation of the entire bourgeoisie was proclaimed just half a year before the most extensive Rectification Campaign of all sought to reform the laggard thoughts of millions of intellectuals. Such frenetic pursuit of statistics apparently stemmed from Peking's determination to fulfill—in appearance, at least—the intellectual preconditions for transition to Communism. There must be universal literacy and a high standard of culture, as well as an expanding economy, it was written.

China was determined to claim at the very least, equality with Russia in her stage of evolution toward the Marxist millennium. She had originally adopted Marxism in order to reassert her quintessential supremacy to the hated West. If she had merely aped the parliamentary democracy of the West, she would have remained forever a follower. By embracing Marxism—an infant and experimental ideology—and carrying it to new heights, China sought to become pre-eminent in the world again. Therefore, the constant assertion that Mao Tse-tung had carried Marxism-Leninism to new heights of creative development. Therefore, the determination to win acknowledgment of Chinese pre-eminence from the rest of the Communist world.

The Maoist strategists further believed that their emphasis upon the cultural and ideological prerequisites for Utopia would appeal greatly to the underdeveloped nations, which could not hope to create the strict material basis for decades to come. It was, after all, easier to establish People's Communes—or to reform intellectuals by making them clean latrines—than to build steel mills.

Other urgent reasons compelled the Maoists' insistence upon their own interpretation of the Marxist scriptures. Khrushchev's espousal of peaceful coexistence made ludicrous the militant posture essential to China's emotional needs. China's secular mystics could endure no modification of their vision of hope. Above all else, they could not even consider the possibility that China might once again have been deceived by the West into adopting doctrines that did not serve China's needs. The enforced alteration of basic attitudes finally came from within China. The pragmatists in the end rose in revolt against doctrinal mysteries, which underlay fanatical and wholly worthless policies. The American demonstration in South Vietnam that people's war was anything but invincible played a significant role in stripping Maoism of its pretensions.

China's relations—or lack of relations—with the United States were long second in importance only to her relations with the Soviet Union. The single constant in the foreign affairs of the People's Republic of China was the mutual enmity she enjoyed with the United States of America. The United States provided the strong external enemy the Maoists required. It also maintained Chiang Kai-shek's government in exile on Formosa, whose mere existence compromised the Communists' accomplishments. Beginning just a year after the regime's establishment, China and the United States engaged each other in a protracted and inconclusive war in the convenient arena of Korea.[3] After the truce in 1953

[3] Exact Chinese losses are unknown, but the Communist generals' lavish use of manpower in place of the equipment and fire power they did not possess makes it likely that those casualties were not less than five times America's —or nearly two hundred thousand killed and missing in action. Adding the

their military units continued to confront each other at a dozen different places along China's extended sea and air frontiers. They came close to open conflict several times.

But the Chinese and the Americans also began talking in 1955. The ambassadorial talks continued at irregular intervals, though neither side was willing to "recognize" the other. Despite the vehemence displayed by both sides, their enmity remained at approximately the same level, without growing noticeably deeper. Each became so accustomed to the existence of a dependable— though potentially dangerous—enemy that large groups in each country would probably have felt a definite sense of loss if the quarrel had been resolved.

The Soviet Union at one extreme and the United States at the other determined the limits within which the People's Republic of China conducted her business with other nations. Those poles were obviously not fixed. But they did mark the rough boundaries, since major changes in China's relations with either the Soviet Union or the United States would have altered totally the frame of reference within which she dealt with all other nations.

China's foreign policies were often naïve, since they were based upon inadequate knowledge of the rest of the world and upon dogmatic appraisals of such information as she did possess. But the Maoist hierarchy was resentfully aware that China could not possibly execute an independent foreign policy as long as her actions were circumscribed by the two great powers. Since the constant demonstration of their relative impotence was a major irritant to the Chinese leaders, they were determined to pursue an effective foreign policy that could attain Chinese aims regardless of Russian or American actions. Their chosen instrument was the oppressed and rebellious masses of the world. They believed that they could triumph internationally by using the massed strength of the common people as their chief weapon, just as they had conquered China with the same weapon.

Within the confining extremes, China's relations with the outside world fell into three categories that were necessarily rough in

likely number of wounded brings total casualties to an even million, an enormous number.

definition and often overlapping. Peking sought, first, to maintain normal and amicable relations with as many foreign countries as she could, both to enhance her own prestige and to diminish the prestige of Chiang Kai-shek's rival regime. "Normal" relations with countries like India, Indonesia, and Burma were often hampered by Chinese activities of the second category, her pressing of the expansionism characteristic of all Chinese regimes. The oldest continuing movement of peoples in the world's history was accelerated by the Communists' accession, for China began to move southward and eastward after a pause of more than a century and a half. The final and crucial area was China's relations with the Communist bloc, which she sought to dominate ideologically and to command strategically.

The three categories were obviously not distinct, for normal diplomatic relations with the new nations of Africa, Asia, and Latin America have served as a channel for infiltration and subversion.[4] In the same manner, the traditional expansionist pressure on neighboring countries sometimes complemented and sometimes hindered Peking's efforts to bring the Communist revolution to the entire world. China's historical drive to dominate Japan, for example, took on new meaning as soon as Peking's strategists seriously envisioned the likelihood of a break with the Soviet Union. China could compensate for that schism only by creating a third center of world power, based upon Japan's industry and China's manpower, the new combination transformed into a vital force by Mao Tse-tung's "uniquely correct" strategy.

The sources of the Maoists' internal compulsions have been revealed by the tortuous dialogue of the Sino-Soviet quarrel. Their plans for the countries which border upon China and, indeed, their plans for the world, have also been revealed by the grand debate. The Maoists have made no secret of their desire to install

[4] Within the limitations imposed by their straitened circumstances, the Chinese have provided economic and technical aid to selected underdeveloped nations. Their primary activity, however, is the attempt to capture the Communist and "progressive" movements in those countries and to convert them to the Chinese line. Chinese agents and propagandists, stressing the joint themes of common opposition to imperialism and solidarity of the colored races, have had many successes in Latin America, Asia, and Africa. They have more and more frequently come into conflict with Soviet agents.

Communist regimes in all nations by all possible means. The Maoists have hoped to accomplish that purpose by sponsoring "united front" movements in the underdeveloped nations and seizing control of all "progressive" forces. Once in command of those forces, the Maoists would lead them in violent revolutions. Peking's strategists have been convinced that the initial disruption and final Communist control of the underdeveloped countries would lead to the collapse of the "imperialist" nations by isolating them from the markets they exploit. The strategy, requiring overt support of the Chinese state for local revolutions, was most likely to result in open confrontations between China and the capitalist nations. The danger that such confrontations might "escalate" into armed conflict was one of the major factors that forced Nikita Khrushchev—and the subsequent Soviet leadership—to dissociate Moscow from Peking. Nor have they attempted to conceal their grand vision of Peking's leading the "new men" of the new world. The traditional concept of China as "all that is under the heavens" and the Marxist dream that "the international Soviet shall be the human race" had become one.

Although the Maoists' words were highly inflammatory, their actions appeared relatively prudent. They always acted up the limits of their military and material capabilities, but they seemed to hold a relatively sober view of those capabilities. The Maoists were dedicated to "protracted wars," to use Mao Tse-tung's own term, which would bring them victory in time. Until the American intervention in South Vietnam beginning in 1965 forced Hanoi to escalate the conventional warfare, the Maoist strategy of conquest by revolutionary proxies was succeeding. Disorganized regimes, newly freed from colonialism, could not reconcile their internal conflicts sufficiently to present effective resistance to the highly organized thrust of Communist subversion and guerrillas. They tottered not so much because they were corrupt, though most undeniably were corrupt, as because they were inefficient. Each new victory in Laos, Vietnam, and Indonesia triumphantly vindicated the Maoists' thesis of "people's war" and encouraged Peking to new adventures.

The American intervention in force in South Vietnam—the "focus of the world liberation struggle," in the Maoists' own description—had an electric effect on Peking. The basic tenets of Maoism were cast into doubt. It was no good to say that the "people" would triumph eventually because the "imperialists" would lose heart. That projection might indeed be correct, but it gave little encouragement to professional soldiers who contemplated with horror the prospect of a direct confrontation between the immensely powerful United States and a weak China as a direct result of the Maoists' foreign policies. The generals protested volubly against a foreign policy which appeared to them to embody many risks and few benefits. They were joined by practical politicians who felt that Chinese support of "wars of liberation" cost much more in risk of total war and diversion of material resources than the hypothetical prize of world hegemony was worth. Though almost all yearned in varying degrees for such hegemony, the practical men felt that the prospect of its attainment was too remote to justify the enormous drains upon China's resources. The pragmatic men therefore argued for "accommodation with the Soviet Union and the United States, accompanied by significant reduction of Chinese support for militant revolutionary movements abroad."

They had much evidence to offer in support of their argument. Indonesia had slipped from the Chinese embrace; Cambodia was growing cool; Burma had turned away from Peking; indeed almost the only nation in the entire world with which the Chinese maintained good relations in 1967 was their insignificant client and ally Albania, far away in the Balkans. Even the North Vietnamese, dependent upon Peking for material support, were turning away from the nation they felt had prevented their victory in South Vietnam by initiating the disruptive Sino-Soviet quarrel. Outer Mongolia and even North Korea were setting their faces against Peking in a demonstration the Maoists could only view as the blackest ingratitude. Had China not given generous aid to Outer Mongolia and, beyond question, saved North Korea from American occupation?

A significant majority of Chinese thinkers from 1966 and 1968 questioned the very bases of the Maoist foreign policy. Instead of Marxist solidarity, China had encountered the basest ingratitude. Instead of a craven American withdrawal, the Viet Cong had encountered the greatest concentration of firepower in military history. Realists within the hierarchy came to the conclusion that the goals of the Maoists were probably unattainable—and were, in any event, not worth the immense price China must pay for their attainment should they prove attainable. Domestic problems, aggravated by foreign involvement, demanded much greater attention. It was not so much isolationism as a withdrawal from exposed positions the pragmatists advocated. However, the fact of their active opposition was producing profound consequences at home. Once more the actions of other nations were gravely affecting internal affairs in China, instead of China's altering the character of other nations as the Maoists dreamed.

EPILOGUE

The Chinese people stand today erect!

MAO TSE-TUNG
October 1949

Do we not have a bellyfull of rage? That is magnificent. Our rage will drive us onward. We will strive for eight more years, perhaps ten years or a while longer. Then we will let the world see what kind of people we Chinese are!

MAO TSE-TUNG
July 1960

18

The Grand Climacteric

The Great Proletarian Cultural Revolution,
Beginning in 1966, Overturns All Structures
of Power and Almost All Institutions

It all seemed more like an Antonioni film with a script by
Kafka than any political development conceivable in any civilized
nation of the twentieth century. China was exploding in a gaudy
conflagration of verbal pyrotechnics accompanied by vicious
street fighting. Old revolutionary comrades howled for each
other's heads, and industrial workers, the "vanguard of the proletariat," fought with wrenches and handmade knives against Red
Guards, the adolescent "little generals of disorder sworn to die to
defend Mao Tse-tung." The cataclysm that began in 1966 might
have been the characteristically confused death throes of one
more Chinese dynasty—and the anarchy that broke in 1967 could
have engulfed more than 700 million people. It might, rather,
have been the violent birth throes of a new totalitarianism, more
rigid, more dedicated, and more dangerous than any the world
has ever seen—the hordes of Genghis Khan inspired by an im-
placably militant ideology and armed with nuclear weapons.

The first alternative was more likely, though the People's Liberation Army managed to preserve a certain aloofness from the
struggle and to maintain its chief units intact. Nonetheless, the
confusion was total and the price in lives and treasure was fearful.
The Maoists had mounted an attack that was determined to destroy the corrupt structure of the Communist Party itself. Dedicated to extirpating every scrap of "bourgeois influence," the Mao-

417

ists ended by attacking the foundations of Chinese civilization. Mao Tse-tung and his followers went to war not only with the Chinese Communist Party and the People's Government, but with China itself.

The phenomenon called the Great Proletarian Cultural Revolution would probably fall short of either extreme. But no one could be quite certain. Observers—both outside China and within the tormented nation—were dependent for their information on the hysterically ranting voices, primarily female, of the Chinese radio network; on the shifting obscurities of the official press; and on the leaves of Great Character Posters that blossomed on Peking's walls like some new tropical creeper, infinitely luxuriant and infinitely malevolent.

In those circumstances confusion was unavoidable. It was impossible to distinguish absolutely between what was fact and what was merely propaganda. The fascinated audience could not even be sure who was speaking with which voice, since even Mao's bitterest opponents declared themselves loyal advocates of the canonical Thought of Mao Tse-tung.

Only one thing was quite clear. The myth of the seamless unity of the Chinese Communist Party had been exploded, and the shock waves of the explosion were sweeping destructively over the entire Chinese nation. Two groups of dedicated Communists were joined in a struggle to determine not only who would rule China, but what fundamental policies the country would pursue—and by what political philosophy it would test those policies. A number of serious attempts at conciliation had failed, making the prospects for final compromise slight.

In Peking, the cold, beautiful capital on the edge of the Asian steppes, men who had campaigned together for decades were assailing each other in language more vicious, more vituperative, and more violent than they had ever addressed to their enemies— the Chinese Nationalists, the American "imperialists," or the Russian "modern revisionists." From the fetid depths of the ancient well of Chinese invective they were fishing out expressions like "ogres with the spirits of oxen" and "monsters with the souls of snakes." The Chairman of the People's Republic, Liu Shao-chi, was identified by the *People's Daily* as "a great heap of stinking, rotting garbage." He had, it was discovered, been "a traitor and a bourgeois agent" for decades. His adherents were removed from their regular positions within the party and government structures by assaults of "revolutionary rebels" under the command of the Party's new and sole Vice-Chairman, Lin Piao. Other senior officials were paraded through the ice-rimed streets in dunce caps, their faces painted with red ideographs reciting the details of their "crimes."

Waving pocket-sized red-plastic volumes of *Quotations from Chairman Mao Tse-tung*, millions of Red Guards, most of them under eighteen, behaved like the country's true rulers and described themselves as "the arbiters of China's ancient civilization, the arbiters of all civilizations." They straggled in weary columns across the frozen yellow landscape of north China and paraded along the miniature dikes dividing the rice fields of south China. They stalked arrogantly through the great cities, challenging their elders' doctrinal purity and occupying governmental and Party offices. They beat respected Communists and burned their possessions; they taunted the police and mocked soldiers; they destroyed ancient works of art and proclaimed themselves the precursors of a new civilization.

Wherever they were, they recited *en masse* their awesome liturgies of hate and self-encouragement from the plastic-covered Maoist texts—their young, unformed voices cracking in proud hysteria. They carried pennants inscribed with fierce slogans and waved portraits of their "great leader, great generalissimo, great helmsman, and great guide—Chairman Mao Tse-tung." They sang martial songs like the favorite that began: "The East is Red and the Sun Is Risen, China Has Produced a Mao Tse-tung."

The Red Guards believed themselves "the revolutionary vanguard, the selfless embodiment of the future." The Maoist leaders who had created the Red Guards and ordered them to "dare to rebel, dare to spread disorder" had told them that they were the only hope of the great nation. In the few months after its creation in August 1966 the movement developed a force of its own which often evaded the control of its creators. The Red Guards were the most obtrusive political spectacle in China, but they were not the government of China. There was, in fact, no effective government in operation over most of the vast country.

The ether surrounding China was charged with words in May, June, and July 1966, words alternately bitter and boastful—and often as tantalizingly indistinct in meaning as the Herzian emanations caught by the astronomers' radio telescopes. Distorted not by time and distance but by passion, the words were intended for the Chinese. Still, any simple radio receiver would intercept them for the listener in Hong Kong on the edge of the far side of the moon, which the People's Republic had become to the rest of the world.

From the beginning of May there was but one chief theme, which developed and widened frenetically. Waves of denunciation resounded across China from the broad plains of Manchuria to narrow, rock-bound farms set among the misty crags of Kweichow Province. Harsh male shouts contended with sharp female cries above the dark muttering of the throngs. Mass meetings bellowed their spontaneous indignation at the "traitors, the anti-Party, anti-Socialist elements, the devils with the spirits of snakes and the souls of oxen, the bourgeois agents, who plotted in coordination with international revisionism and imperialism to destroy socialism and bring back capitalism." Giving only perfunctory attention to their familiar antagonists, "Khrushchevite revisionism and American imperialism,'" all radio programs hailed the "great new victory for the Thought of Mao Tse-tung" which was won in Peking, the holy city of Chinese Communism.

It was a strange victory.

At the beginning of June 1966 a brief announcement noted the dismissal of Peng Chen, Mayor of Peking and First Secretary of the Peking Municipal Committee of the Communist Party. The entire Peking Municipal Committee, which ranked equally with twenty-seven other provincial-level committees, was also dismissed. For the first time in the history of the People's Republic, an erring group had resisted reformation *en masse*. All members of the committee were denounced as henchmen of a "black gang" that had deliberately set out to thwart the Party's will—and to bring about the "recrudescence of capitalism" by curious means.

On the far side of the moon the pen was, it appeared, still more dangerous than the sword, and the pen was the chosen weapon of the "anti-Party group." In their journalistic commentaries, in their collections of essays, and in their historical plays writers under the protection of the Peking Committee and its allies in the central hierarchy had sought to undermine the confidence of the Chinese masses in the canonical Thought of Mao Tsetung and to supplant that doctrine with a "bourgeois view of the world." Not only the ranks of the Communist Party but the "power of the state" itself had been shaken by the ruthless attacks of the squadrons of bourgeois penmen, the Maoists averred. They further warned that socialism in China was engaged in a conflict with capitalism graphically described in Chinese as a "You live, I die; I live, you die" struggle! After the debate on the Great Leap Forward the pragmatists within the Central Committee had contrived a gradual—but marked—economic advance by ignoring the Maoists' visionary and impractical directives. They had also restored to a certain extent both the morale of the masses and the masses' good relations with local cadres. The Maoists, deeply alarmed by such "revisionism and *embourgoisement*," were counter-attacking.

The victorious legions of Marxist (read: Maoist) orthodoxy did not grow complacent with the "defeat" of the hapless Peking Committee and the suppression of its sinister publications. As its first official action the new Municipal Committee removed other "bourgeois agents" from control of Peking University, the intellectual seedbed of the Communist revolution. In the provinces vice-governors, Communist Party cultural directors, senior academicians, and newspaper editors were relieved of their duties to the accompaniment of "drums and dancing," as Chinese has the term Peking usually translates as "fanfare." No drums or dancing enlivened the quiet meetings of regional committees which plucked dissidents out of the economic structure throughout China. But those sessions were an essential and integral complement to the process of removing from critical positions discredited professional writers, academicians, journalists, managers, and technicians. The ultra-orthodox Maoist faction affirmed that the only wisdom which was valid in the new age was the wisdom of the "worker, peasant, soldier masses."

All persons possessing skills derived from higher education were considered in greater or lesser degree corrupted by "bourgeois thought." Even those who came of "pure proletarian backgrounds" had been contaminated by the "bourgeois savants" who were their teachers. Many of the erring intellectuals were dismissed; others were "struggled with," as the stark Communist phrase has it, until they recognized their faults. Seeking to avoid the labyrinthine difficulties imposed on totalitarian regimes by the recalcitrance of the essential managers and technicians—in brief, the independent educated class—the Maoists had already been lured a long way way down the road toward dependence on the "innate" technical skills of the masses, who are presumed to be ideologically pure. From 1958 to 1961, during the Great Leap Forward, that road had led not only to a great victory for the Thought of Mao Tse-tung but to economic and administrative chaos.

The pragmatists had sought to recoup that chaos by measured and reasoned means. At the beginning of 1965 it had appeared that China was finally attaining stability. The body politic had begun to recover from the severe trauma of the Great Leap Forward, the simultaneous effort to create modern industry by massed human labor and to impose a Utopian new social system. The Communist Party no longer devoted its chief energies to the imposition of absolute ideological uniformity. Dissident voices were heard on the airwaves and in the press, though their criticism was invariable couched in Aesopian language. Even Mao Tse-tung was criticized—directly within the inner circles, obliquely in public. A measure of *laissez faire* had replaced rigid economic organization, and many individuals—particularly among the peasantry—were permitted to spend part of their time working for their own profit. Industry was progressing slowly.

Although the pace of industrialization was so slow that it could not, within the conceivable future, make China a great industrial and military power, the people were enjoying an increased flow of consumer goods. Within the limits imposed by an omnipresent and officious bureaucracy, the Chinese masses were happier than they had been since their honeymoon with the Communists ended in 1957. For the first time since 1956 things were working well in China. Contrary to the impression conveyed by the Maoists' foreign sympathizers or the many innocents abroad in China, the relative well-being and substantial popular contentment were not the results of fanatically doctrinaire policies. Nor could the Maoists' striving for total thought control be justified by the undeniable material progress. It was the significantly less doctrinaire pragmatists—already non-Maoist, though not yet anti-Maoist—who had contrived such substantial progress. By their own testimony the greatest obstacles they met were thrown up by the doctrinaire Maoists.

One group was increasingly unhappy at the spectacle of material gratification they saw everywhere around them. Their mentor was the seventy-three-year-old Chairman of the Communist Party, Mao Tse-tung, the creator and ruler of the realm. He himself was disturbed by three chief irritants:

(1) His own physical and mental faculties were fading. The severe illness he apparently underwent late in 1965 compelled his attention to the pressing problem of insuring that he would be followed by a worthy "revolutionary successor."

(2) His power over events in China had been eroded by the new atmosphere of relaxation in Peking itself, as well as by the growing tendency of provincial and municipal Party officials to disregard Central Committee directives calling for the renewal of hard-line policies.

(3) An amorphous—but irresistible—psychological transformation was occurring throughout China. The emphasis was upon orderly—if slow—material progress attained by pragmatic measures, rather than upon dedication to perpetual revolution at home and abroad. Revolutionary fervor had decayed, and the determination to create a society that would be a model for the future had all but withered.

While Mao brooded, knowledge of his illness spurred the powerful pragmatic faction within the regular Party apparatus to its own thoughts of the future. The group which had presided over the *de facto* change in the condition of China began to make its own plans for the succession. Those plans did not include Mao's own candidate, fifty-nine-year-old First Vice-Premier and Defense Minister Lin Piao. A field marshal until he had abolished formal military ranks in mid-1964 in order to assert his own personal control of the military establishment more forcefully, Lin had also purged the Army for Mao after the upheavals of 1958–59 demonstrated that the military were a center of "revisionist" thinking.

The contest over personalities and policies was precipitated by the grave ailment—probably arteriosclerotin Parkinson's disease—which deprived Mao of much of his vigor and made it appear that he might soon die. The Maoist group struck first, vilifying and deposing the entire Peking Municipal Committee of the Communist Party at the beginning of June 1966. Swept from their desks shortly thereafter were more than two hundred of China's leading propaganda directors, writers, editors, motion-picture directors, and educators. The generic charge: plotting like the writers' Petöfi Club of Hungary to prepare public opinion for "peaceful evolution" to capitalism. The opposition was both stunned and incoherent. Only after August did it begin to rally.

At the beginning of August the Maoists intimidated a meeting of the Central Committee, which ordered sweeping changes in the structure of the powerful Political Bureau. Lin Piao, hailed for the first time as Mao's "closest comrade-in-arms," became sole Vice-Chairman of the Party, while Chairman (President) of the People's Republic of China Liu Shao-chi was dropped from second to eighth place in the hierarchy. The military command was also completely reshuffled, since Lin Piao's hand-picked chief-of-staff had sided with the pragmatists and the "professional" generals. Premier Chou En-lai retained his third rank, but two Mao adherents, Tao Chu, a practical politician from southern China, and Chen Po-ta, Mao's secretary and ideological mentor, were elevated to the fourth and fifth places in the central hierarchy. Tao Chu also became chief of the Party's Propaganda Department, replacing Lu Ting-yi, while Chen Po-ta was named Chairman of the new Group Directing the Cultural Revolution. Chiang

Ching, Madame Mao Tse-tung, became First Vice-Chairman of the Group. Her strength was her relationship with Mao; her virulence in goading the extremists arose from bitter frustration. She was an unsuccessful motion-picture actress professionally and privately an ambitious wife who had been deliberately kept in the background by her husband.

The Maoists called the Red Guards into being and staged a series of turbulent mass rallies in Peking extending from August to November—all to show their strength. School was out—for more than a year. The adolescents began rampaging through the cities of China and across the countryside.

Red Guard terrorism at the beginning of the Cultural Revolution was intended to paralyze the intra-Party opposition to Maoist policies and to clear the ground for a wholly new political system. It was intended neither to destroy wholly the normal structure of the Communist Party and the People's Government nor to carry China to the brink of anarchy.

Instead of achieving its sweepingly romantic but still rational objectives, the extremists' pressure forced the crystallization and expansion of the opposition. Instead of a quick victory, the pro-Mao forces faced a pitched battle, and they then moved to destroy the Party apparatus utterly. Above all, they had by their erratic violence forfeited the respect of the Chinese masses. Popular support rallied around the pragmatic local cadres and their pragmatic anti-Maoist superiors.

The Red Guards' purpose had been to terrorize the opposition into compliance. But their tactics had had the opposite effect. Not only the conventional apparatus of the Party but also the working masses were alarmed by the new excesses. Slowly the opposition began to take form, and the Maoists realized that they would have to destroy the entire structure of the Communist Party if they were to prevail.

Thereafter, the conflict shifted back and forth, with the anti-Maoists' strength increasing gradually. The final battle was provoked by the Maoist decision to carry the fight into industry and agriculture, areas that had been specifically exempt from the ravages of the Cultural Revolution. The opposition, grown powerful,

riposted with strikes in Shanghai and other major cities. The Maoists, in turn, threatened to use the Army against their opponents.
January and February of 1967 were the critical months.

The entire Municipal Committee of the Communist Party of
Shanghai, the nation's largest city, was denounced by the Maoist
press and radio as a band of traitors who "followed the bourgeois
reactionary line." The great port city was shaken by widespread
strikes that interrupted its communications with the rest of China.
Water and electricity supplies operated intermittently, and many
factories were closed down. The stalwart railway workers—some
of them the same men who had been the backbone of the Communist labor movement for decades in the struggle against the
Nationalists—left their throttles. Stevedores refused to work, and
the rhythm of the docks along the muddy Whangpoo River slowed
convulsively like the pulse of a dying giant.

The "revolutionary rebel faction," loyal to Mao Tse-tung and
his heir presumptive, former Field Marshal Lin Piao, thundered
threats of dire punishment for all supporters of the traitorous Municipal Committee and ordered instant arrest of all its adherents.
Not a single regular organization of the Communist Party, the
People's Government, or the People's Liberation Army appeared
on the list of thirty-two signatories to the Maoist rebels' Urgent
Proclamation on the state of Shanghai. Instead, that list was com-
prised of newly constituted, somewhat amorphous groups like the
Shanghai Branch Committee of the Peking Aeronautical Insti-
tute's Red Flag Struggle Team, the Shanghai Branch Committee
of the Harbin Military Engineering Institute's Red Rebellion
Group, and the United Shanghai Municipal Units to Bombard the
[Rightists'] Headquarters.

Fighting in streets and factories was kept from becoming a
total battle within the city only by the control exerted by the
Army. The generals, however, did not take sides. They sought
chiefly to preserve a modicum of order and to ensure that the
economy would not cease functioning entirely.

The controlled press and radio made a *cause célèbre* of the
Shanghai "counter-attack of the reactionaries" in the hope that the
severe repression they essayed would serve as a warning to all
China. But similar declarations of independence by municipal and

provincial Party branches and by government organizations elsewhere in China were not publicized by the Maoists for fear that
the news would reveal the true state of anarchy upon which the
nation verged.

The formal structure called the Government of the People's
Republic of China still existed in Peking. The buildings remained,
and some of the bureaucrats sat behind their desks. Directives
continued to be issued in the name of its Cabinet under Premier
Chou En-lai, just as the Central Committee of the Communist
Party and its appurtenant bodies still issued directives. The People's Government also maintained formal relations with other nations through its ministry of Foreign Affairs under Foreign Minister Chen Yi. But the true impotence of the People's Government
in foreign affairs was indicated by the recall to Peking of great
numbers of Chinese diplomats from abroad. The Maoists appeared determined to destroy everything they could not control.
Sanguinary incidents between Chinese students and "diplomats"
on the one hand and the local populace and authorities on the
other flared in Russia, Burma, Czechoslovakia, Britain, and Indonesia—to give only a few examples. China's international prestige
plummeted, and a half-dozen embassies in Peking were attacked
by Red Guards.

The violent verbal assaults by Red Guards in Great Character
Posters against both the Premier and his Foreign Minister were,
however, merely a symptom of the decay of the government's authority. The real cause was the cutting of the wires that led to the
central switchboard. The provincial and municipal agencies of the
government were, quite simply, no longer responsive to the orders
of a government which was itself harassed unmercifully by Maoist
hooligans. The provincial agencies of the Communist Party were
even less responsive to the directives of a Political Bureau and a
Central Committee which had both been reorganized by *force
majeure*.

It would have been the peak of folly for provincial officials to
obey a small Party clique which had seized the central apparatus
with the avowed purpose of destroying the men and the institutions that had ruled China for the last seventeen years.

Things had not quite worked out according to Lin Piao's

grand design. Instead of terrorizing the opposition, he had inspired it to the first collective resistance ever mounted in the People's Republic. Instead of intimidating the people into sullen obedience or evoking spontaneous support, he had aroused deep anger. A coherent—if poorly organized—opposition force began to take form round the old Party structure, which still existed despite the Maoists' vicious assaults upon it. The people rallied to the local authorities they knew rather than to the distant fanatics of Peking.

A degree of restraint had marked the actions of both sides until mid-December 1966. Above all, the People's Liberation Army had remained aloof from the quarrel. The area of battle had also been limited. The Red Guards, Lin Piao's political shock troops, were deployed primarily in urban areas, and they were ordered not to harass industrial workers and farmers. Both the bases of the economy and the overwhelming mass of China's population had been carefully isolated from the struggle over power and policy. The Maoists' attack had been concentrated on the Party itself. Although China was close to chaos administratively and institutionally, the daily life of large areas of the country had been virtually untouched.

The situation was radically altered just after Christmas, when the dwindling Maoist leadership saw that it was in danger of losing. Sweeping changes in the leadership presaged the change in tactics. Tao Chu, who had in August been abruptly promoted from the satrapy of the Central-South China Region to the fourth position in the national hierarchy and the direction of all propaganda agencies, was deprived of those posts in December. His character and his politics were attacked in the wall posters of Peking, those sometimes erratic weathervanes of changing political winds. At the same time Chiang Ching, Madame Mao Tse-tung, rose ever higher, becoming adviser to a new committee set up to purge the Liberation Army and, shortly thereafter, chairman of a wholly new purge committee with Premier Chou En-lai as her "adviser." The Cultural Revolution, the Maoists abruptly decreed, must purify both industry and agriculture. The newly purged People's Liberation Army was ordered to intervene in support of the Maoists. The power struggle was verging upon civil war.

An incident in Shanghai reflected the new aspect of the struggle. In the courtyard of their school, which was closed for the Cultural Revolution, a dozen teen-aged boys and girls surrounded a middle-aged teacher. While the older man tried to protect his head from their blows, other teachers stood by, afraid to intervene. The attack might have gone on until the teacher fell, the culmination of many similar incidents. But a half-dozen workmen from a neighboring factory burst into the courtyard and dispersed the "young rebels."

By extending the Cultural Revolution to industry and agriculture, the Maoists had finally aroused the Chinese people's bitter anger. With few exceptions, the working and farming masses rose behind their local leaders against the Maoists. They were inspired not only by fear of the new fanticism, but also by the practical benefits offered by the anti-Maoist cadres. In factories workers were granted shorter working hours, higher wages, longer vacations, and a number of fringe benefits. On rural People's Communes the "year-end sharing out" of profits was remarkably more generous than it ever had been—at the expense of the state. Farmers were promised that they could keep—and even enlarge —the prized private plots they farmed for their own profit. After first having disregarded the economic effects of the Cultural Revolution, the Maoists had proclaimed their determination to "increase production," and the people had realized that they would work much harder for much less if the Maoists triumphed. They remembered the rigors of Maoist economics during the Great Leap Forward.

The Maoists found themselves in an extremely weak tactical position. They railed against the opposition's tactics as "economism," angrily predicting that the new prodigality would ruin the Chinese economy. But they had few effective weapons with which to counter the opposition's moves except an appeal to patriotic and doctrinaire dedication—and the masses no longer listened to such abstract pleas.

Woes worse than "economism" befell the Maoists. General strikes paralyzed rail transport, the seaports, and many factories. Peasants formed their own armed units and defied the Maoists. In Kiangsi Province, the cradle of the Liberation Army, more than twenty thousand veterans formed the Army of Righteous Uprising. In many cities angry workers broke into banks to take back the wealth they felt had been stolen from them over the years. Anti-Maoist Scarlet Guards, formed months earlier, fought hand to hand with Red Guards.

Although they were not in full control, local Communist Party secretaries and their adherents administered their own districts—even entire provinces—as independent entities. The First Secretaries of the Party's Regional Bureaus in the Northwest and the Southwest—each ruling an area of five provinces with a population of hundreds of millions—were denounced for their lack of fealty to the Maoists. Pockets of Maoist influence remained in their areas, and the opposition could enforce no orderly rule—if indeed it wanted to. The final disposition of the fate of China passed into the hands of the aroused masses. It was wildly ironic that Mao, who had placed all his confidence in the "wisdom of the masses," should be directly contending with them for power.

Irony even more grotesque soon shrouded Mao's position. He had orginally won control of China by mobilizing the oppressed peasants as guerrillas to strike against the "bourgeois cities" and their regular troops—a strategy that Lin Piao had later declared the perfect pattern for the Maoists' "world liberation struggle." Yet in February 1967, Mao was reduced to attempting to "seize power" in those same cities with the might of his own regular army. He hoped that his control of those urban centers would in time enable him to regain control of the countryside. It was a curious reversal.

The Maoists' response moved slowly and badly. Two months after the campaign to "retake power" began, they claimed only four provinces and the two major autonomous cities of Shanghai and Peking. A full year was to pass before they could even claim half the twenty-eight administrative areas of China.

Their power was, however, by no means firmly established even in those scattered areas. When the Maoist "revolutionary rebels" succeeded in taking over factories or government and Party offices, they could not manage them with even minimal efficiency. Bedeviled by the crippling lack of trained administrators and technicians who had gone over to the opposition, the "revolutionary rebels" themselves began to split. In March and April, Maoist organs of publicity frantically inveighed against "extreme democracy . . . individualism . . . anarchism" within their own ranks. Peking appealed for "revolutionary discipline," but anarchy spread. A full year later the Maoists were still pleading for unity and inveighing against "factionalism . . . anarchism . . . economism. . . ."

An even greater disappointment awaited the Maoists. The essential support of the Liberation Army was given sparingly and grudgingly. The military, it appeared, was willing to help preserve a pro-Maoist status quo or to put down civil disorder in some cities. But it would not throw itself into the battle to "seize power"—even in the cities. The position was worse in the countryside. Commanders of a peasant army would not hazard their control of that army by ordering their men to attack dissident peasants. Besides, the Liberation Army itself was badly split. Having been subjected to a major purge, it was simply not prepared to risk all in support of the Maoists against the majority or the Party. The loyalty given to Lin Piao and his adherents weighed less than the traditional loyalty to the aged Generalissimo Chu Teh and his field marshals. Besides, intelligent commanders knew that keeping their forces intact and uncommitted was the best hope of avoiding full-scale civil war—and perhaps the only hope of perpetuating Communist rule in China. Some commanders, particularly in outlying and border areas, made common cause with the anti-Maoist cadres.

Haunted by the specter of defeat, the Maoists again modified their strategy. The new tactics resembled the devious intriguing characeristic of Mao himself more than it did the frontal attacks of Lin Piao. In mid-February a "threefold alliance" of the young mobs with "loyal revolutionary cadres" of the Communist Party and "responsible commanders" of the Army was proclaimed. The "revolutionary rebels" were seeking to win new allies from among the undecided and the disaffected. The Maoists promised rewards for defectors from the opposition and leniency for all but the "most stubborn and persistent" of their enemies. Most erring cadres would not only be forgiven, but would be permitted to retain their positions if they repented. Such promises had already been made in late 1966; their substance did not alter substantially in 1967, but their tone became ever more conciliatory as the Maoists grew more vividly aware of their own weakness.

The new approach epitomized by the "threefold alliance" was a tactical change of direction. Realizing that their frontal assault was creating new enemies, the Maoists shifted to flank attacks. The strategy displayed an enhanced recognition of political realities. It finally represented a withdrawal from the Maoist objectives: total defeat of all Mao's enemies and the creation of a new social and political structure. The Maoists formally conceded all their major policies in order to preserve their power.

While the Maoists experimented with these new tactics, the centrist group under Premier Chou En-lai was striving, as it had on several earlier occasions, to moderate the conflict. "Speaking as the representative of Chairman Mao, Vice-Chairman Lin Piao, the Party center, the State Council, and the Party's Military Affairs Commission," Chou implicitly counseled moderation. The Red Guard movement, he said, had been a great success: the Cultural Revolution had already won great victories. He had spoken in almost the same terms in November—and he had failed. Besides, he had finally forfeited the trust of the anti-Maoists by his own attacks on their position.

Some defections to the Maoist camp followed the promises of amnesty for defectors, since the complex factors in play in different areas of China sometimes made that course attractive to individuals. But the earlier savage repression of tens of thousands of hard-working officials was hardly calculated to entice other officials into the Maoist ranks. Besides, bureaucrats and generals have a penchant for order, and the Maoists offered only the prospect of increasing disorder.

Unable to retake control of the conventional machinery of either the state or the Party, the Maoists were at the same time attemping to create an entirely new framework, beginning with "provisional power structures" formed by the threefold alliance. But the inherent liabilities of those provisional governments made them incapable of ruling effectively. They possessed neither technical skills nor popular support. In any event, it soon became clear that the Maoists were too weak to establish even the formal strucures of the new authority. They were isolated from the true sources of power, though they still controlled the propaganda apparatus.

The confused process of disintegration proceeded ever more rapidly and ever more obscurely from April to August. The Maoists proclaimed "military control" of all China, but the People's Liberation Army still did not support them. The Maoists launched open attacks on Chairman (President) Liu Shao-chi of the People's Republic and Secretary-General Teng Hsiao-ping of the Communist Party, but the masses and the apparatus remained inclined toward the pair. On May Day only 28 percent of the Central Committee turned out to honor Mao Tse-tung, and a good number of the senior generals and officials were really in Peking to reach a non-Maoist understanding among themselves.

In July two Maoist emissaries were sent to Wuhan, the triplet cities of central China which are the nation's industrial heart. Their mission was to win back to the Maoist camp the dominant political and military figures of central China. Both men had shown a tendency to associate themselves with the alliance of generals that was taking form along the Yangtze River and in the Northwest and Southwest Regions. The Maoist envoys failed so badly that they found themselves held prisoner for a time by troops in open revolt. For the first time, the Maoists acknowledged active and violent opposition within regular units of the People's Liberation Army. The Wuhan Rising was a signal to other generals in other areas.

Even before consolidating the "victory" they claimed over the disaffected troops and civilians of Wuhan, the Maoist clique issued two startling warnings to its adherents. The "grave political incident" of Wuhan, they said, was likely to occur again elsewhere, since it was by no means "an isolated, chance phenomenon." One day later the virulently Maoist newspaper *Wen Hui Pao* of Shanghai warned that "evil elements" were plotting a second great upheaval in that premier seaport of China.

Having departed almost as far from private recognition of reality as they had from objective truth in their public utterances, the Maoists were concerned primarily—although not exclusively —with the propaganda effect of their words. As a maneuver in the psychological war it made perfect sense for them to claim a sweeping victory over their enemies in Wuhan. It would obviously be highly useful for the Maoists to convince the people that they had in truth regained control of the three cities which together are the single most important communications complex in China—and the key to the populous, wealthy, and disaffected Yangtze Valley. Although the Maoists had made sweeping concessions in return for their opponents' reducing the pitch of open defiance of the presumed central authority, there was no reason for the clique's propagandists to let the reality of compromise shadow their claim of triumph.

At first glance it was more difficult to understand why the Maoist publicity organs should have followed that sweeping proclamation of victory with warnings that the disastrous events of Wuhan could recur in more virulent form elsewhere—or, for that matter, why their cries of victory should gainsay themselves by their continuing frantic appeals to Wuhan itself to recant its heresy. Instead of spreading confidence and creating a bandwagon psychology, those statements could only sow apprehension in the hearts of loyal Maoists.

One reason for the Maoists' laxness was obvious: since almost everyone in China took official statements as conondrums from which the underlying truth must be extracted, they could not hurt themselves much more by the warning. But there was another— and more immediate—reason for the apparent ineptitude of Maoist propaganda. The press and radio, still in Maoist hands, were the clique's chief means of communication with its dispersed followers. The Maoists warned of recurrences of the Wuhan Incident because it was imperative that they prepare their adherents for the new revolts they could not prevent. Fighting a rear-guard action, they apparently judged it wiser to rally their ranks against new setbacks rather than risk the dismay the sudden and unexpected manifestation of these setbacks would engender.

The Great Proletarian Cultural Revolution had passed through a kaleidoscopically confusing multitude of stages in little more than a year's time.

It had started as a mass purge of all Chinese society, the

waves of "rectification" spreading outward from the nucleus of the Communist Party. It was soon transformed into a fierce struggle for power between two hostile groups. The Maoists had initially refrained from using the full coercive power of the People's Liberation Army because they felt that the employment of total force was unnecessary. They had attempted to substitute terror, mass persuasion, and social pressure for the naked might of the bayonet and the gun which they nonetheless hailed as the basis of all political power.

They subsequently had good reason to shrink from indiscriminate use of the Liberation Army's guns. If they had ordered troops to crush every manifestation of opposition, the guns might have been turned against the Maoists themselves. Even in the summer and autumn of 1967, when the conflict was slowly approaching its climax, the Maoists were debarred from unlimited use of those troops who would still obey their orders. Open civil war between troops supporting the two different factions could have followed such a deployment—and civil war would have destroyed all that still remained of the accomplishments of the preceding two decades. Moreover, civil war would almost certainly have destroyed the Maoists' last remaining political strongholds. By the spring of 1968 the Maoists no longer controlled sufficient troops to "crush" the opposition. The Liberation Army had become a semi-autonomous organism seeking order rather than revolution.

Preaching violence, but debarred from the ultimate violence, the Maoists were forced to sit by and watch their opponents' strength increase. The Maoists themselves finally acknowledged their enemies' great strength by warning that the anti-Maoists' "appearance of total superiority" was illusory. Self-contradictory again, they warned further that the struggle would be protracted and bitter because the anti-Maoists were by no means in a state of "anarchy." The Central Political Department of the People's Air Force described the opposition as "a kind of government of its own."

To an outsider that analysis might have appeared to overstate both the power and the cohesiveness of the anti-Maoist camp. But the Maoists' estimate of their enemies' power deserved the most serious consideration, albeit consideration conditioned by recognition of their propensity for alternately exaggerating and deprecating the enemy's power for propaganda purposes. The Maoists' own statements indicated that anti-Maoist or "neutralist" officials exercised a high degree of power in most of the twenty-eight provinces, special administrative areas, and autonomous municipalities into which China was divided. It was also safe to conclude that those dissident authorities were in communication and that the actions they initiated, as well as their responses to Maoist pressures, were coordinated to a certain degree.

The force that bound those local authorities was not only dedication to common purposes, but the only functioning nationwide structure in China—the People's Liberation Army. The Liberation Army was not necessarily totally anti-Maoist in its philosophy, but the majority of generals in the provinces were without question non-Maoist in action. Since Maoist pressures insisted upon separating all China into unquestioning supporters and outright foes, the generals were compelled either to support the Maoists unquestioningly or to make common cause with the self-consciously anti-Maoist and neutralist civilian officials in their respective localities. They tended to the latter choice.

The shape of the new shadow government was highly confusing. It consisted, by and large, of what had been the normal structure of government before the Maoists proclaimed the Cultural Revolution and commanded their followers to "revolt against the holders of power within the Party." The Maoists were therefore not being misleading when they described themselves as the "rebel revolutionary group" and declared that they must "seize power." Although they retained the formal appurtenances of the central authority and presided in Peking, the Maoists were in truth a minority group that sought to conquer the real power of the shadow government. That government itself was not actively seeking to overthrow the Maoists, in part because such aggressive action might splinter the tenuous unity of its disparate elements. It was, instead, content to fight a battle of attrition, maintaining its positions while it waited for the Maoists to destroy themselves.

The Maoists, in turn, alternated between evenings of doctrinaire intoxication and lucid mornings when they glumly acknowledged reality. Sustained by their dogmatic belief in ultimate victory because "the revolution can triumph only by struggling against obstacles," the Maoist leadership alternately pressed the attack against its enemies and offered them inducements to change sides. Because of that vacillating Maoist strategy and the peculiar composition of the opposition, the battle for China became a series of brief, violent engagements interspersed with discussion and compromise. The process was not unlike the open warfare, regularly broken by negotiations, which brought the Communists to power in the face of the material and martial preponderance of the Nationalists. Only this time the Maoists were losing.

The unique situation explained in good part why China, having stumbled to the brink of civil war several times since the acute phase of the struggle began in January 1967, had always managed to draw back at the edge of the precipice. Despite the vicious antagonism between the leaders of the contending factions, neither side wished to risk the civil war that could sweep Communist rule from China—and leave the country fragmented and naked to its enemies. Besides, most generals were sufficiently detached from the purely ideological aspects of the conflict so that they saw their primary mission as preserving their own forces and maintaining order. They were not committed to smashing the opposition at all costs.

The struggle dragged along at its own pace. Its manner was terribly confusing to the outside world—and to many of the participants. Dramatic confrontations like Wuhan were succeeded by face-saving compromises. The Wuhan Incident itself was obscured by rhetoric—and by the fact that outsiders heard only the Maoists' side of the story. The Incident was, therefore, most significant as confirmation of the highly volatile state of China which had already been deduced from official reports and affirmed by unofficial reports. It was, it appeared, not the climax of the struggle for all China.

There would probably be no sharp climax to mark the abrupt end of Maoism. Instead, the "local power-holders" excoriated by the Maoists were likely to pursue their policy of doing as they wished within their own areas and saying what the Maoists wished for consumption elsewhere. Backed by the popular will, their stubborn resistance would finally begin to shape a new, non-Maoist China.

Contemplating a cataclysm of the enormity of the Great Proletarian Cultural Revolution, one could not help feeling that the fate of individual leaders had already become somewhat irrelevant. Nor could one regret the fact that history's most sweeping and most reckless attempt to remake a nation would probably end not with a bang, but with a sigh of relief.

The Great Proletarian Cultural Revolution had already revealed itself not only as the grand climacteric of Maoism, but also as a climactic clash between the two great Chinese traditions of thought and politics. The orthodox central tradition, authoritarian in essence regardless of whether it called itself Maoist or Confucianist, was engaged against the continuing protestant and pragmatic tradition, which was, in essence, *laissez faire* regardless of whether it called itself Marxist or Taoist.

Despite its institutional uniformity, the glory of Chinese civilization has always been its protestant tradition. Under the most stringent repression of the Confucian empire, courageous men with independent minds had always dared to challenge official stubbornness, complacency, and obduracy. Courageous men— officials or private individuals—had always dared to speak out against oppression. They were often forced to make their points by indirection in the settings of novels or plays. They were often punished for their effrontery.

No more than the empire was the Communist state a seamless unity. Despite the most intense intellectual repression China had ever known, courageous and independent men managed to publish their reproaches in oblique form. The Party had discerned a deep-laid plot in the works of a few writers who dared to follow the old tradition of criticism after the Great Leap Forward. It is, however, more likely that those men came together informally, drawn to each other by their common concern for the future of their country.

Mao Tse-tung's withdrawal from the day-to-day business of the state, in part because his health was failing, had transformed such opposition into a major crisis within the leadership of the Party. Peng Chen, fifth after Mao in the Party, had allied himself with the moderate group, perhaps because it represented his best chance of attaining power. He had apparently felt that he enjoyed substantial support—and, further, that he had to act immediately or be swept away himself. Peng—and other leaders—therefore joined with the men who cried out against the prospect of another Great Leap Forward, arguing: "My God, not again! The people are reasonably happy, and the economy is reasonably stable. Let us build on what we have already built. Let us not essay another wild leap into chaos in pursuit of an unattainable ideal."

So spoke the pragmatists. They challenged the hyperorthodox, who knew that the preservation of their own power required of them the strictest adherence to the extreme policies of Mao Tse-tung. Even in death, the shade of Mao Tse-tung was to protect his successors, who were aware that his personal prestige was a chief buttress of the regime. He was therefore canonized in his lifetime, and his works were enshrined as the highest expression of human wisdom.

The Maoists were, further, mesmerized by their own obsessions. They could not abandon their purposes without negating the endeavors of their entire lives. They were therefore compelled to one more attempt to remake both the Chinese people and the Chinese economy through another great convulsion. Because Mao Tse-tung told them so, they knew that all things would be possible once they had "completely remade the thinking of the masses." Because they had no choice, they had to believe that they could accomplish miracles of industrialization and agricultural expansion by the intensive application of human labor under the proper intellectual and administrative conditions. Then China would be the compelling model for the entire world.

Mao Tse-tung's purpose was nothing less than the creation of the first perfect government for mankind. His model was the Paris Commune of 1871, created when the working class led by the radical left of the time took arms against the bourgeois National Assembly and sought to create a wholly decentralized government. Karl Marx called the Paris Commune "history's first true proletarian government." The monument of Mao Tse-tung was not to be merely a revitalized China. It was to be a new era in the annals of mankind, characterized by perfect equality, perfect democracy, and the total absence of exploitation.

The organizational and doctrinal principles of the experiment called the Paris Commune were to guide the creation of the new government. China would not, strictly speaking, be a national state at all, but a popular confederation wherein all authority proceeded directly from the people. Provinces, cities, and rural counties were to be governed by groups of officials selected from among the proletariat through direct universal elections and combining in themselves the legislative, judicial, and administrative functions. Factories, universities, hospitals, and newspapers—indeed, every purposeful grouping of human beings—were to be similarly administered by officials serving brief terms under the constant threat of referendum and recall and enjoying no privileges, monetary or ceremonial, that would set them off from the commonalty. All China was to become a Great Commune.

The new-model officials—legislators, executives, and judges in one—would receive salaries no higher than those of any other worker and would enjoy no special privileges. Most would function from their workbenches. In time new popular bodies would replace the People's Government and the Communist Party itself. They would be called the "groups, committees, and congresses" of the Proletarian Revolution. Guiding all men under this perfect government would be the perfect altruism and utter dedication that arises from expunging all personal desires and devoting oneself solely to the common good. The perfect "new Communist man," possessing no property whatsoever, would be inspired by the canonical Thought of Mao Tse-tung.

The opposition considered this plan to be, at the very least, visionary. It argued that ideal systems could be only ideals and could not work in practice. It believed that material incentives were essential to both industrial and agricultural production, and that industry must be managed by specialists. It contended that Maoist fervor was no substitute for specialized training.

The opposition was also opposed to the Maoist policy of fostering "people's wars"—guerrilla uprisings and political mass movements—throughout the world. Professional soldiers in the opposition argued that China was too weak to thus dare the risk of war with either the United States or the Soviet Union. Specialists in foreign policy contended that the quarrels with those two countries harmed China immeasurably. The professional propagandists among the opposition attacked Mao's absolute control of the arts. The Maoists, their critics said, defeated their own purposes by producing works that no one would read.

Above all, the opposition wanted a reasoned and practical approach to the government of China. It was bored and irritated by the unending claims that China could move mountains, build steel mills, conquer all enemies, and remake mankind—if each Chinese only read, reread, and memorized the works of Mao Tsetung.

The great majority of the Chinese people—peasants, workers, intellectuals, even *apparatchiks*—were also utterly disillusioned with grotesque intellectual gyrations under the unremitting physical and spiritual pressures of Maoism. Thus their support for the opposition. That support forced the compromise which offered the chief hope of ending the disruption of the Cultural Revolution. When violence and economic dislocation became intolerable, the military attempted to bring the forest fire under control.

Fights between different factions, all avowedly "defenders of Chairman Mao," had given most of China's major cities the alternating appearance of battlefields and ghost towns. Strikes, sabotage, and lockouts had destroyed the normal functioning of the economy. Farmers were producing more because they were left alone, and they were cheerfully selling much of their produce on the free (read: black) market. Individual artisans and traders were also setting themselves up in small-scale private business. The cities, however, knew sharp alterations not only between violence and apathy, but between abundance—for those who could afford the black market prices—and severe rationing. So many factional leaders commanded their own armed troops that China was in immediate peril of returning to the days of the warlords. In Peking itself, the Maoist hard core was at once dwindling and at odds with each other. The writ of the Maoist Party Center did not run even in all Peking.

The solution that was being worked out early in 1968 was

typically Chinese. Under the red flag of the Thought of Mao Tse-tung, generals and old-line cadres were establishing Revolutionary Committees—as prescribed by the Maoists. The purpose of those Committees was not to enforce the Utopian vision of Mao Tse-tung, but rather to impose a modicum of civil order. The task was not easy, but the efforts of the generals appeared to be averting complete anarchy. They were concerned not with ideology but with minimal administrative and economy efficiency. They were neutralists and anti-Maoists quoting the sacred books of Mao for their own purposes. The rush to Utopia was, once again, postponed.

The Cultural Revolution, seeking to make the Thought of Mao Tse-tung all pervasive and all powerful, had virtually destroyed ideology as a significant force in China. It appeared that Mao Tse-tung's greatest contribution might prove to be forcing the Chinese nation to abandon illusion for reality.

19

*Can China Become a Normal Member of
the Comity of Nations?*

No people is fonder of reading the future from the past than
the Chinese, perhaps because no other people possesses a past
which has been as minutely recorded and as consistently glorious
for more than three millennia. The passion for their own history
has bred a propensity for repeating both the triumphs and the
mistakes of the past. Until the end of the nineteenth century the
Chinese were in many ways in thrall to their own voluminous and
detailed chronicles. When the intellectual sat down to the obliga-
tory study of those chronicles, the profuse commentaries thereto,
and other quasi-sacred works of great antiquity, he was quite consciously performing an act of affirmation. He was at once affirming his personal commitment to the spiritual and political values
of the great central tradition and renewing that two-thousand-
year-old tradition. He was excluding any radical change in those
values or the society based upon them, and he was severely re-
stricting the possibilities of evolutionary change. Alterations did,
of course, occur—some of them quite sweeping. But they occurred within the framework of the central tradition—or, at the
least, the Chinese could pretend that they occurred within that
framework. When they considered the probable shape of the future, they could therefore assume that it would, with some variations, repeat the past in perpetuity.

Since the beginning of the twentieth century, the politically engaged vanguard of China has deliberately sought to destroy both traditional society and the moral values on which it rested. Long before the establishment of the Communist Party in 1921 activists and idealists were laboring to prepare a site for a wholly different future by leveling the customs and the laws of the past. When, at the start of the Great Proletarian Cultural Revolution, the adolescent Red Guards raised the slogan "Wipe out the old civilization!" they were bringing to its ultimate expression the overriding political and cultural preoccupation of twentieth-century China. By the end of 1967, the old civilization had been virtually shattered; the Cultural Revolution had also blasted the new society developed since the Communist "liberation" of 1949.

Changes even more sweeping than those envisioned by the Maoists appeared to be in train. After devoting the first two-thirds of the twentieth century to sweeping destruction, the Chinese appeared to be escaping from total bondage to their own past—although their direction was still, in part, determined by that past, just as a fugitive is impelled to put the greatest possible distance between himself and the jail. The moral and political values which had been sustained through all the changes of the past and which limited those changes were finally discredited. Attempting to read China's future from China's past—immediate or remote —was, therefore, a more hazardous undertaking than it had been in the days of the Confucian Empires.

The People's Republic established by Mao Tse-tung in 1949 was disintegrating in much the same manner previous short-lived and radically innovating dynasties like the Chin (221–207 B.C.) and the Sui (A.D. 589–618) had disintegrated. Nonetheless, changes in the fundamental matrix of Chinese civilization have rendered the events that followed the collapse of those dynasties but an uncertain guide to the events that will follow the Maoists' collapse. Enduring a few years longer than Adolf Hitler's thousand-year Reich, the "wholly new organization of human society based upon a wholly new kind of human being" Mao Tse-tung offered as the model for all mankind was passing. The Maoist experiment could prove no more than a thorough catharsis of traditional Chinese civilization—an essential, but hardly a glorious process. Nonetheless, the phase of destruction appeared to be drawing to an end. The Chinese people appeared ready to give themselves once again to the great work of construction.

Their first task must be to create a wholly new system of values and bring them to general acceptance. Other nations can, perhaps, live without a minutely formulated political and moral creed. The Chinese have never been able to do so in the past, and it is unlikely that they will be able to in the future. The historical phase that is most nearly analogous to the present radical transition was the change from the repressive Chin, with its strictly codified laws, to the significantly less intrusive Han Dynasty, which endured from 206 B.C. to A.D. 221. The Han was based upon general acceptance of the five sacred relationships among men which had been defined by Confucius four centuries before the dynasty appeared. The Han's succession to the Chin represented a fundamental alteration of both social values and administrative institutions. All subsequent dynastic changes, including the transition from the Sui to the Tang (A.D. 618–805), occurred within the broad political and moral framework established by the Han. New men took power and adjusted the system. They did not contrive a wholly new system as the Han did—and the successors to the Maoists must.

The Han, finding both its sanction and its model in the Confucian canons, nonetheless embodied many administrative devices of the Chin. It is likely that the successor to the Maoist dynasty will utilize many organizational principles developed by that state. The great problem the new regime will face is the absence of any well-developed model such as the Han found in the Confucian doctrine and all its Imperial successors followed until the Ching Dynasty fell in 1911.

A period of intense disorganization is likely to follow the People's Republic of China, even though a presumptive government still exists in Peking and still calls itself the People's Republic of China. The necessity to shape a new order, regardless of what it calls itself, will force upon the country's new rulers a problem which no Chinese government before 1900 truly acknowledged and no subsequent government solved—the nature of China's relationship to the outside world. Even before the emergence of an effective government, the Chinese attitude toward other nations will demonstrate whether the world's largest nation is truly entering a new epoch or is merely repeating the distressing recent past once again.

The Chinese state was for two thousand years aloof and self-centered as no other great realm has been. It developed in substantial isolation from any realms which could claim to be its material or cultural equal, and it was, quite self-evidently, vastly superior to all its neighbors in power, culture, and wealth. The concept of the nation-state therefore never took root in Chinese minds. The Confucian Chinese were not merely incapable of grasping that specific concept of the nation-state, which was a product of the Renaissance and the Reformation in Europe, but were incapable of recognizing the existence of distinct—but equal—national or racial entities.

China was, until the late nineteenth century, a realm without diplomats. Only one relationship was possible between the Great Empire and other peoples, near or far—subordination to the Chinese. Believing themselves the center of a world which would, in time, be brought into harmonious order under their suzerainty, the Chinese could not conceive of entering into relations of equality with other self-avowed nations. The few visitors who were permitted to penetrate the forbidden vastness of China came as "tribute-bearing envoys"—neither as ambassadors nor as traders or tourists. China was *Tien-hsia,* all under Heaven, and the *Ta Tung,* the Great Unity, was the proper goal of humankind—a Utopia spanning the entire world and enforced by Chinese wisdom. When Mao Tse-tung promised to "liberate" all mankind and create "a wholly new era," he was reaffirming the fundamental Chinese view of the world which rose before Confucius and ended with Kang Yu-wei, who tried in vain to reform the structure of the Ching Dynasty in 1898. Implicit in the Confucians' doctrines—and expressed in their actions—was sanction for the use of armed force when force was necessary to move mankind toward the state of unitary blessedness. Mao Tse-tung's theses on "people's war" explicitly declared that force, deceit, and subversion originating in China were essential to the "liberation" of mankind from the exploitation of the past. "Power grows out of the barrel of the gun,"

Mao asserted. "Force is the midwife of the new era," his followers echoed.

The crucial problem of China since the realm first came into sustained contact with the intrusive West in the eighteenth century has been its inability to adjust to existence as an equal member of the comity of nations. There were, however, signs amid the turmoil of the last days of the Great Proletarian Cultural Revolution that a profound change in the Chinese approach to the outside world was occurring. Pragmatists were being forced toward recognition that China was not so powerful—morally or materially—that she could impose her own order upon mankind. The same men were moving toward the corollary recognition that the outside world was composed not of evil midgets to be controlled by China, but of equal nations with which China *must* live on amicable terms. Although the vision of millennia would not dissipate wholly for many decades, the auguries were favorable for the essential psychological adjustment without which China could neither build a viable nation, untormented by a Messianic mission, nor cease to torment the world.

The chief attack leveled by the Maoists on the foreign policy proposals of their opponents, "the power-holders within the Communist Party who follow the capitalist road," was compressed in the Chinese phrase "three harmonies and one reduction." The bald official translation charged the anti-Maoists with championing "the idea of doing away with struggle in our relation with the [American] imperialists, [all] reactionaries, and the [Soviet] modern revisionists, and of cutting down our assistance and support to the militant revolutionary struggles of other peoples." By the Maoists' own admission, the group that advocated such a radical change was a strong majority of the officials of both the Communist Party and the People's Government. The Chinese masses, though bemused by visions of the Great Unity, have never displayed any great desire to sacrifice either their lives or their comfort for its attainment. The official pragmatists were forced to alter their approach to the outside world by the realization that China could afford neither the enormous costs nor the great risks inherent in Mao Tse-tung's policy of perpetual revolution. They recognized that they must choose between China and the world—and they chose China. They had learned that China could not remake the world and that, in any event, the pursuit—or even the attainment—of that purpose did not necessarily serve China's own interests. Recognizing that much of China's agony of deprivation and disorder was due to the sacrifices demanded by Mao's forward policy, the pragmatists were moving toward a non-ideological foreign policy. The conviction that China's activities should seek to advance China's self-interest, rather than to found a world-wide Utopia under Chinese hegemony, was the beginning of a new wisdom. It was based upon the realities of the modern world, rather than upon the internal compulsions of men like Mao Tse-tung.

In the beginning the new Chinese foreign policy was likely to march behind the militant slogans of its aggressive predecessor. But little force was likely to back those slogans. By mid-1968 there was much concrete evidence that Peking was already either too weak or too indifferent to intervene effectively in the "liberation struggles" it supported verbally in Hong Kong and Burma. As new men reshaped the mechanism of power and recast foreign policy, the slogans would become less strident. They would in time subside to whispers.

Any Chinese government must provide for the country's defense by denying possession of North Vietnam to a powerful and hostile power like the United States. But the tenor of support to North Vietnam was likely to change. Hanoi's total commitment to "liberation" of South Vietnam at all costs and Peking's belief that the victory of the "National Liberation Front" must be won by internal "people's war," rather than outright invasion, had come into conflict even before the Cultural Revolution began. Under the pragmatists Chinese support of Ho Chi-minh's war to take South Vietnam would slowly diminish. A foreign policy based upon Chinese self-interest would be forced to make that adjustment during a transitional period in which all China's resources were urgently required for reconstruction. Besides, the most pressing problem of foreign policy would be to reduce the vicious mutual antagonism that made the Chinese fear American invasion.

The Chinese would in the early 1970s come into possession of a nuclear arsenal adequate for defense of their own borders—and adjacent areas of primary interest like North Vietnam. They could then be able to take a more relaxed and more confident view of their position in the world. With the passing of the obsessed Maoists, Chinese foreign policy would at once be less aggressive and more wary. If—as was unlikely—the "power-holders" were to come to total power, China would not rush back into Moscow's arms. The Chinese had learned too much of the world—and of themselves—since 1949 to subordinate themselves again to "Big Brother" Russia. Although the transition was likely to be protracted, the Chinese would probably seek more normal relations with the Russians, just as they would, in time, seek better relations with the United States. Still feeling themselves encircled by the two great powers, they would be determined to keep their guard up. But they would also wish to reduce acute tension. That tension would, of course, diminish when China's foreign policy no longer proceeded from an absolute determination to assert the absolute supremacy of China.

Lingering Marxist commitment to the world revolution might prevent rapid thawing of Sino-American relations. But in time Peking and Washington should be progressing toward the same kind of understanding that prevailed between Moscow and Washington in 1968. It might actually take longer to restore "fraternal" relations between Moscow and Peking than to arrive at an armed truce between Washington and Peking. Any Chinese government was likely to be wary of the Russians for some time because of its memories of the Russian "betrayal" of China—the "betrayal" having been Russian refusal either to give Peking nuclear arms or to underwrite Chinese preponderance in the underdeveloped world. Besides, the four thousand miles of Central Asian border between China and the Soviet Union would remain a potential source of trouble—just as China's resentment of Russian control of much territory that was once Chinese would remain an irritant.

Tremendously important in itself, the new direction of foreign policy would also indicate the general orientation of their rulers to the Chinese people. If the new Chinese regime could shake off the millennia-old obsession with imposing a Chinese-directed Utopia on the world, all things would be possible to it. But pure pragmatism, which can provide guidance for an *ad hoc* foreign policy, is an inadequate foundation for a consistent internal policy. The fundamental assumptions and basic moral values from which China's new government proceeds would therefore be at least as important as the exact composition of that government and the name by which it called itself. The nature of those assumptions and values was also the single most difficult projection to make. The difficulty stemmed from the fact that the Chinese themselves would find it exceedingly difficult to create a satisfactory new doctrine—if, indeed, they could finally create such a doctrine at all.

The Chinese have for millennia been an ideological people because they were not a formally religious people. Confucianism provided them not only with a minutely detailed moral code and an intricately organized political system shaped after a legendary Golden Age, but also with spiritual sustenance and a satisfactory relationship to the supernatural. Acknowledging the possible existence of "spirits," the Confucian Mandarins nonetheless felt that the self-conscious worship of such spirits was fit only for the lower orders. The philosopher-officials, who managed society by example as much as by authority, derived their own spiritual satisfaction from the unending progression of mankind through this world. Albeit naïvely, the masses also shared that satisfaction.

The spiritual pragmatism of Confucianism stemmed from posterity worship rather than the ancestor worship the West discerned in the doctrines. The past, the present, and the future were inextricably linked by the unbreakable continuity of custom and the obvious immortality of humanity. Starting with Darwinism, modern science has depreciated that doctrine, for an ignoble beginning implies the likelihood of an ignoble end. Modern power has further depreciated the spiritual worth of Confucianism by destroying the political system which was at once its expression, its affirmation, and its indispensable matrix. Deprived at once of their temporal grandeur and their spiritual certainty, the Chinese have in the twentieth century tested a wide range of substitutes. Communism was the last and the most sweeping of those substitutes, which ranged from parliamentary democracy to science and aesthetics. The failure of Maoism either to achieve its objectives or even to endure finally deprived the Chinese of their last ideology.

Lacking a generally accepted formal religion to provide both purpose and reassurance, the Chinese will find it difficult to make do with the materialistic pragmatism which is the secular creed of both Western nations and the Soviet Union. The new generation of Chinese leaders is almost certain to be pragmatic in the sense that it will test policies by their accomplishments, rather than by towering goals they *should* ideally attain. Nonetheless, the Chinese will always be driven back to the question: Pragmatism for what end? Even if they could transcend the common human need for submission to a power and a purpose greater than the individual and, ideally, greater than mankind itself, the Chinese could hardly devote themselves totally to the pursuit of material betterment. China's prospect of creating an affluent society within the foreseeable future is so remote as to be almost non-existent. It would, therefore, hardly be pragmatic for the Chinese to dedicate themselves to making such a society. That is not to deny that gradual material betterment is one of the few clear-cut, concrete purposes on which all Chinese pragmatists can agree when they contemplate the deprivation of their compatriots. In any event, even dwellers in an affluent society need to believe in—or, at least, to believe that they believe in—some supernatural sanction.

The working doctrine, which will probably never be quite satisfactory, will include elements from all China's past ideologies, as well as Western and Marxist thought. It is, however, almost impossible to anticipate the nature of the unifying central principles that will give life to the complex substance of that doctrine. Indeed, the fundamental question remains whether the Chinese will be able to create such principles or whether they will, over an extended period, learn to live without a codified doctrine. Above all, the country which is by far the greatest and most highly civilized of the economically underdeveloped nations must somehow find a new basis for belief in its own greatness. The traditional glories of Chinese civilization may provide some inspiration for a new doctrine, though the specific institutions of Confucian civilization have been discredited. In addition, certain organizational principles developed by the Communists are likely to endure, making for greater efficiency in the long run. After the first total revulsion from the dogmatic Thought of Mao Tse-tung, the virtues of altruism, honesty, and hard work so assiduously preached by the Maoists and the "power-holders" alike will probably be assigned the honored position they always just failed of attaining under Confucianism. But those virtues, like the organizational devices, will be purified of much of the compulsion and extremism the Maoists attached to them.

The Han Dynasty similarly diluted the harsh repressiveness of the totalitarian Chin's system of meager rewards and extreme punishments when certain aspects of that system were combined with the Confucian doctrine in a functioning political organism. But the new quest for an underlying doctrine will be protracted and arduous. Its chances of ultimate success are, at best, questionable. Pragmatic because they must be pragmatic, severely limited by their material incapacity, humiliated by their past failures, the Chinese are likely to remain an unstable element in the world for some time to come as they press their search for a satisfactory ideology.

The reaction to the Great Proletarian Cultural Revolution will nonetheless shape the China of the immediate future because of the intensity and the viciousness of the Cultural Revolution's attempt to destroy all existing institutions—traditional or Communist. Words like "anarchy," "confusion," "upheaval," and even "chaos" are too abstract to convey the reality of life in a country where almost all acceptance of authority—moral or temporal— had vanished. Even reporting pitched battles between supporters of the half-dozen-odd feuding groups could give no more than an impression, nor could the Maoists' own anguished appeals to their presumed followers to "restore revolutionary discipline" within their own ranks. An exceedingly minor incident in Shanghai, one of the few cities the Maoists claim to rule, may obliquely illuminate the state of China under the Great Proletarian Cultural Revolution.

A sympathizer of the "power-holders" entered a local branch of the Public Security Office to apply for an exit visa that would permit him to visit Hong Kong. His aged father was ill in the British Crown Colony, he told the sympathetic policeman who inter-viewed him.

"I'm sorrry, but there's nothing I can do for you," the police-man said. "That fellow over there is a 'revolutionary rebel,' the next one is with us, and so on. The whole office is split."

"Well," the applicant finally asked, "who's in charge?"

The policeman put on a sorrowful face. "I guess nobody's in charge here," he answered.

The episode revealed not only the breakdown of order, but the immense effort that would be necessary to re-create an effec-tive structure of authority. The Maoists had fought a losing battle to impose their own Utopian extremism on China; and they were treading the dreary path to political annihilation. The anti-Mao-ists too had been battered. The formal structures of both the Peo-ple's Government and the Communist Party had been gutted, and leaders like President Liu Shao-chi and Secretary-General Teng Hsiao-ping had been publicly humiliated. In the West a leader like Liu Shao-chi, who had borne the most vicious calumnies with dignity, restraint, and the determination not to yield, would prob-ably emerge from his ordeal much revered and much respected. He might come to power on a wave of enthusiastic support from a public that had repudiated his predecessor. Normally such a reac-tion would be most unlikely in China, where the man's weakness, rather than his strength, would be most apparent. The Maoists had tried to reduce Liu Shao-chi to an unperson in the eyes of the Chinese masses. Those masses, of course, wondered how Liu could possibly endure all that he had endured without striking back. But the manner of the Maoists' attack had the curious effect of increasing Liu's stature—a fact most simply attested by the growing support his faction enjoyed among the people. (The conviction of the growth and increasing stubbornness of that pop-ular support was derived neither from the accounts of refugees nor by inference from Peking's reports, but from the Maoists' di-rect admissions.) Many Chinese found in the matter of the Maoist attacks on Liu renewed reason to support him. Liu became the symbol of rational and courageous resistance to the extremist poli-cies of Mao Tse-tung which had spread deprivation and disorder throughout China. The Maoists themselves have repeatedly declared that Liu opposed rigid economic policies at home and an aggressively messianic policy abroad. Since the people, concerned primarily with their own well-being, shared those attitudes, Liu's personal prestige rose. It was, however, questionable whether he could overcome the great practical obstacles to a resurgence of his power. Although the anti-Maoist forces managed to maintain themselves in many areas, they possessed neither a coherent organization at the provincial level nor any national structure of power. It would, therefore, be precipitous to predict that the so-called "power-holders" would inherit authority over a united China, particularly since the military remained the key to the immediate future of China.

The People's Liberation Army managed to avoid an open civil war in which units supporting different political groups fought each other. It also, by and large, managed to retain those units intact. Nonetheless, the Liberation Army was also riven by the contention of the Cultural Revolution. It was bewildered by external events and tried by internal strains. The Army nonetheless remained the closest thing to a functioning nation-wide institution in China. It was, therefore, not unreasonable to expect the Army to play a major role in the consolidation that would follow the Cultural Revolution. That consolidation would begin when the exhausted combatants realized that neither side could win because they had destroyed the very structure of power for whose possession they fought.

Six of the ten men who held the rank of Field Marshal until formal military ranks were abolished by Mao's chief lieutenant Lin Piao were disaffected from the Maoists. They were not necessarily supporters of the anti-Maoists, a term which, in any event, described a loose alliance of men whose opinions and allegiances covered a broad spectrum—rather than the coherent group the term implies. Possessing a wide-meshed—if tenuous—network of allies, clients, and supporters throughout the military establishment that covered all China, those former Field Marshals could form the nucleus of a military *junta*. When the declining personal prestige of Mao Tse-tung had fallen even further, they might even make a coup at the center. Either displacing Mao or capturing him, they could then attempt to rebuild the Chinese power structure.

Regardless of whether a military *junta* actually seized the tattered shreds of central power, the immediate prospect for China was the erection of three separate façades of power—with a complex reality half-revealed behind them.

The first façade would be the "Victory of the Great and Invincible Thought of Mao Tse-tung." There were no avowed anti-Maoists in China, and all the contending groups fought in the name of Mao and his canonical Thought. Unless anarchy destroyed all semblance of the institutions of power, a victory for the doctrines of Mao Tse-tung would be proclaimed and Mao himself would be hailed until his death as "the supreme leader, the helmsman, the great teacher." Since all his extreme policies had already been conceded by the Maoists themselves, Mao would be even more of a figurehead than he had been in the recent past. The rapid decline of Mao's personal prestige, however, meant that the first façade would be gossamer-thin. In certain areas where Mao's name had already become an object of opprobrium, the authorities might spare themselves the bother of maintaining the pretense.

Behind the Great Victory of the Great Thought of Mao Tse-tung would stand another façade, hardly more substantial than the first. A government calling itself the Central Government of the People's Republic of China would exist in Peking. Its authority was, however, likely to be limited to certain sections of Peking, though it would perform the ceremonial functions of a central government at home and abroad. Unless the Maoist mania destroyed China's relations with almost all foreign nations—a prospect not wholly unlikely—the Peking government would maintain embassies abroad and would treat with foreign embassies in the capital. It would most closely resemble the government maintained by successive warlords in Peking from 1916 to 1928, when the Nationalists under Chiang Kai-shek took the city. Cut off from effective authority over the great mass of China, that government nonetheless maintained the dignity of sovereignty—and, occasionally, extended its sway beyond Peking.

Regardless of whether a *junta* of generals made a coup at the center, the third and final façade would be the most substantial, though it too would be a façade. Since the People's Liberation Army was the only coherent institution remaining in a chaotic China, it would appear that the country was under effective, centralized military rule. But the Army would be unable to rule China effectively for a number of reasons. It was itself too badly split to act in a coordinated fashion throughout the country. It was also too heavily committed to regional loyalties and to alliances with local "power-holders" to function as a wholly independent organism. Besides contending with the problems produced by the shattering of normal communications and lines of command, the Liberation Army would have to settle its own struggles between pro-Maoists and anti-Maoists before it could act effectively as an integral force.

The reality behind the three façades was likely to resemble the reality that existed behind the façade of central rule by the Manchu Dynasty as it lay dying between 1890 and 1900. Groups of four or five provinces, perhaps corresponding to the six Regions into which the Communist Party divides China, would resemble the viceroyalties of the Ching's last days. No more than the viceroys controlled their sub-realms wholly would the rulers of the new sub-divisions exercise total power in every country and prefecture. They would however, make their political decisions and manage their economies in substantial independence of the ineffective central government. Just as the great viceroys possessed their own semi-autonomous armed forces, their own treasuries, and their own powers of life and death, the new satraps would hold almost complete discretion. Their relations with the armed units within their territories were likely to be complex and to assume divergent forms in in each of the satrapies. But those satraps who were not themselves generals would be dealing with generals who had been stationed so long in specific localties that their dominant, immediate loyalties also were regional rather than national. The satraps on the borders, like the viceroys of the Ching, might even manage their own relations with neighboring countries.

The process of growing together of those semi-discrete parts of China was likely to take some time. Perhaps the Army would become so strong and so unified that it could impose an apparent unity and a degree of centralization upon the vast country. The regionalized structure was, however, likely to endure for some time. One of Mao Tse-tung's chief errors had been his attempt to impose complete centralization and total conformity upon a nation and a race which feel themselves one but cherish their differences above their similarities in times of crisis like the present one. China is almost too vast and too disparate to be ruled from a single center even by a government that possesses both popular support and the full paraphernalia of modern science for communicating its decisions and processing the information on which those decisions are based. It certainly cannot be ruled in an intrusive and totalitarian fashion from a single center by a government that possesses few of those devices. A federal pattern of rule was, therefore, likely to emerge in time from the confusion of regionalization.

In the long run the temper of the Chinese people would determine the shape of the Chinese nation. The greatest achievement of Mao Tse-tung was, ironically, the very factor that insured his downfall. That achievement was summed up in the injunction: "Let the masses manage the great affairs of the state!" Brought into the political turmoil by the Maoists, who believed the popular will would support them, the masses turned against the extremism of the Maoists. Since the masses decided the outcome of the struggle, the remaking of the nation would depend largely upon their wishes. They must be wooed with measures of which they approve, since they can no longer either be hypnotized by demagoguery or be compelled by coercion.

The question of the future of China, therefore, reverts to the problem of forging a new moral consensus that is accepted by most Chinese. The Cultural Revolution at once splintered Chinese society and created a new unity of opinion arising spontaneously from the people, rather than imposed from above. The Red Guards, the adolescent symbol of the Cultural Revolution, began by supporting the Maoists without reservation. But as they became aware of their own intellectual and physical powers, they tended to carve out new positions which the essentially authoritarian Maoist leadership found antipathetic. The Red Guards finally escaped from the Maoists' control. Despite the mindless enthusiasm and the vicious vandalism that characterized their early activities, the Red Guards did not withdraw from Chinese society, but became totally involved. Despite what the Maoists call their "indiscipline," the Red Guards were not alienated, but *engagé*. Although most Chinese would emerge from the turmoil desiring only a quiet life, both industrial workers and young farmers had realized that they could affect the course of "great affairs"—and their own lives—by their own actions. They would not be content to be quiescent in the future, particularly if they objected to the direction the nation was taking.

The so-called intellectuals were always a group apart in China, although, by the Chinese definition, they ranged from high-school graduates to professors with three doctorates. One of Mao's greatest failures was his inability either to arouse the enthusiasm of the intellectuals or to bring them to unwilling cooperation. The intellectuals, too, were united by their revulsion from Maoism. They had actually converted senior Party officials by their example and their stubborn advocacy of reasoned policies. Although the intellectuals were not likely to form a new center of power, the new rulers would depend upon their managerial and technical skills if they were to create a nation out of the debris of power.

A host of outside factors could, of course, vitally influence the future course of China. The Nationalists, for example, might seek to reassert their authority. They might possibly succeed in reasserting their authority over a number of coastal provinces. The Russians might tinker with the northern tier of provinces, since Moscow abhors a political vacuum. American intervention of some sort was most unlikely but not totally impossible. Given the state of critical equilibrium of the present mixture, insertion of such outside catalysts—even in minute quantities—could have profound effects.

Regardless, of the outside influences and the maneuvers of men seeking power, however, the new state of China would be shaped by the forces released by the Cultural Revolution—and, above all, by the will of the Chinese people. It would be excessively optimistic to declare definitely that China was coming to the adjustment with the outside world—and her own complex character—she had sought by so many different roads for the past century and a half. It would be excessively cynical not to recognize that she was moving in that direction.

Bibliography

I have listed below only English-language sources which are generally available to the reader—and only a few of them. Works cited in the text have not been listed again. The volume of English-language material on China, most of it highly specialized, has reached the point where the best one can do is to offer a few samples of useful books, each of which will lead the reader on to other works. The list is intended as a partial guide to reading, rather than a list of sources. I have depended largely on primary sources for my own material.

I have seen no point in listing the Chinese and Japanese sources employed, since they would be of value only to specialists, who are already aware of them. A large body of English-language material presenting the Communist regime's point of view is available from the Foreign Languages Press in Peking. I have, therefore, listed only a few samples of that genre. In addition, magazines like *China Reconstructs* and the weekly *Peking Review* regularly offer Peking's viewpoint and statements on internal and external matters.

One of the best running commentaries on Chinese affairs is the *China News Analysis,* published weekly in Hong Kong under the editorship of Louis Ladany, S.J. Translations of the Chinese press published by the American Consulate-General in Hong Kong are also of great value.

Among the most useful Chinese periodicals employed were: *The Peking People's Daily,* the organ of the Central Committee of the Chinese Communist Party; *Red Flag,* a fortnightly theoretical journal; and *China Youth,* a monthly directed to members of the Youth Corps. Specialized journals and the provincial press, available irregularly, were also of much value, as were a variety of books in Chinese published by the regime.

The most significant portion of the reporting on affairs of the last five years, however, has come from hundreds of interviews with refugees, businessmen, diplomats, and others who have lived in different parts of China during the period. In addition, a constant flow of information came from the letters received by inhabitants of Hong Kong from relations living on the mainland.

It would be impossible to list the scores of colleagues, specialists, and diplomats who have given me their counsel and assistance in the preparation of this book. I am, however, particularly indebted to Howard L. Boorman of Vanderbilt University and to Joseph Agassi of Boston University for reading the manuscript and making invaluable suggestions for changes which either corrected errors or enhanced clarity. Robert A. Burton, then of the American Universities' Field Staff and now of the University of Kansas, was generous enough to make available to me the manuscript of Chang Kuo-tao's memoirs, the publication of which will be a major contribution to the understanding of modern China. Beyond that, I am deeply grateful to Mr. Burton for his constant encouragement and for the stimulating opinions he has, over the years, offered out of his own great knowledge. Sydney Liu, former editor of the *New Life Evening Post* and later correspondent in Hong Kong for the *Hindustan Times* and *Newsweek,* was always ready with his unique insights, with unstinting assistance, and with profoundly helpful guidance. This note may, perhaps, serve as a small installment on a debt which cannot really be repaid.

ANONYMOUS, *Ten Glorious Years,* 368 pp., Peking: Foreign Languages Press, 1960.

BARNETT, A. DOAK, *Communist China and Asia,* 574 pp., New York: Harper & Row, 1960.

BOORMAN, HOWARD L., *et al.*, *Moscow-Peking Axis*, 231 pp. New York: Harper & Row, 1957.

BRANDT, CONRAD, *et al.*, *A Documentary History of Chinese Communism*, 552 pp., London: George Allen and Unwin, 1953.

BRANDT, CONRAD, *Stalin's Failure in China 1924–27*, 226 pp., London: Oxford University Press, 1958.

CH'IEN, TUAN-SHENG, *The Government and Politics of China*, 526 pp., Cambridge, Mass.: Harvard University Press, 1950.

DEPARTMENT OF STATE, *United States Relations with China*, 1054 pp., Washington, D.C.: Department of State Publications, 1949.

ELEGANT, ROBERT S., *China's Red Masters*, 264 pp., New York: Twayne Publishers, 1951.

———— *The Dragon's Seed*, 319 pp., New York: St. Martin's Press, 1959.

EPSTEIN, ISRAEL, *From Opium War to Liberation*, 146 pp., Peking: New World Press, 1956.

FAURE, EDGAR, *The Serpent and the Tortoise*, 205 pp., New York: St. Martin's Press, 1958.

FEIS, HERBERT, *The China Tangle*, 445 pp., Princeton, N. J.: Princeton University Press, 1953.

FITZGERALD, C. P., *Revolution in China*, 299 pp., London: The Cresset Press, 1952.

FLEMING, PETER, *The Siege at Peking*, 273 pp., London: Rupert Hart-Davis, 1959.

FUNG, YU-LAN, *A History of Chinese Philosophy*, Derk Bodde, trans.; Vol. I, 454 pp., Peiping: Henri Vetch, 1937; Vol. II, 783 pp., Princeton, N. J.: Princeton University Press, 1960.

———— *The Spirit of Chinese Philosophy*, 224 pp., London: Kegan Paul, 1947.

HSIA, C. T., *A History of Modern Chinese Fiction 1917–1957*, 662 pp., New Haven, Conn.: Yale University Press, 1961.

HSU, FRANCIS L. K., *Under the Ancestors' Shadow*, 317 pp., New York: Columbia University Press, 1948.

HU, CHANG-TU, *China, Its People, Its Society, Its Culture*, 611 pp., New Haven, Conn.: HRAF Press, 1960.

ISAACS, HAROLD R., *The Tragedy of the Chinese Revolution*, 382 pp., Stanford, Calif.: Stanford University Press, 1951.

KIANG, WEN-HAN, *The Chinese Student Movement*, 176 pp., New York: King's Crown Press, 1948.

LANDON, PERCIVAL, *Lhasa* (2 vols.), London: Hunt and Blachett, 1905.

LEVENSON, JOSEPH R., *Liang Ch'i-ch'ao and the Mind of Modern China*, 265 pp., London: Thames and Hudson, 1953.

LIN, MOUSHENG, *Men and Ideas*, 256 pp., New York: The John Day Co., 1942.

LINDSAY, MICHAEL, *China and the Cold War*, 283 pp., Melbourne: Melbourne University Press, 1953.

LU HSUN, *A Brief History of Chinese Fiction*, 462 pp., Peking: Foreign Languages Press, 1959.

MARCUSE, JACQUES, *The Peking Papers*, 351 pp., New York: Dutton, 1967.

MAO, TSE-TUNG, *Selected Works*, Vols. I–V, London: Lawrence and Wishart. (In Chinese, same works in 4 volumes.)

MARX, KARL, *Marx on China 1853–1960*, 98 pp., London: Lawrence and Wishart, 1951.

NORTH, ROBERT C., *Moscow and Chinese Communists*, 306 pp., Stanford, Calif.: Stanford University Press, 1953.

PAVLOV, I. P., *Selected Works*, 653 pp., Moscow: Foreign Languages Publishing House, 1955.

ROSTOW, W. W., *et al.*, *The Prospects for Communist China*, 376 pp., New York: John Wiley, 1954.

SCHRAM, STUART, *Mao Tse-tung*, 351 pp., London: Penguin, 1967.

SHIH, VINCENT Y. C., *The Taiping Ideology*, 553 pp., Seattle: University of Washington Press, 1967.

SMITH, ARTHUR H., *Chinese Characteristics*, 342 pp., New York: Fleming H. Revell Company, 1894.

SNOW, EDGAR, *Red Star Over China*, 528 pp., New York: Random House, 1938.

THOMSON, LAWRENCE G. (trans.), *Ta T'ung Shu, The One-World Philosophy of K'ang Yu-wei*, 300 pp., London: George Allen and Unwin, 1958.

TING, YI, *A Short History of Modern Chinese Literature*, 310 pp. Peking: Foreign Languages Press, 1959.

WALEY, ARTHUR, *The Opium War Through Chinese Eyes*, 257 pp., London: George Allen & Unwin, 1958.

WHITE, T. H. & JACOBY, A., *Thunder Out of China,* 304 pp., London: Victor Gollancz, 1947.

WHITING, ALLEN S., *Soviet Policies in China 1917–1924,* 348 pp., New York: Columbia University Press, 1954.

WU, YUAN-LI, *An Economic Survey of Communist China,* 365 pp., London: Constable, 1956.

YANG, C. K., *A Chinese Village in Early Communist Transition,* 284 pp., Cambridge, Mass.: Technology Press, 1959.

—————— *The Chinese Family in the Communist Revolution,* 246 pp., Cambridge, Mass.: Technology Press, 1959.

INDEX

Index

Abahai, 44

Academia Sinica, 309, 362

Africa, 168, 397, 401, 404, 411, 411n.

Afro-Asian Conference (Bandung), 165

Agrarian Reform Law, 277, 279

Agriculture, 217, 333; crop failures, 348–351; expansion of, 57, 57n., 58

Aid Korea-Resist America Movement, 164

Albania, 172, 396, 397, 413

Algeria, 404

All-China Labor Federation, 147

All-China Union of Writers, 374

Alliance of the Working Class and the Peasantry, 395

All Men Are Brothers (Buck), 204

Amherst, Lord, 70, 75

Analects (Confucius), 38, 185–192

Ancestors, reverence for, 15, 151, 190, 331, 385

Anti-despot Campaign, 278–279

Aristotle, 184, 406

Army: as basis of Mao's power, 246–247; Long March, 159–161; Red (Chinese), 156; Righteous Uprising of, 430; Support withdrawn from Mao, 431–433; threat of Junta, 354–356; *see also* People's Liberation Army

Arrow incident, 76

Arts, 373–378

Asia, 397, 401, 404, 411, 411n.

Association of Righteous Harmony, 101; *see also* Boxers

Atomic testing, moratorium on, 398

Australia, 348

Behavior, individualism, 180, 180n.

Belgium-China trade, 76

Bhutan, 54, 104

Birth Control Campaign, 275, 289–292

Boorman, Howard L., 359–360

Borodin, Michael, 134n., 147, 150

Boxers, 101, 101n., 102, 107; indemnity, 141; Peking, 77–78

"Brainwashing," 293, 296; *see also* "Thought Reform"

Bramah, Ernest, *Kai Lung*, 67

Brook Farm, 179

Bucharest Conference, 394

Buddhism, 102, 193, 373; Mahayana, 194

Burma, 53, 77, 168; and China, 94, 411, 413; and U.S., 429

Burton, Robert A., 105n.

Bygor, 10, 56

Cadres, 12, 12n., 13, 270, 270n., 271ff., 284ff., 299, 301, 321ff., 328–329, 340, 344

Cambodia, 54, 168

Campaigns, 274ff., 35–52; *see also under* CPC

Canada, 348

Canton, 32–33, 60, 61; behavior, 75, 76; Commune, 152; Five-Antis Campaign, 286–288; judges, 266–267; *Nanfang Daily*, 232; Sun Yat-sen government, 119

Capitalism, Mao on, 206

Capitalists, 282ff.

Cathay: name, 29, 30, 34, 39; wealth, 73; *see also* China

Catherine the Great, 255

Catholic missionaries, 62, 73; Communist action against, 378–379, 380–381

Central China Normal College, 358

Central Committee, 154, 155ff., 230, 231, 237, 242, 337, 338ff.

Central Kingdom, 193–194

Chang Chih-tung, 88, 89–90

Chang Kuo-tao, 105, 106–107, 128n., 130, 135, 136, 136n., 137, 137n., 140, 141, 158, 160–161, 208n., 237

Cheng Cheng-kung (Koxinga), 48–49

Cheng Feng Movement, 207, 207n., 237

Cheng Ming, 207

Chengtu-Lhasa Railroad, 103–104

Chen Kuang, 224

Chennault, Clare, 162

Chen Po-ta, 424

Chen Tu-hsiu, 122–125, 128, 131–133, 136, 136n., 137n., 139, 140, 144ff., 152, 156

Chen Yi, 141, 234–236, 246, 285, 427

Chen Yuan, 368–369

Chiang Ching, *see* Madame Mao Tse-tung

Chiang Hsueh Hui (Reform Club), 97

Chiang Kai-shek, 147, 148–151, 156, 159, 161–163, 183, 217, 248,

256, 383, 409, 411, 455; Comintern, 147; defeat, 163; exile, 409; Japanese, 161–162; kidnapping, 162; and Mao, 158–159; Northern Expedition, 148–150; Whampoa Military Academy, 147–148

Chiaotso Mining College, 369

Chien Lung, 50, 52, 56, 69, 72, 87, 113, 345, 384

China: Age of Reason, 72; affluence of Empire, 56, 73; characters, 15, 16; Civil Service Examination System, 36, 37, 43, 96, 102, 106, 109, 116, 124, 185, 186, 351; Communist Party (*see* CPC); crop failures, 348–351; economy, 344–354; emigration, 78; empirical research, 87; expansion, 53–54; famine, 66–67; future of, 443–459; intellectuals, 179–182, 294–297, 307–309, 313–314, 315, 372ff.; Japanese regime, 130–131; malnutrition, 344–348; patriotism, modern, 120; population, 19, 54, 55; post-Revolution, 119ff.; reformers, 93–101; revolution, *see* Sun Yat-sen; spheres of influence, 78–79; social order, 84; strikes, 429, 430; superiority, feeling of, 70, 71, 73, 109, 114, 116; tradition, 175–176; West, 69, 70, 71–72, 75–77, 81–83, 90–91, 95, 121; World War I, 128–129; World War II, 196, 402; *see also* Chinese People; People's Republic of China; Ming Dynasty

Chin Dynasty, 40, 385, 444, 445, 452

Chinese People: behavior, 68–71; character, 195; characteristics, 195; Communists, understanding of, 351–352; intellect, obsession with, 180, 182; language, 121, 122n., 182, 182n.; religion: attacks on, 378–381, tolerance of, 14; Talmudic mind, parallel, 182

Chinese Revolutionary Party, *see* Kuomintang

Ching Dynasty, 38, 44, 53, 55, 57–58, 60, 66, 79–80, 87ff., 99, 111, 113–114, 188, 445, 446; Civil Service Examination System, abandonment of, 185–186; *Tsung-li Yamen*, 90, 90n.

Chou En-lai, 141, 164, 234, 382, 396, 404; education system, 370; Northern Expedition, 148–150; Premier, 427, 428; relations with Soviets, 157–159; State Affairs Council, 258, 432; underdeveloped countries, 168–169; urban bourgeoisie, 284; Whampoa Military Academy, 147–148

Chou Li-fan, 249, 350

Christ, 102, 183, 184

Christianity: in China, 22, 31–33, 61, 80, 120; Hung Hsiu-chuan, 61, 63, 64; Peking war against, 378–381

Chu-Mao Army, expansion, 153–154

Chungking, urban communes, 340–342

Chung-kuo Ko-ming-tang, 109, 109n.

Chung Tsai Ling incident, 271–274

Churchill, Winston, comparison with Mao, 213–214

Chu Teh, 151–152, 153–154, 158, 160, 214, 234, 247, 259, 431

Civil Service Examination System, 36, 36n., 37, 37n., 93, 96, 102, 106, 109, 116, 124, 185, 186, 192, 351

Co-hong, 76, 78

Collectivization, 281–282, 344–345

Columbia University, 299

Columbus, Christopher, 29

Comintern: Chinese Marxist movement, 141; CPC, 133, 135, 137, 142, 152, 156–158; KMT, 142, 145, 147–148, 150; *see* CPC

Communalization, *see* Communes

Communes, People's; creation, 247; example, 321–325; failure, 335–339; "foreign cadres," 322; Great Peace and Prosperity Commune, 321–323, 324, 325; individualism,

conflict with, 325–327; logic of, 329–330; People's Militia, 325, 333–334; ration tickets, 347; reaction to, 322–323; resistance, 327–328; Sputnik Commune, 328; urban, 16, 339, 340, 342–343; villages, 319–323

Communism: Catholic Church, 379–381; Confucianism parallels, 196–197; individualism, conflict with, 325–327; national interests, 384–387

Communist bloc: -Mao, 383; uncommitted nations, 397

Communist China, *see* CPC; People's Republic of China

Communist Party of China, *see* CPC

Confucianism: ancestor worship, 15, 190; code of behavior, 39, 43, 44; disapproval of trade, 70; Doctrine of Rectification of Names, 192; downfall, 80, 102; ethos, 48, 49, 66; family, 13, 40, 187, 187n.; government, 42–43; ideology, 188, 193; intellectual basis, 191–192; life of official man, 188; and Mao, 196, 198; morality, 186, 188; Plato, 189; pragmatism, 450; shaping public character, 195; system, 95; Taoist, school of, 185, 192; Utopia, 180–181, 197–198

Confucius: *The Analects*, 38, 185–192; Golden Age, 38, 45, 138, 185, 194; *The Great Learning*, 295n.; ideal, 184–186, 204; influence, 183; and Marx accord, 317; mystique, 177–198; life of, 184–191; superior individual, defined, 40; time of, 180

Constitution, People's, 261–265

Cooke, C. Wingrove, 70–71

"Corrective labor," 351

Couéism, 333

Courts, People's, 264–267

CPC (Communist Party of China): Army, break with, 245–246; birth

CPC (cont.)
of, 96, 117, 133, 134–137, 145;
campaigns, 274ff., 350–352; *Cheng
Feng* Movement, 207, 207n., 237;
Central Committee, 154, 155ff.,
230, 231, 237, 242, 337, 338ff.;
chronology (1949–1968), 163–
173; Comintern, 141, 142, 133–
137, 145, 147–148, 152, 156–159;
constitution, 136; crises, 335–341;
factions, 155–156; Fifth Party
Conference, 148; First Party Conference, 135, 407; Five Year Plan,
360; judiciary, 265–269; junta,
threat of, 454–456; and KMT, 142,
146, 148, 150, 162; loans, from
Russia, 391–392; Long March,
159–161, 235, 236; Marxism, 138,
407–409; membership, 242; Municipal Committee (Shanghai),
426; nuclear development, 172,
249; problems, 231–232; Red
Guards, 171, 224, 417–427, 430,
432, 444, 457ff.; "Russian faction,"
156–157; Soviet Union, relations
with, 387–401; structure, 242–244;
"thought reform," 292–314, 408;
tribunals, 209, 275; 21st Congress,
393; 22nd Congress, 396; Youth
League, 262, 321; *see also* Communes; People's Republic of China
Cuba, 348
Cushing, Richard Cardinal, 31n.
Czechoslovakia, 427

Dalai Lama, 165, 166
Darwin, Charles, 195, 295n., *On the
Origin of Species*, 95
Dialectical materialism, Pavlov and,
309–310
Dream of the Red Chamber, The,
373
Dynasties, morality of, 59–61

East German Party Conference
(1963), 397

Eberhard, Wolfram, 43
Economy, 344–354
Education: academic system destroyed, 355–358; campaigns, 35–
52; dichotomy, 360, 361; Great
Leap Forward, 366, 367; Half-
Work Half-Study Program, 361,
363–367; psychological basis, 355–
356; "Red before Expert" principle, 361; 2nd Five Year Plan, 360;
students, 357–360, 371; reactions,
368–370; teachers, 311–314, 356–
358, 360–361
Ehih, Vincent Y.C., 62n.
Eisenhower, Dwight D., 203, 394
Empress Dowager, 93, 99–101, 102,
111
Engels, Friedrich, 138, 309, 401,
407; population, 292
Euclid, 29
Europe, 68–70; *Chinoiserie* craze,
36n.–37n.
Everywhere the Red Flag Flutters,
330–331
Evolution and Ethics (Huxley), 95

Family: communes, 338; Confucian-
ism, 187, 187n.; destruction of,
11–13; Mao, 324; model, 13; se-
curity, 191; traditional, 19, 20
Farmers, Communes and, 319
Feng Pai-chu, 239–240
Feng Shui, 106, 106n.
Feng Yu-hsiang, 130n., 144
Feudalism, 37
Five-Antis Campaign, 275
Flying Great Leap Forward, *see un-
der* Great Leap Forward
Ford, Henry, 117
Foreigners, attitude towards, 81–88
Foreign relations, 383–415
Formosa, 48, 77, 94, 306, 335, 346,
346n., 383, 386, 388, 409
France: Chen in, 124; and China,
94; concessions, 76–77; Tientsin
Massacre, 81–83, 85

Fung Yu-lan, 181n., 190, 369
Future, of China, 443–458

Geneva Conference (1954), 164
Genghis Khan, 66, 417
George III, King of England, 74
Germany, concessions to, 77
Gordon, Charles George, 64, 88
Government, Communist pattern of, 193–217
Great Britain: and China, 64, 65, 68, 73, 74–75, 76; Opium War, 75–76; Soviet Union, 427
Great Commonwealth, 179, 181, 197–198
Great Constitutional Dynasty, 118
Great Depression, The, 154–155
Great Leap Forward, 158, 166, 168, 173, 331, 345, 353, 360, 374, 390, 421, 422, 424; admission of error in, 372; failure of, 345, 346; Flying, 331–332, 337, 359
Great Learning, The (Confucius), 295n.
Great Proletariat Cultural Revolution, 36n., 171, 196–197, 297, 339, 372, 418ff., 428–442, 447, 452; as climax of China, 438–442; stages of, 435–442
Great Wall, 40, 45, 48, 385
Gregory XIII, Pope, 31
Guerrillas, handbook for, 402–403

"Halls of Happiness," 303, 319, 325
Halls of Learning, 40
Hammarskjöld, Dag, 165
Han Chun, 223
Han Dynasty, 38–39, 185, 211, 385, 444, 452; Civil Service Examination System, 39–40
Han Fei-Tzu, 212
Hangchow, 5, 56
Hankow, city, 112; Middle School, 359
Han Yu, 194
Hitler, Adolf, 131, 256, 444

Ho Chao-ting, 271–274
Ho Chi-minh, 448
Ho Lung, 245
Honan Revolt, 241
Hong Kong: Great Britain, 75–76, 136n.; missionaries, 32; Queens College, 107
Hoshiht'ai, 70
Hsiaoching, 32
Hsiao Shu, 224
Hsien Feng, 99
Hsuan Tung, 113, 113n.
Hsun Tzu, 181, 189
Hunan Daily, 342
Hundred Flowers Movement, 165, 264, 313–314, 332, 345, 357, 358
Hungarian Revolt, 202
Hung Hsiu-chuan, 60–65, 66; visions, 63–64, 63n.; see also Tien Wang
Hung Liang-chi, 58
Hun Wan-chun, 376
Hu Shih, 122, 126–127, 132, 307–308
Huxley, Julian, Evolution and Ethics, 95

India: attacks on China, 167–168, 248, 411; birth control, 290; opium, 75; Soviet Union, 385
Individualism, Communism conflict with, 325–327, 328; loss of, 15–16
Indo-China, 77, 94, 164
Indonesia, 411ff., 427
Intellectuals, 179–182, 274–297, 307–309, 313–314, 315, 372ff., 458
I-wu (Barbarian affairs), 97

James, Henry, 117
Jao Shu-shih, 236
Japan: anti-, war, 242; -China, 128–130; Communist Party, 404; concessions, 77; conflict, 91–92; Formosa, 94; Korea, 94; Meiji Restoration, 84, 100, 121; Sino-Japa-

Japan (cont.)
nese War, 77, 84ff.; "Twenty-one Demands," 129, 131
Jesuits: in China, 22, 30, 31–33, 34, 66; expulsion from, 73, 379; Confucianism, 39, 41, 44; Manchu Emperors, 87; Western ideas, spreading, 33, 41
Jews, parallel with Chinese mind, 182–183
Joffe, Adolf, 134n., 146
Judiciary, 265–269
Julius Caesar, 184, 203
Junta, threat of, 454–456

Kai Lung, 67
Kang Hsi, 48, 49–50, 52ff., 85, 292
Kang Yu-wei, 97–98, 99, 100ff., 179, 181, 197, 198, 446
Kao Kang, 236
Karakhan, Leo, 141
Kashmir, 53
Khampas, 160
Khrushchev, Nikita, 166, 168, 194, 200–203, 385–387, 388–389, 392, 394, 396–397, 409, 412
Kia King, 70
Kiangsi Soviet Area, 154, 159, 234, 235
KMT, *see* Kuomintang
Korea, 53, 72, 77, 92, 94, 302; Tong Hak Society, 92
Korean War, 163, 164, 245, 248, 283–284, 306, 383, 390, 409, 409n.
Kowloon, 77
Kowtow, 70
Koxinga, *see* Cheng Cheng-kung
Kuang Hsu, 99, 100, 101, 102
Kung Fu-tze, 183, *see* Confucius
Kuomintang (KMT), 110, 117n., 118, 119, 130, 142, 145–146, 147ff., 161ff., 164, 235, 242, 250, 253, 264, 284, 298, 313, 327, 359, 373, 374, 384
Ku Ta-tsun, 239, 240
Kwan Yin, 195

Lam, Herbert, 348–349, 350, 351–352
Land Reform Movement, 274, 275–282, 284, 289; Agrarian Reform Law (1950), 277, 279; Anti-despot Campaign, 278–279
Language, 121–122, 182, 182n., 369
Laos, 396, 414
Lao Shaw, *Rickshaw Boy,* 67, 375
Latin America, 130n., 397, 401, 411, 411n.
Latourette, Kenneth Scott, 35n., 144
Law courts, 255, 266–269
Lee Hsin-min, 363–366
Lee Teh-ming, 322–327
Legalist School, of political philosophy, 211–213
Legal system, 264–266
Lenin, N., 141, 148, 260, 309, 383, 395, 401, 407
Li, 177–178, 185, 212
Li, Bishop, 379
Liang Chi-chao, 96ff., 109–110, 114, 122ff., 197, 295n., 306
Liang Shu-ming, 307–308
Liberation Daily, 252
Li Chi, 177, 190, 197–198
Lifton, Dr. Robert J., 299–304; *Thought Reform and the Psychology of Totalism,* 300
Li Li-san, 154–157, 157n., 214, 234–235
Lincoln, Abraham, 203
Lin Piao, 152, 169, 170, 171, 203, 242n., 243ff., 252, 253, 330, 335, 339, 419, 424, 426, 428, 430ff., 454
Lin Shu, 95
Li Ssu, 212, 212n.
Li Ta, 136, 136n.
Li Ta-chao, 128, 131, 147
Literacy: relationship of birth control to, 290, 290n., 291
Literary Leap Forward, 332
Literature: New Movement, 125ff., 298; renaissance of, 373–378

Li Tzu-cheng, 45–47, 60, 86

Liu, Judge, 267–269

Liu Shao-chi, 141, 156, 166, 171, 214, 232–234, 236, 257–258, 309, 369, 382, 387, 418, 424, 433, 453

Li Yuan-hung, 112, 119, 144

Lo Jui-ching, 247, 247n., 253

Lolos, 160

Long March, 159–161, 235, 236

Low, F.F., 82–83

Loyang Agriculture Machinery Institute, 369

Lu Ting-yi, 356, 356n., 360, 361–362, 368, 378, 405, 405n.

Macao, 22, 77

Macartney, Lord, 69, 74, 78, 113

Malnutrition, 344–348

Manchu Dynasty, 50–51, 79–80, 87, 105, 107, 108, 385, 456

Manchuria, 44, 77, 236

Manchurian Candidate, The (Richard Condon), 293

Manchus, 44, 48, 49; bannermen, 59; Mings, 59; Mukden, 44; Opium War, 76; overthrow of, 80; rule, 44ff.; *see also* Ching Dynasty

Mao Jen-shen, 214, 215

Mao Tse-tung: academic system, destroyed, 355–358; adulation, 199–200, 201; aims, 18–21, 22, 172; *All the Reactionaries Are Paper Tigers*, 330; alter ego, 336 (*see* Liu Shao-chi); army, 246–247, 253–255, 431–433; ascendance, 58–60; biographer, 204n.; brothers, 215–217; character, 206–207; childhood, 215–217; compared to Winston Churchill, 213–214; Community Party, 137; Confucianism, 43n.-44n., 196–197; "creative philosophy," 227; cult of, 201–202; differences with Khrushchev, 199–201; education of, 204–206; errors, 381ff.; dictatorship,

255–256; failure, 423, 450–452, 457; father, *see* Mao Jen-sheng; ideological defeat, 171–173; infallibility, conviction of, 203–206; "Internal Contradictions," thesis, 165–166; Land reform, 276–278, 280 (*see also* Land Reform Movement); literary reputation, 50; Marxism-Leninism, 206–208; materialism, disturbed by, 423–425; military doctrines, 334–335; Nationalists, 161–163; opponents, attacks on, 447; peasants, 137, 218–219; People's Communes, 198, 206, 209, 317–319, 322; "people's wars," 173, 249, 440, 446; "Quotations," 419; resignation, 335–337; rural faction, 155, 157, 159; Russia, defiance of, 167, 383–384, 386–388; "Russian Faction," 235–236; *Thesis on Contradiction*, 261; thought, 294–295, 354, 440, 442, 452, 455; tragedy of, 206–210; Utopia, 180, 181, 206, 208, 343; withdrawal, 439–442; world, in today's, 219–221; Yalu, swimming, 203

Mao Tse-tung, Madame, 425, 428

Maring, 134, 134n., 135

Marshall, George C., 163

Marx, Karl, 33, 117, 138, 139, 209, 309, 310, 320, 401, 407, 439–440

Marxism-Leninism, 21, 65, 201, 203, 206–208, 408, 449

Matsu, 317, 327

May Fourth Movement, 132, 312

"Memorial," 89, 89n.

Mencius, 181

Middle East, opium, 75

Mif, Pavel, 157

Ming Dynasty, 33, 35–37, 50, 54ff., 60, 62n., 64, 69, 87; Civil Service Examination System, 36n.-37n.; Emperors, 41; -Europe, contrast, 36–37; government, 37–40; population, 54; Sacred Edict, 50

Missionaries: Catholic, 62, 73, 81; expulsion, 378–381; Protestant, 95–96; Tientsin Massacre, 81–83, 85; trial of Canadian Sisters of Mercy, 33

Mohammed Ali, 245

Mohism, 210–211

Mongol Empire, 44, 85, 114–115, 385

Monlin, Dr. Chiang, 290n.

Montgomery, Viscount, 113

Morrison, Robert, 62, 63, 96

Moscow, Declaration of (1957), 394–395

Mo Tzu, 210, 211

Mystique: Mao, 199–200; nature of man (Confucianism), 177–198

Nanchang Rising (1927), 152, 153, 234

Nanking, 33, 64–65; Treaty of, 75

National Defense Council, 257

"National Humiliation Treaty," see Shimonoseki, Treaty of

Nationalism, see Chiang Kai-shek; KMT; Sun Yat-sen

National Liberation Front, 448

National People's Congress, 256–258; Standing Committee, 259

National People's Party, see Kuomintang

Nehru, Jawaharlal, 164

Nepal, 53, 104

Nerchinsk, Treaty of, 73

Netherlands, -China trade, 73, 75

New Literature Movement, see under Literature

New Youth, 125, 126–128

Noreay, China trade, 76

North China Revolutionary University, 300, 307

North Korea, 413

North Vietnam, 248, 413, 448, 449

Northern Expedition, 148–149

Nuclear development, 249, 250; H-bomb, 172, 249

Nurhachi, 44, 48, 53

Okuma, Shigenobu, 129

On the Origin of Species (Darwin), 95

Opium War, 75–76; first, 84, 92; second, 82, 84, 85

Outer Mongolia, 396, 413

Owens, Robert, 179

Pan Fu-sheng, 240–241

Paris Commune (1871), 13, 140n., 172, 209, 439–440

Patriotic Catholics Association, 378

Pavlov, I. P., 24, 294, 309–311, 356–357; research committee, 309

Peaceful coexistence, 400, 409; panch sheel, 164

Peking: allied capture (1860), 86; Boxers, 77–78; Committee, 420, 421; modern, 225–226; regime (see CPC); Ricci in, 33–35; Treaty of, 77; see also People's Republic of China

Peking-Moscow quarrel, see Sino-Soviet quarrel

Peking Normal School, 361, 368

Peking Opera, 5

Peking University, 47, 69, 101, 101n., 128, 130, 217, 309, 310, 358, 369, 386, 421; May Fourth Incident, 132; Russians, 383, 386

Peng Chen, 170, 420, 439

Peng Jui-ching, 224

Peng Teh-huai, 164, 166, 214, 246, 339

People's Air Force, 247, 435

People's Communes, see Communes, People's

People's Daily, 291, 333, 341, 358, 375

People's Liberation Army (PLA), 5, 156, 170, 171, 176, 217, 243, 244, 246ff., 250–254, 334, 402, 431–433, 435–437, 454

People's Militia, 325, 333–335;

Everyone a Soldier Movement, 333-334

People's Navy, 248

People's Republic of China: Chinese Peoples Political Consultative Council, 257; constitution, 261-265; daily life, 3-13; "democratic centralism," 260; established, 163; government, 260-261; judiciary, 264-267; National Defense Council, 257; National Peoples Congress, 242, 257, 258-259; State Affairs Council, 258; superiority, 20-21, 109; Supreme State Conference, 257

Pescadores, Japan and, 94

Philosopher's Stone, 84-85, 90, 125, 138, 321

Plato, 36, 39, 189

Pliny, 406

Political philosophy: Legalist School, 211-213; Mohism, 210-211; *wu wei*, 194, 353. *See* Confucian ethos; Mao

Polo, Marco, 29, 30, 34

Population, 19, 54, 55, 55n.; *see also* Birth Control Campaign

Portugal, 31, 33; -China trade, 73; concessions, 77

Potemkin, Count, 255

Pravda, 398

Private enterprise, 282ff.

Production: failures in, 336-337; quotas, 331

Propaganda, 332-333, 373-377

Protestant missionaries, 95-96

Purges: *Cheng feng*, 237; Maoist, 261; "persuasion corps," 288; technicians, 330; *see* Education, People's Liberation Army

Pu-yi, Henry, 113; *see* Hsuan Tung

Quemoy, 166, 248, 317, 327

Queues, 110

Railways, nationalization plan, 111

Ration tickets, 347

Rebel Emperor, The (Anderson), 62n.

Rectification Campaign, 284-285, 306-308, 343

Rectification of Names, Doctrine of, 192

Red China, *see* Peoples Republic of China; CPC

Red Flag, 318, 333, 402, 403, 404

Red Guards, 17, 171, 224, 417, 419ff., 425-427, 430, 432, 444, 457, 458; embassies attacked, 427; Great Character Posters, 418; motto, 224; terrorism, 425

Religion, 14, 378-381, 451; *see also* Confucianism

Republic of China, 109-130, 123ff., 142ff.

Revolution, *see* Chiang Kai-shek; Kuomintang; Mao; Sun Yat-sen

"Revolutionary University," 299-301

Ricci, Matteo, 7, 9, 32-36, 41ff., 53, 55, 69, 173-174

Rickshaw Boy (Lao Shaw), 67, 375

Roberts, Rev. Issachar, 63

Romance of the Three Kingdoms, 204

Roumania, 399

Roy, M.N., 151

Russell, Bertrand, 69

Russia, 76, 77, 94; *see also* Soviet Union

Sakhalin Island, 53, 72

San Min Chu Yi (Three People's Principals), 114

Sargant, William, 297, 304

Scarlet Guards, 430

Schaal, Adam, 85

Sebastian, King, 31

Shanghai: bourgeoisie, 283-285; Catholic stronghold, 378; -Hangchow Railway, 135; Kiangnan Arsenal, 90, 96; rising, 149-150; urban commune, committee, 426

Shang Yang, Lord, 210, 211, 212

Shen Nung, 24

Shih Huang, Ti, 37

Shimonoseki, Treaty of, 77, 94, 96

Shun Chi, 48, 53

Siao San, 216

Siao-yu, 204n.

Siberia, 54

Sikkim, 54, 104

Sinkiang (Chinese Turkestan), 49, 53–54, 77

Sino-Japanese War, 109, 161–162

Sino-Soviet quarrel, 168, 314, 384, 385–401

Sino-Soviet Treaty of Friendship and Mutual Defense, 163

Sneevliet, Hendricus, *see* Maring

Socialist Youth League, 133

Socrates, 38, 39

Southeast Asia: China in, 78, 78n., 385, 394, 412; official corruption, 188; U.S. policy, 412–413

South Vietnam, 167, 169, 412, 413, 448; *see also* Vietnam

Soviet Union, 72, 73, 76, 141, 386, 387–401, 447; *see also* Comintern

Stalin, Josef, 150–151, 200, 202, 203, 236, 309, 386, 387, 390, 397

State Affairs Council, 258, 432

Stillwell, Joseph, 162

Strikes, 429–430

Sui Dynasty, 38, 444

Sung Dynasty, 38, 385

Sun Soong Ching-ling, 110

Sun Yat-sen, 103–104, 107, 108, 109–120, 123ff., 130, 130n., 142ff.; *see also* Tung Men Hui

Sun Yat-sen, Madame, 401

Sun Yat-sen University, 286, 316, 358

Supreme State Conference, 257

Sweden, -China trade, 76

Swift, Jonathan, 95

Ta Ching, 50, 52

Tagore, Rabindranath, 375

Taiping Empire, 63–66; *see also* Hung Hsiu-chuan

Taiping Rebellion (1851), 54, 63, 68, 94, 183, 215

Taiwan, 77, 346, 346n.; Krushchev, 385–386; U.S. position, 409; *see also* Formosa

Taku Forts, 76–77

Tamerlane, 66

Ta Ming, 50

Tang Dynasty, 38, 445

Tao-chu, 424, 428

Taoists, 193, 194–195

Ta Tung, 179, 446

Teachers, 355–359; shortage, 360–361; Socialist Education Campaign, 362–367

Technical Innovations Movement, 352

Teng Hsio-ping, 333, 382, 398, 433

Teng Tze-hui, 267

Thailand, 54

Theatre, 377

"Thought Reform," 293–314, 408; failure, 297; Rectification Campaign, 306–308

Thought Reform . . . (Lifton), 299–304

Three-Antis Campaign, 164

Tibet, 49, 103, 104, 163–166, 246

Tien An Men (Gate of Heavenly Peace), 47, 225

Tientsin: massacre, 81–83, 85; Treaty of, 77

Tien Wang, revolution, 60–61

Ting tax, 54

Tong Hak (Korean secret society), 92

Treaty ports, 75–78, 120

Trotsky, Leon, 105, 155

Tsao Kun, 119

Tsinghua University, 357

Tsung Chen, 46, 47

Tsung-li Yamen, 90, 90n.

Tsunyi Conference, 235, 336

Tuan Ch-jui, 119, 129–130, 143

Tuchun (warlord) government, 119
Tung Meng Hui, 110, 111, 125
Tung Pi-you, 288
Turkestan, see Sinkiang
Tzu Hsi (Yehonala), see Empress Dowager

Uighur tribes, 385
Underdeveloped nations, 168–169
United Arab Republic, 391
United States (U.S.): attitude towards China, 384, 409, 410, 449; concessions, 76–77; Civil Service Examination System, 37n.; Nationalist, 409, 411; Open Door Policy, 79, 129; Southeast Asia, 448; stock market crash, 154; U-2 incident, 395, 404; Vietnam, 412–413, 449, 458
Utopias: Anglo-Saxon, 179; Chinese, 179ff.; Communist, 139, 140, 140n.; Confucian, 180, 194; Great Commonwealth, 179, 197–198; longing for, 298; Mao, 180, 181, 186, 206, 208, 343; Russian views on, 387–389; West, 179–180

Vanderbilt University, 356
Vatican, 73, 378, 379–381
Versailles, 131, 139
Viet Cong, 169, 173, 413–414; Spring offensive (1968), 156n., 173
Viet Minh, 166, 167
Vietnam, 344, 395, 409, 412, 448, 449, 458; see also North Vietnam, South Vietnam

Wang Ching-wei, 148, 151
Wang Mang, 181
Wang Ming, 156, 156n., 157, 158
Wang Po-hwai, 350
Wang Tsun-ming, 303, 303n., 304–306

Ward, Frederick Townsend, 64
Warlords, 117ff., 128–129, 142, 143
Warring States, Period of, 117
Washington, George, 98, 203
Water Margin Tale, The, 204
Wen Hui Pao, 433
West: -China relations, 68–90, 95; hatred of, 81–83, 121; militant approach to, 67–80; Utopia, 179–180
Whampoa Military Academy, 147–148; Nanchang Rising, 151–152, 217
Williams, S. Wells, 72
Wilson, Woodrow, 140
Women: Army, 65; mother-in-law dominance, 8–9
Woo Ming-way, 366–367
Workers and Peasants Red Army, 154
World War I, 128–129; II, 196, 402
Wuhan Revolt, 119, 433, 437
Wuhan University, 24, 357
Wu Hsiu-chuan, 168, 397
Wu Hsun, 306
Wu Pei-fu, 119, 144
Wu San-kuei, 47, 48
Wu wei (doctrine of inaction), 194, 353

Yalu, Battle of (1894), 92–93
Yen Fu, 95
Yen Hsi-shan, 117
Yi Ho Tuan, 77–78; see also Boxers
Young, Brigham, 179
Young Communist League, 321
Young Pioneers, 7
Yuan Dynasty, 38
Yuan Shih-kai, 112, 113ff., 117–119, 125, 129, 142
Yugoslavia, 397
Yung Cheng, 50, 56
Yun tung (Campaigns), 274, 274n., 350, 351ff.

"Zhukovism," 334